D1029926

# POLITICS AND THE PEOPLE OF LONDON

# POLITICS AND THE PEOPLE OF LONDON

## THE LONDON COUNTY COUNCIL 1889-1965

EDITED BY

ANDREW SAINT

THE HAMBLEDON PRESS

LONDON AND RONCEVERTE

Published by The Hambledon Press, 1989

102 Gloucester Avenue, London NW1 8HX (U.K.)

309 Greenbrier Avenue, Ronceverte WV 24970 (U.S.A.)

ISBN 1 85285 029 9



*British Library Cataloguing in Publication Data*

Politics and the People of London:
the London County Council, 1889-1965.
1. London County Council to 1965.
I. Saint, Andrew.
352. 0421

*Library of Congress Cataloging-in-Publication Data*

Politics and the People of London:
the London County Council, 1889-1965/
edited by Andrew Saint.
Includes bibliographical references.
1. London County Council – History.
2. London (Eng.) – Politics and government.
I. Saint, Andrew.
JS3625. P65 1989
320.9421 – dc20 89-20024 CIP

Typeset by Vitaset, Paddock Wood, Kent.
Printed and bound in Great Britain on acid-free
paper by The Camelot Press, Southampton.

## *Contents*

# *Notes on Contributors*

**Mark Clapson** is working for the Charles Booth Project at the Open University. He has recently completed a doctorate on popular gambling and English culture.

**Gloria Clifton** is a temporary lecturer in the history of London at Queen Mary College, University of London. She is writing a book on the Metropolitan Board of Works.

**John Davis** is a Fellow of The Queen's College, Oxford. His *Reforming London* (Oxford University Press) was published in 1988.

**James Gillespie** works in the School of Philosophy and Politics at Maguire University, Sydney. He has written a book on health policy in Australia.

**Helen Jones** is a lecturer in social policy at the University of Liverpool. Her doctorate and other publications are in the field of the history of health policy.

**Sue Laurence** is a social historian and museums consultant. She completed her Ph.D. on the politics of housing at the London School of Economics in 1987.

**Ellen Leopold** is an economist. While working for some years in the Industry and Employment Branch of the Greater London Council she wrote *In the Service of London*, a history of employment by the LCC and GLC.

**John Mason** began his career in urban planning. His work has included research into Manchester's housing problems and into the issues of homelessness in London.

**Malcolm Richardson** teaches part-time at Middlesex Polytechnic. He has recently completed a Ph.D. at the Institute of Education, University of London.

**Andrew Saint** is a historian with the London Division of the Historic Buildings and Monuments Commission. He was previously architectural editor of the *Survey of London*.

**Terry Segars** is a firefighter with the Essex County Fire Brigade and an Executive Council member of the Fire Brigades Union for East Anglia.

**John Sheldrake** is Senior Lecturer in Politics and Industrial Relations at the City of London Polytechnic. He has published books on industrial training, municipal socialism, industrial relations and corporatism.

**Chris Waters** lectures on history at Williams College, Williamstown, Massachusetts and has written a doctorate on culture, politics and leisure at the turn of the nineteenth and twentieth centuries.

# *Introduction*

In 1939 Sir Gwilym Gibbon and Reginald Bell published their 696-page *History of the London County Council*, celebrating a half-century of the LCC's existence. Labour had then been in office at County Hall for six years. Herbert Morrison was at the height of his prestige as 'Leader of the Council' – the most powerful-seeming boss ever to emerge from the muddle of modern London politics. The picture of the LCC which Gibbon and Bell, working in haste, assembled was of a mighty, just, clean, smooth-running bureaucratic machine of limitless capacity, ever-eager to take on more of the manifold tasks of urban social administration which governments might entrust to it – housing, education, health, the poor law, and so on. The sole product of all this activity was intended to be the benefit of the people of London (to whom the book was dedicated). If the tenor of the fifty-year *History* was too factual and its tone too modest to suggest that the LCC might hold sway over London for as long as the 'thousand-year Reich' then so much on people's minds, yet the scent of solidity and permanence exuding from Gibbon and Bell's pages was pervasive. The future for metropolitan London government seemed to promise only growth and expansion. Even such a squib as W.A. Robson's *Government and Misgovernment of London*, published in the same year as Gibbon and Bell, reinforced their conclusions. Robson's was the clearest of early voices calling for a Greater London Council. By demanding better co-ordination of the capital's services and a wider geographical locus for the LCC or some such other body, he in effect was saying that what London wanted was more and better government.

Fifty years later again, with the LCC itself an increasingly remote and obscure body, with its successor the GLC three years abolished, and with Britain's whole tradition of municipal autonomy in tatters, it is well to remember that the collapse of confidence in London-wide government is very recent. When the project to commemorate the LCC's centenary was conceived in 1984, there were no firm proposals to dismantle the GLC. That body had been finally established as recently as 1965, as part of the first phase of the Conservative Party's post-war reforms of local government. It was set up for a variety of reasons – among them to break Labour's thirty-year control of the LCC. In the event, the GLC proved an incoherent institution which satisfied nobody, since constant changes of political control led to discontinuities in its policies and widened the rift between the inner and outer London boroughs which had dogged it from the first. But the view that London, in contrast to other great capitals of the world, either did not deserve or did not need representative metropolitan government remained until the mid 1980s a heresy of extreme localism. It was a view that had a history going back to the early days of the LCC. In 1899 Lord Salisbury's Conservative administration attempted to rein in metropolitan ambition by turning the London vestries into boroughs and boosting their powers. But calls at the time actually to abolish the LCC went unheeded. Even in the 1960s, that end could only be achieved by the device of appearing to turn the LCC into something bigger and better, with the same staff working from the same offices, only greatly enlarged and with added responsibilities.

A masterly statement of the LCC's self-image as a benevolent institution of indestructible permanence was furnished, late in its history, by the evidence of the Centre for Environmental Studies given in 1959 to the Herbert Commission. This was the Conservative-appointed body whose recommendations on the future of local government in Greater London were to lead to the LCC's demise six years later. Discovering that most of the evidence heard by the Commission was not particularly scientific or academic but either party-political or in some sense localist in slant, with the exception of the expansionist urgings of W.A. Robson's Greater London Group, the Centre for Environmental Studies hastily put together a document in defence of the LCC's continued existence. A rising historian, Asa Briggs, wrote the section directly concerning the LCC and its past. With Lord Briggs's kind permission, it is reprinted as an appendix to this book.

The essays in this book do not deliberately aim at overturning the 'triumphalist' image of the LCC presented by Gibbon and Bell and epitomized by Asa Briggs. Only a full historical study of London's government in the twentieth century, on the scale of Gibbon and Bell's book or longer, could properly assess that view of the Council and its work. It is a sign of current political apathy at metropolitan level that no such study, nor apparently the enthusiasm to support one, seems to exist at present. A selection of essays can only give clues and point in new directions. But it will be readily apparent that this book, produced during and in the immediate aftermath of the abolition of metropolitan government for London, often highlights the frailty of the LCC, its limitations, and the obstacles which it encountered. The sturdy institution depicted by previous writers often turns out, under critical scrutiny of its record, to have been weak, vulnerable and cautious.

Thus, for instance, the image of a 'new start' for London in 1889, so effectively canvassed by the Progressive Party, conceals many continuities with the habits and policies of the supposedly discredited Metropolitan

Board of Works. Nor did the Progressives, for all the vigour of their propaganda, succeed during their heyday in carrying out more than a small fraction of their vaunted programme of municipalization. When they left power in 1907, the LCC had failed in its bid to control water supply and the docks, had made little ground over local taxation and rate equalization, and had only a toehold in the tramway system to show for all its battles over transport. Its wider ambitions to influence the London labour market had had to be demonstrated by example, and were only intermittently effective. Some services which the LCC had inherited and was supposed to run, like the fire brigade, enjoyed semi-independent status and had proved difficult to direct and control. Had responsibility for education not been conferred on the Council in 1904, the appearance that metropolitan government in London still consisted of a ragbag of responsibilities, as it had done in the despised era of the Board of Works, would have been hard to avoid.

The period of Municipal Reform control of the LCC, between 1907 and 1934, remains the least studied of the three into which the Council's political history so neatly falls (Progressives, 1889-1907; Municipal Reformers, 1907-34; Labour, 1934-65). Undoubtedly Municipal Reformers, as London Conservatives called themselves during these years, were not so keen on the concept of metropolitan government as their Progressive predecessors had been and their Labour successors were to be again. The Progressives' sense of ambition largely dissolves during this period of the LCC's history; there is much concern that the Council's expenditure must be curbed in the ratepayer's interest, and that the prerogatives of the boroughs shall be safeguarded. When governments enjoin municipal activity, as in the case of the post-war housing programme or the expansion of the education service, or transfer of the poor law to municipal control (as happened in 1930), the duties are undertaken, but cautiously and without broader or more integrated vision. Thus Becontree, the LCC suburb which might have shown a national lead in town planning, declines for reasons of economy into a vast, monotonous housing estate. During these years the LCC, through lack of heart and unanimity in the Municipal Reform Party, lost its best opportunity to extend its boundaries and powers at the time of the Ullswater Commission on London Government (1922-3). Once this opportunity had been missed, the LCC's attempts to influence such essentially regional matters as town planning and transport were bound to be flawed. Some of the essays in this book stress the conservatism of Morrison and his Labour successors at County Hall after 1934 and the continuities with past policies, despite their claims to socialist progressiveness. One reason for that was the London Labour Party's constant preoccupation with party discipline as a key to electoral respectability and success. Another was that Morrison, Latham and Hayward found the fiefdom of the LCC insusceptible of extension, and so accustomed themselves to limited progress within the sphere which they knew they could control. When the prospect of an enlarged political map for London finally became a reality in the 1950s, Labour was unsure of its ability to control an area larger than the LCC and therefore fell back on the stale task of defending its own record. Despite this, it was Labour which won the first GLC election in 1964.

The underlying reason for the LCC's weaknesses through all three periods of control was that it never functioned as an autonomous body. During the Progressive and Labour years, majority-party members and more ambitious officers liked to think of the LCC as the government for London, in contradistinction to unfeeling national governments so palpably close at Westminster and petty local politicians in the boroughs. In reality, the LCC was awkwardly sandwiched between two rival tiers of government. Almost no large question could be decided upon without consultation with the other tiers. Furthermore, both Progressive and Labour administrations at County Hall suffered from the misfortune that the periods when sympathetic administrations held power at Westminster were slim indeed – 1892-5 and 1906-7 for the Progressives, and 1945-51 for Labour. National governments of all complexions were, in any case, notorious for their reluctance to let London look after itself. Not only were the services which the LCC ran a peculiar, constantly varying and far from logical assortment, but the actual powers which the Council enjoyed to get and spend money and to exercise its initiatives were acutely limited. No wonder, then, that those who determined policy at County Hall found it easiest in the end to acquiesce in the conception of local government as the exemplary execution of strategic decisions made at national level. In this way, the LCC came to see itself as the 'flagship' of British local government, larger, more adventurous, more intelligent and better organized than other town and county halls across the country, but essentially performing the same tasks. This was a far cry from the concept of self-determination for London which the more 'advanced' Progressives brought to their task in 1889. It marked, in essence, the acknowledgement that in 'central-local relations' the national government of the day would always have the whip hand over the LCC.

If the propaganda of strength and solidity put about by the LCC is misleading, why then commemorate its centenary? Answers to this are not difficult. First and most important of all, the Council remained for all its weaknesses Britain's second most important institution of representative democracy. If the history of British electoral democracy is to be taken as more than a mere chronicle of Parliaments and their decisions, and if any credence is given to the belief that healthy societies should have a plurality of representative institutions based on topography, then the case of the LCC merits examination.

Secondly, the LCC dominated London's politics for the term of its existence. Its activities had a vast if unquantifiable effect upon inner

London and its people. All serious books on twentieth-century London's history refer in one way or another (if usually in passing) to the Council's endeavours. By focussing on the LCC itself, but not to the exclusion of other bodies and without the self-congratulation of earlier accounts, it is possible to grasp something of the Council's impact, however dimly perceived at the time or blunted by compromise. Some classes of Londoners and some parts of London – usually the poorer ones – were more touched by the LCC's services than others. Kensington, for instance, had almost no LCC housing and few maintained schools. A borough like Lambeth had much of both, while some of the large outlying housing estates resembled colonies paying tribute to their distant rulers at County Hall. Because of this uneven, intermittent distribution of activity, because too of the continued significance of borough politics and the bizarre survival of the City Corporation, the LCC was never able to act as the coherent force in defining an 'identity' for London which some might have wished and which would have been the ultimate tribute to its influence. Yet it did undoubtedly have some unifying effect on the inner area, whether through its timid attempts at redistributing rate-income or through the simple mechanism of administrative continuity. The geographical area which the LCC inherited from the Board of Works survived the huge expansion of London and still continues as an entity, at least in the sphere of educational administration; only when the Inner London Education Authority is abolished in 1990 will it cease to have political meaning. Arguments can still be made that the inner London boroughs have a natural community of interest which requires joint political expression – in other words that something like the LCC could have a future, while something like the GLC could not.

Thirdly, the LCC in many spheres embarked on social, political and technical initiatives which are of abiding historical interest, whether for their own value or for the influence they had on policy and administration elsewhere in Britain. This is a variant of an argument advanced by Asa Briggs to defend the Council in 1959. By virtue of its size, he claimed, the LCC was able to experiment in ways with which other local authorities could never compete. Many examples of this could be found, and some are discussed in the essays that follow. During the Progressive era, for instance, there was the early institution of a fair wages clause, later taken up by national as well as other local administrations; and there was the inauguration of a regular programme of municipal housing, with the monumental LCC estates of Boundary Street and Millbank in the van. Later, the teaching policies of the inter-war LCC, the post-war drive for comprehensive schools and indeed the whole ambitious venture of post-war planning and building are other spheres in which the Council was able because of its unique size and position to experiment. Some of the LCC's cultural policies, from its support for the *Survey of London* to its building of the Royal Festival Hall, are also sufficiently remarkable and might have been explored in this book, had space allowed. The size of the staff and its work, too, encouraged new and sometimes very successful and smooth-running organizational arrangements, of which perhaps the most notable was that of the cost-effective Supplies Department. To an extent, professional officers and members of the later LCC who possessed wider vision liked to think of such ventures as initiatives freely undertaken by London on behalf of the nation, in default of adequate national policies for administration, research and experiment. This perhaps was to be blind to the amount that the LCC itself borrowed or adopted from elsewhere. But there can be no doubt that the balance of creativity, if that is the appropriate word, was in the LCC's favour.

That is not to say that one must endorse everything original which the Council adopted. Much that it tried ended in failure, or simply could not be carried on to a successful conclusion because of the range of social problems and adverse political and economic forces which the LCC faced. It is perhaps more accurate to see the Council's experimentalism as a series of bold attempts to take advantage of puffs in the political wind rather than as a continuous, well-grounded set of ventures towards social progress for Londoners. Sooner or later the wind would drop and the experimenters would be exposed, ground between the upper and nether millstones of national and local government. Whether viewed as failures, successes or something in between, these experiments nevertheless remain of extraordinary interest in British social history.

## *Acknowledgements and Philosophy*

This book began with the belief of four people, John Mason, Susan Pennybacker, Andrew Saint and Robert Thorne, that the centenary of the London County Council should not pass without some considered publication. The original goal was a new centenary history of the LCC. To that end, interested parties came to a meeting at County Hall in 1984. This led to the establishment of an LCC Centenary History Group, composed of people from differing walks of life and with diverse interests. The Group met regularly in 1984-5 and in due course applied to the Greater London Council for a grant to fund the work, on the understanding that the project was not in any way to be an 'official' one. The GLC was able to offer a year's grant, on which basis work began in autumn 1985, with Andrew Saint as editor, Sue Laurence and John Mason as assistant editors and Mark Clapson as research assistant. Accommodation and some administrative support were generously provided by the Institute of Historical Research.

In the event it proved impossible to pursue the project on the scale envisaged. Difficulties with funding, stemming from curbs put upon the GLC just before its abolition, limited the original grant to a six-month period, and other bodies proved unwilling to fund the project. So the Group had to content itself with a book of essays, contributed without payment by those with a strong commitment to the project.

The philosophy of the project was much discussed in the Group and by the team working in 1985-6. Two consistent principles emerged from these debates. Firstly, the Group felt that Gibbon and Bell and most previous writers had ignored or at any rate underplayed the important political element in the LCC's history. By examining the nature of the political parties which ran the Council and their relations to other groups within London or their own internal relations, it was hoped that a clearer sense of the LCC's policies and priorities would emerge. Secondly, contributors were concerned that the essays should not concentrate too much on County Hall itself, on the grounds that the value of local government resides ultimately not in what it says or how it is organized, but on how it touches the people whom it claims to represent and serve. This second goal has proved far harder to achieve. Short essays, which were agreed to be the only possible format for a subject of such potential breadth, scarcely allow the writers to get beyond the immediate, bureaucratic nature of most of the evidence and the claims and bickerings of the politicians. Only the full history of the Council which remains to be written can seriously begin to assess its impact on Londoners.

As completed, then, this book stands as a series of critical reflections on important aspects of the LCC's life and work. It cannot claim to be comprehensive; many very important aspects of the Council's massive range of activities have had to be omitted. But we hope the essays will stimulate those many Londoners – be they young or old, politicians, academics, journalists, teachers, students or laypeople – who appreciate that, more than ever today, the whole problem of local government in London deserves hard, honest and serious thought, and that the history of London government must be starting point for that thought.

It remains to thank the very many people who have helped us over the last five years. During a difficult period, Dr. Alice Prochaska and other members of the staff of the Institute of Historical Research were always patient and helpful. At an early period, the Group established a panel of advisers who generously contributed their wisdom and ideas: this consisted of Professor Michael Thompson, Dr. Geoffrey Crossick, Dr. Gillian Sutherland and Dr. Francis Sheppard, later assisted by Professor Michael Port. Michael Ward, Deputy Leader of the last GLC administration, has also been very supportive of the project, and David Reeder supplied advice on publication and some other matters.

Special thanks are due to the Arthur McDougall Fund for generous financial support at a critical stage in the project.

Among members of the LCC Centenary History Group who did not in the end contribute essays, we would like to single out Susan Pennybacker, Denise Riley and Robert Thorne for their special encouragement and companionship; also David Englander, David Feldman, Tony Green, Carl Levy, John Marriott, Deborah Thom and Deborah Weiner, who came to many of our meetings and were for some time potential contributors. The contributors themselves must be thanked for their perseverance over a long period and for their acceptance of limitations imposed and revisions suggested for the greater coherence of the book as a whole. Readers will find that the language of the essays has been kept simple, and the apparatus criticus light, in the interests of accessibility and brevity.

Many former officers and members of the LCC were consulted during the period of the project's gestation. Among members we should especially like to thank Molly Bolton, Lady Denington and Lady Pepler; and among former officers, Alan Neate, the GLC's Record Keeper. A feature of the 1985-6 period was a conference at County Hall, just before the GLC's abolition, concerning the post-war LCC and its history. This was addressed among others by Ken Livingstone, then the GLC Leader.

Many former officers and members attended the conference; subsequently, some of them kindly sent in written reminiscences and opinions, which have been most helpful to contributors. These will in due course be lodged with the Greater London Record Office, to be placed among its records of the LCC – a uniquely, formidably voluminous archive on local government which contributors to this book have hardly been able to do more than scratch at.

## *Acknowledgements of Illustrations*

All illustrations come from the Greater London History Library's Photographic Collections, where we gratefully acknowledge the help of Chris Denvir, with the exception of 7a (Dorothy Peirce) and 16b (Birmingham City Libraries).

# *Chapter 1*

## *Members and Officers of the LCC, 1889-1965*

Gloria Clifton

The objectives of the London County Council depended ultimately on the attitudes of its members, but their decisions were often influenced by the advice received from officers and could only be carried out efficiently by a competent and committed staff.* Understanding the dynamics of the LCC, its strengths and weaknesses, depends on a knowledge of the participants. This chapter sets out to explore the background of the members and officers, the qualities and experience which they brought to the work of local government, the relations between them, including the Council's methods of recruiting and managing staff, and their respective roles in decision-making. Since the numbers involved are so large only the white-collar staff in the central departments of administration will be considered, as they were most concerned with day-to-day policy decisions.

Initially the LCC consisted of 118 Councillors, elected for a term of three years, and nineteen Aldermen chosen by the Councillors and serving for six years, with half retiring every three years. Since the number of Councillors was defined as twice the number of Members of Parliament returned by the constituencies in the County of London, the total varied with alterations in parliamentary representation. The area represented by each Councillor was the same as the parliamentary constituency. The number of Aldermen was defined as not more than one-sixth of the number of elected Councillors.

### *Party Affiliations of Members*

Party politics were a feature of the London County Council from the beginning. In this respect it was very different from its predecessor, the Metropolitan Board of Works (MBW), which had not been organized on

*I am extremely grateful to a number of former LCC members and officers who agreed to be interviewed or who wrote to me and the LCC History Group, notably Molly Bolton, C.D. Andrews, Pat and Sylvia Bacon, M.A. Freedman, A.J. Fry, P. Johnson-Marshall, K.S. Mills, I. Murphy, A.D. Nicholls, A.G. Stokes and S. Tickner.

party lines. However, there had already been signs of the intrusion of party politics into London local government in the School Board elections of the later 1880s, and the interest aroused by the creation of the LCC accelerated this trend.

The formation of the LCC was greeted as a victory by those who had long been campaigning for the reform of local government in London. The reform agitation in the 1880s had been led by the London Municipal Reform League, founded in 1881 by John Lloyd and J.F.B. Firth. Many who stood in the first LCC election on 17 January 1889 were supporters of the League's aims, a loose alliance of Liberals, Radicals and Socialists, co-operating as 'Progressives'.[1] Their opponents chose the name 'Moderates', changed in 1907 to 'Municipal Reformers'. In 1889 some local Conservative Associations put up independent candidates, but such individuals were soon sucked into the party politics of the LCC and at subsequent county elections Conservative groups supported Moderates.[2] The extent to which the LCC was run on party lines made it stand out from most other local authorities in Britain which, even if party politics played a role, still retained a substantial number of independent Councillors well into the twentieth century.

The first election returned a clear Progressive majority, which used its voting strength to ensure that all but one of the Aldermen were of its own persuasion. This, together with the Progressives' determination to carry out their programme, helped to polarize party feeling and to ensure that the new Council would be run on party lines. Party discipline was relaxed at first and during the first term Members often voted according to conviction rather than party, but gradually party divisions hardened, and by the later 1890s party meetings and whips had appeared. The political organization of the Council meant that its history fell into three distinct phases according to which party was in power: the Progressives from 1889 to 1907; the Municipal Reformers from 1907 to 1934; and the Labour Party from 1934 to 1965. The party balance on the Council after each election is set out in Table 1. Elections were suspended during the two world wars and vacancies were filled by co-option.

The most striking change in the party balance on the LCC was the rapid emergence of the Labour Party after the First World War to replace the Progressives as the main opposition to the Conservative Municipal Reformers. A similar process was taking place in local government in other large towns, with Labour taking control of Sheffield, Leeds and Coventry in the 1920s and 1930s. While this mirrored the eclipse of the Liberal Party in parliamentary politics the process was completed much more quickly, with a majority Labour administration taking over some local councils more than a decade before a Labour government achieved an overall

[1] See John Davis's contribution to this book for a fuller discussion of Progressivism.
[2] K. Young, *Local Politics and the Rise of Party*, 1975, pp.44-6.

## Table 1

*The Party Balance on the LCC after each Election**

| *Year* | *Moderate Municipal Reform or Conservative* | | *Progressive or Liberal* | | *Labour*** | | *Independent* | | *Number of Elected Members* | *Number of Aldermen* |
|---|---|---|---|---|---|---|---|---|---|---|
| | *Cllr.* | *Ald.* | *Cllr.* | *Ald.* | *Cllr.* | *Ald.* | *Cllr.* | *Ald.* | | |
| *1889* | 46 | 1 | 72 | 18 | — | — | — | — | 118 | 19 |
| *1892* | 35 | 2 | 83 | 17 | — | — | — | — | 118 | 19 |
| *1895* | 59 | 7 | 59 | 12 | — | — | — | — | 118 | 19 |
| *1898* | 48 | 8 | 70 | 10 | — | 1 | — | — | 118 | 19 |
| *1901* | 32 | 6 | 86 | 12 | — | 1 | — | — | 118 | 19 |
| *1904* | 35 | 6 | 82 | 13 | — | — | 1 | — | 118 | 19 |
| *1907* | 79 | 11 | 37 | 8 | 1 | — | 1 | — | 118 | 19 |
| *1910* | 60 | 17 | 55 | 2 | 3 | — | — | — | 118 | 19 |
| *1913* | 67 | 15 | 49 | 4 | 2 | — | — | — | 118 | 19 |
| *1919* | 68 | 12 | 40 | 6 | 15 | 2 | 1 | — | 124 | 20 |
| *1922* | 82 | 12 | 26 | 5 | 16 | 3 | — | — | 124 | 20 |
| *1925* | 83 | 13 | 6 | 3 | 35 | 4 | — | — | 124 | 20 |
| *1928* | 77 | 12 | 5 | 1 | 42 | 6 | — | 1 | 124 | 20 |
| *1931* | 83 | 13 | 6 | — | 35 | 6 | — | 1 | 124 | 20 |
| *1934* | 55 | 9 | — | — | 69 | 11 | — | — | 124 | 20 |
| *1937* | 49 | 8 | — | — | 75 | 12 | — | — | 124 | 20 |
| *1946* | 30 | 6 | 2 | — | 90 | 14 | 2 | — | 124 | 20 |
| *1949* | 64 | 5 | 1 | — | 64 | 16 | — | — | 129 | 21 |
| *1952* | 37 | 6 | — | — | 92 | 15 | — | — | 129 | 21 |
| *1955* | 52 | 8 | — | — | 74 | 13 | — | — | 126 | 21 |
| *1958* | 25 | 7 | — | — | 101 | 14 | — | — | 126 | 21 |
| *1961* | 42 | 7 | — | — | 84 | 14 | — | — | 126 | 21 |

* In the early years of the LCC the party affiliations of some of the Members were not very clearly defined and cross-party voting in Council divisions was common.

** The term 'Labour' is rather ambiguous until about 1910. Some trade unionists elected before then considered themselves representatives of the interests of Labour, but as most of them also operated as part of the Progressive group on the LCC they have been counted with that party.

SOURCES: K. Young, *Local Politics and the Rise of Party*, 1975, p.223; G. Gibbon and R.W. Bell, *History of the London County Council 1889-1939*, 1939, p.677; London County Council, *General Election of County Councillors*, 1949, 1952, 1955, 1958 and 1961.

majority in Parliament. Not surprisingly those who formed the Labour administration at the LCC in 1934 saw themselves as pioneers, believing that their success or failure would affect the prospects of the Labour Party nationally.[3]

Once Labour won a majority on the LCC, party politics became even more firmly embedded into the organization of Council business. The machinery of party control had gradually become more formal. The Progressives' caucuses and whips had gradually tightened their hold, but when the Municipal Reform administration took over the LCC external party organizations came to exercise more explicit control through the London Municipal Society, whose Executive agreed the general policies to be followed by London Conservatives. Similarly, the London Labour Party dominated the LCC Labour Group and largely determined its policies. Under both Progressive and Municipal Reform control it had been usual to appoint a few members of the minority party as committee chairmen, giving them a major role in the management of Council work, but when Labour came to power this practice was ended and committee chairmanships were confined to members of the majority party.

As soon as the LCC had been set up it was clear that the leading Progressives formed an unofficial policy-making 'inner cabinet'. They were by no means a united group. There were tensions between those like the first Progressive leader, Sir Thomas Farrer, who supported a unified government for London but opposed what he regarded as excessive spending, and the exponents of municipal ownership of public utilities and taxation of land values, such as the socialist John Burns and Charles Harrison, a radical solicitor. As party organization hardened the 'party committee' played an increasingly important role. It reached its apogee during the period of Labour control, when all the committee chairmen came from the majority party. As Labour consolidated its hold on the Council and seemed increasingly unlikely to lose control, so the chairmen increasingly dominated their committees. The leading figures remained on the LCC for decades and rotated the committee chairmanships among themselves. Together with the Leader of the Council and the whips they formed a close-knit group who kept all the strings of Council business in their hands and spent much of their time at County Hall. For example, in the 1950s and 1960s figures such as Helen Bentwich, Florence Cayford, Evelyn Denington, Reginald Goodwin, Sir Isaac Hayward, Victor Mishcon, Norman Prichard and Albert Samuels could be identified as members of an 'inner cabinet' on the LCC.[4]

[3] Interview with Mrs. I.M. Bolton, 1 June 1987.

[4] B. Grocott, 'Leadership in Local Government', University of Manchester MA, 1967, pp.68-9.

### *Background and Occupations of LCC Members*

The London County Council was always a middle-aged body. About half of the Councillors and Aldermen elected in 1889 were aged between forty and sixty years, and the average age of the committee chairmen was fifty-three. By the time the LCC came to an end in 1965 the average age of committee chairmen had crept up to fifty-eight. While the majority of Councillors served for less than ten years there were always a few who remained for twenty or thirty years and worked their way up through committee chairmanships to become Chairman or Leader of the Council, such as Sir Evan Spicer, who served from 1889 to 1919, or Sir Isaac Hayward, first elected in 1928 and Leader of the Council between 1947 and 1965.[5]

The occupations of Members of the LCC are set out in Table 2.[6] Councillors' paid employment was usually in the professions, business or administration. The Progressives in the 1890s included a small but significant contingent of representatives from the labour aristocracy, who had come to local prominence through their involvement in trade unions and radical politics. But even when Labour took control members from manual occupations remained a tiny minority. The proportion of members from the professions fluctuated a little but in both 1889 and 1965 represented just under a third of the total. This was a rather higher proportion than was found on provincial town councils, even in prosperous cities like Birmingham, where the professions never formed more than a quarter of the Council over the period 1839-1966. This contrast reflects the strength of the professions in London. While the proportion of professional people on the Council remained stable, there were marked variations in the relative strengths of the administrative and business contingents. In 1889 and 1907 administrators and managers formed 11 per cent of the Council, compared with 24 per cent in 1925 and 22 per cent in 1961. By contrast there was a very marked reduction in the numbers of manufacturers and wholesale traders on the LCC. In 1889 they formed just over a quarter of the total, whereas by the 1950s and 1960s there were just one or two individuals. In part this reflected changes in the organization of business and commerce, with public companies replacing privately owned firms, and industry moving out of central London. But the extent of the decline indicates that there was also a growing reluctance to participate in local government on the part of owners of businesses. This pattern of a rise in the proportion of

[5] *Pall Mall Gazette 'Extra', No.47, The Popular Guide to the House of Commons, 1889; and to the London County Council*, 1889; Grocott, *op. cit.*, p.69; W.E. Jackson, *Achievement*, 1965, app.II.

[6] Table compiled from sources in note 5 and London County Council Minutes of Proceedings, 1889-1965.

Table 2

*Occupations of Elected Members and Aldermen of the London County Council, 1889-1961*

| OCCUPATION | *1889* | *1907* | *1925* | *1934* | *1952* | *1961* |
|---|---|---|---|---|---|---|
| MEN | | | | | | |
| Peers and peers' sons | 3 | 8 | 3 | 3 | 2 | 2 |
| Private income | 9 | 24 | 16 | 10 | 2 | 1 |
| MP (no other occupation) | 2 | 8 | 2 | 2 | 1 | 2 |
| Professions | 42 | 47 | 34 | 42 | 36 | 38 |
| Administrators and managers | 15 | 15 | 34 | 32 | 34 | 34 |
| Employers and proprietors | 46 | 19 | 18 | 9 | 2 | 4 |
| Clerical workers | — | 1 | 2 | 2 | 5 | 6 |
| Retired employers, managers, professionals and clerks | 14 | 13 | 9 | 14 | 9 | 13 |
| Foremen and supervisors | 1 | — | — | 1 | — | 1 |
| Skilled and semi-skilled manual workers | 2 | 2 | 2 | 6 | 8 | 5 |
| Unskilled manual workers | — | — | — | — | 1 | 1 |
| Total men | 134 | 137 | 120 | 121 | 100 | 107 |
| WOMEN | | | | | | |
| MP | — | — | — | — | 1 | 2 |
| Professions | — | — | 3 | 3 | 4 | 9 |
| Administrators and managers | — | — | — | — | 1 | — |
| Clerical workers | — | — | — | 1 | — | 2 |
| Retired professionals and clerical workers | — | — | 1 | 1 | 1 | — |
| No paid employment | 3 | — | 20 | 18 | 43 | 27 |
| Total women | 3 | — | 24 | 23 | 50 | 40 |
| TOTAL LCC | 137 | 137 | 144 | 144 | 150 | 147 |

SOURCES: See text.

Councillors from white-collar employment and a diminishing percentage of manufacturers and merchants has also been found in other studies of municipal authorities since the late nineteenth century.[7]

Another major group on the LCC were those without a formal job. In the early years they were mostly peers, younger sons of peers, gentlemen with private incomes, and those who had retired from business. But as changes in society and in taxation eroded the numbers living on capital, and the laws about women's eligibility for election were reformed, married women and retirement pensioners came to form a substantial part of the membership. Council meetings began at 2.30 or 3 pm and it was easier for those without full-time paid employment to attend. Even when payment for lost earnings was allowed in 1948 there was not a major increase in the number of manual workers who became Councillors, though it was only after that date that the first members from unskilled manual occupations were elected.

In both 1889 and 1965 about a third of the members of the LCC had previous experience of local government. In 1889 they had held office on parish vestries, as guardians of the poor or on the London School Board. In 1965 they combined being County Councillors with membership of a metropolitan borough. As far as the LCC was concerned there was general agreement that there was no shortage of good quality candidates and that, particularly in the period after the Second World War, London fared rather better than most.[8]

### *Women Councillors*

The first London County Council had three women members: Lady Sandhurst and Jane Cobden, daughter of the Liberal MP Richard Cobden, as elected representatives, and Emma Cons, well-known for her charitable work, as an Alderman. They were the only women returned in the first county council elections: there were just two other women candidates in the rest of the country and they were both defeated. The women members' right to sit on the LCC was immediately challenged. C.T. Beresford Hope, Lady Sandhurst's defeated opponent, took action in the courts to have her election declared invalid because she was a woman. By 1889 women's right to sit on boards of guardians of the poor, school boards and municipal councils had been established, and there were already precedents for women's election to a London-wide local

[7] E.P. Hennock, *Fit and Proper Persons: Ideal and Reality in Nineteenth-Century Urban Government*, 1973, pp.42-8; M. Elliott, *Victorian Leicester*, 1979, pp.161-4.

[8] LCC Minutes, 14 July 1959, p.480; Greater London History Library (GLHL), typescript by the Council Clerk, O.W. Holmes, 'History of the London County Council', 1957; Grocott, *op. cit.*, pp.40-3; *Pall Mall Gazette 'Extra'*, 1889; interview with Mrs. I.M. Bolton.

authority, the London School Board. But the Act setting up the county councils had not specifically confirmed women's eligibility for election. In May 1889 the Appeal Courts held that in the absence of provision within the Act for women to stand as candidates Lady Sandhurst was not qualified, and Beresford Hope was declared elected. Jane Cobden and Emma Cons then took no part in Council work until the year during which their election could be challenged had expired. But when they resumed their seats another anti-suffragist on the LCC, Sir Walter De Souza, took further successful legal action in 1890 against Jane Cobden for acting while disqualified. Jane Cobden and Emma Cons still attended Council and committee meetings but refrained from signing the attendance book! When their term of office ended the LCC became an exclusively male body for over a decade.[9]

Women began to participate in Council work once more by the back door, as co-opted members of the new Education Committee, set up in 1904 when the LCC took over responsibility for education from the London School Board. From the start women played a full role, with Dr. Sophie Bryant and Maude Lawrence acting as vice-chairman of sub-committees in the first year. In 1909 (Dame) Jessie Wilton Phipps, another co-opted Member, became the first woman to chair a sub-committee, the Special Schools Sub-Committee. These developments made an anomaly of women's exclusion from the full Council, and helped to create a climate more favourable to a change in the law. The Qualification of Women (County and Borough Councils) Act was passed in 1907 but it was not until the LCC election of 1910 that women were once more returned as full members. Two women candidates were successful at the polls, Susan Lawrence, who had already served as a co-opted member of the LCC Education Committee, and Henrietta Adler; a third, Lady St Helier, well-known for her work for the poor, was chosen as an Alderman. Henrietta Adler was a Liberal, the other two were Conservative Municipal Reformers, but Susan Lawrence had become a convert to Labour by 1913, when she stood in the LCC election at Poplar, a transformation which was partly a result of her experiences as a member of the Education Committee, when she became appalled at the conditions of employment of women school cleaners.[10]

Women rapidly became a significant element on the LCC, but at first their main contribution was to those aspects of Council work which were considered especially appropriate, such as education and other matters connected with children. Here their practical experience was invaluable. Margaret McMillan, a pioneer of children's clinics and nursery

[9] LCC Minutes, 9 June 1891, p.597; P. Hollis, *Ladies Elect*, 1987, pp.307-11.

[10] *Dictionary of Labour Biography*, vol.3, 1976, pp.128-32; B.M. Allen, *Down the Stream of Life*, 1948, p.86.

education, played an important role on the Children's Care Sub-Committee just after the First World War.[11] The first full committee to have a woman in the chair was the Midwives Act Committee with the selection in 1915 of Jessie Wilton Phipps, who had been elected Alderman two years earlier. Nevertheless, women members soon won a wider role for themselves. By the end of the First World War the LCC had its first female Deputy Chairman, Katherine Wallas, and in 1923 two important committees, Education and Parks, had women as chairmen, Jessie Wilton Phipps and Lady Eve. By 1931 the chairs of five committees were occupied by women and in 1939 Eveline Lowe became the first female Chairman of the Council.

During the inter-war years women became an accepted part of the LCC. In 1919 there were eleven female members and by 1925 the figure had risen to twenty-five, but what was more important was that the majority remained on the Council for twelve or more years, participating fully in committee work and earning the respect of their colleagues. Many of these women had no paid employment and, whatever their political affiliation, were prosperous enough to afford domestic help, leaving them ample time to devote to Council work and master the details. Herbert Morrison appreciated the contribution they could make, particularly those who had received a good education, and as Secretary of the London Labour Party made a deliberate policy of encouraging able women to stand in LCC elections. It was as a result of Morrison's persuasion that Molly Bolton became a candidate in the LCC election of 1934; she remained on the Council until its abolition, serving as Chairman of the Council in 1953-4.[12] The effect of Morrison's policy was that by 1934 the Labour group had a much larger proportion of women than the Municipal Reformers, 23 per cent compared with 8 per cent. Women continued to play a much larger role on the LCC than on most local authorities. The Redcliffe-Maud Commission on Local Government in England and Wales reported in 1969 that 12 per cent of council members were women. On the LCC women formed almost 27 per cent in 1963 and chaired several important committees, forming part of the key policy-making group on the Council.

## *The Size and Structure of the Staff*

The staff of the LCC grew at an enormous rate in the early years as it took on new responsibilities, particularly housing, tramways and education. In April 1890 there were 3,369 Council employees and by 1898 their

[11] E. Bradburn, *Margaret McMillan: Framework and Expansion of Nursery Education*, 1976, pp.20ff., and appendix.

[12] B. Donoughue & G.W. Jones, *Herbert Morrison: Portrait of a Politician*, 1973, pp.30, 73; interview with Mrs. I.M. Bolton.

numbers had increased to 6,311. The take-over of the tramways after 1898 helped to push the Council's total staff up to almost 12,000 by 1904 and during that year its workforce tripled when the schools previously run by the London School Board came under LCC control, bringing the total to 35,316 by April 1905. In 1909 the LCC claimed to be the largest employer in London.[13]

In the early 1890s its employees had represented about 1 in 519 of the London workforce, but by the early 1920s they were approximately 1 in 38. The staff averaged a little over 56,000 in the 1920s, until the transfer of the administration of the poor law to county councils brought another influx of employees in 1930, pushing the total workforce up to 83,846. This compares with 111,000 non-industrial staff employed in all central government departments except the Post Office in the same year, and gives some indication of the significance of LCC employment in the 1930s. In 1933 the maximum size of the LCC staff was reached: 85,676. Then the tramways were transferred to the new London Passenger Transport Board and the number of LCC employees fell. The process of removing functions and staff from the LCC continued after the Second World War as services previously provided by local authorities were taken over by central government, a trend which has continued up to the present. In April 1948 a total of 79,435 people were employed by the LCC but by July the transfer of hospitals to the new National Health Service, and of the relief of poverty to the National Assistance system, reduced their numbers to 58,899. But in the 1950s and early 1960s the staff once more grew steadily, reaching 74,300 in January 1963.[14] Clearly, throughout its life, the LCC was a major London employer whose methods of dealing with staff were bound to be influential.

There has been a tendency to see the creation of the LCC as marking a completely new departure in metropolitan local government, but although the system of direct elections for a general London-wide local authority was an innovation, and only five former MBW Members were returned at the first LCC poll, there was in practice substantial administrative continuity. The LCC inherited a ready-made staff from its predecessors, the Metropolitan Board of Works and the County Justices. They ranged from gardeners and labourers employed in the parks and pumping stations, through members of the fire brigade and skilled engine drivers, to clerks, administrators and highly qualified professional men.

[13] S.D. Pennybacker, 'The "Labour Question" and the London County Council, 1889-1919', Cambridge University, Ph.D., 1984, p.x.

[14] GLRO, LCC Clerk's Department, Establishment Branch Papers; London County Council, *Facts and Figures About the Council's Services in 1963*, p.19; H. Llewellyn Smith (Director) for London School of Economics, *New Survey of London Life and Labour*, 1930, vol.I, p.327; Department of Employment and Productivity, *British Labour Statistics: Historial Abstract 1886-1968*, 1971, table 154.

To begin with all the administrative staff were male, the only female employees being housekeepers, charwomen, lavatory attendants, and asylum and industrial school staff. Here the main focus of attention will be the senior white-collar officials, who had the most contact with elected Members and whose advice was most likely to influence policy.

The Metropolitan Board of Works had already developed its own bureaucracy with the typical features, notably a hierarchical organisation which divided the majority of the clerical and administrative staff into four classes, combined with rules to govern recruitment, promotion and other conditions of service. The LCC retained this bureaucratic structure and gradually adapted it to meet the growing demands of Council work.

The MBW system of four classes provided a starting salary of £80 a year and a maximum of £300, though heads of departments and senior assistants earned substantially more, as much as £2,200 including travelling expenses for the Engineer, and there were always a few junior clerks and messengers who earned as little as 10 or 12 shillings a week. The Council decided to keep the four classes and the same upper and lower limits for the salaries of the majority of permanent staff, but tried to make some saving by dividing the first class so that, instead of a scale rising by £20 a year from £200 to £300, there would be a lower section with a starting salary of £200 and annual increments of £15 to £245, an an upper section with a first increment of £15 and subsequent annual increases of £20 up to the maximum. Office staff normally worked thirty-nine and a half hours a week, including Saturday mornings, but were expected to do some overtime without extra payment. Saturday working was limited to one week in five in 1956 and finally abolished in 1963, in line with national trends in office hours. Initially the highest paid chief officer of the Council was the Solicitor on £1,750 a year, but soon the leading chief officers were earning £2,000. LCC salaries compared well with those offered by the other major contemporary employers of clerical and professional staff, such as the railways and insurance companies.[15]

Another feature both of LCC policies towards its clerical staff, and of the attitude of the officials themselves, was the tendency to imitate the Civil Service rather than to look to local government experience elsewhere. This was not surprising given that the LCC was competing in the same metropolitan job market as government departments and that a few of the oldest officials, such as the first Cashier, Henry Edwards, had

[15] GLRO, Metropolitan Board of Works, Minutes of Proceedings, 2 March 1877, pp.326-30; LCC Minutes, 16 July 1889, pp.575-7; G.C. Clifton, 'The Staff of the Metropolitan Board of Works, 1855-1889: the Development of a Professional Local Government Bureaucracy in Victorian London', London University, Ph.D., 1986, chapter 3; *London County Council Services and Staff for the Year April, 1909, to March, 1910*; T.R. Gourvish, 'The Standard of Living 1890-1914' in A. O'Day (ed.), *The Edwardian Age: Conflict and Stability 1900-1914*, 1979, pp.23-4.

begun their careers in the administration of London affairs as actual civil servants working for the Metropolitan Commission of Sewers, whose employees had formed the nucleus of the staff of the MBW. Like the Civil Service the LCC was large enough to offer a lifetime's career, with reasonable prospects of promotion. By contrast, local government employees in other parts of the country usually had to move between authorities to secure a satisfactory rate of promotion. The tendency to see the Civil Service as a model can be seen in attitudes both to recruitment and to salaries, with Civil Service pay being used as a yardstick for Council pay.[16]

Some of the changes which the Council made in the structure of its staff were prompted by a desire to maintain the flow of promotion which its classified employees expected and at the same time to economize on the costs of administration, in order to appease the ratepayer. But in the process it abandoned the unified service inherited from the MBW, which made it relatively easy to rise from the very bottom to the top of the hierarchy, as did (Sir) James Bird who joined the staff on the MBW in 1877 when not quite fourteen years old, as a junior messenger earning twelve shillings a week, and rose to be Clerk of the LCC from 1915 until his death in 1925.[17] Instead of retaining a unified clerical staff the LCC hived off certain types of work into separate grades and placed barriers in the way of promotion to the mainstream.

The major staffing problem faced by the Council in the early years was coping with the growing volume of routine clerical work such as making fair copies of minutes, reports and letters. Increasing the classified staff for this purpose would be expensive and would also mean that the bottom of the pyramid would be so wide that promotion prospects would be severely curtailed, so other devices were sought. The first experiment was to set up a new grade of boy labour in 1891. The boys concerned were considered temporary employees who could be dismissed at a week's notice, and if they did not succeed in passing the Council's examination for permanent staff they would have to leave when they reached twenty years of age. There was considerable contemporary concern about the use of boys as cheap labour in dead-end jobs and the Council hoped to provide its boy clerks with reasonable prospects by encouraging them to take its competitive examination. But full-time work left little time for study and many could not qualify for a permanent post. The Progressives on the Council were concerned to provide fair conditions of work and disliked the way the boy labour scheme operated. They searched for an alternative method of coping with the mounting volume of routine work.

[16] London County Council Staff Association, *Progress Report, 1909-59: the First Fifty Years of the London County Council Staff Association*, 1959, pp.34-5.

[17] MBW Minutes, 2 August 1878, pp.195-7; *London County Council Staff Gazette*, March 1925, pp. 58-9.

The next experiment was to employ female typists to do fair copying. Although they were not the LCC's first female employees it was the first time that the Council had hired women to do routine clerical work, and other London employers were ahead of them in recruiting female office workers. In 1898, after some investigation of the conditions offered to women typists in the commercial world, the Council decided to employ three at a minimum salary of a pound a week for a trial period. This proved more economical than sending copying work out and the section was made permanent in 1899. More lady typists were employed, their numbers reaching forty by 1914. They gradually superseded boy clerks, who were no longer employed by 1905.

Even with the success of the typewriting department the volume of routine work remained a problem and was greatly enhanced when the Council took over responsibility for education, prompting a further change in the organization of the staff. Instead of the old four classes, there would be a Minor and a Major Establishment, with promotion from the lower to the upper grade dependent upon passing the Council's open competitive examination. The Major Establishment consisted of the old four classes of the established staff, consolidated in 1908 into only two with a break at £200 a year. The Minor Establishment recruited from a separate examination requiring a lower level of education and was divided into two sections, the starting salary in the lower half being fifteen shillings a week for boys aged over fifteen and under eighteen years old, rising to £2; pay in the upper section ranged from £2 to £3 a week. In 1912 the division of the Minor Establishment was removed after a petition from the staff.

Increasingly, as the Council's operations grew, and especially when political control passed from the Progressives to the Municipal Reformers, there developed a conflict between the Council's wish for economical administration and the officials' desire for an organizational structure which offered them good promotion prospects. This conflict was seen clearly in 1908 when the Moderates, taking a leaf out of the Civil Service book, imposed a £200 promotion barrier on Major Establishment staff, preventing any further advancement beyond that limit unless there was a definite vacancy at higher levels. This caused enormous resentment, particularly as it came at a time when living costs were rising, and prompted the first serious attempt at collective organization among the senior administrative officials, with the setting up of the London County Council Staff Association in 1909. Although some individuals on the Minor Establishment decided to become members of the National Union of Clerks, the fact that the majority of LCC officials preferred to set up their own organization rather than join an established union is revealing, confirming their sense of detachment from the local government service elsewhere in the country. The Staff Association subsequently affiliated to the National Association of Local Government Officers, but full amalgamation was resisted, despite a vigorous campaign by NALGO in the 1930s.[18]

In the inter-war years the basic staff structure established in the decade before the First World War was retained, though the Minor Establishment was renamed the General Grade and in 1935 a new Higher Clerical Class was set up, recruited by the promotion of employees from the General Grade. There was considerable conflict over salary levels and the arrival of a Labour administration at County Hall in 1934 made little difference to attitudes towards white-collar staff.

The rising cost of living during the First World War created pressure from the staff for increases in pay, especially when Civil Servants were granted a bonus. The Council made some concessions, but the Staff Association and trade unions decided to go to arbitration under wartime regulations, and secured bonuses for all males earning up to £300 a year. Women employees also received bonuses, but at a slightly lower rate than men. These awards excluded those LCC employees such as teachers and asylum staff who had already received pay increases under national agreements.

After the First World War more formal machinery was created for negotiating pay and conditions. The committee under J.H. Whitley set up by the Ministry of Reconstruction to consider labour matters had reported in favour of joint industrial councils consisting of representatives of both employers and workers. In response the LCC agreed to set up an Interim Joint Committee of Members and Staff in 1920. This proved to be an effective negotiating body and was made permanent in 1927. It succeeded in maintaining the war-time cost of living bonuses and in converting these into improved salary levels in 1930.

For most of the 1920s there was a very complicated structure of payments, with considerable discrepancies between official salary scales and take-home pay for the vast majority who earned less than £2,000 a year. The official pay scales in operation from 1921 to 1929 are set out in Table 3.[19] However, the various additions meant that when Thomas Bullivant was appointed Solicitor to the LCC in 1926 his official salary was £1,500 but he actually received £1,686 6s 1d a year. There was no bonus on salaries of £2,000 a year or more, and when permanent increases in salary were adopted in 1930 all temporary additions ended.

Complications of a different kind appeared in the economic crisis of the early 1930s, when local authorities were forced to make economies. Salary cuts were imposed, but those already in the service of the LCC on 31

[18] G. Anderson, *Victorian Clerks*, 1976, pp.56-8; Pennybacker, *op. cit.*, pp.23-38, 70-82; E. Leopold for Greater London Council, *In the Service of London: Origins and Development of Council Employment from 1889*, 1986, pp.30-40; LCC Minutes, 6 October & 3 November 1891, pp.948-9, 1079-80; 21 February 1905, p.482. W.G. Wilmot, *The London County Council Staff Association: the Story of its Inception and Progress from 1909 to 1935*, 1935, and see n.17.

[19] Table compiled from *London County Council Services and Staff on 1st April, 1927.*

Table 3

*Annual Salaries of LCC Officers in 1927*

| | *MEN* | | *WOMEN* | |
|---|---|---|---|---|
| | *Minimum* £ s | *Maximum* £ s | *Minimum* £ s | *Maximum* £ s |
| *General Grade (paid weekly)* | 52 0 | 208 0 | 44 4 | 174 2 |
| *Major Establishment* | 120 0 | 350 0 | 120 0 | 350 0 |
| *Head of Department* | 1000 0 | 2500 0 | | |

Table 4

*Annual Salaries of LCC Officers, 1 June 1930*

| | *MEN* | | *WOMEN* | |
|---|---|---|---|---|
| | *Minimum* £ s | *Maximum* £ s | *Minimum* £ s | *Maximum* £ s |
| *General Grade (paid weekly)* | | | | |
| Employed by 31 March 1930 | 78 0 | 338 0 | 65 0 | 280 16 |
| Employed after 31 March 1930 | 78 0 | 312 0 | 62 8 | 260 0 |
| *Major Establishment (First Class)* | | | | |
| Employed by 31 March 1930 | 160 0 | 540 0 | 160 0 | 540 0 |
| Employed after 31 March 1930 | 160 0 | 500 0 | 160 0 | 500 0 |

March 1930 received more favourable treatment than new recruits, including those transferred from the poor law authorities. From 1930 two salary scales operated, as shown in Table 4,[20] the rate depending on the date the officer entered the Council's service. On top of this in 1931 the Staff Association volunteered a 2½ per cent salary cut for those earning up to £250 a year to try and forestall a more severe reduction. This cut

[20] Table compiled from *London County Council Services and Staff on 1st June, 1930.*

operated from January 1932 until March 1933, and went up to 10 per cent on salaries over £750. The dual pay scales continued to operate throughout the 1930s and the Labour administration which took control in 1934 showed itself no readier than the Municipal Reformers to end the inferior treatment of post-March 1930 entrants.

Compared with the position before the First World War by 1937 there had been some narrowing of differentials, as there was a 100 per cent increase in Minor Establishment and General Grade pay compared with a 50 per cent improvement in the salaries of the leading chief officers, who earned between £1,400 and £3,000 a year. The purchasing power, or real value, of salaries declined between July 1914 and July 1920 as the cost of living rose by 152 per cent, but by 1930 it had risen above the 1914 level through the combined effect of salary increases and a fall in the cost of living.

Despite the gradual improvements in real earnings in the 1930s there was growing resentment of the continued discrimination against post-1930 entrants. Eventually the Staff Association decided to act. In 1938 it issued a Post-1930 Report on the grievances of junior and transferred staff. The outbreak of the Second World War interrupted negotiations on this report and when the Council eventually offered minor concessions in 1940 the Staff Association rejected them and called for domestic arbitration. This request was refused. Representatives of the junior staff stepped up their campaign and when the next Staff Association elections took place in 1941 candidates who favoured a more vigorous approach won control of the main committees. The Council agreed to resume discussion of the Post-1930 Report and eventually conceded higher pay scales for those affected, though they still did not receive complete equality.

The Staff Association maintained its more militant approach after the end of the Second World War, feeling that a dictatorial line was being adopted by the Council side, headed by the LCC's Leader, Lord Latham. It mounted a campaign to back the demand for equal treatment of post-1930 entrants and a mass meeting took place in January 1947 at Kingsway Hall, attended by about 3,000 of the staff. This show of solidarity persuaded the LCC to be more conciliatory and after further negotiations it was finally agreed to end the post-1930 dual pay scales and to raise salary levels generally. As the cost of living continued to rise, the Staff Association sought further pay increases, but although they had some success they were not able to maintain the 1947 value of salaries. In money terms, by 1961, salaries ranged from £305 to £855 a year for the clerical grades, formerly the General and Higher Clerical Grades, £630 to £1,250 for administrative officers, formerly the Major Establishment, and up to £6,250 for the best-paid chief officers. These figures represented a further narrowing of differentials compared with the pre-war position. The reduction in differentials between clerical and professional employment was part of a national trend, and LCC salaries remained comparable with those which could be earned in similar occupations.[21]

### *Staff Recruitment and Promotion*

The LCC's methods of recruiting permanent staff resembled those of the Civil Service and in the early years contrasted markedly with the practice of other Victorian local authorities. The Metropolitan Board of Works had pioneered the use of open competitive examinations for the recruitment of permanent junior clerks from the 1860s onwards and the LCC retained and developed this system, another example of administrative continuity. The examination was sufficiently demanding to require education beyond the elementary level and the fee was a guinea, with a further five shillings for each additional optional subject. The compulsory subjects were English composition, English dictation, arithmetic, compound addition, geography and either shorthand or book-keeping. The composition was normally on a subject of contemporary debate; for example, in 1898 candidates had to write on either 'The importance of the increased efficiency of the Navy to the commercial interest of Great Britain' or 'Will the Central Electric Railway assist in relieving the congested traffic of London, or what other means may be suggested for the purpose?' The LCC was the only local authority to recruit by competitive examination in the late nineteenth century. Not until after the First World War did the practice spread more widely, and even then it was by no means universal.[22]

When the Minor and Major Establishments were set up, recruitment to the bottom rung of both was by separate competitive examinations. At first Minor officials who wanted to be promoted to the Major Establishment had to compete with outside candidates in the same examination for the limited number of places available. The resulting slow rate of promotion caused resentment and, spurred on by the disruption to career patterns caused by the First World War, the Council changed its policy in 1920 and reserved 80 per cent of vacancies in the Major Establishment for what were now called the General Grade, chosen by an internal competitive examination. In practice, between 1922 and 1935 only 9 per cent of Major Establishment vacancies were filled by outside candidates.

[21] LCC Minutes, 14 December 1920, pp.1009-20 and 23 November 1926, pp.638-9; Department of Employment and Productivity, *op. cit.*, table 89; G. Routh, *Occupation and Pay in Great Britain, 1906-1960*, 1965, pp.51-108; Pat Bacon (former Secretary of LCC Staff Association), unpublished and untitled typescript of reminiscences, 14 April 1986, sent to the LCC History Group.

[22] MBW Minutes, 6 March 1863, p.246, and 2 March 1877, pp.326-30; LCC Minutes, 16 July 1889, pp.575-7 and 10 December 1889, p.969; W.A. Robson, *From Patronage to Proficiency in the Public Service: An Inquiry into Professional Qualification and Methods of Recruitment in the Civil Service and the Municipal Services*, 1922.

This change did not however satisfy the hopes of the staff. Promotion by competitive examination only when vacancies occurred meant that their chances fluctuated enormously from year to year. In 1935 the Council decided on a further change. The entry standard for the General Grade was lowered so as to recruit candidates for routine work, and the reservation of places on the Major Establishment for internal candidates was to be phased out by 1940. From the 1930s onwards a number of graduates were taken on to the Major Establishent on the basis of interview, without further examination, and by the 1960s graduate entrants made up about half the total. To begin with the graduate entry scheme caused some friction, with senior officials arguing that if graduates were given accelerated promotion it would cause resentment among the other staff, while the new intake became frustrated by spending long periods doing relatively routine work. This pattern of growing graduate entry mirrored developments in other professional and managerial occupations since the Second World War, but promotion into the administrative grades by passing the Council's examination remained an option.

Recruitment to senior and professional posts followed the same pattern throughout the LCC's existence and was also modelled on the practice established by the MBW. Many senior vacancies, especially those of an administrative character, were filled by internal promotion. But where professional expertise or wide experience was required, the post was usually advertised in the press and a candidate chosen by competitive interview. Up to the Second World War recruitment and promotion of permanent staff were handled either by the Establishment Committee or by the General Purposes Committee. But after the war most of the work was delegated to senior staff for posts below assistant chief officer level. For example, entrants to the general clerical class were chosen by a panel of three senior officers and simply recommended to the Establishment Committee for formal appointment.[23]

### *Women Staff*

The first woman to be employed by the Council in an administrative or clerical capacity was an inspector in the Public Control Department in 1894. The immediate reason for her appointment was the passing of the Shop Hours Acts of 1892 and 1893, as it was felt that it would be useful to have a woman to check on the hours worked by female shop assistants, though she was also to help implement the Infant Life Protection Act, alongside the male inspectors already employed. Her starting salary was

[23] LCC Minutes, *passim*, specifically 2 February 1904, pp.111-12 and 14 December 1920, pp.1008-20; Gibbon & Bell, *op. cit..*, pp.205-77; P. Bacon, *op. cit.*; Clifton, 'Staff', pp.137-8; Grocott, *op. cit.*, p.20.

to be £100 a year, two-thirds of the sum received by men in the same grade.[24]

The next major experiment with women clerical staff was the employment of 'lady typists' to do fair copying. They remained a separate all-female grade in the Clerk's department, but they were recruited by methods similar to those used for male clerks and quite a high standard of education was demanded. Candidates had to pass either matriculation or the Council's preliminary examination in English composition, arithmetic, English history and geography, and then take a competitive examination in general subjects as well as typing and shorthand. One of the conditions of employment for women typists as soon as the section was made permanent was that they should resign on marriage, apparently following the example of the Civil Service where such a marriage bar for women already existed. In 1906 a standing order was passed applying the marriage bar to all women subsequently employed by the LCC, except teachers and any others specially exempted. The marriage bar was a symptom of the contemporary determination that women should not be allowed to compete directly with men, however well qualified they were.

In local, as in national employment, the First World War began to change attitudes towards women at work, though many of the advances into new areas of employment were only temporary. As far as the LCC was concerned it was not until after the Second World War that formal equality of treatment was conceded. Even then there were few women in senior positions and the Council never had a woman chief officer, a figure still a rarity in local government.

During the First World War women were brought in by the LCC to replace men who had joined the armed forces, but they tended to be confined to routine work, while men who were too old for military service took the more demanding responsibilities. Women were generally paid less than men of the same grade, though this was often justified by allowing them shorter hours or exempting them from certain heavy duties. There were some exceptions to this rule, especially in professional posts; for example, in the Public Health Department women medical officers were paid the same as men.

The wartime experience created an atmosphere in which women's role in public and economic life was more fully accepted and prepared the way for the Sex Disqualification (Removal) Act of 1919, which provided that sex or marriage should not disqualify a person from holding any civil post or profession. But there was an escape clause which allowed the Civil Service to be excluded from the operation of the Act and the LCC too continued to operate a marriage bar, despite efforts by Councillor Susan

[24] LCC Minutes, 13 February 1894, pp.156-7, 20 February 1894, p.175 and 10 April 1894, pp.403-4. Miss Isabel Grinton Smith was appointed.

Lawrence to have it rescinded. As far as the Council was concerned there were good practical reasons for maintaining the bar, for it meant that women in their mid-to-late twenties, who had moved up the salary scale, were continually replaced as they left to marry by younger women receiving the minimum pay. This helped to ensure that women continued to act as a source of cheap labour.[25] The women themselves often accepted the bar, partly because they received a lump sum (called a dowry!) if they had served six years or more when they left to marry. However, there were also steps to recruit women to a wider range of posts in the Council's service. In 1919 women were admitted to the Major Establishment, competing in the same examination as men, and though they were limited to 10 per cent of vacancies, they did receive equal pay. They were also allowed to compete in the examination for the General Grade, and could take up to 30 per cent of the posts available, but they were paid less than men. The restrictions on the proportion of women recruited were removed in 1928 for the General Grade and 1930 for the Major Establishment, but it was not until during and after the Second World War that the other disadvantages suffered by women were removed. By the inter-war years several important branches of the LCC's responsibilities were heavily dependent on female staff, notably primary education, children's care work, hospitals and routine clerical work. But staff regulations treated them as a marginal workforce.

The wartime demand for labour meant that the marriage bar had to be suspended, and it was finally removed in 1945. Equal pay was eventually conceded in 1952, somewhat to the astonishment of the Staff Association, who had renewed their demand without much hope that it would be accepted. This was an important point of principle, but it did not benefit those women who were in exclusively female grades, such as typists.

How good an employer was the LCC? Pat Bacon, who was in a position to form a judgement, as Secretary of the Staff Association from 1946 to 1949 and later editor of the staff journal *London Town*, came to the following conclusion:

> [The LCC] strove to be fair to its staff, though never extravagantly so, and yet was capable of tolerating for long periods injustices like the marriage bar, unequal pay and other less obvious forms of sex discrimination, and dual scales – and occasionally of engaging in unworthy pettiness. It was not a model employer . . . but it was never a 'bad' employer.[26]

[25] This point was made by Sylvia Bacon in a typescript 'Service or Slavery: Women Workers', sent in 1986 to the LCC History Group.

[26] P. Bacon, *op. cit.*, p.11; see also LCC Minutes, 11 December 1906, p.1468; Leopold, *op. cit.*, pp.50-60; Pennybacker, *op. cit.*, pp.292-9.

### *Staff Attitudes and Professionalization*

Competition for employment with the LCC was intense, particularly at the higher levels. There was usually a pride in working for a leading local authority and a corresponding dedication and sense of service. Officials who had begun their careers under the MBW recalled the new team spirit and enthusiasm which emerged in the early years of the LCC. Up to the period of the Second World War most officials had a strong commitment to their work and a desire to make local administration efficient and effective.

By the last decade of the LCC there was some feeling among the staff of the larger departments, such as the Architect's, that the bureaucracy was growing too rigid and it was becoming increasingly difficult to change established procedures. The problem was worse because there was no prospect of change in political control to shake things up.[27]

Another trend, which the staff of the LCC shared with employees in other forms of administration and in the commercial world, was the growing importance of professional training and values. Gradually more and more senior appointments required membership of recognized professional bodies. At the start of the LCC the Architect, Chemist, Engineer, Medical Officer, Solicitor and Valuer were all expected to have received a formal professional training, but it was not considered necessary for the Clerk, the Chief Officer of the Fire Brigade and the Comptroller. The LCC and the MBW, unlike most local authorities, had separate chief officers for administrative and legal affairs, instead of making the Clerk responsible for both. Consequently a legal qualification was never a formal requirement for the Clerk, though it was an advantage, and the final two Clerks had both had a legal training. However, by the inter-war years the Chief of the Fire Brigade was expected to have an engineering qualification, and after the Second World War the Comptroller was expected to be a member of one of the institutes of accountants. A similar process occurred with newer departments: the first Chief Officer of Stores, appointed in 1909, had worked his way up through the LCC hierarchy; the final official to hold the same position, renamed Chief Officer of Supplies, had professional accountancy qualifications. This was part of a trend among the emerging professions to control the entry of new recruits and to establish their claim to be on an equal footing

[27] P.C.E. Dimmick, 'Spring Gardens in 1891', *The London County Council Staff Gazette*, January 1936, p.30; Laurence Gomme, 'A Retrospect', *LCC Staff Gazette*, June 1915, p.89; G.A. Joce, 'Spring Gardens Again', *LCC Staff Gazette*, July 1936, p.238; reminiscences of K.S. Mills; A.D. Nicholls, 'Working for London', typescript dated 3 March 1986; P. Johnson-Marshall, 'The King is Dead – Long Live the King', typescript dated March 1986, all sent to the LCC History Group.

with the well-established vocations, such as medicine and the law.[28]

### *The Background of the Officers, 1889-1965*

Apart from the tendency for a growing proportion of chief officers to be members of professional institutions the other main change which occurred in their background was in their education in the broader sense. In 1890 three out of ten chief officers had a degree or had passed examinations of equivalent standard, such as those for admission as solicitor. But the proportion of chief officers with similar qualifications had risen to 44 per cent by 1927, and to about 50 per cent by the early 1960s. There were also changes in the types of schools chief officers had attended, reflecting changes in state provision for education. There was always a proportion from public schools, but whereas in 1890 the majority for whom information exists attended private schools, by 1964 a grammar-school background was the most common. The best chances of rising from the ranks without the benefit of a good education existed for those who were young in the 1890s and became chief officers in the 1910s and 1920s, such as the Clerk, James Bird, who started work when he was just under fourteen years old, and the Valuer, F.W. Hunt, who had attended Peckham Wesleyan Higher Grade School.

Like the Councillors, the majority of chief officers whose background is known came from middle-class homes, most of their fathers being in the professions or in business. A few, like J. Bird, F.W. Hunt, and C.D. Johnson, the Comptroller in the 1920s, were sons of skilled artisans or shopkeepers.

Chief Officers tended to be slightly younger than the leading Councillors, averaging fifty-one in 1890 and fifty-five in 1965. When first appointed to head a department they were usually in their late forties or fifties, but some talented individuals reached the top in their thirties: Harry Haward was only just thirty when promoted to the post of Comptroller in 1893 and P.F. Stott became the LCC's last Chief Engineer at thirty-seven years of age.

The route to headship of a department remained varied throughout the LCC's life. From the beginning some vacancies for chief officers were advertised in the press and outsiders were appointed, while others were filled by promotion. It was slightly more likely for posts requiring professional qualifications to be advertised, but after the Second World War recruitment was often at assistant or deputy chief officer level, with the final elevation to head of department coming by promotion. For example, in 1964, the Comptroller, the Education Officer, the Chief

[28] LCC Minutes, *passim*; *Who Was Who*, vols.I-VII; R. Lewis & A Maude, *Professional People*, 1952; G. Millerson, *The Qualifying Associations*, 1964; Grocott, *op. cit.*, p.18.

Engineer and the Medical Officer of Health had all entered the service as second or third in their respective departments. While it was still possible to spend a lifetime's career with the LCC and eventually reach chief officer level, as did T.G. Randall, appointed Children's Officer in 1962 after over forty years' service, this pattern became less common in the post-war years. Seven out of the sixteen departmental heads in 1927 had begun their careers as fourth-class or junior clerks in the service of the LCC or one of its predecessors, whereas by 1964 only two out of sixteen had worked their way up in this manner.

Administrative staff below the level of head of department tended to come from slightly humbler homes than their chiefs. Of the twenty-three successful candidates for fourth-class clerkships in 1890 twelve, or roughly half, were sons of clerks, shopkeepers, and commercial travellers, while three were sons of skilled artisans. About half went to minor public schools. By 1913, when the LCC was under Municipal Reform control, entrants to the lower rung of the Major Establishment were slightly more likely to come from middle-class homes. Only one out of twenty-seven was the son of a skilled artisan, twelve were sons of clerks, foremen, shopkeepers, and teachers, while thirteen were sons of professional men, managers, merchants and manufacturers; one father was retired. Twelve had been to public school. After the First World War LCC application forms no longer asked for fathers' occupations, so only the education of candidates can be compared. By the 1930s entrants from public schools were in a minority, and most came from grammar, county and other secondary schools and this remained the pattern after the Second World War. Before the graduate entry scheme was set up in the 1930s only a few candidates had university degrees, though others worked part-time for degrees and professional qualifications while employed by the LCC. Throughout the LCC's existence the vast majority of candidates at the lower levels came from the London area.

In the early years many new recruits to the LCC staff were attracted by the pioneering nature of the work and tended to be sympathetic to the Progressive outlook. Both before and after the First World War there was a minority of socialists, but if the contents of the *London County Council Staff Gazette* are a fair reflection the majority were more interested in hobbies and sports than in political activism.[29]

### *Relations Between Members and Officials*

When the first London County Councillors took their seats in 1889 they were suspicious of the administrative staff they had inherited from the

[29] *Who Was Who*; LCC Minutes, *passim*; LCC Clerk's Dept. Papers, Original Applications for Appointment.

MBW, and took steps to ensure that the reforms they wanted to carry out would not be blocked by official inertia or obstruction. They assigned to the new post of paid Deputy Chairman of the Council the duty of supervising the staff. The Deputy Chairman took over many of the functions carried out by the Clerk under the MBW and emphasized the point by occupying the former Clerk's room. The new elected Members had clear ideas about what they wanted to do and were less dependent on the advice of officials than their Board of Works predecessors. They resisted delegation of powers to committees or to chief officers. They also felt that the officials had been unduly privileged under the old regime, and proceeded to vote that any new staff they appointed should not be entitled to the non-contributory pension enjoyed by those originally recruited by the MBW.

The Councillors soon discovered that their distrust of the staff was unfounded. The leading officials were much more efficient and eager to co-operate than they expected. Even those who did not share the Progressives' views impressed the elected Members with their anxiety to provide an impartial service. Heads of department inherited from the MBW showed considerable energy in putting together teams to carry out new policies, such as the building of housing for the working classes. The Councillors also discovered some talented, sympathetic and enthusiastic figures among the younger staff and encouraged their rapid promotion to senior positions. So the changes in London's local government brought to the fore officers such as Laurence Gomme, Edgar Harper and Harry Haward, who were to play a leading role in the implementation of Council policy in the Progressive period. Harper, for example, provided much of the detail for the Progressives' abortive plans for the taxation of site values. Even though the Councillors kept a firm grip on policy they still had to rely on the technical advice of officials. The success of the policy of purchasing London tramway operations depended on the arguments marshalled by the Valuer, Andrew Young, to convince the arbitrator that only plant and not goodwill should be included in the valuation. The original policy ideas might come from Members but the skills of the officials were still essential to put them into effect.

The growing confidence of the Members in the officers was shown by the ending of the close supervision by the Deputy Chairman in 1896 and by giving the Clerk responsibility for the administrative staff. But the Councillors retained a distrust of delegation right up to the Second World War, and the growing strength of party organization also helped to restrict the influence of the staff on policy. It was only in post-war years that substantially more routine decisions were left to officers. One result of the reluctance to delegate was an enormous volume of paperwork as officials had to write formal reports for committees on even the smallest details. Much of this had little effect on what the Council actually did, as in all routine matters the officials' advice was usually followed. But elected

Members tended to be busier than their colleagues on other leading local authorities, and senior staff who joined the LCC after service elsewhere found it difficult to adapt to the limitation of their discretion.

Even though formal delegation was limited, the chief officers remained influential figures. As the Council became responsible for a wider range of services the Members inevitably became more dependent on the specialized knowledge of the senior staff. There developed very close working relationships between the committee chairmen and the relevant heads of department, and between the Clerk and the Leader of the Council. However, under Morrison's leadership it was made clear that Members and officials should not have any social contacts, so that the staff could more easily maintain the impartiality of their advice.

A study made at the end of the Council's life by B. Grocott, a junior LCC official studying for an MA, found that the relative positions of the senior staff and Councillors had changed dramatically compared with the 1890s. By 1964 there had been much more delegation of routine work to the officials, and heads of department were able to exercise considerable influence on policy matters. The reasons for this development were the growing need for professional advice on complex issues and the long period of Labour control. The Council appointed chief officers who were in close sympathy with their political outlook and could therefore leave much business to the staff with considerable confidence. Senior staff with clear views could often guide policy, as in the case of some of the Education Officers, but such an approach could also lead to disagreements such as those over housing densities in the Planning Committee under Mrs Bolton's chairmanship. A determined committee chairman could normally resist staff policy initiatives, unless the officer was supported by the Leader of the Council.[30]

The LCC was sometimes an unwieldy body, and relations between Members and staff over conditions of work were not always harmonious, but both sides shared a determination to make local government work. There was a tendency for senior positions to be filled by candidates who were sympathetic to the outlook of the majority on the Council, but even in the early years there was none of the jobbery which characterized much Victorian local government, and the LCC set an example in methods of recruitment which became the model for other authorities to follow. From the beginning of the LCC there was considerable continuity in local government with both leading Councillors and officers serving the

[30] Harry Haward, *The London County Council From Within: Forty Years' Official Recollections*, 1932, pp.52-71; A. Offer, *Property and Politics 1870-1914: Landownership, Law, Ideology and Urban Development in England*, 1981, pp.198-9; *The Times*, 25 February 1916, p.5, 24 January 1934, p.6, and 10 September 1953, p.10; *LCC Staff Gazette*, August 1901, pp.92-3 and June 1906, p.85; GLHL, M. Bryant, 'Andrew Young: A Brief Account of His Life and Work as a Public Officer of London', 1924, pp.16-20; interview with Mrs. I.M. Bolton, 1 June 1987.

Council for long periods. Even when the LCC was abolished in 1965 there remained a strong element of continuity, just as there had been in 1889, for most of the staff, and many of the Members, went on to serve the new Greater London Council.

## *Chapter 2*

# *The Progressive Council, 1889-1907*

John Davis

Much was expected of the early London County Council. It was a new local authority, created when expectations of local government stood at their highest – when the constraints of mid-Victorian parsimony were loosening, but before responsibility for social policy had begun to fall to central government. Excepting the London School Board, it was the capital's first democratic metropolitan authority, attracting a degree of publicity unprecedented in British municipal history and a cluster of celebrity councillors rare in local government. It was invested by many with the task of bringing to London the sort of energetic administration that had transformed Britain's provincial cities since the 1840s – a municipal gospel which included public health reform and slum clearance, the provision of gas, water, electricity and transport, and urban regeneration through street improvements, parks and other amenities.

With its police force under central government control and its gas and water supply, its markets, docks and tramways and even some of its bridges and parks in private hands, London was a municipally backward city in the 1880s. The LCC's predecessor, the Metropolitan Board of Works, had built the Thames embankment, the main drainage system and some major new streets, but as an indirectly elected body it was subject to growing public suspicion as its expenditure inevitably rose. Doubts about the MBW's accountability led to its being denied gas and water purchase in the 1870s, and limited still further its value as a municipal body as it became engulfed in scandal in the 1880s.[1] The immediate effect of the MBW's decline was the creation of a climate favourable to municipal enterprise, and the LCC began life with as comprehensive a mandate for action as any British local authority can ever have been given. The Liberal/Radical Progressives who controlled the Council for its first eighteen years – and many of the officers who served them – believed that municipal activity could provide an efficient collective response to modern social problems without undue dependence on the state. In eighteen years their achievements were to be considerable,

[1] D. Owen, *The Government of Victorian London, 1855-1889*, 1982, chapters 8 & 9.

but I will argue here that their success was necessarily qualified. The Progressive LCC stands as one of the benchmarks of British municipal development, but it is perhaps more significant as a demonstration of the *limits* to local collectivism.

Victorian municipal enterprise depended upon the efforts of local councillors, and most of its students have emphasized the victory of municipal visionaries over obstructionists and 'economists'. It has not always been obvious that local authorities operated within a statutory framework – that the ground rules were made at Westminster. Much routine work was, of course, carried out without reference to Parliament, and even housing schemes and tramway purchase could be effected under existing general Acts, but most of the major projects which characterized Victorian municipal enterprise required separate parliamentary sanction. This was never the obstacle that it might have been to provincial municipalism, largely because Parliament had tended to defer to the petitioning authority and its representative MPs as arbiters of the local interest. Though the Victorian municipal revolution might now be seen as a stage in the growth of the British state, nineteenth century observers tended to see the expanding role of local government as evidence of the pluralistic nature of the British democracy, and were not unduly worried by its interventionist implications. Bitter hostility might be voiced by interests threatened by municipal proposals – particularly gas and water companies – but provincial municipalism encountered very little disinterested ideological opposition at Westminster. The battles over the adoption of contentious schemes in the cities concerned raised few echoes in the national Parliament.

This was possible because for most of the nineteenth century the conventional distinction between local and national politics had some basis in fact. While parliamentary politics revolved around matters of denominational rivalry or trade policy, municipal activity was not easily given political colour: 'gas and water socialism' emanated from Tory as well as Liberal councils. By the 1890s, though, national politics embraced questions of urban poverty and unemployment, the rights of organized labour and the role of government in alleviating social distress. These were questions more likely to have a municipal dimension, and for the first time it became possible to interpret municipal policy in terms of the philosophies of the major political parties. The Conservatives, at both national and local level, came to represent the propertied middle class. The Liberals' identification with the working class and their adoption of interventionist social policies emerged more painfully from their years of introspective opposition after 1886, but among the leading advocates of movement in that direction were the London Radicals who dominated the LCC. The LCC Progressives added to the traditional elements of provincial municipalism an emphasis upon the local authority's role in tackling social problems – a direct response to the widespread public concern about London's poverty, overcrowding, unemployment and sweated labour in the 1880s. Their adoption of this agenda emphasized the developing similarity of local and national politics, particularly in the larger cities. As national politics became more urban, urban politics became more national, and the Victorian assumption that national politics was irrelevant to local government was steadily undermined.

In the first LCC elections in 1889 party labels were less important than they would become later. Local prominence could still carry a Tory employer, W.P. Bullivant, to the top of the poll in working-class Poplar, and allow the Liberals W.H. Dickinson in Wandsworth and T.H. Williams in North St Pancras to be asked to stand by both Conservative and Liberal Associations.[2] Personal charisma brought the election of the Liberal Lord Rosebery as an independent in the Conservative City of London and the Socialist John Burns in Battersea, but most of those returned in 1889 were party candidates, demonstrating the advantages enjoyed by political organizations in managing a large urban electorate. 'In the absence of an accredited non-political organization, it was inevitable that party machinery should be used in the selection of candidates', H.J. Powell, elected for Dulwich in 1889, acknowledged in his election address.[3] Powell was one of thirty-two candidates to admit party sponsorship. Others, who claimed to be standing at the request of 'numerous influential friends in the Division',[4] or resorted to similar euphemisms, were urged by one Tory MP to 'have no more of this humbug'.[5] A week before the poll it was accepted that 'most people regard the election as a semi-political affair, and will . . . vote for candidates according to their political views'[6] and the claim of the *South London Press* after the election that every successful candidate in its area had had party backing applied equally north of the river.[7] The formation of party groups on the new Council was therefore inevitable,[8] and the LCC was hardly unique in this respect. What was distinctive was the fact that 'the party system of the Council was carried to much greater lengths than it is in provincial municipalities where, although the elections are usually fought on political lines, there is less rigorous party division subsequently, when

[2] *The Metropolitan*, 22 December 1888.

[3] Bristol University Library collection of LCC election addresses, 1889.

[4] Address of W. Johnson & J. Lowles (Central Hackney), 1889, *ibid.* Johnson and Lowles had been adopted by their local Conservative Association two months earlier: Borough of Hackney Central Division Conservative Association Minutes, 16 November 1888, Rose Lipman Library, Hackney.

[5] A.A. Baumann, quoted in *South London Press*, 12 January 1889.

[6] *The Metropolitan*, 12 January 1889.

[7] *South London Press*, 26 January 1889.

[8] 'It would be as unwise to quarrel with the caucus as to complain of the equator', W. Saunders, *History of the First London County Council*, 1892, p.vii.

the members settle down to their administrative work'.[9] Most of the members of the early LCC saw Council work as intrinsically political.

Party politics tarnished the Council's image of itself as a Platonic elite, answering Victorian concern about the calibre of local politicians. In the eighteen years covered here LCC membership included two dukes, a viscount and thirty-seven other members of the peerage, one serving Prime Minister (Rosebery in 1894-5), several other cabinet ministers and MPs from all parties, former Governors of New Zealand and New South Wales, a member of the Judicial Committee of the Privy Council, four retired Permanent Secretaries, a Director of the Bank of England, two Fellows of the Royal College of Surgeons, the first Professor of Applied Mechanics at Cambridge, and such *literati* as Frederic Harrison, Sidney Webb and Graham Wallas. Yet power within the Council did not automatically reflect status, intellect or even administrative experience. It depended before all else upon membership of the Progressive group ('the LCC consists of the Progressive portion of it', as Beatrice Webb recorded),[10] acceptance of most of its objectives and a willingness to spend unpaid hours promoting them. Those celebrities who, like Webb and Lord Carrington, met these requirements were influential, but most of those who ran the LCC in the Progressive years did not belong to the list above. Men like John Williams Benn, Edwin Cornwall, B.F.C. Costelloe, W.H. Dickinson, Charles Harrison and Thomas Mackinnon Wood were closer than most of their contemporaries to the modern 'professional councillor' – living for their municipal work and involving themselves to a degree that could only be sustained by political conviction.

Governing London was arduous work. It meant four days' 'close attention' each week for a conscientious rank-and-file Councillor,[11] while the workload for even the less prominent chairmen was 'stupendous', 'downright slavery'.[12] Leading Councillors suffered burdens which turned Burns grey, gave Benn migraines and Allen Baker headaches and dyspepsia, led Arthur Hobhouse to a serious breakdown and perhaps hastened Joseph Firth's death.[13] The Council depended upon its

[9] Sir H. Haward, *The London County Council From Within: Forty Years' Official Recollections*, 1932, p.23.

[10] N. & J. MacKenzie (eds.), *The Diary of Beatrice Webb*, vol.II, 1983, p.33 (30 July 1893).

[11] F.W. Soutter, 'George Joseph Cooper, LCC, MP, Citizen, Radical, Democrat', in his *Fights for Freedom*, 1925, p.167.

[12] William Phillips in his autobiography *Sixty Years of Citizen Work and Play*, 1910, pp.36-7, and Evan Spicer, quoted in *South London Press*, 21 March 1891.

[13] K.D. Brown, *John Burns*, 1977, pp.60-1; typescript reminiscences of Sir J.W. Benn by Ernest Benn, n.d., Stansgate Papers (House of Lords Record Office), ST/286/3; E.B. Baker & P.J. Noel Baker, *J. Allen Baker, MP, a Memoir*, 1927, p.104; L.T. Hobhouse & J.L. Hammond, *Lord Hobhouse, a Memoir*, 1905, pp.173-4. For the claim that Council work had helped kill Firth, who had led the movement for a London municipality in the 1880s, see Lord Hobhouse, 'The London County Council and its Assailants', *Contemporary Review*, LXI, 1892, p.337.

workhorses who in turn made it into something of an oligarchy of committee chairmen. This may have been, as Beatrice Webb thought, a means of 'dodging the democracy (in a crude sense) by introducing government by a select minority'.[14] Certainly it was a means of resisting interference from outside and asserting the LCC's political independence.

In the first place this meant independence of the official Liberal Party. When the Council was created the Liberal hierarchy had seen it as a vehicle for the party's metropolitan recovery: Rosebery stood for election and accepted the Chairmanship in 1889 on Sir William Harcourt's insistence that 'the advance of Liberalism in the Metropolis will do much for the party',[15] while both Carrington and James Stuart first ran for the Council at the instigation of the Liberal grandees.[16] At the same time, London Radicals saw their comprehensive victory in 1889 as evidence that 'a really Radical programme would carry 20, or at least 15, more London seats' in the next general election.[17] Men who tended to attribute the Liberals' failures in London parliamentary contests to the 'milk and water policy' adopted by the leadership[18] feared that manipulation by the national party implied the emasculation of Progressive policy. The relationship between the LCC Progressives and the national Liberal party deteriorated steadily from 1892, when the party was bounced into acceptance of a comprehensively Radical manifesto for the second Council election,[19] and reached its nadir as the minority Liberal government of 1892-5 failed to satisfy many Progressive demands. The LCC Progressives provide the first instance of a local party using their position on a local authority to advocate the radicalization of party policy. Control of the Council gave them a greater independence of the party leadership than most of the pressure groups and regional lobbies clinging to the Liberal skirts, especially as repeated Progressive electoral success down to 1904 contrasted with the Liberals' parliamentary weakness. By 1899 Webb felt confident enough to tell Campbell-Bannerman and other senior Liberals that 'the leaders would have to make it clear that they meant business on London questions'.[20] The image of the Progressives as

[14] *The Diary of Beatrice Webb* (see n.10), II, pp.34-5.

[15] Harcourt to Rosebery, 25 January 1889, Rosebery Papers (National Library of Scotland), RP 10035, 21.

[16] For Carrington see his diaries in the Bodleian Library, 25 September 1891; for Stuart, S. Webb to J.R. MacDonald, 22 January 1890, in N. MacKenzie (ed.), *The Letters of Sidney and Beatrice Webb*, vol.I, *Apprenticeships*, 1978, p.130.

[17] *The Star*, 19 January 1889.

[18] B.T.L. Thompson, quoted in *East London Observer*, 13 April 1889.

[19] See Sidney to Beatrice Webb, 15 November 1891, in *Letters* (see n.16), p.328. The manifesto was reprinted in Sir J. Lubbock, 'A Few Words on the Government of London', *Fortnightly Review*, LVII, 1892, pp.166-9.

[20] Sidney to Beatrice Webb, 21 June 1899, in N. MacKenzie (ed.), *The Letters of Sidney and Beatrice Webb*, vol.II, *Partnership*, 1978, pp.109-10.

a ginger group on the Liberal left, anxious to drive the party in Radical or even 'socialistic' directions, was more than an invention of their political opponents: it was accepted by many of the Progressives themselves.

A large proportion of the Progressive rank and file consisted of men prominent in their local constituency Liberal and Radical Associations – in modern terms party activists. Their municipal policy was an activist's combination of backward-looking fundamentalism and visionary radicalism. Most of the Progressives were Radical Liberals. The party on the Council included a sprinkling of Liberal Unionists, who had broken with the national Liberal Party over Irish Home Rule, a more significant group of trade unionists – some of them socialists – from 1892, and individual Fabians like Webb and Wallas who distinguished themselves from conventional Radicals, but conventional Radicals always formed the bulk of the party and set its direction. Like many Radical groups in this period they distanced themselves from the parody of pitiless individualism that they stigmatized as 'Old Liberalism', and their knowledge of the depth of London's social problems led them to emphasize the role of the public authority in fighting distress. This implied active municipal intervention in the fields of sanitation and public housing, and inspired the attempt – arguably the Progressives' most important innovation – to make the local authority a model employer, both in the adoption of fair wages and hours for its own employees and in the imposition of similar terms upon its contractors.

Linked to this interventionist social policy was an enthusiastic advocacy of municipal trading. At its heart was the traditional municipal ambition – associated with Joseph Chamberlain's mayoralty in Birmingham and central to municipal activity in the provinces – of taking existing gas and water monopolies into public hands, fuelled by the London consumer's resentment of the cost of private supply. The case for public utility purchase was strengthened by its relevance to the labour policy, particularly in the case of the tramways, whose employees were 'among the hardest worked, most cruelly treated and worst paid of London's wage slaves'.[21] In the more adventurous Progressive fantasies it developed into a general vision of municipal direction of the local economy, embracing municipal bakehouses,[22] municipal pawnshops,[23] even Lord Monkswell's idea of a 'practical socialism' leading men 'to such a state of mind that private property might be usefully and considerably diminished and public property increased.'[24]

Usually, though, the Progressives did not stray far beyond the municipalization of natural monopolies. Though they sometimes called

[21] S. Webb, *The London Programme*, 1891, pp.73-4.

[22] The brainchild of Frank Sheffield, *East London Observer*, 26 June 1895.

[23] W.H. Dickinson, quoted in *London*, 26 July 1894.

[24] *Hackney and Kingsland Gazette*, 29 May 1893.

themselves socialists they did not display any sophisticated vision of the municipality as redistributor of wealth. Most of them subscribed, some obsessively, to the doctrines of the American land reformer Henry George, who had drawn attention, in his British tours in the early 1880s, to the windfall gains made by urban freeholders,[25] but their advocacy of George's single tax, designed to intercept such gains for the benefit of the community, allowed them to beg the question of how far their activity should seek to redistribute non-landed wealth. They showed little interest in graduating the rating system,[26] and resisted any suggestion that Council rents be directly subsidized from the rates, although the policy of making LCC housing pay its way put it beyond the reach of the very poor.[27] They showed few qualms about applying tramway profits in aid of the rates and hoped to do the same with water and gas, though this implied taxing the working-class consumer to support the householder.[28] At the same time, attempts to force them into the fashionable 'national efficiency' mould, such as the future Lord Rothermere's intriguing offer to Mackinnon Wood in 1901 to throw his newspapers behind a Progressive programme combining 'advanced social legislation' with 'a policy of sane and unaggressive imperialism' were misplaced.[29] Essentially the Progressives sought to adapt traditional Radicalism to a modern urban setting. If they had rejected *laisser faire*, they remained committed to the ethical foundations of what Dickinson called 'our older Liberalism', with its respect for 'the abstract rights of mankind'.[30]

The Progressives claimed for this programme the kind of consensual approval which they believed to have sustained municipal enterprise in the provinces. Their rhetoric was pervaded by the assumption that they spoke for the London community as a whole and that opposition to their policies was prompted by the naked self-interest of ground landlords, public utility companies, the City Corporation and its livery companies, the House of Lords, dock owners, the holders of market rights and other metropolitan parasites. Consensus was not entirely illusory. The first council elections were held at the height of the social concern that suffused London in the 1880s, which demonstrated that metropolitan opinion could attain a kind of unity in response to an evangelistic appeal to social duty. The gas and dock companies who faced the strike of 1888-9 were

25 For George, London and the LCC see A. Offer, *Property and Politics*, 1981, chapter 12.

26 Though graduated rating was advocated by Burns ('Let London Live!', *Nineteenth Century*, XXXI, 1892, p.681) and B.F.C. Costelloe (*The Incidence of Rating*, 1893, p.5).

27 Dickinson said that building on the rates 'would be the destruction of the entire Progressive party', *London and the Municipal Journal*, 8 December 1898.

28 Though Webb advocated free gas, water and tramways: Royal Commission on Labour, *Parliamentary Papers*, 1893-4, XXXIX, Part 1, QQ. 3863-8.

29 H. Harmsworth to Wood, 4 March 1901, Mackinnon Wood Papers, Bodleian Library, Oxford, MS Eng. Hist. c.499.

30 W.H. Dickinson, *London and Liberalism*, 1902, p.7.

bewildered by the hostility of the London public: as Stedman Jones has commented on the dock strike, 'there have been few strikes in British history which have been helped by subscriptions from the City, cheered on by the stock-brokers, and won in an atmosphere of carnival'.[31] *The Star*, the aggressively Radical evening paper founded in the previous year, was playing to an appreciative gallery when it urged voters in 1889 to:

> think of London's poor, of the overworked bus and tram driver, of the dweller in the Whitechapel slums, of the sweated tailoress in her den, of the unskilled labourer hungrily watching for his turn at the docks, of the rent-crushed toiler for daily bread, which he can scarce snatch out of his landlord's maw, of the multitudinous oppressions of this great wealth-ridden city.[32]

But the bipartisan social concern to which this sort of hyperbole appealed was essentially transient, an effect of the sudden re-emergence of urban poverty as a political issue in the 1880s. By the turn of the century the philanthropic consensus of that decade seemed to Masterman 'so incredibly distant from us', [33] a victim of the developing polarization of London politics. London's politics were not naturally consensual. London was too large and too socially diverse for this sort of unitary civic ethos to be plausible. Almost any municipal action was redistributionary in its effects, between classes and between social areas. In more compact and cohesive communities the inevitable reaction of those aggrieved might have given way to an overriding local patriotism, but London's metropolitan awareness was too weak to be invoked with confidence; civic pride was still primarily parochial, and if anything divisive in its effects.[34]

The social segregation that had created the concentrations of poverty so prominent in the 1880s had also produced homogeneous middle-class areas with their own political priorities. The interests of the working-class voter and the middle-class ratepayer, the demands of the East End and the West, were different and potentially antagonistic. It is true that the concern of the middle-class householder for lower rates and municipal economy was not unqualified: muted by the vogue for social reform in the 1880s, it was offset by his consumer's interest in the cheaper water, gas and transport promised by municipalization. Purely negative retrenchment would remain a minority cause for twenty years, but London was an expensive, high-rental city whose rate burden rose by 160% over the last quarter of the nineteenth century;[35] the politics of economy could always find a constituency. The Progressive ascendancy

[31] G. Stedman Jones, *Outcast London*, 1971, p.315.
[32] *The Star*, 7 August 1889.
[33] C.F.G. Masterman, 'Realities at Home', in C.F.G. Masterman *et al.*, *The Heart of the Empire*, 1901, p.2.
[34] See J.H. Davis, *Reforming London*, 1988.
[35] *Ibid.*, Appendix 3.

reflected, if not a bipartisan consensus, at least majority support for an active municipal programme, but their hegemony was achieved at the expense of the alienation of a minority whose opposition was ideological rather than self-interested, and who were ready and able to renew municipal battles in the parliamentary forum.

The evaporation of the consensus created by 'Outcast London' in the 1880s drove both Progressives and Moderates back to their political roots. For the Progressives, whose clear lead in working-class seats in 1889 became a near-monopoly in 1892, this meant a more explicit identification with working-class material interests. The philanthropic tone of the early days gave way during the 1890s to a more straightforward concern to advance the interests of London labour. For the Progressive Councillor T.B. Napier, speaking on 'Ideals of Local Government' in 1894:

> Local Government means very little indeed for rich people, but the poor man is dependent for his happiness upon Local Government, for cheap water, cheap gas, cheap and efficient means of locomotion, pleasant parks, pleasant streets, these are essential to a poor man's life.[36]

The labour Progressive Will Crooks spoke of bringing the County Council right into the working-man's home:

> We not only protected poor tenants from house spoilers and extortionate water companies, we gave a helping hand to the housewife. We saw that the coal sacks were of proper size, that the lamp oil was good, the dustbin emptied regularly, that the baker's bread was of proper weight, that the milk came from wholesome dairies and healthy cows, that the coster in the street and the tradesman in the shop gave good weight in everything they sold.[37]

John Benn anticipated the day when 'no middleman would stand between the poor and the article of food or of necessity'.[38]

This municipal consumerism was complemented by co-operation with organized labour. In 1892-3 the enlarged Progressive majority, now including a trade unionist contingent, passed two of the most controversial measures of the second Council – the decision to link LCC wages to the rates claimed by trade unions and 'in practice obtained' in the trades concerned, and the conversion of the Stores Department into a direct-labour Works Department to carry out Council building and engineering operations.[39] Burns considered the Works Department 'the biggest thing yet done for Collectivism', which 'properly developed will do more for labour in England than any other piece of work I have ever set my

[36] *London*, 25 January 1894.

[37] W. Haw, *From Workhouse to Westminster, The Life Story of Will Crooks, MP*, 1907, pp.92-3.

[38] *East London Observer*, 16 February 1895.

[39] LCC Minutes, 22 November and 13 December 1892.

hand to'.[40] It emphasized the Progressives' move from philanthropic reformism towards policies aimed at the working-class vote, while Moderate opposition to the most innocuous Progressive aspirations was hardened by their fear of 'a great army of working men in the direct employment of the County Council – a special and privileged class, exercising a great, perhaps an overwhelming influence over the elections'.[41]

The cost of this move to the left was the loss of much of the bipartisan sympathy that had attended the Council's creation. This showed itself first in the developing scepticism of much of the national and metropolitan press. A press corps forced to endure four or five hour debates in 'the worst . . . Press Gallery of any great municipal authority in the country'[42] consoled itself by creating an image of Progressive pedantry and political posturing that was refined by its Conservative majority into an extravagant attack upon the Progressive Council. A press consensus hostile to Progressivism developed virtually without reference to public opinion, so that in the 1898 election the Progressives achieved a landslide victory though supported only by the minority of explicitly Radical papers.[43] Within a few years press treatment of the Council was determined largely by mechanical prejudice on both sides. In consequence both parties became fixed in hardened rhetoric. The Progressive litany of opposition to the monopolist and the ground landlord changed little in eighteen years, leaving them intellectually unprepared for the 'ratepayers' revolt' of 1907. The Moderates' increasingly negative attitude towards Progressive initiatives harmed them severely until then.

One Moderate Councillor warned his party of the dangers of 'promiscuous abuse' of the LCC as early as the summer of 1891,[44] but it remained the easiest option for all those Conservatives whose political hatred of Progressivism reflected deeper opposition to municipal intervention. Lord Salisbury and others on the Conservative right had always harboured misgivings about the democratic potential of a single directly elected metropolitan authority.[45] Some Conservative MPs had responded to their party's failure to win the 1889 election by sniping at almost every LCC initiative requiring parliamentary sanction. Ratepayers and local politicians in the West End – the most highly

[40] John Burns' Journal, 18 October and 22 November 1892, British Library Add. MSS. 46312.

[41] Devonshire, quoted in *Local Government Journal*, 19 February 1898.

[42] Arthur Arnold, quoted in *London*, 16 May 1895.

[43] *London*, 10 March 1898. Cf. Lord Hobhouse's criticism of the 'Tory Press, the predominant press of London', *London Government. A Speech to the Eighty Club*, 1892, p.12.

[44] W.M. Acworth, quoted by J. Stuart, 'The London Progressives', *Contemporary Review*, LXI, 1892, p.529.

[45] P. Marsh, *The Discipline of Popular Government*, 1978, pp.163-4.

assessed residential district in London which consequently carried the greatest share of the LCC's demands – became obsessed with the need to curb Progressive 'extravagance'. Their rational objections to municipal enterprise developed into an often hysterical hostility to the Progressive LCC; the Moderates, denied power and influence on the Council, became increasingly susceptible to the appeal of purely destructive opposition.

In 1892 they effectively sub-contracted their campaign to Lord Wemyss and the libertarian eccentrics of the Liberty and Property Defence League.[46] In 1895 and 1898 they identified themselves with proposals to emasculate the Council by devolving many of its powers to enlarged borough authorities.[47] In 1902-3 they were seduced by the campaign against municipal enterprise waged by *The Times* and leading industrialists, and in 1906-7 they put themselves at the head of the retrenchment movement. They turned Council politics into an artificial debate over the principles of municipal activity – principles enshrined in statute, adopted widely in the provinces and held by many metropolitan Conservatives.

This helped the Progressives to maintain party discipline and court the London electorate. The Progressive group contained all the ingredients of Liberal fragmentation familiar from the national politics of the 1890s – some Gladstonian traditionalists, a significant employer group, 'social purity' Nonconformists and a semi-independent labour bench. All accepted, though, that the local authority had the power to ameliorate social problems and the duty to do so – a belief that had brought many of them into municipal politics in the first place. As long as a section of the Moderate party sought to neutralise the Council and deny it standard municipal functions, attention was deflected from policy differences which might have threatened party unity.

The only Progressive to cross the floor in this period was Sir John Lubbock, who was in any case a Liberal Unionist, a banker, a representative of the City and 'the politest reactionary that ever lived'.[48] Other Liberal Unionists like Richard Roberts and Alfred Hoare remained Progressives even when their metropolitan organization declared for the Moderates.[49] A traditional Gladstonian like Sir Thomas Farrer, 'still one of the pillars of free trade' in 1889,[50] was suspicious of Progressive enthusiasm in general and the wages policy in particular,[51] but his

[46] J.H. Davis, *Reforming London*, 1988, pp.187-9.

[47] See *ibid.*, chapters 7 and 8.

[48] John Burns' Journal, 29 October 1891, BL Add. MSS. 46311.

[49] In 1898 the Central Liberal Unionist Association took no official part in the LCC election, but several local associations declared their support for Moderate candidates and none supported Progressives: see the interview with Roberts in *London*, 17 February 1898.

[50] Pall Mall Gazette 'Extra', *The London County Council*, 1889, p.96.

[51] Royal Commission on Labour, *loc. cit.* (n.28), esp. QQ 7858ff; *Local Government Journal*, 17 December 1892.

'undiminished zeal for Progress' even in his mid-seventies meant that 'if the question is between Progress and Reaction, then a thousand times rather with John Burns than with the Reactionaries'.[52]

The same was true of the significant industrialist group within the party. London lacked the sort of Liberal industrialist caste that might have mounted a dogmatic defence of *laisser faire* in a provincial authority. Most Progressive employers treated Council service as part of a wider civic duty entailing local charitable and philanthropic work as well as membership of vestries and boards of guardians. James Branch, one of the largest employers in Bethnal Green, who believed that 'the day would not be far distant when the wealthy, the middle and the labouring classes would be found to possess an identity of interests',[53] joined the LCC with 'perhaps too ambitious hopes of bringing the millenium to the teeming poor of the East End'.[54] In a smaller community he might have become another Salt or Cadbury, pursuing a private philanthropy which did not compromise his essential individualism. In London, employer philanthropy was constrained both by the relative poverty of the capital's employers and by the sheer scale of its social problems, and an acceptance of municipal collectivism was inevitable. The Progressive labour policy strained the loyalty of many. T.H.W. Idris, founder of the soft drinks firm, who believed that 'it hurt nobody to be compelled to give good wages'[55] but did not want wage rates dictated by trade unions, and Richard Roberts, 'that rarity of rarities, an honest builder with a conscience',[56] registered their doubts in the division lobbies.[57] Burns' journals suggest considerable intra-party bitterness on labour questions in committee,[58] but such outspokenness was largely confined to the committee room. In Council, faced by an obscurantist Moderate opposition, most Progressive employers were ready to compromise rather than jeopardise all municipal work.[59]

The Nonconformist Progressives threatened not so much resistance to municipal collectivism as the promotion of potentially unpopular ethical crusades. London Nonconformity in the generation after Spurgeon was theologically liberal and politically Radical. C. Fleming Williams, a Hackney Congregationalist minister and an LCC alderman from 1889 to

[52] Farrer to Collins, 11 April 1894, Sir William Collins Papers, Senate House Library, 812/15.

[53] *East London Observer*, 15 December 1888.

[54] Pall Mall Gazette 'Extra', 1889, p.94.

[55] *London*, 17 December 1896.

[56] J. Burns, 'The London County Council: 1. Towards a Commune', *Nineteenth Century*, XXXI, 508.

[57] LCC Minutes, 13 December 1892.

[58] See e.g. the entries for 26 February 1891, 6 April 1892, 27 May 1892, 16 May 1899.

[59] See the debate on Frederic Harrison's amendment in *Local Government Journal*, 17 December 1892.

1904, was typical. Having 'drifted away from his old moorings; preaching originally "Salvation by the blood of Jesus", he is now evidently one of the broad school in the free churches' who aimed 'to show that without a church, without a chapel, without a bible I could still, through the lessons taught by our social and political activities, lead people to the Highest, that we call God.'[60] The LCC provided a platform for this sort of humanitarian evangelism, and men who convinced themselves that 'to cause a drain to be remedied was doing God's service'[61] provided almost uncritical support for the Progressive social programme throughout the 1890s.

Trouble was threatened, though, by their ethical preoccupations, and the disproportionate controversy generated by theatre and music hall regulation[62] suggests that the Council was fortunate not to be a liquor licensing authority. The LCC could impose a temperance regime upon the captive inmates of its asylums, 'to the marked physical and mental advantage of the patients'.[63] It could extinguish licences compulsorily purchased for slum clearance schemes and could contemplate municipal coffee houses in place of the vanished pubs.[64] It could even rechristen tramway stops named after public houses,[65] but it could not launch a general crusade.

Education was a more serious danger. The LCC's acquisition of the powers of the London School Board in 1904 worried many London Nonconformists, as hostile as their provincial counterparts to the 1902 Education Act.[66] Their opposition almost encouraged the Conservative government, legislating separately for London in 1903, to deny the Council education powers as it had earlier denied it water control,[67] and Sidney Webb was impelled to negotiate surreptitiously with Conservative ministers and Moderate Councillors to ensure that education devolved to the LCC.[68] His belief that 'the Nonconformists on the Council don't give a button about education as such'[69] underestimated, though, the extent to which Nonconformist Councillors saw education as a social service,

[60] For this portrait of Fleming Williams see the interview by A.L. Baxter for the Booth survey, Booth Papers, British Library of Political and Economic Science, B195, ff.3-19.

[61] N.W. Hubbard, quoted in *London*, 29 October 1896.

[62] W. Saunders, *History of the First London County Council*, 1892, pp.xii-xiii.

[63] London Reform Union Leaflet No. 59, *The Social and Moral Issues of the London County Council Election*, 1895.

[64] *London*, 17 May 1894.

[65] *Municipal Journal*, 9 October 1903.

[66] D.W. Bebbington, *The Nonconformist Conscience*, 1982, pp.141ff.; H. McLeod, *Class and Religion in the Late Victorian City*, 1974, p.178.

[67] W.A. Robson, *The Government and Misgovernment of London*, 1939, pp.114-6; A.G. Gardiner, *John Benn and the Progressive Movement*, 1925, chapter 16.

[68] *The Letters of Sidney and Beatrice Webb* (see n.20), II, pp.148-9.

[69] Sidney Webb to G. Wallas, 4 September 1903, *ibid.*, pp.193-4.

whatever their misgivings about Balfour's Act. The 'slump in Webbs'[70] caused by Sidney's duplicity appeared deserved in 1906-7, when the Progressives themselves came under attack from militant nonconformity outside the Council for implementing the Act.[71] The violent attack upon the LCC by the Nonconformist *British Weekly* in 1906-7 was tinged by a general distrust of 'New Liberalism': the paper sought a return to 'the old Liberal watchwords, Economy, Efficiency and Publicity' and welcomed Moderate gains in 1906 Borough Council elections.[72] Those Nonconformists who still saw social reform as a prerequisite for moral regeneration were aware that only 'the publican, the tipster and the monopolist' would benefit from the return of a Moderate Council.[73]

The labour Progressives were the only group within the party to affect a separate organization, but the inherent weakness of their position made them the least likely to break ranks. London unionism was a fragmented collection of small craft associations and the metropolitan branches of larger unions whose centre of gravity lay elsewhere. Trade unionists involved themselves in municipal politics because the failure of London's New Unionism in the early 1890s had demonstrated 'the relative weakness of union effort as compared with political action',[74] and the need to co-operate with conventional Radicalism. The Progressives courted labour candidates in 1892 as part of a policy of matching candidates to constituencies which also sent a number of Liberal peers to electoral slaughter in the West End,[75] but they were not forced into an accommodation with labour, as the Liberal Party was to be nationally in 1903, by any serious concern that independent labour candidatures would lose them seats. For the labour men it was 'a great financial help to fight side by side with a Progressive'[76] even for those who could expect a trade union salary once elected. Those who could not – Burns, Will Crooks and Will Steadman – lived off 'wages funds' and required regular donations from middle-class Progressives to continue unpaid Council work.[77]

The labour men were therefore vulnerable to the charge from the left that they were 'mere decoy ducks for political wire-pullers',[78] but their

[70] *The Diary of Beatrice Webb* (see n.10), II, p.273.

[71] See the circular, 'The London Liberal Federation and a Separate Education Authority', ?1906, in the McKinnon Wood Papers, Bodleian Library, Oxford.

[72] *British Weekly*, 8 November 1906.

[73] F.B. Meyer, *ibid.*, 28 February 1907.

[74] Burns to J. Chamberlain, 20 September 1892, John Burns Papers, BL Add. MSS. 46290, f.317.

[75] A. Morley to Rosebery, 7 January 1892, Rosebery Papers (see n.15), MS 10090, f.13; A. Morley to J.W. Benn, 12 March 1892, Benn Papers, Tonbridge, vol.3.

[76] H. Gosling, *Up and Down Stream*, 1927, p.82.

[77] See e.g. *London*, 16 January 1896, 5 March 1896; Gosling, *op. cit.*, p.84; Burns Journal, 9 January 1897, BL. Add. MSS. 46315, for the precarious nature of wages funds.

[78] H.M. Hyndman, quoted in *Daily Chronicle*, 19 March 1892.

position was much strengthened by Moderate nihilism. The Moderates' devotion to middle-class and ratepayer interests strengthened the Progressive claim to be the party of the working man, and Progressive success in working-class seats which consistently returned Conservatives to Parliament was one of the bases of their strength. Only in 1895 did the Moderates make any significant gains in working-class areas, and the return of a clutch of East End Moderates anxious to commit the party to a more popular programme only emphasized the Moderate leadership's hostility to municipal enterprise.[79] The problem was cruelly underlined by the failure of the East End's water supply in three consecutive summers in the mid 1890s. The Moderate leadership disliked water municipalization more than any other Progressive ambition except police control, but the Tower Hamlets were not 'inhabited by people who like being deprived of water as an antidote to socialism',[80] and the Moderate gains of 1895 disappeared in 1898. Moderate attacks upon the Progressive labour policy made it easier for labour Progressives to claim, as Steadman did in the 1898 election, that 'Trades Unionism at Spring Gardens during the last six years had done more in the direction of fostering municipal socialism than any other socialist party in Europe'.[81] The Independent Labour Party's rejection of Cornwall's invitation to fight that election on a joint 'Labour and Progressive' platform[82] left its candidates to be flattened by the Progressive juggernaut as working-class districts responded to Salisbury's threat to dismember the Council. It acknowledged engagingly that it could have done no worse with 'a programme in favour of devastating London with cholera',[83] and by 1901 had accepted that Moderate support 'for reaction, for anti-municipalism and for the continuance of capitalist, landlord and publican exploitation of the community' made it 'most inopportune' to split the Progressive vote.[84]

If the Moderates' negative stance helped consolidate Progressive unity, it also helped clarify policy. As the Moderates identified themselves with retrenchment and the interests of the ratepayer, so the Progressives shed their initial misgivings about expensive projects. On the first Council, street improvements, and the Holborn to Strand scheme in particular, had been deferred in the hope of securing power to levy a 'betterment' rate

[79] See e.g. the Council debate of 10 November 1896 in *London*, 12 November 1896; Onslow's speech at Bow, *Local Government Journal*, 31 October 1896; Lionel Holland's attack on water monopolists in his letter to Bow Vestry (*East London Observer*, 14 September 1895).

[80] *Daily News*, 5 March 1898.

[81] *East London Observer*, 15 January 1898.

[82] For Cornwall's invitation see *London*, 17 February 1898.

[83] *ILP News*, March 1898.

[84] *Ibid.*, March 1901.

on owners benefiting from enhanced land values.[85] A minority of Progressives had opposed the Boundary Street housing scheme out of a reluctance to pay compulsory purchase prices to slum landlords, and attempts were made to push some of the cost on to the second tier authorities.[86] The massive expense of the projected Thames tunnel at Blackwall – a legacy of the Metropolitan Board of Works – frightened many.[87] The original proposal to devote the proceeds of the Beer and Spirit duty to technical education in 1891 encountered opposition from much of the Progressive leadership, and the Council initially resolved to apply half the money to lower the county rate.[88]

In time, though, a succession of critical decisions established the Progressive Council as an interventionist and high-spending authority; the 1889 decision that working-class housing at Hughes Fields, Deptford, should be built by the Council itself rather than a private agency,[89] the decision to press on with the Blackwall Tunnel in 1891, the resolution in the same year to acquire tramway undertakings as they became available under the 21-year purchase option of the 1870 Tramways Act[90] and the decision to work the lines directly in 1896,[91] the eventual establishment of the Technical Education Committee and the Technical Education Board by the second Council in 1892-3,[92] the creation of the Works Department in 1892. The government's concession of the principle of betterment in 1895 led to the approval of the Holborn-Strand improvement (christened Kingsway on its opening in 1905) even though the new levy would cover only a small fraction of the scheme's cost. The pursuit of water control throughout the 1890s was undertaken in the knowledge that purchase would cost at least £30 millions, while the attempt to acquire London's electricity undertakings in 1906-7 was made in the face of the Finance Committee's warning of the 'considerable financial risks . . . inseparable from the establishment of an undertaking of this nature and extent'.[93] Dock municipalization and a public telephone service were mooted at various times,[94] and the Thames steamboat service – which was to make massive losses – inaugurated in 1905.[95]

Few Progressives went as far as Costelloe in suggesting that the Council

[85] Saunders, *op. cit.*, pp.175-6; LCC Minutes, 5 November 1889; Lord Hobhouse, 'The House of Lords and Betterment', *Contemporary Review*, LXV, 1894.

[86] Saunders, *op. cit.*, pp.350-9.

[87] *Ibid.*, pp.78-9, 240-1, 246-7, 252-3, 404-6.

[88] *Ibid.*, pp.400-2, 423-5.

[89] *The Metropolitan*, 6 July 1889.

[90] Saunders, *op. cit.*, pp.473-5, 496-8, 552-4.

[91] Gardiner, *op. cit.*, p.226.

[92] G. Gibbon & R.W. Bell, *History of the London County Council, 1889-1939*, 1939, pp.246 ff.

[93] Quoted *ibid.*, p.629.

[94] *Ibid.*, p.643, 639-41.

[95] *Ibid.*, pp.612-15.

knew better than the ratepayer how to spend the ratepayer's money, 'at least for the higher purposes of his life'.[96] Few went as far as Richard Strong in arguing that high rates would force a change in the system of local taxation.[97] Most continued to anticipate windfall rate relief through absorbing public utility profits, plundering the City's cash or taxing ground landlords, but as it became clear that these funds would not be forthcoming, the Council grew into the role of a spending authority. Increasingly clear evidence that this expenditure was not electorally damaging made this easier.

An initial concern for the plight of the poorer ratepayer gave way to the realization that Progressive social policy was winning working-class votes. The working-class elector was being made increasingly aware of the benefits of municipal action without, in most cases, feeling the incremental burdens. Compounding, the system by which rates were paid by landlords rather than occupiers of poor property in order to ease collection, prevailed in most working-class parishes. In the early 1890s it was estimated that rates for at least 450,000 of the 800,000 houses in London were paid by landlords,[98] and in working-class Bethnal Green more than 80% of properties were compounded.[99] In theory landlords recouped their payments in their tenants' rents, but in areas that were already rack-rented it was difficult to pass on rate increases. Technically their tenants were ratepayers, and entitled to the vote as such, but occupiers paying weekly rents, often in arrears, could not easily be made to feel increases in quarterly or half-yearly rate payments made on their behalf. They continued to see the landlord as predator, and responded to Progressive anti-landlordism rather than Moderate demands for retrenchment.

Lord Onslow's claim that 'the Moderates were returned by those who paid their own rates, but the Progressives by those who had their rates paid for them by other people'[100] therefore had some force, but Progressive control of the Council also depended upon recurrent successes in a number of suburban, middle-class seats, solidly Conservative in parliamentary elections.[101] Suburban householders were generally direct ratepayers, but they were less highly assessed than West End occupiers

[96] B.F.C. Costelloe, *The Incidence of Taxation*, 1893, p.10.

[97] *South London Press*, 11 April 1891.

[98] *The Metropolitan*, 19 December 1891.

[99] C. H. Campbell's figures in *Local Government Journal*, 28 April 1894.

[100] *London*, 12 November 1896. Onslow was Moderate leader from 1896 to 1899.

[101] In each of the first six Council elections the Progressives won both seats in North Islington and both seats in Peckham, although neither of these constituencies returned a Liberal to Parliament before the landslide of 1906. They won one or both seats five times in North Hackney, Fulham and Greenwich, and four times in Brixton, Lewisham, Norwood and North Kensington – all Tory strongholds in Parliament. Only six of London's 58 constituencies never elected a Progressive between 1889 and 1904.

and more conscious of the benefits of municipal enterprise. 'Municipal trading', Robert Donald argued, 'was invented by the middle classes for the middle classes'[102] as water rate payers or suburban tramway passengers; 'gas and water socialism' had been a movement of householders and public utility consumers long before it was invested with the collectivist overtones of Progressivism.

In 1901, after the Moderates' fourth landslide defeat in five contests, Conservative correspondents to the *Pall Mall Gazette* argued that 'the ratepayer . . . does not mind another halfpenny on the rates if he believes he will get his money's worth in cheap trams, good streets, good lighting and the active repression of gas, water and omnibus monopolists',[103] and that 'if the Moderates would undertake to do what other municipal authorities are actually doing . . . they would go to the County Council with a majority'.[104] Progressive-voting Conservatives were probably not common, but there were enough of them to bring regular Progressive victories in unlikely places – Clapham with a labour candidate in 1892, Hampstead, East Marylebone, North Paddington, Wandsworth and Dulwich in 1901, West Marylebone and Dulwich again in 1904. Thus although Council elections reflected national political movements to some extent – strong Liberal performances in 1892 and 1904, Conservative gains in 1895 and Liberal disaffection helping both the Conservatives and Independent Labour in 1907 – the Progressives started from a higher base than their Liberal counterparts in London. In the bad year of 1895 they were merely reduced to parity with the Moderates; in the good years they were swept to landslide victories. Progressive landslides reduced the Council Moderates to a West End rump, which itself made the development of a positive Moderate municipal policy less likely. In any case, by 1900 – arguably by 1892 – the Progressives had identified themselves so completely with municipal enterprise in the minds of metropolitan voters that belated Moderate moves in that direction appeared unconvincing; unable to reorient their policy, the Moderates had to wait until retrenchment became a vote-winner.

That this happened in 1906-7 is familiar enough. The nationwide campaign against municipal 'extravagance' found an electoral strength that had not been evident in earlier campaigns, and in March 1907 the LCC Progressives became its most prominent victims. The 'ratepayers' revolt' of 1906-7 is probably best seen as a consequence of the accelerating cost of living in the mid 1900s, a response to inflation comparable to the ratepayers' movements of 1919-20 and mid 1970s, and in itself as

[102] Lecture on 'Municipal Effort and its Critics', *Daily Chronicle*, 7 December 1906.

[103] Letter from 'Flat', *ibid.*, 6 March 1901. Similar points were made by F. Smith Osler after the loss of one of the Hampstead seats, *Hampstead and Highgate Express*, 9 March 1901, and see also the editorial comments on the 1898 results in the *Times*, 4 March 1898.

[104] Letter from 'A Regular Reader', *Pall Mall Gazette*, 5 March 1901.

transient. In London its significance lay in propelling the Moderates – now renamed Municipal Reformers – into office and releasing them from the cycle in which defeat induced sterile opposition and sterile opposition induced defeat. Suburban Progressivism waned rapidly, and the Progressives were forced back to a working-class electoral base which could not ensure control of the Council. 1907 would prove a permanent defeat for the Progressives, but it did not reverse the upward movement of London local taxation and it would be wrong to see it as inescapable retribution for municipal extravagance.

What it does show – and what the Moderate gains of 1895 had shown in a more limited way – is how close an active, high-spending urban authority stood to the margins of ratepayer tolerance. Under normal circumstances the electoral advantage lay with an active municipal party, and the Progressives were never forced into candle-end economies, but throughout their term they were inhibited in the major projects that most of them considered central to municipal enterprise. Street improvements were balked from the start by the accelerating cost of central London land, so that the Council's record in this respect compared unfavourably with that of its reviled predecessor. The social objectives of municipal housing were similarly thwarted by the high rents necessary to repay loans for the central blocks. After 1900 the LCC's housing strategy came to concentrate upon the building of cottage estates outside the county, preserving the goal of municipal housing but abandoning that of slum-clearance. If the cost of education 'crushed' the Council after 1904, as James Stuart claimed,[105], the LCC was perhaps lucky to be spared water purchase and police control.

Consequently the Progressive era was marked by continuous calls for reforms in the structure of local finance: the taxation of ground rents, a municipal death duty on estates,[106], 'betterment' levies to defray the cost of street improvements, an increase in London's share of Exchequer rate support,[107] the absorption of the City Corporation and guilds with their private estates, or of the public utility companies with their monopoly profits. It is doubtful whether much relief could have come from any of these sources other than the Exchequer grants; it was certain that nothing could be achieved without parliamentary approval.

The Progressives could not 'build the new Jerusalem on both sides of the river'[108] without the co-operation of a central government that was not

[105] J. Stuart, *Reminiscences*, 1911, pp.237-8.

[106] B.F.C. Costelloe, 'Memorandum, as to Legislative Reports Concerning the Powers of the Council', 1892, published as *LCC Official Report* no.52, pp.5-6. Costelloe to Harcourt, 24 October 1892 and enclosure, Bodleian Library, MS Harcourt, Dep. 187, ff.85-93.

[107] E.g. Webb in *London*, 27 April 1893; Stuart to Harcourt, 21 April 1894 and enclosure, MS Harcourt, Dep. 122, ff.155-9.

[108] Gosling, *op. cit.*, p.104.

only sympathetic, but also prepared to provide the parliamentary support needed for measures certain to meet energetic opposition. It was the Progressives' misfortune, of course, that Conservative governments held office for fourteen of their eighteen years. Within the Council's first year Whitehall's resistance to technical changes designed to facilitate LCC borrowing drove Rosebery to public criticism of the 'pedantry of the present government' for insisting that provisions 'framed for the smallest rural county council shall be applied in all their strictures to the London County Council'.[109] As the LCC grew more ambitious, Salisbury's and Balfour's governments became more ready to use their parliamentary majority to block Progressive projects. Their undeclared reason for resisting the Council's water purchase Bills was that 'any support given to these Bills by the Government would be a reversal of the policy of the Moderate section of the Council, and consequently . . . most serious and embarrassing to that section when future County Council contests take place':[110] water was eventually consigned to a special purpose 'quango' in 1902. The LCC's scheme for electricity purchase in that year was blocked by the introduction of a government Bill which was then dropped.[111]

Tory obstruction thus became more blatant over time, but even the minority Liberal government of 1892-5 hesitated to set sweeping precedents in local finance for the sake of the LCC[112] and stalled over water purchase.[113] Progress depended upon more than political sympathy. The fundamental problem was that parliamentary procedure offered too many openings to those anxious to obstruct local authority projects. C.T. Ritchie, the Council's creator, and more sympathetic towards it than most Conservative ministers, acknowledged this in 1891 by refusing to lift the Council's obligation to introduce annual Money Bills, as London's sixty or so MPs 'would never forego the opportunity of *annual* criticism' that this provision – introduced to shackle the undemocratic Metropolitan Board of Works – provided.[114] Many London measures were intrinsically contentious, and many which were not still faced politically motivated obstruction from backbench London Conservatives ('on whom the Council had the effect of a red flag on a

[109] Saunders, *op. cit.*, p.180.

[110] Memorandum by R.W.E. Middleton on the London County Council Water Bills, 9 February 1897, Cadogan Papers, House of Lords Record Office, CAD/1040/i.

[111] Gibbon & Bell, *op. cit.*, p.628.

[112] 'If London desires special powers of taxation of their own the County Council must introduce their own Bill and the Govt. will then consider how far they can support it. I have told Costelloe & Co. this over and over again', Sir William Harcourt to Buxton, 18 April 1893, Sidney Buxton Papers, Hassocks.

[113] Shaw-Lefevre to Farrer, 23 March 1894, copy in Rosebery Papers (see n.15), MS 10092, f.247.

[114] Lingen to Lubbock, 24 January 1891, Avebury Papers, BL Add. MSS. 49656, ff.20-3 (original emphasis).

bull')[115] or from the House of Lords, which blocked six major LCC measures in the Council's first five years.[116] Whatever advantages the Progressives gained from their political stance at the local level, their militancy encouraged their opponents to renew the battles in Parliament, where LCC initiatives were most vulnerable. Only government support could obviate this difficulty. It was provided as a matter of course for the Money Bills to keep the Council solvent, but there were limits to the parliamentary time that even a sympathetic government could devote to the ambitions of a single local authority.

The Progressive era had proved that the process of municipal reform in the metropolis involved more than the ritual triumph of a united community over sinister interests. Big city government was inescapably political. The advantages enjoyed by party organizations in mobilising a large urban electorate meant that parties were immediately formed on the Council. London's pronounced social and spatial segregation ensured that these parties reflected class differences too substantial to be buried in the kind of collective civic ethos that the Progressives sought to cultivate. What the Progressive era did show was that a political ascendancy could be built upon majority support for municipal enterprise, despite the embittered hostility of a minority forced to bear the rising cost of local government. The Progressives' outspoken partisanship, far from being a liability, actually goaded their opponents into an unpopular opposition to legitimate municipal projects, leading the Moderates to repeated defeats in a Conservative Metropolis. But the politicisation of local government also ensured that parliament became less likely to rubber-stamp LCC projects, and the need for parliamentary sanction – a negligible obstacle to municipal enterprise in the past – became a substantial barrier to Progressive ambitions.

This accounts for the ambiguity of the Progressive Council's record. Controversy was the basis of its popularity, and the extraordinary degree of publicity which it generated made the LCC familiar to a wider public than had previously interested itself in local affairs: 'the "man in the street" now sees that his preconceived idea of municipal work being wholly concerned with drainage and paving is entirely wrong'.[117] The East End Councillor who received more than fifty letters – 'the great majority of them . . . begging letters' – on the first Monday after his election in 1892,[118] the housewife who asked a canvasser in the same

[115] Lingen to Lubbock, 18 June 1891, *ibid.*, f.165.

[116] Listed in 'London and the Lords', *London*, 15 February 1894. Hobhouse cited five instances in which the Lords vetoed powers granted to the LCC by the Commons in the 1893 session alone: 'The House of Lords and Betterment', *loc. cit.*, p.449.

[117] *Municipal Journal*, 2 January 1903.

[118] *East London Observer*, 26 March 1892.

election to mend her tap because he had 'come from the County Council',[119], the 'animal lover' who sent a letter about a homeless dog to 'The County Council, Poplar', and the postal workers who directed it to Will Crooks[120] all bear witness to a general awareness of the LCC's existence and an exaggerated faith in its power. The breadth of Progressive municipal ambition had, as one Councillor argued, 'given encouragement to the idea that for every wrong there is a remedy', and if it generated more bad publicity than good, 'the manner in which the Council is held liable for every abuse . . . is gratifying evidence of what it is expected to accomplish'.[121]

Yet the Progressives' actual accomplishments were limited. Within established statutory limits the LCC was an extremely energetic and effective authority, assiduous in its performance of the routine duties of an urban authority, and innovative where existing legislation allowed, as with housing and tramways. But by 1907 the LCC did not control the police, it did not supply London with gas, water or electricity, or run the capital's docks or markets. It had not built itself a county hall and it had left fewer tangible municipal monuments than its predecessor. On these terms London compared badly with most of the larger provincial cities. By 1901 Burns had become nostalgic for the vision of 1889: 'when he thought of the men who in the early days of the Council had helped to form its policy he could say with Wordsworth: "Bliss was it in that dawn to be alive".'[122] Behind his nostalgia lay an awareness of ideals unattained.

If there is something 'modern' about the Council's political militancy and its successful self-promotion, there is also something modern about its limited record. Though many of the features which impeded Progressivism were distinctively metropolitan, the combination of financial pressure, parliamentary obstruction and central government hostility has hampered local initiatives ever since. Perhaps the Progressive LCC represents less the consummation of the municipal achievements of the nineteenth century than a foretaste of frustration to come.

[119] Interview with W.H. Dickinson in *Women's Signal*, 21 February 1895.
[120] *London*, 8 July 1897.
[121] W. Saunders, *op. cit.*, p.xxii.
[122] Quoted in *Hampstead and Highgate Express*, 2 March 1901.

# Chapter 3

# Progressives, Puritans and the Cultural Politics of the Council, 1889-1914

Chris Waters

In 1891 Sidney Webb wrote *The London Programme*, a brief but important work which echoed many of the demands put forward by the Progressive faction on the London County Council (LCC). While calling for the municipalization of public services, Webb also believed that 'public ownership of the means of enjoyment will . . . outstrip public ownership of the means of production'. Firmly committed to the expansion of municipal activity in the cultural arena, Webb called for more public libraries and reading rooms, which he hoped would 'go far to cut out the tavern . . . as the poor man's club . . .' He also called for the provision of music in parks, for municipal fetes, and for firework displays on Labour Day. For Webb, these were all particular instances of what he termed the 'communalization of the means of enjoyment'.[1]

When the London County Council was established in 1889, London lagged behind many provincial towns in its provision of what were increasingly regarded as the necessary social amenities of a 'civilised' life. This was recognized by many Londoners. Frederick Dolman, Progressive Councillor for Brixton (1901-7), surveyed the achievements of other towns in order to contrast them with those in London. All inhabitants of Birmingham, he claimed, lived within a few minutes' walk of a public park, while in Glasgow the local corporation had constructed several municipal concert halls in which it offered inexpensive, popular concerts. Dolman summed up the history of provincial municipalism:

> From the provision of Baths and Parks, municipal policy proceeded to Libraries and Art Galleries; and it is now the boast of the best Corporations that they care as much for the culture of the citizens as for the cleaning of the streets, that the recreation of children is . . . a matter of no less importance than the organization of police.[2]

I would like to thank Peter Bailey, Susan Pennybacker, members of the History of Social Policy seminar at Liverpool University, and members of the History Department at the University of Florida for their useful suggestions concerning this chapter.

[1] Sidney Webb, *The London Programme*, 1891, p.212.

[2] Frederick Dolman, *Municipalities at Work*, 1895, p.123. See also Albert Shaw, *Municipal Government in Great Britain*, 1901.

London embarked upon the crusade to develop and implement its own cultural initiatives relatively late, but under the auspices of the Progressives on the LCC it did so with great gusto. Indeed, throughout the 1890s the Progressives pointed in each of their election manifestos to their accomplishments. In 1895, for example, they claimed to have been successful both in purging music halls of their more disreputable elements and in providing Londoners with many new parks.[3] Looking back on the achievements of the decade, one historian claimed that the Council worked 'to provide wholesome substitutes for the streets and the public-houses'.[4] In this endeavour, he suggested, the LCC had met with success. But had it? In this chapter I would like to examine this claim by focusing on the LCC's cultural policy, exploring the aspirations which shaped its development, the history and consequences of its implementation, the various criticisms it evoked, and finally its effects on working-class life in London.

The London County Council was established at a time when the state and various municipalities were beginning to intervene more directly in working-class culture than had been the case earlier in the century, assuming responsibilities which had formerly been the preserve of private philanthropy. In the early Victorian period middle-class reformers attempted to influence working-class behaviour by providing programmes of rational recreation. By the 1880s and 1890s, however, many of these programmes were in disarray, often ignored by workers who appeared to be devoting their time to spectator sports, music halls and the tabloid press. Social reformers thus turned to political leaders, hoping that such individuals might succeed in creating a more moral populace where they had failed. In particular, they turned to the new county councils. As the Fabian Sidney Dark remarked, commenting on the need for the elevation of the masses, 'Failing the private philanthropic capitalist, I contend that there is an obvious duty for the County Council'.[5]

This is not to suggest that prior to the 1880s the state – at either the national or local level – played no role in the cultural and recreational affairs of the nation. But before this decade its aims were limited and its legislation was little more than a response to immediate and pressing social concerns. State encouragement of the provision of parks, open spaces, baths and wash-houses, for example, more often than not originated quite simply in a practical concern for public health. By the 1880s, however, various social theorists were beginning to conceive of new roles for the state. The Darwinian focus on social evolution fuelled the

[3] Robert Donald, *Six Years' Service for the People*, 1895, pp.5, 30.
[4] A.G. Gardiner, *John Benn and the Progressive Movement*, 1925, pp.486-7.
[5] Sidney Dark, 'The Demoralisation of Public Amusements', *The Commonwealth* 3 (October 1898), p.296.

quest to discover ways of intervening positively in the environment in order to promote 'higher' forms of civilization. And the Arnoldian belief in the 'elevating' nature of 'culture' influenced those who suggested ways in which the state might encourage the growth of social harmony by promoting a 'national' culture, available to all its 'citizens'. In short, while social reformers, evangelicals, factory owners and even utilitarians had all contributed to the notion of an interventionist state in the early Victorian period, in terms of cultural policy it was only towards the end of the century that municipal forms of intervention can be viewed as a conscious articulation and practical realization of dominant modes of social thought.[6]

Samuel Barnett, the East End settlement house worker, summarised in his own work the various strands of thought which were concerned with the cultural responsibilities of the municipality. Barnett's 'ideal city' would provide halls, galleries, libraries, baths, colleges and concert rooms which would serve to 'catch and raise the thoughts of men'. Parks in such a city would be plentiful, public gardens would be adorned with all the trappings of civic grandeur, municipal bands would perform daily, artists would be hired to brighten the streets, galleries would open on Sundays, and the drink trade would be placed in municipal hands.[7] Other writers echoed Barnett's sentiments.

> Some of us look forward to the time when joy will be considered as much a necessity in a city as anything else. In that time the citizens, well convinced that all the prime necessities of life must be municipalized, will not fail to demand that this great necessity of joy, or . . . the means of joy, be also supplied by their local councils.[8]

Such ideas permeated the thought of many Fabians, including Sidney Webb. But they did not emerge solely from the ranks of the Fabian Society; similar ideas – albeit less elaborately developed – can be found in J.F.B. Firth's *Municipal London*, the work which laid the foundations of London's progressivism in 1876. As a strategy for determining social progress by intellectual endeavour and the rational persuasion of a democratic electorate, progressivism, as Peter Clarke has defined it, united Gladstonian Liberals, 'New' Liberals, socialists and trade unionists in support of policies which called for a progressive

[6] For an elaboration of these themes, see Stuart Hall and Bill Schwarz, 'State and Society, 1880-1930', in Mary Langan and Bill Schwarz, eds., *Crisis in the British State, 1880-1930*, 1985, esp. pp.16-24.

[7] Samuel Barnett, *The Ideal City*, 1894, *passim*.

[8] 'Outlaw', 'What We Can Do To-Day', *Clarion*, 8 June 1901, p.181. See also 'W.F.B.', 'Municipalities and Leisure', *Labour Leader*, 12 March 1904, p.6; [William Stewart], 'Should Amusements be Municipalised?', *Labour Leader*, 2 December 1904, p.420; Charles Charrington, 'Communal Recreation', *Contemporary Review* 79 (June 1901), pp.839-54.

reorganization of society along collectivist lines.[9] In the cultural arena London Progressives hoped in particular to embark upon a series of municipal programmes which, while they extended earlier initiatives, must be seen as a response to a growing crisis of mid Victorian laissez-faire individualism. In 1889 many Londoners eagerly anticipated the implementation of new, far-reaching municipal policies. Even the radical Social Democratic Federation saw the advent of the London County Council as the herald of a new democratic age in which the municipality would now minister to the recreational tastes of its inhabitants.[10]

### *The Promise of Open Spaces*

The work of the Council in the provision and maintenance of open spaces was praised by friend and foe of the Council alike. As George Haw wrote on the eve of the 1907 election:

> If the parks are the lungs of London, the lungs must have been in a very weak condition before the LCC was created. That body came along like a benevolent physician with healing in its train. It might be said that it found London suffering from the shortcomings of one lung, and has since restored it to the blessings of two lungs.[11]

Throughout the 1890s, the 'benevolent physician' added some three or four acres per week to London's 'breathing grounds', as Sidney Webb called them. After expenditure on main drainage, technical education and the fire brigade, the financing of open spaces topped the list of municipal expenses. Lord Meath, an important figure in the public parks movement and the first chairman of the Parks and Open Spaces Committee of the LCC, suggested, after a visit to the United States, that London required both a green belt around the metropolis and a formal parks department, run by experts trained in the scientific management of open spaces. The Council decided to establish a parks department in 1892, placing it under the direction of Major J.J. Sexby, a prodigious worker who wrote the definitive history of London's parks while building up a small empire of park superintendents and custodians that more than tripled in size during

[9] Peter Clarke, 'The Progressive Movement in England', *Transactions of the Royal Historical Society*, 24 (1974), esp. pp.164, 172, 181.

[10] 'Popular Pleasure', *Justice*, 15 June 1889, p.1. See also Paul Thompson, *Socialists, Liberals and Labour: The Struggle for London, 1885-1914*, 1967, chap. 6. Thompson claims that the SDF greeted the Progressive electoral victory of 1889 as a triumph of social democracy. Only later, especially after the dismal performance of SDF candidates at LCC elections in the 1890s, did the organization begin to view Progressive policy as inadequate.

[11] George Haw, *'The Daily News' Lantern Lecture. London County Council Election, March 2nd, 1907*, 1907, p.6.

the Progressive tenure of office.[12]

Despite the claims made by the Progressives on behalf of the LCC's parks policy, the groundwork for that policy had been prepared by the Metropolitan Board of Works (MBW), the predecessor of the LCC. In 1857 the Board opened Finsbury Park and in 1864 it dedicated Southwark Park. Two years later Parliament passed the first Metropolitan Commons Act, which allowed the Board to assume control of most remaining large open spaces in London, including Hampstead Heath, Blackheath and Hackney Commons (1871), Tooting Bec Common (1873), Clapham Common (1877), Plumstead Common (1878), Streatham Common (1884) and Wandsworth Common (1887). The final step in the Board's acquisition of open spaces was taken in 1887 when Parliament transferred the control of Battersea, Kennington and Victoria parks from the Office of Works to the Board. By 1889 the MBW was spending some £50,000 per year on the maintenance of more than 2,500 acres of park land (see Table Five) – a significant achievement for a body that had been thwarted in its plans for open spaces by jealous vestries and would later be attacked by the Progressives for accomplishing so little.[13]

Under the Progressives the LCC never assumed control of as many acres of open spaces as had the old Board. In fact, the real success of the LCC rested less in the number of acres acquired than in the new kind of policy advocated. From its earliest days, for example, the LCC encouraged the provision of small recreation grounds in working-class districts of the city. Even in this, however, Council policy drew heavily from the successes of voluntary organizations such as the Kyrle Society and the Metropolitan Public Gardens Association (MPGA). Established in 1882 by individuals who believed that the Board of Works had been inactive in providing parks in the East End, the latter organization had urged philanthropists and local government to combine their efforts in the provision of more working-class playgrounds.[14]

Initially the LCC was enthusiastic about the work of the MPGA, although it didn't warm entirely to the idea that it might assume control of

[12] For Meath's U.S. tour, see *Report to the Parks and Open Spaces Committee of the London County Council by the Rt. Hon. The Earl of Meath on the Public Parks of America*, 1890. J.J. Sexby's survey is *The Municipal Parks, Gardens and Open Spaces of London*, 1898. For a history of the work of the Parks Department in the 1890s, see LCC, *Note Book of the Parks, Gardens, and Open Spaces of London*, 1897. For a list of all open spaces managed by the LCC in 1913, along with their history and cost, see LCC, *Report of the London County Council to 31st March, 1913*, 1913, appendix VIII.

[13] For the history of open spaces under the Board, see LCC, *Statement as to the Existing Arrangements with Respect to the Parks, Gardens, Commons, and Open Spaces . . .*, 1889; David Owen, *The Government of Victorian London, 1855-1889*, 1982, pp.145-53, 358.

[14] The work of Meath and the Metropolitan Public Gardens Association (MPGA) is discussed in H.L. Malchow, 'Public Gardens and Social Action in Late Victorian London', *Victorian Studies* 29 (Autumn 1985), pp.97-124.

the small open spaces established by voluntary effort. The Council eventually decided to take responsibility for eleven playgrounds that had been set up by the MPGA for a limited period of time, although at the end of the period representatives of the vestries claimed that they should maintain the smaller parks that lay within their boundaries. This initiated a dispute between vestries and the Council in which the Council became adamant about the need to implement its own programmes for the efficient management of the metropolis – its parks included. In 1897 the LCC instructed its Parks Committee to prepare a plan for the transfer of all open spaces under ten acres in London to the Council, but a revolt by the vestries forced the Council to back down. Thus, by 1903, while the LCC maintained 55 small open spaces, the local authorities maintained an additional 152. Despite this friction, the Council managed to continue the efforts of voluntary associations, providing many small parks in crowded districts of the city: Wapping Recreation Ground was opened in 1891, Island Gardens in Poplar in 1895, Nelson Recreation Ground in Bermondsey and Walworth Recreation Ground in Southwark in 1899 – and a score of others in the early years of the new century.[15]

The Council also attempted to control much of the activity that took place in its parks. A 'municipal tariff' was established for all refreshment rooms in the early 1890s, while the Parks Committee also sought to provide free concerts in many of its open spaces. As early as 1889 Lord Meath argued that while the LCC should not be in the business of providing *panem et circenses*, it should offer music 'of a high and noble character' because such music served an educational purpose and could 'be brought to bear in a very agreeable manner on large masses of people'.[16] While various bands had performed voluntarily in the parks under the auspices of the Board, in 1890 the Council obtained the power to use public funds for the provision of free concerts. By 1907 the Council was spending more than £10,000 per year on some 1,200 summer concerts in it parks.

The expenses involved in park maintenance and recreational provision grew rapidly under the Progressives. While the annual maintenance bill amounted to some £40,000 per year during the final years of the Board of Works, it had nearly tripled by the time the Progressives left office in 1907.

[15] On the LCC and the MPGA, see Meath, 'The London County Council and Open Spaces', *New Review* 43 (December 1892), pp.701-7; Greater London Record Office (GLRO), LCC Parks and Open Spaces Committee, Minutes, 13 April 1889, 31 May 1889, 26 July 1889. On the LCC and the vestries, see: LCC, *Annual Reports*, 1898-9, pp.125-6; 1899-1900, p.138; 1903-4, pp.73-4; LCC, *Conference on Small Open Spaces*, 1899; LCC, *Open Spaces Under 10 Acres*, 1903.

[16] 'Works for the London Council', *Nineteenth Century* 25 (April 1889), pp.508-9. See also J.C.B. Tirbutt, 'Municipal Music', *Municipal Journal*, 28 April 1905, pp.421-2; 5 May 1905, p.452.

More alarming was the fact that while it cost less than £18 to maintain an acre of open space in 1884, it cost more than £28 in 1902. As early as 1895, Sir Arthur Arnold, Chairman of the LCC, complained that while park acreage had risen by some 50% since 1889, maintenance costs had risen by over 100%. Part of the increase was due both to the greater attention the LCC lavished on its parks than had the MBW and to the higher wages the LCC paid its park workers. Part, however, was due to the fact that the new, small open spaces were costly undertakings: while, in 1904-5, it cost £8 to maintain each of the 267 acres of Blackheath, it cost £115 per acre to maintain the Wapping Recreation Ground and £409 per acre to maintain the Walworth Recreation Ground.[17] Progressives and Moderates often commented on the rising costs associated with the Council's parks policies, although the LCC incurred a heavy financial burden in other areas as well. Overall, LCC budgetary requirements helped fuel the attack on the spendthrift nature of the Progressives, thereby assisting their defeat at the polls in 1907. Although Progressives predicted a catastrophe were they to lose the election, Moderate expenditure on the parks continued to rise after 1907.

Moderates and Progressives could work together on the Parks Committee, believing that open spaces would improve public health. As Lord Meath wrote, 'That exercise in the open air is necessary for [London's] . . . growing boys no one can doubt who has seen how short the stature, how narrow-chested, how physically weak is the average . . . town-bred lad when compared with his country . . . cousin'.[18] On the one hand, Meath and his colleagues viewed London's parks policy in terms of its contribution to the improvement of public health. Often, however, this was couched in terms of the struggle to overcome physical degeneration by a policy of national efficiency: as the MPGA put it, the provision of parks was a 'vital question of social economy and efficiency'.[19] The health of Londoners was obviously related to the availability of open spaces, although in the final analysis it was more dependent on adequate nutrition and housing than anything else. And to some extent East End parks policy, like the policy of street clearing in the 1870s and 1880s, actually exacerbated overcrowding in some of the poorest parts of the city. While the large tracts of land acquired by Londoners in the 1870s seldom required the displacement of local residents, such was not the case with many of the smaller recreation grounds acquired in the 1890s. Some were constructed on the sites of disused burial grounds, but others were laid out in areas which were being redeveloped by the Council, resulting in a lower

[17] For Arnold, see LCC, *Annual Report*, 1894-5, p.6. Maintenance costs per acre of park land are drawn from LCC, *London Statistics, 1905-6*, vol.16, pp.150-3.

[18] Meath, 'County Council and Open Spaces', p.705. See also *London*, 30 November 1893, p.697.

[19] Quoted in Malchow, p.109.

Table 5

## Parks and Open Spaces: Statistical Summary

| *Year (ending March)* | *Acreage of Parks and Open Spaces* | *Annual Maintenance Costs (except music & boating [in pounds]* | *Maintenance Costs per Acre [in pounds]* | *Number of Outdoor staff* | *Acres per Staff Member* | *Net capital Expenditure (since 1856) [in pounds]* | *Profits on Boating [in pounds]* | *Net cost of Music in Parks [in pounds]* | *Number of Band Concerts* | *Number of Games Facilities* |
|---|---|---|---|---|---|---|---|---|---|---|
| **London Under the Metropolitan Board of Works** | | | | | | | | | | |
| *1884* | 2,244 | 40,152 | 17.89 | 217 | 10.34 | | | | | |
| *1887* | 2,506 | 40,305 | 16.08 | 238 | 10.53 | | | | | 111 |
| **London Under the London County Council (Progressive Majority)** | | | | | | | | | | |
| *1890* | 2,985 | 52,751 | 17.67 | 400 | 7.46 | 752,327* | | 1,313** | 446** | 691** |
| *1893* | 3,423 | 82,993 | 22.71 | 608 | 5.63 | 1,065,501 | | 4,188 | 635 | |
| *1896* | 3,686 | 98,489 | 26.72 | 737 | 5.00 | 1,308,843 | | 7,780 | 767 | |
| *1899* | 3,751 | 107,480 | 28.65 | 758 | 4.95 | 1,416,122 | | 7,477 | 852 | |
| *1902* | 3,832 | 109,501 | 28.58 | 787 | 4.87 | 1,577,137 | | 9,814 | 1,202 | |
| *1905* | 4,933 | 116,711 | 23.67 | 930 | 5.30 | 1,802,470 | 2,053 | 10,154 | 1,274 | 1,274 |
| **London Under the London County Council (Moderate Majority)** | | | | | | | | | | |
| *1908* | 5,046 | 119,579 | 23.70 | 919 | 5.49 | 1,855,494 | 1,887 | 10,761 | 1,209 | 1,342 |
| *1911* | 5,070 | 128,855 | 25.42 | 958 | 5.29 | 1,901,725 | 1,871 | 10,513 | 1,254 | 1,505 |

* figure for 1889
** figures for 1891, the first year of LCC-funded band concerts

SOURCES used in the compilation of these figures: LCC, *Annual Reports*, 1889-1912; LCC, *London Statistics*, vols. 1-23; LCC, *Statistical Abstract for London, 1901*, vol. 4; Sidney Webb, *Three Years' Work on the London County Council: A Letter to the Electors for Deptford*, 1895, p.9; Sidney Webb, 'The Work of the London County Council', *Contemporary Review* 67 (January 1895), p.137; William Saunders, *History of the First London County Council, 1889-1890-1891*, 1892, pp.616-7.

population density which often exacerbated overcrowding in surrounding neighbourhoods.

Although the rhetoric of improved public health often accompanied Progressive parks policy, that policy also grew from the belief that healthy, outdoor amusements might reduce the influence of the street and the public house in the recreational life of the London worker. Such ideas certainly played a role in the Council's Boundary Street redevelopment programme. In 1890 the LCC drew up plans to demolish fifteen acres of some of the worst slums of Bethnal Green, an area described as 'a veritable sink of iniquity and forcing-house of crime'.[20] Overcrowded tenements were replaced by new blocks of flats which surrounded a central, circular park, crowned by a municipal bandstand. In demolishing the area, the Council acquired the licences of a dozen public houses, none of which were rebuilt. Members of the LCC clearly viewed rational recreation, enjoyed on the grassy centre of this urban village, as an advance over the kinds of activity the old inhabitants of the area engaged in.

The parks policy of the Council was also aimed at encouraging the development of healthy citizens in London, a goal first articulated in the 1870s by those who believed that citizenship 'could neutralize class consciousness and play a crucial role in integrating the working class into the state'.[21] Progressives on the Council often deployed the rhetoric of citizenship, believing that organized games in parks were essential 'if London's children are to be developed into the race of sturdy citizens we would all like them to be'.[22] And games were indeed to be organized: in the early 1890s the Parks Committee wrote to many individuals, reprimanding them for playing games on unauthorised sites; and it also rewrote the bye-laws of the parks, making them more stringent and prohibitive of certain kinds of behaviour.[23] Moreover, the Council also used its control over parks and open spaces in order to extend its powers of surveillance. Thus, when Lord Meath argued for the provision of more

[20] LCC, *Opening Ceremony by His Royal Highness the Prince of Wales of the Boundary Street Area, Bethnal Green*, 1900, p.5. See also R. Vladimir Steffel, 'The Boundary Street Estate: An Example of Urban Redevelopment by the London County Council, 1889-1914', *Town Planning Review* 47 (April 1976), pp.160-73.

[21] David Sutton, 'Liberalism, State Collectivism and the Social Relations of Citizenship', in Langan and Schwarz, p.64.

[22] *Six Years of Progress: A Reprint of a Series of Articles from the Star, Describing the Work Done by the London County Council*, 1895, p.18. See also Shaw, *Municipal Government*, pp.213, 306-7; W.T. Stead, ed., *The Elector's Guide: A Popular Handbook for the Election*, 1892, p.37; and for one of the earliest expressions of the same ideas, B. Holland, 'London's Playgrounds', *Macmillan's Magazine* 46 (August 1882), pp.321-4.

[23] For letters to the guilty offenders, see GLRO, LCC Parks Committee, Minutes, 4 March 1889 to 11 July 1890. For a late edition of the by-laws, see LCC, *Parks and Open Spaces: Regulations Relating to Games*, 4th ed., 1915. As Susan Pennybacker has reminded me, there is some debate as to the extent to which the by-laws were actually enforced.

playgrounds, he claimed that their existence made it much easier for school attendance officers to locate absentee pupils.[24] In short, behind the benevolent-sounding rhetoric of the Council's parks policy lurked a concern with public order and discipline, with the efficient management of people and spaces, and also with the encouragement of responsible citizenship.

### *The Regulation of the Music Halls*

Like its parks policy, the music-hall policy of the LCC was also concerned with the establishment for all Londoners of an ideal code of 'correct' social behaviour and civic conduct. From its beginnings the Council was devoted to the 'moral improvement' of music-hall fare and to the supervision of all places of entertainment. But just as the development of London's parks owed much to the efforts of the Board of Works, it was the Board which also made the first systematic attempts to regulate London's music halls. In 1878, in order to prevent the outbreak of fires in places of entertainment, the Board was given the power to require all theatre and music-hall proprietors to remedy any structural defects in their halls before they could apply to the local justices for an operating licence. In the following decade the Board petitioned Parliament for an extension of these regulatory powers, although it was thwarted in its quest by the efforts of an increasingly well-organized lobby of entertainment interests which objected to municipal interference in the 'business of pleasure'. This initiated a conflict between the music halls and local government in London, a conflict which intensified when the Board and the justices handed their powers over to the Theatres and Music Halls Committee of the new London County Council in 1889.[25]

When this committee was established, many of its members were devoted to purging London of drink and moral corruption, both of which they associated with the music halls. At first the committee attempted to regulate the halls by making use of its inherited powers of structural surveillance. Between 1889 and 1892, the LCC required alterations in 167 music halls and general halls in which music and dancing took place. Most of these halls were located in impoverished parts of the city: of the nineteen outright refusals of music-hall licence applications in 1890, fourteen were denied on account of structural defects, eleven of which

[24] [Meath], 'Public Playgrounds for Children', *Nineteenth Century* 34 (August 1893), p.270.

[25] For the role of the Board and local magistrates in the regulation of places of entertainment, see *Parliamentary Papers* (Commons), 'Report from the Select Committee on Theatres and Places of Entertainment', 1892, vol.18, pp.434-5; Owen, *The Government of London*, pp.117-9; Clarence Hamlyn, *A Manual of Theatrical Law*, 1891, passim.

were located in the East End.[26]

Faced with an extensive bill for alterations, many proprietors of the smaller halls were forced out of business. This led to a rapid decrease in the number of managers who applied for licences. In 1889 the Council received 348 applications for music and music and dancing licences, while in 1893 it received a mere 215. When asked by a Parliamentary Select Committee why the number of applications had fallen so drastically, Thomas Fardell (Moderate, South Paddington, 1889-98), the first chairman of the the LCC's music halls committee, claimed that many smaller halls of questionable character could not carry out the alterations 'which were desirable in the public interest', and hence did not reapply for a licence. Fardell added, parenthetically, that these halls were seldom frequented by 'respectable' people.[27]

The difficulties faced by the smaller halls – particularly those in poor areas and those already suffering from a bad reputation – can be seen by charting the history of the Rose and Crown, a low public house cum music hall in the East End. The proprietor had struggled to raise £1,135 for structural repairs, only to discover that inspectors reported the existence of soliciting by prostitutes in his auditorium. This led the LCC to refuse him a licence. At the 1893 hearings, the Rose and Crown's defence argued that the Council discriminated against such halls by taking no action against the West End halls where prostitutes were also thought to assemble; the Rose and Crown, the defence argued, was unfairly singled out for attack because it was located in a poor district frequented by sailors. Although in the following year the LCC did investigate charges of solicitation in Leicester Square's famous Empire Music Hall, such charges usually meant death to the smaller halls. Thus, after hearing deputations from various religious bodies, the Council once again denied the Rose and Crown a licence.[28]

While the Rose and Crown was unsuccessful in its appeal, at least it could manage – albeit with some difficulty – to afford both the cost of the required alterations and the cost of hiring an attorney to represent it at the licensing hearings. Other halls quickly collapsed, unable to stand up to

[26] 'Report from the Select Committee', pp.389-91, 462-6; LCC, *Annual Report*, 1889-90, p.70.

[27] 'Report from the Select Committee', p.293. For a more elaborate discussion of the use of the Building Regulations Act by the LCC early in its history, see Penelope Summerfield, 'The Effingham Arms and the Empire: Deliberate Selection in the Evolution of Music Hall in London', in Eileen and Stephen Yeo, eds., *Popular Culture and Class Conflict, 1590-1914*, 1981, pp.214-20. For a detailed history of LCC music-hall policy, differing slightly in its conclusions from this brief sketch, see Susan Pennybacker, '"It was not what she said, but the way in which she said it": The London County Council and the Music Halls', in Peter Bailey, ed., *Music Hall: The Business of Pleasure*, 1986, pp.118-40.

[28] LCC, *Sessions of the Theatres and Music Halls Committee Sitting as the Licensing Committee*, October 1893, pp.139-52. See also Pennybacker, p.128.

the might of the LCC. By contrast, the new 'empires' and 'palaces of varieties' were able to undertake any structural alterations the Council might require of them. Moreover, aided by the Music Hall Proprietor's Protection Association, they were also able to put forward a strong case in their defence, thus managing – in most cases at least – to secure an operating licence. This is not to suggest that all of the larger halls came through the licensing proceedings with ease. In 1898, for example, the Holloway Empire Theatre of Varieties was challenged at its hearings by representatives of the nearby Young Women's Christian Association. But the defence mounted by the Holloway Empire was impressive, and in the end the LCC capitulated to its arguments, as it did in the case of most other large halls.[29]

From its earliest days, the Theatres and Music Halls Committee attempted to extend its powers through legislative means. In November 1889 it convened a meeting with theatre and music-hall managers in order to draft a new bill to strengthen its licensing powers. The resulting bill called for the codification of existing law, constant structural supervision of all places of entertainment, the transfer of the power to license theatres from the Lord Chamberlain to the LCC, the right of the Council to add any special conditions it pleased to the licences it issued, and the imposition of fines on the performer of 'objectionable songs' and on the manager of the hall in which such songs were performed. The Bill failed, largely because Parliament refused to expand the scope of the LCC's powers. But its failure led to the appointment of the parliamentary committee which investigated both the grievances of the Council and those of music-hall proprietors.[30]

The LCC's attempt to extend its regulatory powers over the halls was roundly attacked by individuals associated with the music-hall industry. Philip Rutland, solicitor to the Proprietors of Entertainment Association, claimed that passage of the new bill would lead to the sporadic inspection of the halls by 'morally-motivated amateurs' rather than by carefully-trained professionals.[31] Although many members of the LCC didn't care to join the crusade against the music halls, conservative papers were adamant in rejecting what they viewed as the moral interference of the LCC in the entertainment industry. *The Standard* referred to the Council as 'an arbiter of taste and a court of morals'; the *Daily Telegraph* claimed that

[29] LCC, *Sessions of the Licensing Committee*, November 1898, pp.31-42.

[30] The full report of the conference between the Council and the managers of theatres and music halls can be found in GLRO, LCC Theatres and Music Halls Committee, Minutes, 20 November 1889. The text of the resulting bills can be found in GLRO, LCC Theatres and Music Halls Committee, Proposed Legislation. See also 'Report from the Select Committee', pp.1-10; LCC, *Annual Report*, 1889-90, pp.69-70; 1890-1, pp.79-81; Pennybacker, pp.124-6.

[31] See 'Report from the Select Committee', pp.341-5, 435-6.

it wanted to see free trade in amusements rather than the 'Puritan suppression' of entertainment; and the *Financial News* suggested that what 'the Council really wants is to control the amusements of the people'.[32] The parliamentary committee that had been appointed tended to agree with these assessments, asking Thomas Fardell whether the main object of the Council was 'the safety of the public' or 'the control . . . of the performance, in the interest of public morality?' (p.36). Fardell claimed it was primarily the former, although the committee was not convinced and recommended few changes in existing licensing law.

In attempting to extend its authority, the Council also engaged in a liberal reading of its statutory powers in order not to have to apply to Parliament for a change in the law. In 1890 it argued that as Parliament had delegated to the Council the power to license places of entertainment, it had also admitted the necessity of constantly supervising those places of entertainment. The Council thus appointed twenty-three inspectors who would attend music-hall performances and report their findings to the Council. While the inspectors were asked to address structural matters, they were also asked: 'What was the character of the performance?' and 'Had proper means been taken by the management to secure order and decorum amongst the audience?' Of course, the music-hall industry objected to the existence of such an inspectorate. J.L. Graydon, proprietor of the Middlesex Music Hall, called it a 'ridiculous system of uneducated espionage', complaining 'it is inconceivable that men earning 10s 6d a night . . . could possibly be either competent or have any uniformity of opinion apart from the obvious temptations to blackmail and bribery'.[33]

Although criticism of the inspectorate was widespread, a large number of inspectors' reports were filed with the Theatres and Music Halls Committee early in the 1890s. At the Equestrian Coffee House on Blackfriars Road, inspectors drew attention 'to the fact that due steps are not taken . . . to secure propriety on the part of the audience, and as an example of this the Chairman was in the habit of treating the female singers to drink between the performances'.[34] Once filed, these reports could be used at the annual hearings to deny licences to those establishments considered guilty of transgressing the LCC's unwritten guidelines pertaining to the maintenance of public decorum in the halls.

By 1900 the managers of many of the larger halls had come to police their establishments on behalf of the Council. English's New Sebright Wholesome Amusement Temple, for example, allowed 'no offensive

[32] *Standard*, 19 June 1891; *Telegraph*, 12 March 1891; *Financial News*, 21 November 1893.

[33] 'Report from the Select Committee', p.102. For the rise of the inspectorate, see GLRO, LCC Theatres and Music Halls Committee, Minutes, esp. 12 and 17 April 1889, 17 and 24 July 1889, 22 January 1890, 30 April 1890; GLRO, LCC Theatres and Music Halls Committee, Minutes of the Inspection Subcommittee, esp. 1890.

[34] Minutes of the Inspection Subcommittee, 20 August 1890.

allusions' to be made to the Royal Family, German princes, Members of Parliament, police authorities – or to the LCC.[35] Mutual hostility between the Council and the music halls continued and could still lead to bitter arguments during the licensing sessions. But the smaller halls – the principal moral culprits in the eyes of many councillors – had largely vanished, while the large halls had too much money invested in them to ignore the LCC's demands. The Council's music-hall policy had clearly speeded up the transformation of variety entertainment in London: from now on public morality would be assured by the close co-operation of the licensing authorities and music-hall proprietors – two groups who begrudgingly worked together while remaining suspicious of each other's motives.

### *Municipal Puritanism and the Call for Municipalization*

The attack on the County Council's music-hall policy was vociferous and widespread. By 1900 it had given rise to a sustained critique of Council policy by several self-proclaimed advocates of the 'people's pleasure', all eager to denounce the 'municipal puritanism' which they associated – perhaps unfairly in some instances – with the Council. As early as 1892 the drama critic William Archer feared that if the Council triumphed in its music-hall policy it would soon establish vigilance committees which would censor all forms of popular entertainment. Eight years later, the Entertainment Reform League was created – a front for vested music-hall interests – in order to counter every attempt made by the LCC to regulate popular recreation.[36]

What is important about the emerging critique of Council policy is that it fuelled a series of public debates about the legitimate role of the state, local and national, in the cultural arena. These debates brought together individuals of various political persuasions, all in agreement about the potential dangers of Council policy. At one extreme was the Social Democratic Federation. While, in the early 1890s, some members of the SDF had welcomed the new Council, by the end of the decade that organization's enthusiasm had declined dramatically. After the LCC halted the delivery of a series of Sunday lectures arranged by the SDF, the Federation lashed out against what it perceived to be the 'petty Sabbatarianism' of the LCC. Later, on the eve of the 1907 election, the SDF argued that Progressivism had been played out, that its 'smug Puritanism' had resulted in the control of various areas of public life by a new managerial elite, and that this had become a major obstacle to the

[35] 'Report from the Select Committee', pp.440-1.

[36] For Archer's beliefs, see 'Report from the Select Committee', p.281. For the Entertainment Reform League, see *Municipal Journal*, 12 January 1900, p.27.

realization of social democracy.[37] At the other end of the political spectrum was the Liberty and Property Defence League, an organization which supported London Conservatives and which opposed the cultural policies of the Progressives in terms reminiscent of John Stuart Mill's attack on sabbatarianism in *On Liberty*. In an article entitled 'The People's Amusements Threatened', the new libertarians complained about the petty restrictions encountered in London's parks, calling them an infringement 'on the freedom of the people'.[38]

Both conservatives and some (but certainly not all) socialists feared the growth of a collectivist state which would stress the efficient management of popular pleasure through bureaucratic expertise. But while the Right dreamed of turning the clock back to a period when the state remained more or less aloof from involvement in the cultural arena, the Left often wished to see the state continue to intervene in popular culture, albeit in less restrictive ways than seemed the case under the LCC. Such, at least, was the hope of the Christian Socialist, Fabian activist and member of the London School Board, Stewart Headlam. In November 1904 Headlam spoke to the Fabian Society 'On the Dangers of Municipal Puritanism'. Eighteen months later he helped form the Anti-Puritan League for the Defence of the People's Pleasure. Headlam attacked the Council for its tendency to manage 'other people's lives in the interest of a supposed morality . . .'[39] He believed that the Council's strict parks regulations kept many people away from them; that whereas people demanded to play games in parks on Sundays, the LCC forbade such activity; and that, in particular, by spending public money on the acquisition of public house licences, the Council had merely increased drinking in other establishments. In short, Headlam demanded a new municipal recreational policy which would encourage the development of desirable forms of pleasure rather than discourage those forms considered undesirable.

[37] *Justice*, 18 November 1899, p.4; 12 January 1907, p.5; 23 February 1907, p.7. See also Thompson, pp.123-4.

[38] *Liberty Review* 9 (May 1900), p.111. See also 'The True Path of Temperance', *Liberty Review* 21 (March 1907), pp.123-7. On the League, see N. Soldon, 'Laissez-Faire as Dogma: The Liberty and Property Defence League', in Kenneth D. Brown, *Essays in Anti-Labour History*, 1974, pp.208-33. For Mill's attack on Sabbatarianism from the same intellectual standpoint, see the argument in *On Liberty* (Richard Wollheim, ed., *Three Essays*, 1975, pp.106-7).

[39] Stewart Headlam, *Municipal Puritanism*, 1905, p.13. See also *Fabian News*, November 1904, pp.41-2; J.B.G., 'The Anti-Puritan League', *Labour Leader*, 1 June 1906, p.20. On Headlam and the attack on Puritanism in general, see John R. Orens, 'The Mass, the Masses and the Music Hall: Stewart Headlam's Radical Anglicanism', *A Jubilee Paper*, 1979; Ian Britain, *Fabianism and Culture*, 1982, pp.145-62; Chris Waters, 'Socialism and the Politics of Popular Culture in Britain, 1884-1914', Ph.D. thesis, Harvard University, 1985, pp.406-23; Susan Pennybacker, 'The "Labour Question" and the London County Council, 1889-1919', Ph.D. thesis, Cambridge University, 1984, pp.222-7.

Progressives on the Council were eager to defend their record. Frederick Dolman claimed that the Council had been like a 'fairy godmother' to the people of London, providing them with recreational amenities on a scale hitherto unknown.[40] Despite such claims, many Progressives admitted – and some were even proud of the fact – that their policy was often a restrictive one. As Richard Roberts (Progressive, South Islington, 1889-98), a teetotaller who for many years chaired the music-halls committee, claimed: 'As a radical Nonconformist, I do not regret a revival of the puritan sentiment, which has always characterized English Liberalism in its best days'.[41]

It was the sense of moral zeal exhibited by such individuals, their desire to cleanse the moral life of the metropolis, that fuelled so many of their campaigns – and, of course, that drew so much criticism. But seldom did they interpret their activities in terms of imposing their own values on the populace: the LCC, they claimed, was a democratically elected body which merely expressed the ideas of the electorate. As one defender of Council policy wrote, 'Why should we fear that a body which expresses the will of the people should tyrannously thwart . . . [their will] in the matter of amusements?'[42]

Progressives were often singled out for attack by those Moderates who feared the extension of the LCC's powers. Yet many Moderates also supported the general thrust of LCC policy. Prior to the 1892 municipal elections, the journalist W.T. Stead asked the candidates if they approved of the Council's temperance policy, and, in addition, if they approved of continuing the Council's attempt to secure a 'decent and sober' music hall. The vast majority of them, both Progressive and Moderate, answered 'yes' to both questions.[43] Moderate support for what was seen as a series of Progressive policies by their critics was thus widespread, and was often manifested in many votes taken by the Council on cultural matters. For example, in 1898 the LCC voted on a proposal to prevent the Queen's Hall from offering Sunday concerts at which an admission fee would be charged. Forty-five Progressives and seventeen Moderates voted in favour of the measure, a mere sixteen Progressives and sixteen Moderates voted against it.[44]

Moreover, on many occasions the Council implemented a policy not simply because of its members' puritanical impulses, nor because both Moderate and Progressive councillors shared a belief in the importance of

[40] 'In London's Cause', *Echo*, 22 February 1901, p.1.

[41] Quoted in Stead, *Elector's Guide*, p.53. See also the interview with Roberts, 'The L.C.C. and the Theatres and Music Halls', *London*, 11 October 1894, p.652.

[42] William Archer, 'The County Council and the Music Halls', *Contemporary Review* 67 (March 1895), p.322.

[43] Stead, *Elector's Guide*, pp.64, 70-1.

[44] *London and the Municipal Journal*, 1 December 1898, p.766.

the policy, but because pressure was brought to bear on the Council by external bodies. In the early 1890s, for example, the Council was often influenced in its music-hall policy by local vestries, agencies which also demanded more wholesome music-hall entertainment. The policy of the Council was also fuelled by religious, sabbatarian and temperance lobbies. Thus, while the Council prohibited the playing of games in its parks on Sundays until 1922, each time a councillor proposed changing the policy sabbatarian organizations successfully petitioned against it. Most of all, the LCC was encouraged in its work by the social purity lobby – several of its members actually sitting on the Council. This became clear in the mid 1890s in the struggle waged by the National Vigilance Association against the promenade of the Empire Music Hall in Leicester Square. In short, if Progressives alienated a number of articulate critics of municipal puritanism, their policies were not unique, but were part of a much larger, late Victorian movement to purify urban life in general – even if they were not shared by all Council members or by the bulk of the general public.

By the turn of the century, individuals who attacked the Council's licensing policy began to urge the LCC not simply to regulate existing forms of amusement, but to take control of the provision of popular recreations. As early as 1894 James Keir Hardie had praised the music-hall policy of the Council, claiming that public houses might also be placed under the control of 'an enlightened public body, concerned chiefly with promoting the moral and material well-being of the community'.[45] Despite this plea, it was a decade or more before serious discussion of the municipalization of the drink trade in London took place. Headlam encouraged it because he believed that properly managed public houses might become convivial neighbourhood centres, while the SDF believed that municipal public houses would be more effective in curbing abuses of drink than the past policy of the Progressives on the Council had been.[46] Critics of the Council's music-hall policy began to put forward similar arguments to those developed by municipal temperance reformers. In 1910 one of them argued that the municipal provision of 'decent' music halls – unlike the LCC's policy of refusing to renew certain music-hall licences – would offer the most effective means of drawing people out of the squalid, back street holes the Council disliked.[47]

[45] J.K. Hardie, 'The Municipalisation of the Drink Traffic', *Workman's Times*, 3 March 1894, p.3.

[46] Headlam, *Municipal Puritanism*, pp.3, 6-8; Mary L. Pendered, 'The Psychology of Amusement in its Relations to Temperance Reform', *Socialist Review* 3 (June 1909), pp.284-91; 'Socialism and Temperance', *Justice*, 7 May 1904, p.4; Ernest E. Hunter, 'The Puritan Peril', *Justice*, 21 March 1908, p.6.

[47] See P.P. Howe, 'The Municipalisation of the Music Halls', *Socialist Review* 5 (August 1910), pp.424-32.

The call for increased municipalization in the cultural arena, especially when made by individuals such as Headlam, often developed as a response to what was believed to be the failure of municipal puritanism. The thinking behind it would eventually prepare the ground for various state-sponsored cultural initiatives in the twentieth century. But in the early 1900s the LCC was unwilling to move beyond the direct provision of games facilities, edifying music and municipal boating in its parks. Even this level of provision was a significant advance over the older policies of the MBW. But for many critics it was not enough, especially as what was offered was often accompanied by a stern, moralising rhetoric. Many petitions were presented to the LCC, urging it to provide various forms of entertainment. In particular a number of organizations demanded that the LCC retain the drink licences it had acquired and establish municipally operated public houses. But the Council's answer was always the same: there were already too many temptations to intemperance and vice in London, and these needed to be reduced, not supplemented by others operated by the Council.[48] Thus, while conservative critics of LCC policy, such as those associated with the Liberty and Property Defence League, were opposed to the Council's further intervention in the field of popular culture, other critics held up the beacon of municipalization as the light which would lead Londoners out of the puritanical fog which enveloped them.

By the eve of the First World War further calls for the municipalization of popular pleasure had failed to influence Council policy, while the Council's puritanism had elicited little enthusiasm from those who had hoped for a more daring policy. In 1912, one drama critic, W.R. Titterton, called on the people of London both to ignore the calls for municipalization and to reject the puritanical policy of the Council; he urged them instead to devote their energies to the establishment of co-operative, community-run music halls. The LCC, he claimed, had forced music-hall entertainment to become more sombre: the 'happy, rollicking music-hall public' of former days had given way to 'rows of well-dressed solemn people', separated from the performance by a 'fire-proofed LCC curtain'. At some point Titterton joined the Fabian Society, hoping there perhaps to encounter a policy for the rejuvenation of public amusements. He was soon disillusioned: 'We asked for the wine of life', he wrote, 'and they gave us a tract on municipal beerhouses'.[49] For Titterton, the Fabian municipalizers he encountered merely turned out to be 'experts' and bureaucrats of a different kind from those who were behind the Council's municipal puritanism.

[48] See LCC, Minutes, 1901, pp.197, 1296, 1560.
[49] W.R. Titterton, *From Theatre to Music Hall*, 1912, pp.75, 122-3, 221.

### *Cultural Politics and the London Worker*

What were the effects of the LCC's cultural initiatives on working-class life, and what did most Londoners think of LCC policy? It would be easy to suggest that the Council tried to impose its own code of conduct on a recalcitrant working class. To some extent this was indeed the case, for the strict, regulatory policy promoted by the Council rested on a series of values and assumptions which were at odds with those of most workers, who 'were not Christian, provident, chaste or temperate'.[50] But the issue was more complicated than this, for many workers actually supported – and a few even initiated – LCC policy.

The most important source of working-class support for Council policy came from the handful of workers who were elected to the LCC under the Progressive banner. Will Crooks (1892-1910, Poplar) agitated for a municipal gymnasium, a public library and a technical institute in Poplar. During his eighteen years on the Council he was also a tireless crusader on behalf of the Parks Committee's work for the acquisition of open spaces in the East End. And he opposed the drink interest and gave his full support to the Council's attack on the halls.[51] Likewise, John Burns (1889-1907, Battersea) was not only sympathetic to the Progressives' programme, but was one of its chief architects. In an 1895 election address, he claimed that the LCC had already diminished drunkenness and 'checked indecency and gilded vice', had 'saved public amusement from the degredation a few . . . vulgar managers would inflict upon it', and had 'prevented art and artistes from being made mere accessories to drink and debauchery'.[52] Burns believed that drink, betting and vulgar music-hall fare diverted workers from their quest to understand the source of their oppression, and he saw it as the duty of the LCC to protect the worker from the corrupting influences of the leisure industry.

It was the future Prime Minister, James Ramsay MacDonald, who argued most cogently for the Labour Movement's adoption of puritan values, such as those subscribed to by Burns. Rather than being associated with gloom and cant, he wrote, puritanism was an 'incident in the eternal process of perfection', an active weapon of personal

[50] Gareth Stedman Jones, 'Working-Class Culture and Working-Class Politics in London, 1870-1914: Notes on the Remaking of a Working Class', *Journal of Social History* 7 (Summer 1974), p.471.

[51] George Haw, *From Workhouse to Westminster: The Life Story of Will Crooks, M.P.*, 1907, pp.64-5, 71, 92, 98, 162-3.

[52] Quoted in *London*, 14 February 1895, p.108. See also John Burns, 'Brains Better than Bets or Beer', *Clarion Pamphlet No.36*, 1902; Burns, *Music and Musicians*, n.d.; Burns, *Labour and Drink*, 1904. For Burns's puritanism, see Arthur Page Grubb, *From Candle Factory to British Cabinet: The Life Story of the Rt. Hon. John Burns, PC, MP*, 1908, pp.271-301.

transformation, and hence a necessary part of the mental and moral struggle for socialism.[53] MacDonald's argument was perhaps the final gasp of a nineteenth-century working-class autodidact tradition – expressed most cogently in the 'knowledge' Chartism of the 1840s – which emphasized the importance of self-control and self-culture in the quest for personal and social salvation. Some socialists thus welcomed the advent of municipal policies which would assist them in the cultivation of the kind of individual necessary for their vision of social transformation.

It is difficult to measure the extent to which the working class as a whole shared MacDonald's beliefs, or even to locate particular subgroups within the class which were prone to accept his reasoning. Indeed, the evidence of working-class attitudes towards LCC policy is impressionistic at best. But in one illuminating, albeit limited, study of working-class responses to Council policy, a clergyman who opposed licensing the Sadler's Wells Theatre in 1893 surveyed the occupants of two blocks of model dwellings in Clerkenwell. 362 residents opposed the licence, while a mere 112 approved of it (171 claimed to be indifferent, while 54 residents were not at home).[54] Obviously one cannot generalize from a small study such as this. But as model dwellings largely excluded unskilled workers and casual labourers, this survey can at least offer some insight into the nature of skilled working-class opinion.

But what of the rest of the working class, those individuals who didn't have the good fortune to live in model dwellings? C.F.G. Masterman, in his study of *The Condition of England* (1909), claimed that the bulk of the working class wanted to be left alone, free from interference in its daily life. If Masterman was correct, then most workers would have ignored the Council's attempts to reform them or would have remained oblivious to the efforts made on their behalf. In Islington, for example, we know that many poorer inhabitants in a slightly later period rejected dominant social codes and engaged in an active street culture which was rowdy and beset by drunkenness and gambling. They also rejected attempts to eradicate such behaviour, whether they were made by philanthropists, socialists or the LCC.[55] At times the LCC recognized that its efforts were in vain: thus, despite the usual popularity of council-provided music in the parks, the LCC decided in 1903 to halve the number of its band sections 'as it was found that . . . they had to be sent to places where they were not fully appreciated'.[56]

[53] J. Ramsay MacDonald, 'A Plea for Puritanism', *Socialist Review* 8 (February 1912), pp.422-30.

[54] LCC, *Sessions of the Theatres and Music Halls Committee . . .*, October 1893, p.129.

[55] Jerry White, *The Worst Street in North London: Campbell Bunk, Islington, Between the Wars*, 1986, pp.83-5, 104-8, 118, 121. For working-class intransigence in the face of efforts made to change their behaviour in the late nineteenth century, see Stedman Jones, esp. pp.462, 472, 479.

[56] LCC, *Annual Report*, 1903-4, p.79.

Sidney Webb once claimed that 'the use and popularity of the Council's parks among the masses has enormously increased'.[57] But evidence would suggest that Webb's 'masses' excluded many workers who resented the attempts made by the Council to control their behaviour in the parks. Indeed, most LCC-provided games facilities were intended less for a working-class clientele than for the middle class. Despite the importance of football in working-class life, for example, in 1891 the LCC provided 281 cricket pitches, 331 lawn tennis courts and a mere 79 football pitches. While by 1913 football pitches had risen in number to 321 (cricket pitches now totalled 447 and lawn tennis courts 542), like all games facilities they had to be reserved in advance, which did little to end the prevalence of working-class street games, of which the Council so often despaired.

If many workers ignored the cultural initiatives of the LCC, or were disinclined to use the facilities on offer, members of the lower middle class often rallied to support the Council in its cultural work. In a series of letters printed in the *Daily Telegraph* in 1891, such individuals expressed their approval of LCC policy. Some even called on the LCC to expand its activities:

> I have two daughters, who . . . have few chances of social entertainment and meeting nice people. I wish I could afford to take them to theatres and subscription balls; but then my husband's income is . . . not a large one . . . Now, if only there were happy evenings to be spent in the town hall, where young people . . . could meet, I should feel that I was 'doing my duty' . . . providing them innocent and helpful recreation at a very reasonable cost.[58]

While the Council's parks policy may have benefited the middle and lower middle classes more than it did unskilled workers, there was little formal working-class opposition to LCC policy in this arena. But workers' representatives did object to LCC temperance policy. Between 1889 and 1914 the Council acquired 157 licensed premises, allowing 153 of these licences to lapse, the bulk of which were held by publicans in poorer districts of the metropolis which were subject to LCC redevelopment plans. When, for example, the Council built its Boundary Street estate it refused to renew the ten drink licences formerly held by publicans in the area.[59] Ben Cooper, the working-class Progressive Councillor for Bow and Bromley (1892-1907), believed that in acquiring such licences the Council had failed to promote the cause of temperance and had merely intensified drinking in neighbouring communities.[60] Other workers, less concerned with temperance, simply objected to the attempts made by the Council to

57 Sidney Webb, *Three Years' Work on the London County Council: A Letter to the Electors of Deptford*, 1895, p.10.

58 *Daily Telegraph*, 20 July 1891, p.3. See also 18 July, p.2 and 22 July, p.3.

59 LCC, *Licensed Premises Acquired by the Council*, 1914, p.2.

60 *Municipal Journal*, 26 July 1901, p.569.

close down the public houses and music halls in their neighbourhoods. This would suggest that a wide gulf existed between many working-class leaders and members of a labour aristocracy on the one hand, and the bulk of the working class on the other. During the municipal elections of 1895, one journalist asked why working-class leaders had so adamantly supported Progressive policy while watching rank-and-file support drift away. Perhaps, he suggested, their leaders had 'gone too far' for working-class opinion.[61]

Successful or not, the cultural politics of the London County Council marked the beginnings of an era in which the state and the municipality began to intervene more directly in the field of popular culture than had hitherto been the case. Implicit in the Council's policy were a whole series of assumptions as to what constituted 'good' culture, of what the components of a 'civilized' life should be. The LCC emphasized certain cultural forms, encouraging them through public funding, while attempting to eradicate others, largely through its licensing policies. Most obviously, it encouraged workers to engage in more rational, orderly and well-supervised forms of recreation. Less obviously, it played a major role in speeding up the development of highly capitalized forms of mass culture. It did this largely by accepting the arguments put forward by the representatives of those large-scale institutions which claimed to offer wholesome amusement, while discounting the claims made by the owners of the less orderly, small-scale centres of entertainment which had for many decades provided workers with the bulk of their entertainment in local settings. Perhaps, more importantly, the work of the LCC indicated that the field of culture was no longer simply a matter of civil society, of private, individual experience, but was a matter of utmost social – and ultimately political – significance. While social critics like Matthew Arnold had called as early as the 1860s and 1870s for the state to develop a more interventionist strategy with regards to the nation's cultural life, it was the London County Council under the Progressives which first attempted to implement such a strategy on a grand scale.

[61] C.A. Whitmore, 'The Progressive Check', *National Review* 25 (April 1895), pp.241-3.

# *Chapter 4*

# *Technical Education and the Early LCC*

Andrew Saint

In 1892 the London County Council came under sharp attack from the leaders of the burgeoning movement for British technical education. It had shirked its duties, argued Hubert Llewellyn Smith, secretary of the National Association for the Promotion of Secondary and Technical Education (NAPSTE): 'London is the only county in England and Wales that has not hitherto aided technical and secondary education out of the funds accruing to it from the Residue of the Beers and Spirits Duties'.[1]

At that date the LCC, three years of age, neither controlled nor contributed to any place of education. Twenty years later, by contrast, the LCC's Education Officer, Robert Blair, could survey with pride the scene of municipal and technical instruction over which he presided. He reviewed an army of polytechnics and colleges under direct or indirect LCC control, worthy of an imperial capital, alive to the needs of London's population, industries and commerce, and increasingly linked in with the LCC's own schools system and with a reformed University of London.[2] Once notorious for its poor training facilities, London had learnt from countries and cities where governments had put their backs into technical education, and had pulled itself up by its bootstraps. The groundwork done over those two decades was to put London ahead of other British cities in depth of educational resources for years to come. Such was the sketch of early achievements in technical education that adherents of the LCC liked to draw during its years of eminence and authority.

Strictly speaking, the fount of these efforts was not the LCC itself but the small, semi-autonomous Technical Education Board (TEB), which presided over training in inner London from 1893 to 1904. The TEB in its turn drew its initial impetus from a masterly report by the same Llewellyn Smith who had stung the LCC into action, and its drive and sense of direction from Sidney Webb, chairman or vice-chairman of the Board for most of its brief existence. The TEB is often cited as Webb's great

[1] Arthur H.D. Acland and H. Llewellyn Smith (eds.), *Studies in Secondary Education*, 1892, pp.190-1.

[2] *Eight Years of Technical Education and Continuation Schools*, printed report by LCC Education Officer, December 1912, introduction.

achievement while an LCC Member. 'The Board was virtually synonymous with the name of Sidney Webb', concludes the historian who has studied the Webbs' educational work in most depth.[3]

This essay does not reject this triumphal sketch entirely. It tries instead to shade the picture in, so as to convey the complexities of technical education in London at the turn of the century, to explain the situation within which the LCC and TEB were obliged to operate, and so to judge how well they served the industries, employments and population of the city which they endeavoured to represent.

The LCC was a latecomer upon the stage of London's technical education. Few of the elected Members who foregathered early in 1889 can have anticipated educational responsibilities. A directly elected London School Board presided over the parsimonious elementary education which was all that the law then allowed it to run. The Progressive councillors approved of the Board's vigour and ambition, from which they had to a degree taken their political cue. It was not then thinkable that the LCC should establish itself as a rival authority for education.

This perspective very soon changed. Only months after the LCC took office the first Technical Instruction Act passed into law, permitting the new county councils to levy a small rate for the purpose of training. It was smartly followed by a celebrated clause squeezed by educational reformers into the Local Taxation Act of 1890 during its parliamentary passage. This endowed the county councils with the accumulating annual bounty from surrendered licences – the 'whisky money', as it was popularly called – for the purposes of technical education or reducing the rates. A third law, the Technical Instruction (Amendment) Act of 1891, allowed councils to use the whisky money to provide technical training scholarships from elementary schools to 'higher-grade' schools. These measures, all passed under Lord Salisbury's Conservative administration, marked the first legislative triumphs of a national movement for improving British technical education. They were all more or less instigated by the two main 'activists' of the NAPTSE – the Liberal politician Arthur Acland and the proto-Fabian Hubert Llewellyn Smith. The NAPTSE sprang in its turn from the Royal Commission on Technical Instruction of 1882-5, which had revealed deficiency at all levels of British industrial training, in contrast to growing investment and organization among Britain's trading rivals, notably Germany.

The Technical Instruction Acts became the cornerstone upon which

[3] E.J.T. Brennan in *The Vocational Aspect of Secondary and Further Education*, 12, 1960, p.38. Brennan's studies of Webb and the TEB are contained in *The Vocational Aspect*. . . (*ut supra*), 11, 1959, pp.85-96 and 12, 1960, pp.27-43 and in E.J.T. Brennan (ed.), *Education for National Efficiency: The Contribution of Sidney and Beatrice Webb*, 1975, pp.3-56.

the belated and ill-funded reform of British technical education was to rest for a decade. But they were national in scope. They gave powers to the county councils set up in 1889 not because those bodies were well geared to education, but because in many parts of the country they were the only ones able to take the task on. London, Birmingham, Bradford and other major cities boasted active school boards keen to expand and diversify. But elsewhere, in the countryside particularly, the writ of the school boards simply did not run. Had the English school system been less of a hotchpotch or the Salisbury Government more sympathetic to the school boards, technical instruction might have fallen to the county councils in the country and to the school boards in towns. But the school boards, bastions of radicalism and nonconformity, were suspect to Conservatives. So the new acts directed money and powers solely to county councils.

This put the LCC in a delicate position. Relations with the London School Board apart, there were other reasons for the Council to move circumspectly. After years of inertia, technical education had grown rapidly in London since 1880 and other bodies were increasingly active in the field. The City livery companies, for instance, had been bullied into remembering some of their ancestral obligations for education and training. T.H. Huxley, prominent among the first generation of those to raise the alarm about standards of technical instruction, had been explicit in 1879: 'There were in the City of London . . . the possessors of enormous wealth, who were the inheritors of the property and traditions of the old Guilds of London, which were meant for this very purpose, and if the people of this country did not insist on this wealth being applied for its proper purpose, they deserved to be taxed down to their shoes'.[4] Goaded by such critics, the city companies were induced to confer and report on improving opportunities for artisans. They recommended one trade school north and one south of the Thames, and a central institution for teachers. Out of this emerged the City and Guilds of London Institute (1880), with its own training college and teachers, and the Finsbury Technical College (1883), really an expansion of previous trade classes started under the name of the Artisans Institute. By the best European standards these foundations were inadequately funded and equipped, but for the teaching of technology to London's artisans they represented a start. Had the city companies continued to co-operate, the City and Guilds and the Finsbury Technical College could have developed further and quicker. But in the later 1880s they began to dissipate their energies in unco-ordinated ventures; the Drapers Company, for instance, the original mainstay of Finsbury, transferred its support to the People's Palace in Mile End in 1888.[5]

[4] Quoted in C.T. Millis, *Technical Education*, 1925, p.54.

[5] Early City efforts: Millis, *op.cit.*, ch.5; Sir Philip Magnus, *Educational Aims and Efforts, 1880-1910*, 1910, pp.84ff; Jennifer Lang, *City and Guilds of London Institute Centenary 1878-1978*, 1978.

At the time of the LCC's creation, that practically was the extent of City disbursement towards London's technical education. It was not, however, the full story; another reform in the offing promised substantial sums for training to match the whisky money. So far back as 1878, a Royal Commission had begun to look into the decayed state of London's ancient parochial charities. An Act of 1883 directed the Charity Commissioners to devise and run a scheme for the broader use of this money. They moved slowly, for it was not until February 1891 that the scheme was finally approved. It established a City Parochial Foundation, on which the LCC and the City Corporation were equally represented. To promote technical education, it advocated a ring of seven 'polytechnics' around London, on the lines of the successful Regent Street Polytechnic set up by the businessman-philanthropist Quintin Hogg in 1882. In expectation of the scheme of 1891 and with help from some city companies, a few of these polytechnics had already been founded or planned, at Woolwich, Borough, Battersea and Chelsea. So the polytechnic movement was up and half-running before the LCC got drawn into technical education. The siting of the polytechnics was haphazard, nor had agreement been reached about what should be taught where or why. But the 1891 scheme, framed after a period of intense industrial unrest in London, made the purpose of polytechnic instruction explicit – instruction in trade skills for 'the poorer classes', combined with social and recreational opportunties of the kind which Hogg had fostered at Regent Street. In due course this stipulation was to conflict with the LCC's increasing concern for 'higher' industrial training, and to lead to the spectacle of City money going to support basic training for Londoners, while the LCC seemed preoccupied with higher education and research.[6]

From the outset, the involvement of City money and interests in technical education was a political obstacle for the LCC. The Council owed much of its early vigour and ideology to Radical hatred of the unrepresentative City Corporation, the livery companies and all their works. It was a plank of the Progressives' programme to abolish the Corporation and bring the companies to heel. That the LCC should work with them was unthinkable to many Progressives; either the Council should be the sole authority for London's technical education, or the City should pay for it in true proportion to its wealth and former responsibilities.

Such was the reaction when in 1891 the LCC first debated its opportunities under the Technical Instruction Acts. A committee had been appointed the previous autumn to decide how to use the first tranche

[6] Early history of the polytechnics: Millis, *op.cit.*, pp.76-8; Magnus, *op.cit.*, pp.113-5; Ethel M. Wood, *The Polytechnic and its Founder Quintin Hogg*, 1932; Edric Bayley, *The Borough Polytechnic Institute*, 1910; F.G. Evans, *Borough Polytechnic, 1892-1969*, 1969; Harold Silver and S. John Teague, *Chelsea College, A History*, 1977.

of whisky money. London's secondary and technical education, this committee agreed, was 'little short of a disgrace to the wealthiest city in the world';[7] and it noted that foreign competition had badly damaged Clerkenwell watch-making and was beginning to erode the tailoring, baking and shoemaking industries. Should the LCC just support existing institutions or establish schools of its own? Beset by demands for money from the polytechnics, anxious to avoid overlap, and unsure of its relations with the School Board, the committee merely suggested a cautious initial share-out of £23,000 among the polytechnics.[8] But when this recommendation came to the full Council, it was narrowly overturned by a coalition of teetotal and anti-City interests. F.N. Charrington (renegade scion of the brewing family) and Lord Compton felt that to accept money from the drink trade, even indirectly through taxation, was 'a bribe', 'almost immoral'. The ideological leaders of Progressivism, John Benn and Charles Harrison, argued that the LCC should not meddle with technical education until municipal taxation had been reformed, the livery companies disestablished, and the money left for educating the London poor 'and hitherto appropriated for higher education shall have been restored to the classes and purposes to and for which it properly belongs'. And John Burns chipped in with a remark which showed that even skilled workers and committed trades unionists had still to be convinced by the arguments for training. The rage for technical education, he said, was 'nothing more than a craze on the part of a number of honest, well-intentioned philanthropic persons who did not know what they were talking about and had nothing better to do'.[9]

It was this unholy coalition between ideology, temperance and working-class dog-in-the-mangerism that goaded Llewellyn Smith and the NAPTSE into their attack on the LCC in 1892. At the behest of leaders of the polytechnic movement like Hogg, already an LCC Alderman, it led also to technical education becoming an issue in the LCC election campaign of that year. This was how Sidney Webb, then first standing for the Council in Deptford, came to interest himself in the subject. Llewellyn Smith and Arthur Acland (who was to preside over the Education Department during the Liberal Government of 1892-5) seem to have lobbied Webb hard. As a result, it was Webb who after the decisive Progressive victory of 1892 headed a newly constituted committee to reconsider LCC attitudes to technical education in London, and Webb who secured the appointment of Llewellyn Smith to write his great report

[7] Greater London Record Office (GLRO), LCC/MIN 12787, report of special committee appointed to consider application of funds to be received from new duties on beer and spirits, Jan. 1891.

[8] *Ibid.*

[9] William Saunders, *History of the First London County Council*, 1892, pp.399-402, 418-9, 422-4.

on the subject.[10] But he was far from the only influence. Quintin Hogg, who was on the Council till 1895, headed the polytechnic lobby by seniority and experience. He was supported by others who took up the cudgels for polytechnics sited in their district or committed to their sphere of work; Edric Bayley, for instance, championed the Borough Polytechnic, R.C. Antrobus the South-Western Polytechnic at Chelsea. Some were vestry politicians who had got on to the LCC partly to help these institutions, while others, like Evan Spicer and Edward Bond, had been connected with the efforts to reform the use of City money in education.

Llewellyn Smith's report of 1892 became the bible of the early TEB.[11] On the surface, it appeared to have been commissioned, compiled and printed between March and July 1892. In reality, he had already started his fundamental study of London's technical education some time before, so that the LCC was hiring a Toynbee-Hall-trained expert already examining the field.[12] So the report delved far deeper than would have been possible in four months' work. It went beyond previous investigations of London technical education, indeed beyond most British social science at the time, by looking not just at what educational and financial provision was and might be, but at the whole structure of London's industry and population – at a time before the migration of either had taken serious hold. For the first time in the history of London's government, possibly of British local government as a whole, a full, statistically based survey became the foundation for policy. Just to get an accurate picture of the distribution of London's industries and skills proved a herculean task. Smith, like Beatrice Webb, had worked on the analysis of census material for Charles Booth's *Life and Labour of the People in London*, and this was his starting point. Working with Booth's help and advice, he got special access to the occupation sheets for the 1881 census (the last then available) and went through them page by page.[13]

The employment structure of London in the 1890s which Llewellyn Smith revealed affected the prospects for technical training in several ways. Industrially the picture was patchy, localized and specialized, with almost every type of production represented but some much stronger than others. Building, metal-working, furniture-making, printing and binding, chemicals and clothing were the most important trades. Firms were many and small rather than large, few and monopolistic, as in some British towns and cities. This discouraged London employers from promoting

[10] E.J.T. Brennan, *Education for National Efficiency*, 1975, introduction.

[11] H. Llewellyn Smith, *Report to the Special Committee on Technical Education*, London County Council, 1892 (copy in GLRO, TEB 79a).

[12] GLRO, LCC/MIN 12787, minutes of 31 Oct. 1890, when Llewellyn Smith stated that he had been 'for some time past' engaged on a study of London's educational institutions.

[13] Llewellyn Smith, *op.cit.*, pp.12-14.

training, as the apprenticeship tradition withered. So too did the high rents and cramped quarters prevalent in London industries, leading to lower profits; and, above all, the endless influx of skilled labour from the provinces, sucked in by the higher pay, wider opportunities and more independent life possible in London. While employers (particularly in building and engineering) could rely on skilled immigrant labour, what need had they to encourage training for native Londoners?[14] This attitude helped to swell the pool of casual, indigenous labour whose misery and discontent polluted the capital at the turn of the century.

With the backing of this masterly report, Webb was able to overcome remaining opposition and induce the LCC to carry through the first of Llewellyn Smith's recommendations – the setting up of a Technical Education Board on the lines already laid down by other county councils, with delegates chosen from a variety of bodies. The London example was inevitably more elaborate than others. It was devised to minimize rivalry between the various interests, but the final balance differed from Webb's wishes. In the first formulation, the School Board was to have five delegates and the London Trades Council (LTC) one. The working men elected to the LCC in 1892 under the LTC's umbrella objected to this and demanded equal representation with the School Board. They felt that they were best equipped to pronounce on the improvement of working-class skills and opportunities in London, at that stage the most explicit goal of the whole technical education movement. That aim indeed was enshrined in the LCC's original terms of reference to the London TEB.[15] As it turned out, the working men contributed only sporadically to the Board's policy-making. The labour leaders who sat on the early LCC often saw themselves as representing their trades and districts rather than as fighters for the artisan class in London as a whole, let alone for the unskilled. The working man who made most practical impact on the TEB was Will Crooks, not an LTC delegate but an LCC member who seems to have viewed his role on both Council and Board in 'localist' terms, as a means to furthering the interests of Poplar.[16] In due course the LTC delegates were to become disaffected with Webb's priorities and to begin acting together, but they never did so to great effect.

The London Technical Education Board started its work in April 1893. The final number of the Board was thirty-five, consisting of twenty LCC Members and fifteen others: three from the City and Guilds of London Institute and two from the City Parochial Foundation, representing City

[14] See especially F.G. Evans, *Borough Polytechnic, 1892-1969*, 1969, p.2.

[15] LCC Minutes of Proceedings, 18 April 1893, pp.415-6.

[16] George Haw, *From Workhouse to Westminster*, 1907, pp.100ff. Crooks was largely responsible for the opening of the LCC School of Marine Engineering and Navigation at Poplar in 1906.

interests; three from the London School Board, three from the London Trades Council, one from the National Union of Teachers and one from the Headmasters' Association. Sidney Webb was the first chairman. Llewellyn Smith could not be persuaded to become secretary of the Board; in his stead, the post fell to William Garnett, formerly head of the Durham College of Science. Garnett became the *eminence grise* of London's technical education. He planned, worked out and implemented the TEB's detailed schemes over the next decade, with Bernard Allen and C.W. Kimmins as his main lieutenants.[17] Allen's memoir of Garnett and his own autobiography well convey the atmosphere and methods of the tiny Board. Aloof from the burgeoning LCC bureaucracy in Spring Gardens or from the School Board's imposing offices on the Embankment, the Board occupied a few rooms in St. Martin's Place: 'we lived like a happy family together,' recollected Allen, 'not much more than a dozen people all told.'[18] The TEB's staff could be so small because it had few administrative responsibilities for the establishments that it funded in the early years.

At the LCC's request, the Board's first priority became the creation of a 'scholarship ladder', whereby the brightest children were taken on from the board schools and into the few grammar or 'continuation' schools which passed for London's system of secondary education in the 1890s. This 'capacity-catching' (to use the jargon of the time) accorded with Llewellyn Smith's recommendations, and carried out the aims of the 1891 Technical Instruction Act. Narrowly speaking, the scholarship ladder is only incidental to the history of technical education in London. But it influenced the whole educational system. It tied the TEB and the School Board together, and it pointed towards a structure in which elementary, secondary and higher education would be loosely bound together, mixing public and private funding but under single electoral control. This vision was first advanced by Webb and Garnett, representing the infant TEB, before the Royal Commission on Secondary Education in May 1894.[19] The lucidity, circumspection and statistical backing with which they put their views were to have long repercussions. Many Conservatives had feared the appearance of the radical-seeming LCC in the educational arena. Thereafter, London's TEB began to look more and more like an ally, bent not upon universal secondary education at vast expense but selective piecemeal reforms. Possibly, Conservatives began to see, it might prove a means for clipping the wings of the incorrigibly Liberal school board.

After the scholarship ladder, the TEB's next concern was to provide a more orderly and complete framework for technical education in London.

[17] Bernard M. Allen, *William Garnett, A Memoir*, 1933, pp.54-61.
[18] Bernard M. Allen, *Down the Stream of Life*, 1948, p.75.
[19] PP 1895, XLV, 29 May 1894, pp.254-90 and 546-76.

The bare bones, but only the bones, of a polytechnic system existed when the Board took up its work. By law it could not build, but it could offer funds for teaching and scholarships within the subjects prescribed by the Science and Art Department. The whisky money due to London was growing every year and, with the small rate which the LCC could levy for technical instruction, gradually put the TEB in a commanding role. Getting the unbuilt polytechnics going, topping up the funds of existing ones, adding courses relevant and accessible to local industries and labour: these were the bread and butter of Garnett's work in the 1890s. Transport from one part of London was poor and costly for the working man or woman, so local provision mattered more at this stage than the rational distribution of a London-wide framework. Later on, the polytechnics were regarded as having different 'faculties', as one author put it in 1907:

> Thus the Northampton Institute has developed its facilities of metal-working and technical optics; the Central School of Arts and Crafts its silversmith's work. The Borough Polytechnic, besides its large classes for builders and plumbers, has its school of bakery. The Cass Institute, growing up near the Mint, is steadily developing its school of metallurgy. Woolwich Polytechnic, growing up beside the Arsenal, has supplied the scientific instruction needed by the workmen there. Battersea Polytechnic has developed a close connection with the engineering works of the London and South Western Railway, supplying regular day class for their apprentices, as Woolwich's has done for the Arsenal's. So too classes are arranged in dresscutting and tailoring, for Messrs. Selincourt's apprentices. Chelsea Polytechic has adapted itself rather to a clerkly population, while the Regent Street Polytechnic, with its 15,000 students, is almost universal in its range.[20]

Several of the establishments on this list were not polytechnics but technical institutes or 'monotechnics'. They, not the polytechnics, became the Board's chief endowment to technical education during the 1890s. The LTC's delegates on the TEB, all skilled representatives of particular trades, contributed much to this work. Many of these schools, like the polytechnics, were not really new at all, but previous foundations or hole-in-the-corner classes with educational and financial weaknesses which the TEB took up and pressed into shape. One example was the Shoreditch Technical Institute, an early TEB scheme which picked up some poorly funded training classes for the local cabinet-making and furniture industry, found them new premises and equipment and put the school on a few footing. Another was the Hammersmith School of Art, started in the 1880s as the Brook Green School of Art, for and by the aspiring middle classes of West London. Characteristically, this school went through three phases of integration. From 1896 Garnett furnished

[20] G.L. Bruce in M.E. Sadler (ed.), *Continuation Schools in England and Elsewhere*, 1907, pp.136-7.

TEB money for certain classes for which there was no nearby alternative, but the management remained local. In 1903 the Board took over the management of this and other art schools it supported in London, in order to bring them into 'close relation with industrial needs'.[21] New classes in furniture design, writing and illuminating, and artificial flower-making came in, to supplement the amateur pursuits of life-drawing and pottery. Finally, in 1907 the LCC was able to provide the Hammersmith school with a new site and building under the better funded arrangements for technical instruction inaugurated three years earlier. In this way, Llewellyn Smith's recommendation of 1892 that the LCC should itself in the long run have its own technical schools and colleges was fulfilled more by 'permeation' and take-over than by outright establishment.

Various examples could be given of the TEB's attempts to tackle training in particular industries. Its backing of Herolds Institute in Bermondsey, later the Leathersellers College, showed that in certain trades likes tanning quite modest investment in research and training could improve a London industry's whole status and future. At a humbler level was the School of Nautical Cookery in Dock Street, Stepney, set up with a TEB grant in 1893 on the grounds that 'the temper and efficiency of a crew depend a good deal on the capacity of the cook',[22] and long well patronised. The Central School of Arts and Crafts, inspired by the Board's distinguished part-time art inspector W.R. Lethaby, was conspicuously successful as 'a school of University rank for the artistic crafts'[23], notably book-binding and some of the finer building crafts, though its influence on the building industry was more limited.

Perhaps the best example of a 'monotechnic' which fulfilled the Board's hopes was the Bolt Court School of Photo-Engraving and Lithography.[24] Bolt Court was typical in occupying the borders between art and industry and in not being a wholly new foundation but a shot in the arm for existing classes run by a small union, the National Society of Lithographic Artists, in old premises off Fleet Street. The background to the school's proper establishment was a conference held in July 1894 at the LCC's headquarters in Spring Gardens for the book, paper and printing trades. This gathering aimed to ascertain, with the help of unions and employers, what training existed and what gaps needed to be filled, and to reassure those labour representatives who feared that technical training might 'overstock the trade with workmen, consequently bringing down wages and increasing the unemployed'.[25] The printing industry at the time was

[21] GLRO, ED/HFE/12/1 (cuttings on Hammersmith School of Art).

[22] *Eight Years* . . . (see n.2), p.80.

[23] Millis, *op.cit.*, p.87. On Lethaby and the 'Central' see Godfrey Rubens, *William Richard Lethaby*, 1986, pp.175-98.

[24] Bolt Court: GLRO, TEB 80/57-60 and TEB 24 (Minutes of Finance and General Purposes Subcommittee, 1895).

[25] *Journal of the Royal Society of Arts*, 16 July 1897, pp.832-3.

in a volatile state, with rapid changes occurring in illustrative technique. The St Bride Foundation Institute, newly set up with 'city parochial' money in the same district, had a library and social facilities, to which basic printing courses were added with TEB support. But it offered no chance for developing the new techniques, in which France and Germany were markedly more proficient. Bolt Court was bolstered up from 1895 to remedy this. It was managed by a joint committee of the TEB and the union, directed by a lithographic artist who continued to work commercially as well as in the school. At first it was open only to those already in employment. The students must have found it of financial as well as practical benefit, for early attendances were high. By degrees the teaching became broader. Day courses supplemented evening ones, elementary schoolchildren came in to observe the processes, and with the TEB grants for equipment a programme of research was built up. Soon, the Bolt Court methods of instruction spread to provincial centres. By 1912, when the LCC was at last able to provide new premises, still tucked away behind Fleet Street, the claim could be made that 'of all the special schools, it has probably had most effect upon the trade with which it is connected'.[26] The research tradition carried on: in the Second World War the school, then evacuated to Putney, played an important role in developing steel gauges and graticules for optical instruments.

From about 1898, a shift took place in the TEB's priorities. The training of artisans gave way to other preoccupations: commercial instruction, higher types of technical education, research, and university reform. Hitherto the welfare and advancement of London's manual workers had been paramount. Now the national goals of the technical education movement – efficiency, competitiveness, and the demand for a workforce fit to meet imperial obligations – dominated the Board's plans. This shift cannot simply be put down to the attitudes of Sidney Webb and a few Fabian allies like Graham Wallas (briefly a School Board delegate on the TEB). But Webb certainly encouraged this change of tack. In particular it was he who harnessed the growing clamour for commercial education in London together with the 'Hutchinson legacy', left for some unspecified Fabian purpose, in order to found the London School of Economics.[27]

Commerce, though touched upon, had hardly received the emphasis it warranted in Llewellyn Smith's 1892 report. The international transactions of banking, insurance and trade and the co-ordination of

[26] *LCC School of Photo-Engraving and Lithography: Report by the Principal on the War Work of the School*, London County Council, 1945.

[27] LSE's foundation: Brennan, *Education for National Efficiency*, 1975, pp.38-40; Sir Sydney Caine, *The History of the Foundation of the London School of Economics and Political Science*, 1963; Janet Beveridge, *An Epic of Clare Market*, 1960, pp.42-4; GLRO, TEB 24 (Minutes of Finance and General Purposes Subcommittee), 1 May 1895.

London-based companies and official bodies required an army of clerks to deal with the complexities of law, accountancy and book-keeping. In the 1890s the commercial workforce was growing at a rate which far exceeded that of London's industrial employment. As clerks travelled further to their jobs than manual workers and many already lived beyond the LCC's boundaries, Llewellyn Smith's researches shed scant light on their concentration. In Germany and some other European centres, notably Antwerp and Vienna, commercial education was well in hand. In England the London Chamber of Commerce, embarrassed by the low quality of City clerks, was the prime mover but battled in vain for some years. As late as 1893, an American report on European business education felt able to disregard Britain on the grounds that there was nothing to say.[28]

The TEB laboured under a twofold difficulty. Commercial subjects did not fall unambiguously within those sanctioned by the Science and Art Department, the arbiter of the Technical Instruction Acts within which the Board had to operate; and the London Trades Council's delegates on the Board begrudged clerical claims, insisting that technical instruction money was meant for artisans. Webb first raised the subject in May 1895 – a carefully chosen moment, since the third LCC election had just reduced labour representation. He asked the Board for a small grant towards some classes and lectures already operated by the London Chamber of Commerce, but now to be brought within the framework of the London School of Economics (LSE), then just established. The TEB members seem to have been told little at this stage about the Fabian purposes of the new foundation or the depth of Webb's own commitment to the project. Over the next few years further subsidies for LSE were voted, culminating in an effective grant of some £15,000 in 1899 when the LCC agreed to lease a site to the school at nominal rent. This favouring of LSE caused friction. T.A. Organ, the solicitor to the National Union of Teachers, felt that the Board's approach to commercial education should be simpler and broader than what was on offer at LSE, where business instruction was confined to a few 'higher' lines like railway economics. Webb's ideal of research and of a national role for LSE, he believed, was distracting the Board from its obligations towards London's clerks. Webb certainly exaggerated LSE's role in commercial instruction to the Board, and in fundamental research to the Fabian trustees. As a result he came under fire from both sides. In 1898, during a prolonged absence abroad, he suffered the first real damage to his standing on the Board in the form of an attack from Will Crooks and James MacDonald, the LTC secretary, who claimed that Webb had syphoned off TEB funds for the purposes of pure research.[29]

[28] Michael Sanderson, *The Universities and British Industry 1850-1970*, 1972, pp.185-8.
[29] Beveridge, *op.cit.*, pp.42-4; Brennan, *Education for National Efficiency*, 1975, pp.36-40.

At Organ's instigation the TEB set up a subcommittee on commercial education which reported in 1899. Commercial classes of the type already supported by the School Board were increased and diversified, while one secondary school, University College School, agreed to foster commercial teaching and to send on an annual quota of pupils to LSE.[30] But this was a tiny experiment. The Board could make little progress with basic commercial education until a proper secondary system for London schools was developed. Language-teaching, for instance, an essential tool for commerce and available to many Germany children, was still uncommon in London schools at the turn of the century. The key to better education lay, as Webb well knew, in the schools.

Behind Webb's promotion of LSE lay his conviction that the TEB was going to have to support higher education on top of the simpler type of technical instruction – a thought scarcely before the Board's founders in 1892-3. From their enquiries into industrial training, its members had learnt that many London trades could not be helped merely by improving craft skills or widening opportunities for artisans. This was a constant refrain from scientists and teachers of science. Silvanus Thompson, the Principal of Finsbury Technical College, was scathing when a leading LCC Progressive, Sir Arthur Arnold, opined that chemistry could be taught to bricklayers: 'a grosser caricature of the aim and end of technical education could scarcely have been invented'.[31] Dyestuffs, for instance, an industry originated in Britain but largely lost to Germany because of poor research and training, depended on a few highly skilled chemists and a large unskilled labour force. It was in the provision of advanced scientific facilities of this kind, argued Thompson and others, that London was really falling behind Zurich, Munich, Berlin and other cities. The case was first put to the TEB in the course of an enquiry into chemistry teaching (1896).[32] Without municipal backing for research and higher education in technology, London and by implication Britain would trail further behind.

This raised the spectre of the University of London's inadequacies. During most of the TEB's existence, the university was subject to commissions of enquiry and rent by centralizing and localizing factions.[33] Nor did the Board have the right to subsidise the university, until 1898 technically a government department. It could only lobby for a 'teaching university' and foster institutions which, when reform came, might be

[30] GLRO, TEB 20 and 79d (Minutes and Report of Special Subcommittee on Commercial Education, 1897-9); Sidney Webb, 'The Organization of Commercial Education' in Brennan, *Education for National Efficiency*, 1975, pp.172-9.

[31] *Journal of the Royal Society of Arts*, 23 July 1897, pp.870-4.

[32] GLRO, TEB 80/3 and 79c (Minutes and Report of Special Subcommittee on Teaching of Chemistry, 1896).

[33] Negley Harte, *The University of London, 1836-1986*, 1986, pp.138-60.

part of it. Webb, for one, imagined a refashioned university in London both as a national centre for research and intellectual life and as the final rung on the London scholarship ladder, so that the gifted child would proceed first from the board school to a continuation school and hence by a further scholarship to LSE or some other arm of the university. Alternatively, the best polytechnic students might go on to research and, through links with the university, gain academic recognition of the kind that was denied to them so long as polytechnics only trained artisans.

This attitude was to cause something of a rift once the reform of the university had taken place. The creators of the polytechnics like Philip Magnus and C.T. Millis of Borough, supported by the working men on the LCC and to an extent by Garnett, wanted them to keep faith with their social and industrial origins and not be led astray by 'higher' pursuits. They did not want the polytechnics to be taken over by the middle classes, as had happened to the Victorian mechanics' institutes. Webb's supporters, on the other hand, tended to belittle the social side of the polytechnics and were openly university-oriented in their approach. When eventually a scheme was devised to link the polytechnics with the university, Borough and Regent Street stayed out on the grounds that they would best serve their industrial constituency by steering clear of higher education and research.[34]

The recommendations of the 1892-4 Commission for reforming the University of London took years to carry through. The Bill to make them a reality, drafted by R.B. Haldane with Sidney Webb's help, failed three times and only passed in 1898 after the Government had lent it support. In 1900 a new constitution came into force and the university's offices were shifted from Burlington Gardens to the more scientific milieu of South Kensington. Not until 1902 did the TEB, then with only a year to run, persuade the LCC to give the university the municipal grant which under the new legislation it was able to do. It then proffered £10,000, a sum which amounted to about a quarter of the central university's total income. For the next quarter of a century, the LCC was a major source of money for the University of London. By the First World War its 'block grant' had risen to over £25,000, on top of which were occasional grants to colleges.[35] The sums were never huge, but in the context of the poor endowment of higher education in London they were significant. By way of recompense, the LCC acquired a seat on the Senate (Webb was the first occupant). Up to 1914 its influence was strong; it was used, for instance, in 1912 to block a first attempt to move the university's administration back from South Kensington.

As might have been expected, Webb and his ally Haldane spent less

[34] Evans, *op.cit.*, pp.26-7; Silver and Teague, *op.cit.*, pp.43ff.
[35] *Eight Years* . . . (see n.2), pp.67-70.

time in reminding the university of its municipal debt to London and Londoners as a whole than towards making it a centre of national endeavour, through the fostering of favoured institutions like LSE and Imperial College. There were exceptions. One was the drawing into the university's ambit of the London Day Training College, founded in 1902 by the LCC as a teacher training college for the hamstrung London School Board.[36] But even this college gradually lost its relationship with London. By 1927, when it moved into new premises (paid for by the LCC), it became a full part of the university and changed its name to the Institute of Education, its formal links with London's schools had diminished, though it did continue to train many LCC teachers. In all spheres, the University of London showed – and has continued to show – little consciousness of civic obligations. It preferred to leave that to the LCC, with its independent system of colleges and polytechnics.

The TEB's struggle to promote higher technical education in London culminated in its efforts to establish Imperial College as a rival to the Königliche Technische Hochschule at Charlottenburg outside Berlin and other European centres of technological brainpower. This campaign is sometimes depicted as part of a Fabian conspiracy for national efficiency, led by Webb and Haldane and fronted by influential people like Lords Rosebery and Monkswell.[37] Its true origins lay deeper, in the Germanophilia of early activists in technical education and in the disquiet expressed by London's applied scientists to Llewellyn Smith in 1892 and again to the TEB's enquiry on chemistry teaching in 1896. In 1901-2 the Board held a fresh enquiry into the application of science to industry. Before soliciting views, Garnett drew up a memorandum pointing out the limitations under which the TEB worked. The LCC's original reference of 1893 had required the Board just to provide 'further facilities for practical and technical education in the poor and manufacturing districts of London'. In an army, continued Garnett, private soldiers must be well trained, 'but the result of a modern campaign depends far more on the training and foresight of the officers, especially the staff officers, than on that kind of drill which leads to a perfect appearance on the parade ground'.[38] Witness after expert witness, all scientists or businessmen rather than labour representatives, took the same view. In terms still familiar they lamented the indifference of employers, the poverty of

[36] GLRO, TEB 69 (London Technical Education Gazette vol.6, Oct. 1902); Isaac Hayward, 'The LCC and the Training of Teachers 1902-52', in University of London, Institute of Education, *Jubilee Lectures*, 1952, vol.1, pp.23-38.

[37] Imperial College: Brennan, *Education for National Efficiency*, 1975, pp.40ff; A. Rupert Hall, *A Short History of the Imperial College of Science and Technology*, 1932; T.L. Humberstone, *University Reform in London*, 1926, pp.166-72.

[38] GLRO, TEB 80/114 (Report of the Special Subcommittee on the Application of Science to Industry, 1902), pp.110-13.

secondary education, and the inadequacy of facilities and salaries for research. They stressed particularly the collapse of the British coal-tar industry for aniline dyes, which had proceeded from researches started by Hofmann in South Kensington before he returned to Berlin for lack of support. But they also identified important industries which gave current cause for alarm: optical instruments, electrical engineering, pottery, and even brewing. The focus of most of this evidence was national, not metropolitan. As for the belief that money spent on higher education was 'so much lost to the poorer or wage-earning classes', the committee's report of July 1902 argued that ordinary skilled employment would decline if these industries collapsed. The sums needed to rectify matters were far beyond the TEB's range, it concluded: 'We can do no more than report the need, with all the emphasis we can give to our words, in the hope that, either out of private or public funds, something may be done'.[39]

This trenchant report, perhaps drafted by Webb, was shown by Haldane to the South African mining millionaires Alfred Beit and Julius Wernher at the self-consciously imperial moment after the end of the Boer War. Armed with promises of money for buildings (which the TEB was not empowered to provide), Webb and Haldane suborned Lord Rosebery to write to Lord Monkswell, the LCC Chairman, urging the Council to offer £20,000 per annum for maintaining the new institution. This was agreed in principle – a unique coincidence of solidarity between municipal and imperial ambition. But the 'new and separate institution for the highest technical education'[40] then contemplated never transpired. Imperial College, as it emerged in 1907, started as an association of existing South Kensington colleges within the University of London rather than the independent 'Charlottenburg' which the TEB had believed was needed. Vested academic interests contributed to this, along with a cheese-paring financial attitude from the Government which gave the Municipal Reform LCC administrations from 1907 the excuse to cut down on the promised £20,000 on the grounds that the Government was not giving enough. In addition, a less dynamic policy towards technical education prevailed after the TEB ceded its duties to the full LCC in 1904.

The London TEB's dissolution and the take-over of all municipal education in London by the LCC sprang from the national transfer of education from the school boards to the county councils in 1903-4 and, specifically, from the demise of the London School Board. By the nature of the laws which brought them into being, relations between the two London boards had been complex. The School Board, answerable to the Education Department, was supposed to offer a framework of purely elementary schooling on top of which the TEB, authorized by a different

[39] *Ibid.*, pp.7-8.
[40] *Eight Years . . .* (see n.2), pp.70-3.

elected body (the LCC) and responsible until 1900 to a different arm of government, the Science and Art Department, had to supply a layer of technical instruction. Better technical education needed an improved system of secondary schools, but who was to control these? Here lay the nub of the issue between the boards. In many ways it is remarkable how well they got on. School Board delegates sat on the TEB without forming a dissident faction, except when the future of their parent body came into question. The mechanism of the scholarship ladder welded the boards together, and the TEB often helped the School Board to do things it could not do by itself. The London Day Training College, for instance, was the TEB's answer to a plea from the School Board to help it expand teacher-training beyond the 'pupil-teacher' centres which were all it was allowed by statute to have. Even where overlap occurred, as in the provision of evening classes in art, there was no extreme friction. For most of the 1890s both boards were controlled by the Progressives, while all parties on the TEB sympathized with the School Board's efforts to offer opportunities to the working man and woman by way of technically illegal evening classes.

Nevertheless, at the expense of one body or the other, eventual clarification was inevitable. With the Conservatives in power from 1895 to 1906, it was always on the cards that the Liberal-Radical School Board would be the loser. Webb and Garnett's evidence to the Secondary Education Commission was a turning point. Thereafter it became clear that the TEB could work with the Conservatives and vice versa, whereas the London School Board could not. A first bill to assign secondary education to the county councils failed. But in 1897 the ball was set rolling by a clause surreptitiously inserted in the Education Department's 'Directory', allowing county councils to apply for controlling science and art teaching in continuation schools. With Webb away in Australia and Edward Bond, a Conservative, in the chair, the TEB voted to apply in November 1898. Confrontation with the School Board ensued: then the matter was referred to the full LCC, which refused to back off. The issue went to law, resulting in the so-called Cockerton judgement, confirmed on appeal in April 1901. By establishing once and for all that the London School Board was in many respects acting beyond its powers, the judgement made a major educational reorganization inevitable – at least in London. The details of the Cockerton saga are too intricate to recount.[41] Here it need only be said that the TEB's officials, notably William Garnett, were induced by government ministers and civil servants to bring the original test case. As this became known, the TEB appeared to have connived in the Conservative overthrow of the London School Board.

[41] Cockerton judgement: Eric Eaglesham, *From School Board to Local Authority*, 1956, chs.10 and 11, gives a detailed account of the saga. For the LCC's support of the TEB: LCC Minutes of Proceedings, 6 Dec. 1898, pp.1453-5, 20 Dec. 1898, pp.1834-5.

So it was that when the Education Bill for London came forward in 1903, abolishing both the London School Board and the Technical Education Board and transferring all their responsibilities directly to the LCC, it brought the LCC Progressives into delicate relations with the dominant faction on the TEB. They were delighted that so major a service should pass into LCC hands just when other vaunted schemes of municipalization seemed to be faltering. As Laurence Gomme, the Clerk to the Council, put it: 'the Council has already lost the water supply; the Tramways and the Fire Brigade are both threatened, and the Council, if it loses Education, will be little better than a Drainage Board'.[42] Yet the School Board had been a stronghold of Progressivism and a defender of working-class interests in education. Webb and his allies on the other hand were tainted by their dalliance with Conservatives, imperialists and churchmen, and an appearance of increasing indifference to the education of artisans. The line taken by John Burns, the veteran LCC Progressive, seems to have been typical: they would not stab the School Board in the back, but they would not refuse any responsibilities imposed on the LCC by the Government.[43]

Lobbying for the 1903 Bill was the last act Sidney Webb undertook for the TEB and LCC. He was tired of Council politics, believing in his wife's words that 'the ordinary Progressive member is either a bounder, a narrow-minded fanatic or a mere piece of putty upon which any strong mind can make an impression, to be effaced by the next influence'.[44] The atmosphere on the TEB had become contentious, with the labour representatives (egged on from 1901 by Ramsay MacDonald) now openly gunning for Webb. He was content to give up his LCC seat in 1904, hand over the torch and put together his *London Education* as a record of what had been achieved over the previous decade and what had still to be done. For Garnett, the fall-out from the 1903 Bill was severer. To show how the LCC might manage education, he had drawn up a scheme which he sent to the Association of London Unionist Members at a critical moment during the Bill's progress, so that the LCC could count on their support in Parliament. Following his manoeuvres in the Cockerton affair, this so incensed certain Progressives that when the LCC Education Department was formed, they allowed Garnett a backseat role only, as 'Educational Adviser'. In this position he remained until he retired in 1915.[45]

[42] Quoted by William Garnett, 'How the LCC became the LEA for London' in *Educational Record*, 22, April 1929, pp.746-60.

[43] *Ibid.*, p.759.

[44] Norman and Jeanne MacKenzie, *The Diary of Beatrice Webb, Volume 2, 1892-1905*, 1983, pp.286-7. Webb's attitudes and difficulties with MacDonald and others on the TEB and LCC are graphically conveyed by his wife throughout her diary, 1902-5.

[45] Garnett, *op.cit.*, p.760; Bernard M. Allen, *Down the Stream of Life*, 1948, pp.76-7.

As far as technical instruction is concerned, the first decade of full LCC control of London's education was an anticlimax after the ardour of the TEB years. Most of the institutions created by the two boards were up and running; they needed adjustment, co-ordination and cautious enlargement rather than radical renewal. The last years of Progressive rule in London (1904-7) saw a falling-off in initiative, with many of the most energetic LCC Members becoming MPs in the Liberal landslide of 1906 and turning to national rather than municipal answers to social questions. The cost-cutting 'Municipal Reform' administrations which succeeded were better disposed to education than to other LCC interventions, but the improvement of technical training seems to have engaged few Members' interests. The educational bureaucracy inherited from the School Board had large routine responsibilities, a strict discipline, but no very elevated atmosphere. 'Don't work too hard chaps, make a bit of O.T.', quipped a senior colleague to William Kent, one of many new staff brought in to cope with the administrative consequences of the 1903 Act.[46] Over the Embankment headquarters loomed the forceful figure of Robert Blair, brought into the LCC in 1904 with impressive qualifications including technical education work in Ireland. At first Blair answered to Laurence Gomme, the Clerk to the Council in Spring Gardens – an arrangement made to ensure that School Board staff were under the LCC thumb. But Blair and Gomme, past his best and distracted by manifold duties, could not get on. By a reorganization of 1908 Blair became Education Officer, with absolute powers. Garnett, the Educational Adviser, became invisible.[47]

Much energy during this decade went into London's schools system. The LCC had in particular to bring the voluntary schools, for which it was now financially reponsible, into line with the 'provided' schools and ensure that children in them got the same chances of progress to higher grade schools. The secondary network, a *sine qua non* for real advance in technical education, did gradually grow. But the Council never grasped the nettle of a big expansion in secondary provision – the substitution of a 'broad highway' for the scholarship ladder, which the TUC urged upon them at the time of the 1904 election and which a few radicals like Stewart Headlam continued to call for. The costs were too vast, especially for ratepayer-conscious LCC administrations. Instead, London saw the beginnings of a definite system of aided grammar schools, superior in status and number to the few technical schools and the unrivalled target for brighter elementary children. The hallowing of this arrangement had far-reaching implications for London's education and economy alike.

[46] William Kent, *The Testament of a Victorian Youth*, 1938, p.202.

[47] Blair: D.W. Thoms, *Policy-Making in Education: Robert Blair and the London County Council 1904-1924*, Museum of the History of Education (University of Leeds) Monograph No.10, 1980.

One token of the reduced attention paid by the full LCC to training was the ending of the 'select committee' style of enquiry which had been a feature of the TEB's work. Like the Science and Industry investigation of 1901-2, some of these had virtually been national enquiries undertaken by the Board to prick Parliament and Government, and most had led to practical action. But the last of them, an enquiry into technical instruction for women chaired by Ramsay MacDonald, seems to have died with the TEB itself. Its suggestions for developing trade classes in dressmaking, bookbinding and other subjects, improving 'classes in domestic subjects' and opening technical day schools for girls met scant implementation under the new regime.[48]

Nevertheless, technical instruction in London was better funded from 1904 than in the days of the TEB. Many of the special schools got handsome new buildings and equipment to match. Grants to the university and the polytechnics also increased, so much so that with the LCC appearing as London's undisputed educational provider, City money for training began to fall off. Here the weakness of the unwritten partnership between the LCC and the City over technical education exposed itself. The LCC had obligations, the City an amalgam of mainly voluntary commitments which it could scale up and down as it chose.

Co-ordination and rationalization were the hallmark of Robert Blair's years.[49] In 1913 the various schools were recast into groups of junior and senior technical institutes, an arrangement retained until 1949. Thus it became accurate at last to speak of an entire 'system' for technical education in London. This development owed much to cheaper and better transport. Students now often travelled some way for specialized training, and the duplication which had obtained in evening classes and polytechnics in the days of the two rival boards was much diminished. Evening classes, hitherto dominated by science, crafts and art in line with government rules, branched out into leisure and hobby activities. Some of the deficiencies in commercial education which the TEB had never fully addressed were also tackled. In 1910-11, for instance, 223 LCC evening classes were teaching book-keeping – fewer than in 1904, but with a far higher number of students, 18,216 altogether. The next most popular subject of 'higher commercial instruction' was accountancy, taken by 828 students in 25 classes. Commercial law, economics, banking and currency were all taught in evening classes as well as at LSE, though the numbers were much smaller. The difficulty in all these areas, particularly in the basic subjects, was to find and keep good teachers.[50]

48 GLRO, TEB 56 (Minutes of the Special Subcommittee on Technical Instruction for Women, 1902-3).

49 *Eight Years* . . . (see n.2), pp.37-41; Thoms, *op.cit.*, p.33.

50 *Eight Years* . . . (see n.2), pp.85-7, 100-3; W.A. Devereux, *Adult Education in Inner London 1870-1980*, 1982, pp.156-65.

Where the LCC Education Department, like the TEB, never succeeded was in convincing London employers, commercial or industrial, of the need for training. Up to 1914 and beyond they remained complacent, lulled by the continued influx of skilled workers from the provinces. For every large firm which was persuaded to send its young staff to a polytechnic or LCC class, a hundred were negligent. By 1914 this had convinced Blair and many LCC Members that the only answer was compulsory 'day-continuation' classes for school-leavers. The LCC took the lead in calling for such a scheme. In theory, day-continuation classes became a national obligation under the Education Act of 1918, but they were among the many reforms of war undone in the post-war reaction. The LCC struggled on with its day-continuation scheme until 1922 when it was forced to give it up, finding many employers hiring young staff from outside the LCC area in preference to Londoners whom they would have been obliged to send on day release to continuation schools.[51] Here was the first clear warning that provision for training in London needed to be thought through on a regional basis, in line with the regional development of the London economy. Because of its static boundaries and indifferent or hostile neighbours, the LCC was never able to overcome this difficulty. With the signs of its appearance, this account of the early Council's impressive contribution to technical education in Britain may be brought to an end.

[51] Thoms, *op.cit.*, pp.36-45; Devereux, *op.cit.*, 1982, pp.109-10.

## *Chapter 5*

# *Moderates, Municipal Reformers, and the Issue of Tariff Reform, 1894-1934*

Sue Laurence

In 1907, after a bitterly fought election, the Municipal Reform Party for the first time gained control of the London County Council. Its rule was to continue without a break until 1934, just as the Progressives had controlled the LCC without serious challenge up to that point. The Municipal Reform years are easy to characterize as a long, dull interregnum in the LCC's history, when initiatives disappeared from its work, opportunities to expand the council's boundaries and activities were lost, and only housing and education received their due. The Municipal Reformers' Conservative-inspired political programme demanded strict control of municipal expenditure and advocated the defeat of socialism. In particular they opposed the former policy of municipalization which, they argued, created unfair competition for private enterprise. This concept of restriction upon municipal activity lay at the heart of their differences from their Progressive predecessors and Labour successors.

Nonetheless, during their twenty-seven-year administration the Municipal Reformers were better disposed towards municipal activity than their political programme would suggest. In fact as municipalism inexorably grew, they increasingly saw their task not so much as opposing it wholesale as restricting its expansion. This meant that the Municipal Reformers did in practice support the municipalization of those undertakings which could not effectively be run by private enterprise. The key to this flexibility of attitude lay in the doctrines of protectionism and 'tariff reform' – the call for a system of preference for British and Empire goods by means of taxing imports – which were major strands in national Conservative and Unionist ideology from the 1890s.

The LCC's Municipal Reformers owed their organization and coherence to the London Municipal Society, founded in 1894. A Unionist and Conservative foundation, the original aim of the LMS had been to put some stuffing into the Moderates (the precursors of the Municipal Reformers), then a loose-knit, non-aligned group which sought to counteract the radicalism of their Progressive opponents. By 1894 the Moderates had formalized their links with the LMS and acknowledged a direct allegiance to the Conservatives at a national level. The London

Municipal Society represented a broad spectrum of Conservative and Unionist political opinion. Apart from recruiting many of its members from property lobbies like the Liberty and Property Defence League and the Incorporated Society for the Protection of Property Owners,[1] it also depended on the support of many ratepayers' associations. Industry was well represented by members who were also active in the London Chamber of Commerce[2] and the Industrial Freedom League, an organization which aimed to protect private enterprise from state intervention. Support from commerce and industry was particularly important since the LMS depended on such funding for its survival. Indeed the Moderates' decision to keep their name was the only trace of their autonomy from the London Municipal Reform Society and even this independent feature had disappeared by 1907 when they became known as Municipal Reformers.

The London Municipal Society reflected the divisions between free traders and tariff reformers which emerged within Salisbury's Conservative government between 1895 and 1902. Many of the exponents of these conflicting causes were in the cabinet as well as active within the LMS. Free trade was represented within Salisbury's government by four members of the LMS: Lord Onslow, Lord George Hamilton, the Duke of Devonshire and Sir Edward Clarke. Two of these men were particularly prominent within the LMS. These were Onslow, who was president of the LMS and an LCC alderman, and Hamilton who was Chairman of the London School Board.[3] Lord Salisbury himself was an early pioneer of tariff reform but the task of active campaigning was left to Joseph Chamberlain.

During the 1890s these differences were to a degree latent. Chamberlain undoubtedly developed his views on tariff reform during his period as Colonial Secretary after 1895, but it was only after 1900 that he brought the issue into the foreground of national politics. The issue had a particular resonance for those politicians who were becoming increasingly disturbed by the economic strength of Germany and the United States, which were outstripping Britain's productivity rate in areas like coal and steel. Chamberlain believed that duties on goods would not only deter foreign competition but would contribute towards the financing of social reform and municipal enterprise which in their turn would help ensure national efficiency. Although Chamberlain advocated protectionist policies he was concerned that they should not degenerate into a form of Little Englandism. Hence, he visualized tariff reform in terms of imperial preference; this would extend protectionism beyond the confines of

[1] London Municipal Society, Council Minute Book, March 1907, Guildhall Library.

[2] Sir John Lubbock (Lord Avebury) was both Vice President of the LMS and President of the London Chamber of Commerce. See the *Chamber of Commerce Journal*, 1902.

[3] Ken Young, *Local Politics and the Rise of the Party*, 1975, p.17.

England and bring benefits to England while consolidating the Empire. But protection in Chamberlain's view was also vital and integral to the kind of municipal activity he had encouraged in the 1880s as Mayor of Birmingham. Under Chamberlain's guiding hand, the profits from municipal enterprise like municipal gas and electricity had been used to subsidise further municipal projects in Birmingham, thereby reducing the ratepayers' burden. Chamberlain argued that while capital was mobile, labour was not, and therefore required the twin safeguards of social and industrial legislation and of municipal protectionist policies. Applying local preference policies was, in his view, the only way of ensuring certain standards of living and employment for British workers.[4]

Chamberlain was an important figure behind the scenes in the early days of the LMS. He helped formulate its political programme, yet never secured a position on its predominantly free-trade executive committee. This suggests that the free traders deliberately excluded him from the political decision-making of the LMS. While Chamberlain's views on decentralization of government and his unquestioning support of the cities' privileges were compatible with the majority of LMS members (irrespective of their attitude towards free trade and tariff reform), his tariff reform views were more controversial.

These differences between free traders and tariff reformers became more significant after Balfour had succeeded Salisbury in 1902 as leader of the Conservative Party. Balfour himself, after some prevarication and reservations about the effects on the working-class voter, had come over to the tariff reform cause. Above all, Balfour was convinced that it was fruitless for England to pursue the free trade cause in isolation.[5] Balfour's shift in allegiance away from free trade created considerable turmoil within the cabinet and induced two of its free trade members, the Duke of Devonshire and Lord George Hamilton, to resign over this issue. Sir Edward Clarke and Lord George Hamilton extended their protest against tariff reform to the LMS by resigning their positions within this organization. So although the LMS had not pledged itself to tariff reform, the close links among the LMS leaders within national politics meant that the political reverberations surrounding the tariff reform issue had an impact at the metropolitan level.

Among the Progressives who had controlled the LCC since 1889, there had likewise been confusion about the relation between municipal enterprise and the instinct to safeguard London jobs and services through some form of municipal protectionism. In part the issue was submerged because of the relative failure of the Progressive attempts to municipalize. By the time that the LCC came into being, the practice of municipal

[4] Alan Sykes, *Tariff Reform in British Politics*, 1979, p.54.
[5] Ensor Papers, Board of Trade Papers 1903, Bodleian Library.

trading (defined as those municipal services which are partly paid for directly by individual consumers who wish to purchase such products and services)[6] was well established in Manchester, Birmingham and Liverpool. But for all the Progressives' rhetoric in favour of municipalizing London's utilities of supply and their other schemes of municipal enterprise, their plans were often obstructed. Above all, securing government loans was a major obstacle for the LCC, which unlike other urban authorities, could not apply directly to the appropriate government department but had to seek approval from Parliament. Police, paving, cleansing, lighting, waterworks, gasworks, markets, control over the river, burial and registration of voters were all outside its immediate sphere of influence. Yet while the LCC had either an uneven or a non-existent record in relation to municipal trading, it proved more successful in controlling those public utilities which were more heavily financed out of local taxation levied on the whole body of ratepayers, such as slum clearance and public health provision.[7]

The LCC could be characterized as inclining towards free trade during the Progressives' administration. Certainly Sidney Webb, the Fabians' main ideologue, was a convinced free trader,[8] although there was by no means a consensus on this issue within the Progressive ranks. The Progressives' labour policy was in many ways their most significant achievement and on the whole did not reflect a protectionist bias. Although their labour policy had included setting up a Works Department in 1892 and a fair wages policy which included clauses insisting on an eight-hour day at trade union rates, they expressed no particular commitment towards preference for English or London workmen, nor for goods manufactured in Britain or London. This policy was reflected when in 1896 the Progressives purchased Belgian tram rails on the grounds that they were cheaper than British equivalents. However, the Progressives' free trade policy was lukewarm when they were in opposition, and it was left to the more traditional Liberals within their ranks like Sir John Benn and McKinnon Wood to launch the most vociferous attacks on the protectionism of the LMS.[9]

By 1900, municipal trading was coming under critical public scrutiny at just the same time as the tariff reform debate was raging. A number of government committees took up the question, and the Conservative press launched a series of attacks against municipal trading. In one of a series of celebrated anti-municipal articles in *The Times*, the anonymous author claimed that municipal trading would have a direct impact on free trade

[6] For further discussion see S. Laurence, 'Municipal Socialism, Municipal Trading and Public Utilities', *Bulletin For The Study of Labour History*, Vol.52, Part I, 1987, pp.46-9.

[7] W. Eric Jackson, *Achievement: A Short History of the LCC*, 1965, p.26.

[8] Beatrice Webb, *Our Partnership*, 1948, p.267.

[9] LCC Election Leaflets, 23 August 1910, Guildhall Library.

because it would undermine foreign trade and would lead to local authorities being forced to impose a rigid system of protection. This anti-municipal campaign identified the LCC as one of its main targets. For anti-municipalists, the LCC represented an unwelcome rival power to Westminster. They also objected that the LCC occupied a position which was the rightful role of private enterprise. Municipal trading was considered by the anti-municipalists not just to conflict with the interests of private enterprise. It was also thought to be a transitional step to the ultimate aim of municipal socialism, which was a collectivist state.

This burst of anti-municipal propaganda meant that so long as the Conservatives held national power (which they did until 1906) parliamentary approval for schemes of municipalization was not forthcoming. As a result the Progressives could not fulfil election pledges and lost credibility and influence. This opened the way to the Municipal Reform victory in the election of 1907, which was widely fought around these issues and which successfully equated in the public mind municipal socialism with a collectivist state.[10]

No sooner had the Municipal Reformers secured a majority on the LCC in 1907 than they passed a resolution directing the committees of the Council when buying goods to give ten per cent preference to goods manufactured in Britain.[11] They justified this policy by arguing that approximately 70 per cent of the money spent on British contracts represented the wages to the British workman. This policy was specifically intended to court the working-class voter and their run of electoral victories certainly suggests that they were successful in this aim. However, there were other factors which contributed to extending their appeal beyond the middle-class voter. Apart from dwelling on the need to protect British labour from undercutting by aliens, the Municipal Reformers also emphasized the need to provide employment for the growing number of unemployed.[12]

Having quickly imposed a policy of 10 to 15 per cent preference on the British goods consumed by the LCC, the Municipal Reformers found their protectionism soon put to the test in 1908 over the question of tramlines for the municipally controlled LCC tramway system. Unlike the Progressives who had opted for a less expensive Belgian tender, the Municipal Reformers chose the higher price of a British contract, justifying it on the grounds that it would put at least £130,000 into the pockets of the British working-class man in the form of wages and that the work would moreover be done under trade union conditions.

By the next election in 1910, when the Municipal Reformers were

[10] *The Times*, August 1902.

[11] LCC Election Leaflets, 27 October 1908.

[12] London Municipal Society, Borough Council Election Leaflets, July 1906, Guildhall Library; and London Municipal Society Council Minute Book, 24 November 1909.

returned with only a majority of two, links between the LMS and the Tariff Reform League which had been set up in 1903 to promote this cause, had become much closer.[13] The Tariff Reform League was particularly committed to the task of converting the British working class to protectionism and away from their traditional allegiance to free trade. This preoccupation with the working-class voter was perfectly compatible with the Municipal Reformers' own political priorities, since they not only supported trade union wages and conditions but maintained that they were the true representatives of the working class.[14] The LCC as an employer of outside contractors had an excellent wages record under the Municipal Reformers. LCC wages offered to clothing contractors were, for example, 30 per cent higher than the national rates[15] which had been imposed in 1909 with the introduction of the trade boards (which laid down legal minimum wages). The LCC clothing contractors were also paid much higher wages than those contractors who worked for government departments.[16]

Neither the Progressives nor the Moderates and Municipal Reformers in practice pursued a consistent policy of free trade or tariff reform. For example, at the time when the Progressive administration was buying steamships for a Thames river service they chose to depart from their free trade position. The Progressives in this instance pursued a policy of London preference by supporting the Thames shipbuilding industry rather than selecting firms from other parts of Britain. Although the Municipal Reformers were later to pursue similar policies of preference on a much larger scale, they criticized the Progressives for accepting a tender for steam boats well above the lowest available.[17] Yet when the Municipal Reformers were elected for the second time in 1910, they made a show of establishing preference for London as a permanent feature by introducing a standing order which required all men under LCC contracts to have previously been employed in the County of London or else be resident within a twenty-mile radius of Charing Cross. The Municipal Reformers, like their Progressive predecessors, had a more pragmatic approach to local preference than their political propaganda would suggest. In another pre-war decision, the LCC opted to purchase furniture at a more inflated price from the provinces rather than supporting the London furniture trade at half the cost.[18] The Municipal Reformers justified this contradictory policy by invoking evidence from the Royal Commission on

[13] London Municipal Society, Borough Council Election Leaflets, No.7, 1921.
[14] London Municipal Society, Borough Council Election Leaflets, 1906.
[15] LCC Textiles, Soft Goods, Clothing and Leather Goods Reports, 1899-1932, p.7, Greater London Record Office.
[16] *Ibid.*
[17] G. Gibbon and R.W. Bell, *History of the London County Council 1889-1939*, 1939, p.613.
[18] LMS, Borough Council Election Leaflets, 1911, Guildhall Library.

Alien Immigration to support their xenophobic perspective. They maintained that since the London cabinet-making trade was largely in the hands of aliens, a contract with them was tantamount to purchasing the product abroad. In this case the Municipal Reformers departed from a stated policy of London preference in order to ensure that employment went to British labour. Progressive critics were quick to point out how, ironically, it was only workers outside London who benefited from the protectionist policies of the Municipal Reformers.

As the First World War approached, Unionists who supported tariff reform argued that tariffs could assist the financing of Britain's national defence in the face of the growing strength of Germany.[19] Protectionism, apart from benefiting the British worker, could prevent British finance being used by Germany against Britain. Municipal Reform leaders in London echoed these arguments and the LCC gave particular publicity to the rejection of German contracts. In this way, protection served more of an ideological than an economic function for the Municipal Reformers during the war by stirring up patriotic sentiments and anti-German feeling.

The post-war period drew further attention to the contradictions inherent in the protectionist labour policy of the Municipal Reform Party. In theory the Municipal Reformers had become even more protectionist, a stance reflected in the decision to second the secretary of the LMS – Towler – to the Tariff Reform League in 1917.[20] In practice they were forced to abandon their earlier more narrow labour policy of preference for London workers, by giving preference in their labour policy to sailors and soldiers throughout Britain who had been demobilized.[21] While pursuing this policy the Municipal Reformers sought active co-operation between capital, labour and the state. This meant that the Municipal Reform Party was supported in its efforts to protect and defend the interests of ex-servicemen by the Coalition Government and by employers. Their relationship with labour in the form of trade unions was more problematic, however, since the building unions had refused to admit ex-servicemen to their ranks.[22] The Conservative Government intervened in this dispute and the Prime Minister, Stanley Baldwin, issued a statement in the Commons objecting to the building trade unions' treatment of ex-servicemen. Yet although the government offered inducements to the unions in the form of training grants, organized labour still refused to change its attitude to this question.

Shortages of building materials engendered by the war also meant that the Municipal Reformers were often forced to back down from their

[19] John Ramsden, *The Age of Balfour and Baldwin, 1902-40*, 1978, p.31.
[20] London Municipal Society, Election Leaflets, No.7, 1921.
[21] LCC Election Leaflets, 1925.
[22] *Ibid.*, 1925.

preferential position, even though they retained their protectionist rhetoric for propaganda purposes. Since there was an acute dearth of building materials, particularly cement and bricks, the Municipal Reformers, who were under considerable pressure to build 'homes fit for heroes', were forced to secure these items from Belgium and France. The General Strike also highlighted the futility of pursuing a rigidly protectionist policy during periods of national crisis; the shortages generated by the strike meant the LCC Supplies Department was forced to bid for tenders abroad in order to obtain particular necessities and to ensure in some cases an adequate supply of such items as paper.[23]

Thus during the immediate post-war years protectionism was not a viable policy, since the LCC had to continue to buy foreign materials due to shortages. Although the Conservative Party under Baldwin in 1923 had officially abandoned tariff reform, they still dispatched a series of government circulars, directing local authorities as far as possible to place their contracts in Britain. Far from departing from the tariff reform policy of Bonar Law, the Conservative Party was merely continuing this tradition in spite of its national rhetoric to the contrary. Further endorsement of the need of the LCC to adopt imperial preference came from the Imperial Economic Conference of 1923. Municipal achievements on the LCC were increasingly treated as advancing the imperial cause. By 1929 there appeared a slight weakening of the preference policy towards local authorities when the government recommended that where no satisfactory goods of British or Empire origin could be found, the possibility of using satisfactory alternatives might be explored.

By 1929 the Labour Party nationally expressed considerable sympathy for protectionism. Arthur Greenwood, the Minister of Health, issued a circular echoing those dispatched by previous administrations, drawing the attention of local authorities to the necessity of pursuing protectionist policies when purchasing goods and materials. The support of the Labour Government was crucial to the Municipal Reformers on the LCC, since government approval was necessary for them to carry on with protectionism. In contrast, Labour on the LCC, now the main source of opposition to the Municipal Reformers, was divided over the issue of preference. This meant that although the majority of the LCC Labour Group voted against a motion calling for the continuation of the policy of imperial preference, approximately a third of LCC members voted in favour of the motion.[24]

By 1930 the General Purposes Committee on the LCC had agreed in a renewed flush of protectionism to impose a preference policy of thirty-six per cent on British as opposed to foreign goods, while LCC building

[23] *Ibid.*, 1931.
[24] *Ibid.*, p.5.

contractors henceforth had to supply two tenders, one reflecting the cost of using British materials and the second the cost of using foreign materials. However, in spite of these measures, the LCC found that there were considerable obstacles to the enforcement of protectionist policies. Not only did the LCC have the problem of reconciling their preference policies with their sub-contractors who often objected to British materials, but they had to ensure their products were of high quality and their services efficiently run. The Council also had the additional problem of conciliating the ratepayer and consumer. Given these constraints, the Municipal Reformers were forced to make exceptions to their protectionist policy by sometimes allowing the purchasing of foreign products. For example, the threat of delays in the LCC's building programme prompted them to purchase foreign, as opposed to British, timber. Foreign timber was also selected by the LCC's Supplies Department for its furniture in order to satisfy their contractors who were reluctant to buy British. Consumer pressure also meant that the LCC had to abandon buying certain British food products. Bacon and eggs were frequently neither Empire-made nor home-produced,[25] while beef was usually Argentinian since according to a leading Municipal Reformer:

> Some of the Empire beef has not yet quite come up to the standard demanded by the digestion of some of the inhabitants of our institutions and we prefer to look after their digestions rather than go the whole hog of preference in that direction.[26]

Imperial preference played a large role in the LCC elections of 1931. The emphasis now was not so much on London work for London men as on the need for British firms as opposed to foreigners securing LCC contracts. Hence Lord Jessel, who was chairman of the LMS during the LCC election campaign, made great play of the fact that the Municipal Reformers' great pride – Lambeth Bridge – had been built by British steel and British granite.[27] He also claimed that this enterpise put £170,000 worth of wages into the pockets of British steel and granite workers.

In spite of the Labour Party's sympathetic attitude towards protectionism, the Municipal Reformers by 1934 were playing up the free trade current within the Labour Party by identifying socialism with the free trade cause. This merely reflected their increasingly impoverished electoral tactics which continually dwelt on the international aspects of socialism and chose to ignore the protectionist leanings of the labour movement. While the Municipal Reformers stood in theory for protectionist policies, the support of Labour on the LCC for this issue was more lukewarm. Certainly there were sections of the Labour movement

25 *Ibid.*, p.6.
26 *Ibid.*, p.10.
27 *Ibid.*, p.21.

that embraced tariff reform, its most prominent early promoter being Herbert Morrison.[28] G.K. Naylor, the General Secretary of the Tariff Reform Association (an organization set up to recruit Labour to this cause) was also a leading trade unionist and an LCC alderman.

The ideological battle waged by the LCC Municipal Reformers was also fought in the post-war period on the basis that municipal socialism was not merely a metropolitan, nor indeed a national phenomenon, but an international enemy. This was clearly reflected in the Municipal Reformers, political propaganda which by 1925 was exploiting fears of communism by insinuating that municipal socialism would mean Moscow governing London and a municipal dictatorship. Far from ceasing to equate municipal socialism and Labour in particular with direct London government from Moscow, Sir William Ray, a prominent LMS spokesman, as late as 1934 was still giving expression to the following fears at a ratepayers' rally:

> I am afraid that London, organized as it is, would be turned into the closest example of a Soviet that one could imagine. The machine is there. It only wants taking over, it only wants a small enabling Bill in the House of Commons, and the capital city of the Empire could become a model socialist state as easily as possible.[29]

The crudity of such jibes was to lose the Municipal Reformers the LCC election that year, and with it, the Conservatives' chance of controlling metropolitan London for over thirty years.

In conclusion, the LCC Municipal Reformers applied protectionist policies to their limited municipal activities on the grounds that protectionism and tariff reform benefited not just the Londoner but the Englishman and the Empire as well. This, they calculated, had as much if not more appeal to the metropolitan working class than any call for purely municipal preference or enterprise. Where they applied protectionism fairly consistently, as for instance in relation to the Supplies Department and labour policy, it indirectly undermined the Municipal Reformers, economising campaign. Tariff reform was not identified with one particular party, so it was also able to serve the important function of providing a link between the anti- and pro-municipal lobbies within the LCC. It also enabled the Conservative Municipal Reformers to adopt policies that they had earlier regarded as smacking of socialism. Above all, tariff reform served more of an ideological than economic function. Indeed, where the principles of tariff reform conflicted either with the exigencies of national crises, or with the demands of consumers of LCC goods and services, or with LCC contractors, protectionism was abandoned to satisfy these interests.

[28] Bernard Donoughue and G.W. Jones, *Herbert Morrison: Portrait of a Politician*, 1975, p.32.

[29] *The Morning Post*, February 3 1934.

# Chapter 6

## *Municipalism, Monopoly and Management: The Demise of 'Socialism in One County', 1918-1933*

James Gillespie

During the inter-war years London experienced an unprecedented growth in state intervention in its local economy. After the long hiatus since the defeat of the Progressives in 1907, municipal control of key sectors of the local economy returned to the centre of metropolitan politics. Moves towards the public control of the essential services of transport, water, gas and electricity revived the pre-war Progressive and Labour projects of municipalization. This shift in political ideology was reinforced by changes in the machinery of local government. Proposals for the transfer of the administration of the Poor Law to the London County Council and the construction of massive new housing estates seemed important steps towards a reformed and unified local government authority covering the whole Greater London area. By bringing economic activities under control of institutions of local democracy the closely linked problems of urban overcrowding, inadequate transport services, not to mention the high rents and insanitary conditions of slum housing, could be removed from the vagaries of the market and be addressed coherently.[1]

This renewed vigour of municipalization coincided with the formation of the London Labour Party in 1915, which proclaimed itself the inheritor of the Progressive tradition. Many of the founders of the new organization were drawn from the Labour Bench of the LCC Progressives, including Harry Gosling, the leader of Labour's LCC Group. The Manifesto of the London Labour Party at the first post-war election for the London County Council called for 'Home Rule for London', with a 'Parliament for Greater London' accorded full powers to own and manage all major public services within the capital. This programme of municipalization was firmly located within Labour's national objectives of parliamentary

[1] For examples of the manner in which municipalization was linked to issues of town planning and reform of the labour market see London Reform Union, *London Today and Tomorrow: Proposals for the Reform of London Government*, 1908; Sir John Benn, *London Rates and London Industries: the Grievance and the Remedy*, 1912; Benn, *Exploited London*, 1912; on pre-war municipal socialism see S. Laurence, 'Municipal Socialism, Municipal Trading, and Public Utilities', *Bulletin of the Society for the Study of Labour History*, Autumn 1987.

socialism. The extension of the municipal franchise and the confident expectation that a majority Labour Government would shortly legislate the new Co-operative Commonwealth into existence meant that even apparently petty advances in local government enterprise were seen as part of a general movement towards the democratic control of the economy. These themes of democracy and socialism underpinned the debate on municipalization within the London labour movement during the early 1920s, registering a major shift from the utilitarianism of 'gas and water socialism'.[2] By 1934, when Labour at last took power at the LCC, the public control of the major utilities had been achieved. The bulk supply of electricity had been centralized under the London Joint Electricity Authority and London's chaotic transport system was at last on the point of unification with the formation of the London Passenger Transport Board. The development of public control, however, took forms few of the earlier advocates of municipalization would have anticipated. Successive failures of attempts to increase the LCC's area and powers had weakened its ability to manage a regional economy extending well beyond the County's boundaries. At the same time, the dominance of the Municipal Reformers had ensured that the LCC leadership would be antagonistic to any schemes which weakened private capital. Hence, at a time when the necessity of public control of these major utilities was recognized even by Conservative governments, the LCC, a pioneer of municipal socialism, was unable to reap the benefits.

During the years of Progressive control before 1907, the LCC had played a central role in attempts to bring the major utilities under public control. In the long political controversy over the reorganization of the Port of London following the Dock Strike of 1889, for instance, a strong body of Liberal and Progressive opinion had advocated a municipal takeover. The LCC's evidence to the 1902 Royal Commission on the Port of London represented the high point of this position, proposing a new administrative body drawing at least one third of its representatives from the Council. More importantly, all capital raisings were to be carried out by the LCC on the security of London's rates. This effective financial control over the future development of the Port met immediate opposition from City interests as well as from dock companies and wharfingers. When it was advanced in legislative form in 1903 and again in 1905, Conservative majorities in the House of Commons effectively blocked these plans. By 1908, when a more sympathetic Government with Lloyd George at the Board of Trade finally moved to restructure the administration of the Port, the LCC was in Moderate hands, unwilling to support municipal control. In the circumstances, the Government

[2] 'Manifesto to the People of London by the Executive Committee of the London Labour Party', *London Labour Chronicle*, no.41, March 1919.

dropped the municipal guarantee of debt and provided an Authority firmly dominated by Port and City interests; the LCC was given only four out of thirty places. Only two of these were filled by elected members of the Council.[3]

In similar conflicts, LCC attempts to win control over a unified water supply for the capital were thwarted by the jealousy of neighbouring counties, unsympathetic or weak central governments and the determination of Progressive administrations to avoid overgenerous offers of compensation to the private companies. Instead of a centralized system under LCC control, London's water supplies were controlled by the Metropolitan Water Board, a cumbersome joint board of sixty-nine members, only fourteen of these representing the LCC. Similarly, the LCC-controlled tram system, after an efficient and highly profitable start, was managed directly by the Council's Highways Committee. By the 1920s the trams were suffering from underinvestment, fierce competition from the bus companies and the refusal of many neighbouring councils to allow interrunning of services. Again, the apparent way forward, a unification of the private and municipal systems and co-ordination of their services with other forms of transport was blocked by political and commercial rivalries.[4]

The fall of the Progressive Party in 1907 saw the LCC shift to the periphery of political argument about the control of public utilities. In opposition, however, the Progressives continued to argue that social reform in the capital must be preceded by a thoroughgoing reconstruction of local government. In the immediate years after the World War of 1914-18 this theme of administrative reform returned to the centre of political discussion in the capital. The adequate planning of transport, other utilities and housing was seen as dependent on an expansion of the LCC's boundaries. The theme reiterated by Progressive leaders was that only with this reform of the machinery of local government could the LCC confront the interlinked problems of adequate housing and transport. The changing fortunes of schemes for a Greater London Authority set the framework in which questions of LCC intervention in the local economy and municipal control of utilities were posed. The temporary, and increasingly shaky wartime alliance of Progressives and Municipal Reform parties joined briefly with the newly formed London Labour Party to advocate the expansion of the LCC to absorb the City and the urban areas of Greater London.[5]

Despite misgivings expressed from the start by many Municipal Reformers, support for a unitary and strengthened Greater London

[3] J. Broodbank, *History of the Port of London*, ii, 1921, pp.323-4.

[4] G. Gibbon and R.W. Bell, *The History of the London County Council, 1889-1939*, pp.622-7; T. Barker and M. Robbins, *A History of London Transport*, vol. ii, 1974, pp.233-41.

[5] Sir John Dickson-Poynder, *The Housing Question*, 1908, pp.12-13.

Authority was temporarily and grudgingly conceded as the price of political peace. Preoccupied with the problems of post-war reconstruction and the demands of coalition, the Municipal Reform leaders Hayes Fisher and R.C. Norman, working closely with J. Scott Lidgett, the Progressives' leader on the LCC, showed considerably greater enthusiasm than their rank-and-file. Fisher's support for an enhanced LCC was strengthened by his position as President of the Local Government Board where he was responsible for prodding local authorities into action on the housing question. The capital's massive housing crisis, exacerbated by the virtual cessation of new construction during the war, lay at the heart of these political calculations. No authority confined to the limited rate base and expensive land of the LCC area could hope to make a serious impression on the housing shortage. This bipartisan push for amalgamation reached its climax with the Royal Commission into London Government, the Ullswater Commission, established by the Coalition Government in 1922.[6]

The Ullswater Commission proved 'an unmitigated disaster' for the supporters of strengthened metropolitan government. Before its deliberations were completed, the collapse of the coalition at municipal as well as national level destroyed political support for an enlarged authority. Opposition to an increase in the power of the LCC mounted from business interests and within the London Municipal Society. The evidence presented to the Ullswater Commission by the London Chamber of Commerce summed up this growing hostility. The Chamber called for a postponement of any moves towards political reorganization on the grounds that '. . . the mental attitude of the electors towards many questions is abnormal on account of the exceptional economic conditions in which the country at the present time finds itself.'

The revolt of the Conservative rank and file against proposals for a Greater London Authority was part of a more general move against the compromises of coalition politics. W.G. Towler, a veteran opponent of municipal trading and socialism, attacked amalgamation schemes as 'part of a plan for the establishment of socialism', and, under increasing electoral siege from Anti-Waste League candidates backed by Lord Rothermere's *Sunday Pictorial*, the Municipal Reformers repudiated Norman's evidence to the Ullswater Commission, abandoning any support for a strengthened metropolitan government. Bowing to the strength of opposition from extra-metropolitan local governments, business interests and the increasingly lukewarm support emanating from County Hall, the majority report of the Ullswater Commission

[6] J. Scott Lidgett, 'London After the War', *Contemporary Review*, October 1918, pp.358-9; K. Young, 'The Conservative Strategy for London, 1855-1975', *London Journal*, i, 1975, pp.71-3; K. Young, *Local Politics and the Rise of Party*, 1975, pp.115-8; M. Swenarton, *Homes Fit for Heroes*, 1981, pp.163-5.

recommended against change.[7]

With the Greater London scheme abandoned, the LCC's Municipal Reform majority took few initiatives in London's administration. After the failure of a half-hearted attempt to expand its own transport undertakings into the competitive bus services, the LCC confined its involvement to schemes for the transfer of its surviving enterprises to the control of private monopolies. In two areas where major changes occured – the organization of London's electrical and transport utilities – the principal initiative in policy-making shifted to business organizations, the Labour Party and increasingly to Whitehall.[8]

### *Labour and Municipalization in the 1920s*

After decades of factional in-fighting a unified London Labour Party was formed in 1915 to contest LCC elections and co-ordinate Labour within the LCC area. It moved immediately to exploit the problems of the Progressives, who were increasingly beset with the problems that the Liberal Party was suffering nationally and the difficulties of defining their own political position from within the confines of wartime alliance with the Municipal Reformers. For its part, the Municipal Reform-controlled LCC was increasingly defensive, developing policy on public regulation only under strong external pressure and showing stolid opposition to any initiatives towards public control. Its regulatory schemes were *ad hoc* reactions to crises, attempts to avert more thoroughgoing change and marked by a stalwart defence of the interests of the stockholders of privately owned utilities.

Under the energetic leadership of its secretary, Herbert Morrison, the London Labour Party (LLP) resisted attempts to achieve the reorganization of public utilities by handing their management to private monopolies. Aside from a rhetorical assertion of the need for control by the public interest, Labour's alternative remained vague, shifting in rapid succession from demands for municipal control in the early 1920s, trade-union support for a corporatist joint authority run by private capital and trade union nominees, through to the final embrace of the public corporation, an *ad hoc* authority (in modern terms, the quango) run on conventional business lines and insulated from direct political interference. Labour's abandonment of the goal of municipalization and its acceptance of the *ad hoc* authority, previously pilloried by Morrison,

[7] W.A. Robson, *The Government and Misgovernment of London*, 1939, p.294; Evidence of London Chamber of Commerce to Royal Commission on Local Government in London, 11 May 1922; W.G. Towler quoted in K. Young and P.L. Garside, *Metropolitan London: Politics and Urban Change 1837-1981*, 1982, p.137; K.O. Morgan, *Consensus and Disunity: the Lloyd George Coalition Government 1918-22*, 1979, pp.355-6.

were taken at the time as a temporary tactical shift. The failure of administrative reform in London's local government was to deprive Labour of the machinery of government necessary to achieve a reorganization of electricity supply and transport which was both efficient and under the control and co-ordination of popularly elected local authorities.[9]

In the early 1920s Labour's municipal politics was dominated by the demand for an extension of municipal control of enterprises. In many ways this was little more than the adoption of the old Progressive slogan of 'Home Rule for London', reflecting the considerable common ground between London Labour and the more radical sections of Liberalism, a continuity London Labour was eager to emphasize. The leader of the LCC Labour Group, A. Emil Davies, acknowledged in 1925 that:

> Up to comparatively recent times the Progressive Party, in municipal affairs stood practically for what Labour does now. It had vision and imagination, it regarded the job of governing London as a task to be joyfully undertaken, and it stood for that public ownership of vital services that has since become the principal line of cleavage beween Labour and the older parties.[10]

Campaigns for municipal control of transport, distribution and essential services emphasized these continuities to win support and defectors from the more radical wing of the Progressive Party, already concerned at the constraints imposed by alliance with Municipal Reform.

Labour's commitment to municipalization was not merely an expedient electoral tactic. The development of policy at borough as well as LCC level during the war years and the 1920s shows a consistent support for political intervention in the local economy. Labour built its new strongholds in east and south London on interventionist policies in local labour markets, using minimum wage-rates in municipal employment and generous levels of out-relief for the able-bodied unemployed to establish a buffer against the wage reductions which took place in the post-war depression. An essential part of this political programme was the strengthening of existing municipal powers and increased regulation of those forces which were sapping municipal resources.[11]

[8] Barker and Robbins, *A History of London Transport*, vol. ii, p.205.

[9] A.H. Hanson, 'Labour and the Public Corporation', in *Planning and the Politicians*, 1969, pp.143-9.

[10] A. Emil Davies, *The Story of the London County Council*, 1925, p.55; for the strength of these views amongst the more radical sections of London Liberalism see H.L. Nathan (Liberal MP for North-East Bethnal Green from 1929 until his defection to Labour in 1935), 'Home Rule for London: Notes on the Reform and Unification of Metropolitan Government', in H.L. Nathan and H. Heathcote Williams, *Liberalism and Some Problems of Today*, 1929, pp.485-536.

[11] 'Labour and the Cement Ring', *London Labour Party Municipal Circular*, no.118, 7 October 1922; see J.A. Gillespie, *Industrial and Political Change in the East End of London During the 1920s*, unpublished Ph.D., University of Cambridge, 1984, chapter 2.

One of the first public policy statements of the LLP, drafted by Herbert Morrison, pointed to the destructive effects of unregulated competition between the municipally owned trams and the private bus service. The only rational solution, he argued, would require 'the municipalization of the entire London passenger traffic'.[12] This call for local government control of transport and public utilities was central to Labour politics in London during these formative years. These demands rarely extended beyond control of a few key utilities, such as public transport, electricity supply and distribution, and the strengthening of powers over profiteering, including municipal control over the distribution of coal and milk, all themes familiar to pre-war Progressivism or made pressing by the shortages and inflation of the war years. A unanimous resolution at the LLP's 1919 Conference set out the central tenets of this municipal programme:

> London Labour is strongly opposed to the existence and the creation of special bodies for special services – such as Ports, Police, Water and Electricity Supply, Housing and Transit – because they complicate London government, lead to poor citizenship, and keep great public services out of the direct control of the electorate.
>
> This Conference demands from Imperial Parliament local self-government for London, and we deny the right of the central Government to impose nominated representatives of Whitehall on bodies responsible for London's public services.[13]

'Home Rule for London' remained the strongest theme in LLP campaigns of the early 1920s. It carried two major elements, a strengthening of the statutory powers of local authorities and a subordination to control by elected municipal representatives based on an expanded LCC. 'Direct popular control' was counterposed to bureaucratic control by 'gentlemen in Whitehall' or representatives of vested interests. Bureaucratic bodies, including the Metropolitan Police, the Metropolitan Asylums Board, the Metropolitan Water Board and the Port of London Authority were all attacked as 'encroachments upon our rights of local self-government'. In recognition of the problems of managing services covering a far greater area than the LCC, the demand for municipalization was predicated on the expansion of London's municipal boundaries. A report prepared by Morrison in early 1922 argued for a new regional authority for Greater London, a London and Homes Counties Regional Council, vested with full planning powers for roads and housing, and with control over the transport and electricity

[12] H. Morrison, *The People's Roads: An Urgent Question of Municipal Economy*, London Labour Party, 1916, p.3.

[13] 'Manifesto to the People of London by the Executive Committee of the London Labour Party', *London Labour Chronicle*, no.41, March 1919; *Daily Herald*, 26 November 1919; *Home Rule for Greater London*, LLP, January 1920.

enterprises in the region.[14]

In the meantime, Labour campaigned for an expansion of the powers of both tiers of local government to conduct business enterprises and regulate prices and profiteering in essential commodities such as milk. At Morrison's initiative the LLP established a joint buying organization for metropolitan borough councils, to increase their bargaining strength in the face of price rings, particularly in the overstretched building supply industry. The Municipalities Mutual Supplies Company, with a board drawn from the LLP and six of the Labour-controlled borough councils was formed in April 1922, but a boycott by the non-Labour boroughs and the LCC, and determined opposition from suppliers made its progress slow. Labour's losses at the 1922 borough elections sealed this failure.[15]

From the start, schemes to base state control of local services on the County of London were bedevilled by the open hostility or, at best, indifference to the Labour-controlled borough councils. A persistent theme in Labour politics in London during the early 1920s was the conflict between Morrison and the LLP Executive on one side, committed to an expanded LCC as the instrument to implement Labour's programme and, on the other, the Labour boroughs which were deeply suspicious of the weakening of their own power implied by this centralization. Support for Labour's rhetoric of 'Home Rule for London' did not go much further than the confines of Morrison's office when it implied weakening the second tier of London government. This conflict was deeply coloured by clashes between the LLP and the East End boroughs over the administration of the Poor Law and the gaoling of the Poplar councillors for refusing to pay LCC precepts, in protest over the inequity of a system of poor relief which forced already impoverished local communities to bear much of the financial burden of unemployment. At the same time Morrison's repeated unsuccessful attempts to change the Labour Party Constitution to eliminate the borough and sub-divisional parties in London and centralize all power over finances and selection of candidates in the hands of the LLP won him many enemies at the local level.

Consequently, the Labour boroughs displayed little enthusiasm for ambitious plans to restructure London government. Although the Ullswater Commission received a strong LLP submission calling for expanded metropolitan government area and powers, seven Labour-controlled borough councils failed to send representatives to the meeting

[14] Executive of LLP to Prime Minister, Minister of Food, Parliamentary Labour Party, County Councils in London and Home Counties, Municipal Labour Parties in London and Speaker's Conference on Devolution, 9.4.1920; *The Government of Greater London: A Draft Report prepared by a Labour Party Advisory Committee to be submitted to a Conference of Representatives of Local Labour Organizations in the Areas Concerned*, 4 March 1922; Royal Commission on Local Government in London, 1923, *Minutes of Evidence*, pp.681-2.

[15] LLP, *Municipal Circular*, no.117, 31 July 1922; *Daily Herald*, 31 September 1922.

of the Metropolitan Boroughs Joint Standing Committee that co-ordinated evidence to the Royal Commission, thus allowing the better-organized and anti-amalgamation London Municipal Society, the Conservative Party's local government organization in the capital, to dominate proceedings.[16] The Labour boroughs remained preoccupied with the local politics of the Poor Law and suspicious of any reorganization of local government which, in the short term at least, would shift power from Labour's electoral base at borough level. In some cases this indifference turned to open hostility. Bethnal Green, one of the few Labour-controlled borough councils to make a formal submission, called for the retention of London's existing two-tier structure: '. . . all purely local affairs, including Poor Law, Public Health, Education, Building, Drainage and Electricity should be carried out by a Council established on the lines of the present Borough Council and administered on the basis of a further and better equalized rate for the whole area of London'.[17]

There were deeper problems in Labour's municipal programme which opened the way for its steady dilution and final abandonment as the Party assumed greater political power over the future of the capital. 'Home Rule' never really moved beyond a slogan. It promised a democratization of the control of London's economy, but this objective was weakened by the limitation of proposals to the narrow range of activities already included in the legitimate ambit of municipal enterprise before the First World War – public utilities over which there was considerable agreement on the need for monopoly. Labour's blue-prints never went beyond vague generalities on the form of organization to be adopted, the representation of sectional groups, and the relationship of day-to-day administration with political direction. A further dampener on Labour support for a stronger regional government in London came with the national Labour Party's firm opposition to a strengthened and autonomous London Labour Party, and by extension, to the objective of 'Home Rule'.[18]

The Labour movement's suspicion of a strengthened LCC helps to explain the ease with which the LLP shifted under Morrison's leadership from advocacy of the radical democracy for 'Home Rule for London', to support for management of public utilities by the previously anathematized public boards insulated from any direct control by elected representatives. The failure of unification forced a rethinking of objectives based on municipalization. Given the wide geographical area to be

[16] LLP, *Report of Second Municipal Conference*, 15 May 1920; Herbert Morrison, *The Citizen's Charter: Why the Vested Interests Oppose the Labour Party's Local Authorities Enabling Bill*, 1921; LLP, *Municipal Circular*, no.114, 9 June 1922.

[17] London Labour Party's LCC Election Notes, no.20, 1 March 1922; Metropolitan Borough of Bethnal Green, Special Meeting of Council, 5 January 1922.

[18] R. McKibbin, *The Evolution of the Labour Party 1910 to 1924*, 1974, pp.170-4.

administered by an electrical or public transport authority, the existing boundaries of the LCC were insufficient. The immediate alternative, retaining some form of municipal control, was a series of joint boards, with representatives from all the local authorities affected. By late 1924 the London Labour Party had reluctantly accepted that until the political climate for municipal reform improved, joint boards offered the main alternative to control from Whitehall (still anathema) or handing utilities over to private monopolies.[19]

### *Public Regulation of Electricity Supply*

Despite its early start in the 1880s, the supply and distribution of electricity in London had achieved slow progress before the 1920s. Constrained by intense rivalries between competing private and municipal enterprises, the attractions of cheap and efficient gas supplies for domestic fuel and lighting, as well as a restrictive legislative framework, the electricity industry proved unable to develop a unified and inexpensive supply of power. In the LCC area alone distribution remained in the hands of sixteen metropolitan boroughs and fifteen electrical supply companies. The current supplied was direct in some areas, alternating in others, and delivered at a number of different voltages, tariffs and rates. As electricity was initially sold as a means of household lighting the private companies developed the most lucrative domestic markets, while industrial and more sparsely populated areas were left to local-authority intervention. The division between supply by private companies and local-authority control followed the political geography of London. Private companies had flourished in the West End, exploiting the lucrative home and street lighting market, a domestic market which was marginal in working-class areas until after the Second World War. Municipally owned undertakings dominated the East End, outer suburban area and the areas south of the Thames. Their markets were more industrial, and in the 1920s became strongly linked to the political priority of encouraging local employment.

Although in 1902-3 and again in 1906 the Progressive-controlled LCC had put up plans for a unification of London's electricity services under Council control these came to nothing. The first of these proposals was abandoned after an intense campaign of opposition to municipal socialism, led by private electricity companies abetted by an unsympathetic Government. The second scheme was still at a planning stage when the Progressives lost control of the LCC in March 1907. During the long dominance of LCC politics by the Municipal Reformers

[19] A.H. Hanson, *Parliament and Public Ownership*, 1961, p.24; G.H. Ostergaard, 'Labour and the Development of the Public Corporation', *The Manchester School of Economic and Social Studies*, xxii, 1954, p.197.

few initiatives were taken at the local level. The only exception showed the hostility to public ownership within the Municipal Reform Party. In contrast to the schemes of the Progressives, however, recognizing that the private companies and borough council undertakings would never come to agreement of their own accord, in 1913 the LCC sought Parliamentary authority to unify electricity supply and distribution. Following unification the LCC would relinquish all direct control, leasing the industry to a private company. The outbreak of war ended discussion of this scheme.[20]

The antagonism between municipal and private suppliers gave conflicts over the organization of electrical services a strong political edge. Control of distribution within their borough gave Labour councils and their trade union supporters an important lever to influence employment practices and to attract industry. Many of the key leaders of Labour in London had their first experience of the management of publicly owned industry by serving on borough council electricity committees. Clement Attlee and Herbert Morrison were directly involved in the management of the electrical undertakings of Stepney and Hackney in the early 1920s. Municipally controlled electrical undertakings were occasionally more directly involved in local politics. In 1922 the Manager of the Stepney Borough Council Electricity Supply Department placed a notice in the local press warning that:

> Intending consumers, before placing orders for the wiring of premises, should take steps to see that the contractor employs only Trade Union labour. Instructions have been issued by the Union concerned to all its members employed in this undertaking not to connect any installation carried out by non-union labour.[21]

During the General Strike the Stepney Electricity Committee, chaired by Attlee, cut power supplies to local factories rather than employ strike-breakers. Labour's defeat in Hackney in 1922 was due in part to the revelation that Morrison had used profits from the local electricity undertaking to subsidise a pre-election cut in rates. The dominant element in the electrical policies of the Labour-controlled boroughs, however, remained the attraction of new industry to their area. None was willing to relinquish this power over local employment conditions to the Municipal Reform-controlled LCC. This contradiction between the desire for a rationalized regional administration of electricity and the political realities of the post-Ullswater LCC undermined the LLP's

[20] L. Hannah, *Electricity before Nationalization*, 1979, pp.43-8; H. Haward, *The London County Council from Within: Forty Years of Official Recollections*, 1932, pp.357-9; R. Roberts, 'Businessmen, Politics and Municipal Socialism', in J. Turner, *Businessmen and Politics: Studies of Business Activity in British Politics, 1900-1945*, 1984, pp.20-32.

[21] *Eastern Post*, 4 November 1922.

response to post-war schemes for amalgamation of London's electricity supplies.[22]

The reorganization of electrical supplies involved two separate issues. The state control of generation met with no great resistance from within the industry; many saw it as a means to achieve standardization of current and to avoid sharp fluctuations in local supplies. The regulation of electrical distribution, however, provided a more contentious topic. The private companies used the Electricity Section of the London Chamber of Commerce as their major lobbying instrument. Their priority was the preservation of the value of their existing investments, confining public control to the generation and co-ordination of bulk electrical supply.

The first post-war attempt to address the co-ordination of electricity supply came with the Electricity (Supply) Act of 1919. This anodyne attempt at central co-ordination lost its few powers of compulsion in the face of strong opposition by London Conservative MPs with close links to the electricity supply companies. The Electrical Section of the London Chamber of Commerce ran an effective scare campaign amongst London MPs, arguing that the Act could unleash a new wave of municipal enterprise, as its attempts to place municipal trading enterprises on the same financial basis as private companies enabled 'local authorities to raise money on the security of the rates and cut out the specific authority of Parliament as hitherto'.[23] In 1920 the LCC used its powers under the Act to produce a scheme for the joint control of electricity supply in Greater London. Despite their reluctant recognition that the continued expansion of the domestic and industrial use of electricity required state intervention, the Municipal Reformers ensured that the fears of the Chamber of Commerce were not realized. The LCC scheme was based on the principle of 'government by subcontract', the regulation of industry by establishing a privately-owned monopoly, with no local government involvement in day-to-day management. The Council's powers of compulsory acquisition under the Act would be transferred to a new Joint Electricity Authority covering the Greater London region. 40 per cent of the members of the JEA were to represent the LCC and other purchasing authorities, 28 per cent the companies, with the remainder to be drawn equally from local authorities operating their own systems and those giving financial assistance. All electrical holdings, both municipal and private, would be unified in a central holding company and this monopoly would then be leased to a private company.[24]

[22] Hannah, *op. cit.*, pp.98-101, 331-3; T. Burridge, *Clement Attlee: A Political Biography*, 1985, pp.66-7; K. Harris, *Attlee*, 1982, pp.70-1; B. Donoughue and G.W. Jones, *Herbert Morrison: Portrait of a Politician*, 1973, pp.56-7; 'London Electrical Supply', LLP Executive Minutes, 20 April 1920, folios 262-8.

[23] Hannah, *op. cit.*, p.86; Electrical Section, London Chamber of Commerce, *Minutes*, 4 July 1919, 19 May 1921.

[24] L. Hannah, quoted in Turner, *op. cit.*, p.11.

The scheme met with noisy but ineffectual hostility from the defenders of municipal enterprise, who complained that 'the local administration of this great public utility service which is now to come under national ownership is not to be of a popular character. What we are getting here is national ownership and private control'. This feeling was strengthened when the London companies introduced private bills into Parliament to enable amalgamation, with provisions to set further obstacles in the path of municipal control, blocking any move in this direction before 1971.[25] In the view of the LLP, any reorganization must be 'based decisively upon collectivist principles' with public ownership of generation and distribution, the former in the hands of the central government, the latter left in municipal control. London Labour's opposition, however, was undermined by a serious conflict of interests within the Party. The Labour-controlled boroughs were reluctant to relinquish their electrical undertakings to the LCC, even had it been willing to accept the responsibility. With the failure of the Ullswater Commission to support a viable Greater London scheme, no alternative agency for a regionally based administration was likely. At most, the LLP could gain its constituents' agreement to a separate East London Electricity Authority, avoiding the problem of unification with the private companies at the cost of perpetuating the fragmentation of generation.[26]

Because of these internal divisions, London Labour's opposition to the Joint Electricity Authority was short-lived. At a national level the Labour Party supported the scheme, and leading London Labour figures such as Harry Gosling (President of the Transport and General Workers' Union and Minister for Transport) and Attlee assisted the bills in their passage through Parliament. Though Morrison at first loudly opposed the transfer of effective control from local government, he quickly accepted the reality of the new JEA (both Attlee and Morrison were appointed to the Authority). In 1926 what heat remained departed from the issue, when the Baldwin government, with the active support of the Parliamentary Labour Party, established the Central Electricity Board to co-ordinate all bulk supplies of electricity. The failure of the moves for a Greater London Authority had weakened the proponents of municipalization, leaving them with no effective government machinery to replace the chaos of competing borough and private undertakings. In the case of the most fundamental public utility, crucial to the future industrialization of the capital, the proponents of municipal control had been unable to come up with a workable alternative. In 1932 Sir Harry Haward, the former

[25] *Hansard*, vol.115, 14 May 1919, p.1665; Herbert Morrison, 'London Electrical Supply', April 1920.

[26] LLP, *London Threatened by Electrical Trust! A Dangerous Precedent for the Rest of Great Britain*, June 1924; LLP, *Municipal Circular*, no.32, 10 June 1920 and no.123, 13 February 1923.

Comptroller of the LCC, pointed to the continuing failure of divided control of electrical services in London:

> . . . it is a sombre reflection that the expenditure of so much time and money has resulted in so little improvement in the organization of London's supply . . . on the distribution side, matters remain much as they were years ago.[27]

### *London Transport and the LCC*

By the 1920s there was bipartisan agreement on the need for sweeping reform of London's competing and inefficient transport services but deep differences remained over the forms this should take and the proper roles of Whitehall and local government. The metropolitan transport system was organized in five rival groups, controlled by private and municipal interests. Most of the underground railways, bus services and some tram services were under the control of the Underground Electric Railway Companies of London, better known as the Combine. Established in 1915, the constituent companies of the Combine were unified through a central holding company, the Common Fund, chaired by Lord Ashfield and with Frank Pick as general manager from 1928. The Metropolitan Railway drew the bulk of its revenues from suburban services, while other above-ground local passenger rail services were provided by the main-line railways. The majority of tramways were owned by the LCC and other local authorities. Finally, competing bus services were operated by about sixty smaller private companies.

Since the 1905 Royal Commission on London Traffic, all parties had agreed on a need for greater co-ordination of public transport in Greater London. The Royal Commission's recommendation of a traffic authority for Greater London was echoed by the Parliamentary Select Committee on Transport (Metropolitan Area) in 1919 and the Ullswater Commission. The obstacle to rationalization was not identification of the problem but one of political implementation. By the mid 1920s the reorganization of London transport had become the most pressing political problem in the capital. The expansion of the population to the west, north and north east had led to a demand for new underground extensions and the linking up of existing underground lines with the suburban services of London and North Eastern Railway. The Combine refused to make the heavy capital expenditure required to meet these needs, citing poor returns on tube services due to excessive competition from rival buses and subsidised trams. Only with the complete unification of transport services under central control could the economies be made

[27] Donoughue and Jones, *op. cit.*, pp.123-5; Hannah, *op. cit.*, pp.98-100; Haward, *op. cit.*, p.371.

which could enable a viable investment in the expansion of the system. The Combine's case was supported by the Municipal Reformers who agreed that co-ordination of traffic and the expansion of networks into the expanding suburbs of west and north east London could be achieved by transferring all services to the effective control of the Combine, using a holding company vested with all local-authority and private services and leased back to the Combine (a similar arrangement to the LCC proposal for electricity).

In contrast, from its creation the London Labour Party strongly supported central and unified control of transport services. It rejected, however, the LCC and Combine-supported schemes which saw the solution in transfer of a complete monopoly to a private company. Again, the LLP saw a Greater London authority as the ideal body to administer a unified transport system. As with electricity supply, the main political question was not the need for public regulation and monopoly control but the political forms which could best achieve this end and the forms of legal ownership and control to be imposed. Labour's case for public ownership and control drew its force from an attack on the anti-social effects of the Combine's private monopoly, insisting that only under unified political control by elected bodies covering all of Greater London could transport services be both co-ordinated and tied closely to the development of town planning, public health and other amenities under local government control. As Morrison put it to his party executive in July 1923:

> Ratepayers should beware of specialists. Specialists have their uses but if they are allowed a free hand in all directions they will involve us in administrative and financial disaster. The existence of special bodies for special purposes is already overdone in London Government and if the principle is going to be extended we shall have a whole host of separate administrative bodies with their own set of officials, all fighting for their own status and elevation, whereas what we require more than anything else in the interest of efficiency and economy is co-ordination and a sense of relativity between the different departments of Local Government. Consequently the policy of the London Labour Party has been, and continues to be that there should be established for Greater London a directly elected general municipal authority charged with these services, incuding traffic control, which are inevitably large-scale and central in character. *This is the policy emphatically approved by Conferences of Labour in GREATER [sic] London and beyond convened by the National Labour Party.*[28]

Throughout this debate the LLP justified public control with the objective of linking town planning and housing policies, with the transport and social problems of the new LCC out-county housing estates such as Becontree in mind.

[28] Emphasis in original, Herbert Morrison, 'Memorandum on London Traffic Control', 9 July 1923, LLP Executive Minutes, folios 1450-1.

Transport, the LLP argued, could not be arbitrarily separated from other services. Nor could the formal ownership of the transport network be divorced from day-to-day administration. Any central traffic authority must combine financial and executive responsibility for the provision of services; anything less would only confuse the situation by delaying real change while leaving the power of the Combine intact. Secondly, the independence of the proposed company was seen as a step towards centralizing political power and weakening local responsibility and democracy:

> Most strongly do we condemn the bureaucratic nature of the proposal which would set up an Authority neither elected by nor responsible to the people of London, three out of five of its members being Government nominees. This proposal is reactionary and would, if adopted, constitute an addition to the many betrayals by Parliament of London's self-governing rights.[29]

In line with 'Home Rule for London', the area of the LCC should be expanded to cover the entire Metropolitan Police District and the Council should receive powers to own and operate all forms of passenger transit over the region. Labour believed at this stage that any authority controlling transport in London should draw its entire membership from local authorities within the region.

An essential element of this approach was hostility towards the direct representation of special interests, be they the management of the Combine, transport 'experts', or trade unionists. During the discussions of the 1924 London and Home Counties Traffic Authority Bill, this led to a narrowly averted breach with the trade unions. The London and Home Counties Group of Labour MPs prepared a response to the Bill which embodied most of the LLP objections. Bevin expressed such strong hostility to the principle of exclusive municipal control that he threatened to throw his union's support behind the original Conservative scheme of a weak advisory committee appointed directly by the Minister for Transport. Morrison persuaded the MPs to withdraw the demand for municipal control, as a tactical move to retain trade-union support for a watered down but still local government-based scheme.[30]

This emphasis on municipalization as the solution to all London's transport problems was reiterated during the following year's tramways dispute. The Transport and General Workers' Union struck demanding parity with busworkers. The LLP intervened to argue that a deeper problem underlay the wages dispute, and that the pressure on

[29] London Labour Party, 'Statement by the Executive Committee on the Report of the Select Committee on Transport (Metropolitan Area)', 19 August 1919.

[30] Parliamentary Labour Party, London and Home Counties Group, 'Report of the Special Committee on London Traffic Control', 12 February 1924; Notes by Secretary, LLP Executive Papers, folios 1668-72.

profitability of trams was the result of unfair competition by the bus services of the Combine, which used cross-subsidization to undercut trams. Only with a thoroughgoing reorganization of transport services could stable conditions be achieved for the tramway men. The strikers and the government accepted this logic: a clause in the strike settlement promised a move towards the co-ordination of different forms of public transportation.[31]

All sides now agreed that the way forward was for monopoly control of transport services and the amalgamation of smaller concerns with the Combine. The question remained whether this monopoly was to be controlled by local government, another form of public authority or dominated by the privately-owned Combine. Over the following two years moves toward co-ordination were extended. The London Traffic Act of 1924, introduced by the first Labour government but with bipartisan support, introduced three levels of authority: the Minister of Transport was to be advised by a weak London and Home Counties Traffic Advisory Committee on the exercise of his regulatory powers, while executive functions were to remain with the Combine, the main-line railways and municipal undertakings. These moves were taken further by the Advisory Committee's 'Scheme for the Co-ordination of Passenger Traffic in the Greater London Area' (the 'Blue Report'), completed in July 1927 and supported by the Transport and General Workers' Union, the LCC and the Combine. Again, the control of London transport services was to be split three ways. All private and public undertakings were to be placed in a Common Fund, although without disturbing existing ownership. A Public Control Body was to plan a programme of expansion and development, regulate scales of fees and ensure the adequacy of services while a Common Management, based on the existing Combine, was to be responsible for day-to-day management. Although the Baldwin government supported amalgamation on the basis of the Combine, it was reluctant to proceed in the face of intense opposition from Labour, and allowed the Blue Report to die a quiet death. The initiative now passed into the hands of the LCC, which sponsored two private bills to amalgamate its transport holdings with those of the Combine, an arrangement which left the Combine with effective control. The reorganization of London's transport, like its electrical services, was to be achieved by handing them over to a private monopoly.

London Labour's response to the LCC's 1924 Act marked its first move away from the commitment to control by a unified authority. A joint statment by the LLP, the Labour group on the LCC and the London Labour Members of Parliament (almost certainly drafted by Morrison) attacked the LCC proposals. While agreeing that the public suffered from

[31] LLP Executive, 'The Way Out of the London Transport Strike', 17 March 1924.

the existing competition between rival services and endorsing moves towards unification, the Labour statement reiterated the objections to *ad hoc* authorities. Labour administrations at local and national levels would ensure that all such undemocratic bodies would be abolished and replaced by a directly elected Greater London authority controlling all metropolitan-wide services, and smaller local authorities responsible for local services. However, as conditions for such a reorganization were no longer propitious, in the interim Labour would support a special joint traffic authority for London composed of representatives of the LCC and the local councils in the Greater London area. This was seen as an uneasy short-term measure, to last until the Greater London Authority scheme could be revived.[32]

Hence by the end of 1927 Labour's rationale for a public body had shifted fundamentally. As the argument for unification of transport services was no longer at issue, the administrative forms of public regulation had become the central issue. Labour's support for public control remained unshakeable, just as the Municipal Reformers and the Combine contrived ever more ingenious schemes to marry central co-ordination of services with private ownership. Abandoning its arguments for linking traffic control with town planning, Labour employed a narrower justification for public ownership. At present, the LLP argued, the only check on monopoly pricing by the Combine was the keen competition provided by the municipal tramways. If these were transferred to the Combine's control, fare structures would move effectively outside public control. Labour ended its attack on the LCC-Combine scheme with a backhanded compliment to Lord Ashfield's abilities, 'especially those necessary for the management of the Government and Municipal "Reform" politicians'.[33]

The election of the second Labour Government at the end of 1928 shifted the balance against the LCC scheme. Morrison was appointed Minister of Transport, with responsibility for resolving the impasse over the control of London's transport. Although Morrison's position did not hold Cabinet rank, the success of Labour in London in the General Election put the transport services of the Capital high on the new Government's priorities. It also posed a dilemma for the new minister. After a decade of campaigning for local authority control of public utilities he was in a position to implement his vision. However, the most likely beneficiary, the LCC, remained firmly in the hands of the Municipal Reformers, the sworn enemies of municipal enterprise. The immediate

[32] London Labour Party, *London's Traffic Problem: How to Secure Low Fares, Better Services and Greater Comfort*, 1927, pp.8-11.

[33] LLP, *London Traffic: A Co-ordinated Public Service or a Private Monopoly – Labour Party Policy*, 1927; 'Unified Operation of London Local Passenger Transport Services', *LLP Circular*, no.23, 6 November 1928.

political problem was to devise a form of public control which would circumvent the baleful influence of the LCC. When Morrison assumed office the issue of LCC control was relegated to obscurity. The question became the form of state control since both the LCC leader and Ashfield realized that the solution proffered in the two bills was now dead.

The LCC's bills were rejected in the first session of the new Parliament, reopening the question of regulation. As an enlarged London government was not politically feasible, Morrison had to construct a practical form of public control which would not merely hand services over to Labour's political opponents. There was still no inevitability about full public ownership. Morrison seriously contemplated establishing private monopoly on lines briefly entertained by the LLP in the mid 1920s. A union of the LCC and the Combine under a London Traffic Authority, with a local government majority, could provide representation of the public interest without greatly disturbing existing arrangements. A Common Fund would unite the financial interests of the transport undertakings and a strengthened independent regulatory authority could represent the public interest, controlling levels of fares and services.

The advice from the civil servants in the Ministry of Transport, however, stressed that complete control should be vested in the body responsible for the financial outcome, pointing to the Port of London Authority as the most appropriate model. The parallel was clear – both were to co-ordinate well-established and heavily capitalized services held by rival undertakings, a problem of managing a smooth transition to regulation. Ministry officials proposed a body dominated by representatives of the interest groups already involved in transport. Local government was to have a strong presence, with one member from the LCC, one representing the metropolitan boroughs, the City of London and one from each of the county councils and county boroughs in Greater London. The railway companies were to have two representatives, balanced by two trade unionists.[34]

By August 1929 the uncertainty of Labour's policy meant that Ashfield was having commercial problems raising capital for new works. From this point it appears that he was less concerned about the financial question of ownership, as long as the business structure of the Combine remained intact or was strengthened. He approached Morrison, offering his co-operation in return for the Government using its power to bring the hitherto independent underground and suburban services of the Metropolitan Line under Combine control. He offered the Government a political bait. If unification proceeded swiftly and with minimal dislocation of existing business arrangements within the Combine, the new organization could establish new services including an extension of the Metropolitan Line to Edgware, the Northern Line from Finsbury Park

[34] PRO, MT 46/2, Minute, R.H. Hill, 30 August 1929.

and the electrification of Underground lines to Ilford. For Ashfield the most pressing issue was no longer public control of transport but a resolution of the more practical question of

> ... whether the Metropolitan Railway was to be regarded as properly part of London transport or whether it should be left as a distinct and autonomous unit functioning independently as a main line. No doubt what Lord Ashfield had in mind was that if the Metropolitan Railway made application for financial assistance from the Government in connection with this project, which is estimated to cost some £2 millions, it might be possible if you thought fit to bring about some change in the past attitude of the Metropolitan Railway, which has stood out for complete autonomy, and secure some satisfactory arrangement for bringing it within the ambit of a London pool.[35]

Able to use his direct connections with more powerful Cabinet ministers to place further pressure on Morrison, Ashfield made it clear that no new underground works would be commenced until a final plan was agreed for unification. Morrison's initial reactions had an air of reluctant acceptance of an unpalatable necessity. As it became apparent that, whatever ownership structure was chosen, the existing Combine management structure would remain in place, he raised the danger that Government would merely create a new, more powerful monopoly, warning that, 'It is a matter for consideration whether a *complete* fusion of the private traffic concerns is in the public interest'.[36]

It is clear from the course of negotiations that once the option of local government control was abandoned Morrison had few firm proposals of his own, beyond a rejection of the representation of 'interests' on the controlling authority. From his position outside the Cabinet he saw control over the issue slipping away into the unsympathetic hands of the Treasury and the vagaries of an overcrowded parliamentary timetable. To avert this threat of inaction he repeatedly drew attention to the political problems that Labour would face in London if a solution was delayed. The Combine had already refused to carry out further capital works on tube extensions from Finsbury Park to Southgate and west from Hammersmith without a substantial interest-rate subsidy from the Exchequer, citing the alleged difficulties of raising fresh capital when the future of shareholders' investments were in doubt. Secondly, he warned of the political costs if the Labour Party was forced to an election with mounting unemployment while major capital works were postponed by Cabinet's indecision. In November 1929, Cabinet agreed to purchase all London transport holdings except for those of the main-line railways and to establish 'a small board of businessmen of proved capacity' to manage

35 PRO, MT 46/2, Sir Cyril Hurcomb to H. Morrison, 9 August 1929.
36 H. Morrison, note, 12 August 1929, *ibid.*

the new board.[37]

In this manner the scheme for the London Passenger Transport Board was created by a Labour Government, in a form to which Conservative and business interests and the Municipal Reformers of the LCC could have few objections. For this reason, although Labour was to lose office in 1931 before the finalized scheme could go through Parliament, only one major change was made by the incoming Coalition to insulate the Board still further from direct ministerial control. The London Passenger Transport Act passed into law in 1933 essentially as the Labour Cabinet had agreed it. Far from being a carefully thought out response to the modern problems of municipal management, the LPTB was an *ad hoc* answer to a political impasse. The inability to create a Greater London Authority and the rejection of the joint board left Morrison to develop his proposals from political expediency. The repeated failure of schemes for a democratically accountable authority or authorities for Greater London, stemming fundamentally from Labour's failure to control the LCC and the Government at the same time during the inter-war years, had finally led to a Labour Government itself rejecting municipal control.

Morrison, other London Labour MPs, and sections of the labour movement in London did not abandon the eventual goal of transferring control of transport in London to a Greater London Authority. In early 1930 the London and Home Counties Group of the Parliamentary Labour Party proposed a new central authority to cover the London Traffic and Joint Electricity Areas to replace the existing second-tier and *ad hoc* authorities, and to vest control of traffic, public transport and electricity in a directly elected body. Morrison himself qualified the departmental draft of the first Cabinet submission proposing control by an independent board with the words 'pending the reform of local government in London':

> It is with regret that I assume that the creation of a Greater London Authority which would exercise all the functions of local government over the area of Greater London, including traffic operations, is unlikely in the immediate future. If such a development occurred it might be found expedient to merge any *ad hoc* Traffic Authority in the larger authority and it might in any case be thought advisable to insert in any immediate legislation a provision to the effect that an *ad hoc* body should continue in existence until such time as Parliament might provide for the establishment of a Greater London Authority.[38]

Morrison's objections to local authority control remained pragmatic, a question of the adequacy of the existing local-government machinery. With no single authority for the Greater London area, municipal control

[37] PRO, MT 46/2, F. Phillips (Treasury) to R.H. Hill, 18 October 1929; C. Hurcomb to Morrison, 24 October 1929, 26 October 1929; PRO, CP 305 (29).

[38] PRO, CP 305/291, 21 October 1929.

would require the formation of an indirectly elected joint board. Direct experience of the cumbersome Joint Electricity Authority, attacked by Morrison as 'more joint than authority', led to the rejection of this solution of government by 'interests' rather than 'efficient service to the millions of people directly affected [which] must be the first consideration'.[39] Although his opponents were able to make some political capital out of Morrison's inconsistency, recalling his former hostility towards *ad hoc* bodies, the matter was now firmly outside municipal politics. In an interview with *The Times*, Morrison declared his antagonism towards 'the old-fashioned state or municipal socialism'. He continued, however, to express reservations about *ad hoc* bodies outside political control. In 1935 he suggested that if past opportunities to achieve a Greater London Authority had not been squandered 'it is possible . . . that the occasion for the establishment of the London Passenger Transport Board would not have arisen'. He continued his criticism of the tendency towards government by statutory boards:

> Ministers have almost ceased to apologize for creating Greater London authorities for purposes which, if local government were rationally organized in the area, could have been discharged under normal local government auspices. Indeed, some enthusiasts with specialist minds occasionally bob up demanding yet another Greater London authority in respect, for example, of housing or town planning. There are people who believe that the establishment of a special authority will solve most problems for co-ordination, whereas it may have done little more than create a salary list.[40]

Yet the establishment of the London Passenger Transport Board in 1933 had lasting and great repercussions both upon the shape of municipal administration in London and upon Labour's future concepts of nationalization. Morrison's part in the LPTB's creation meant that when Labour finally won power on the LCC in 1934 under his leadership, the Council was not disposed to press the National Government for changes in the arrangements at long last agreed for running transport in London. At national level, the administrative successes, efficiency and strong public profile of London Transport under the LPTB in the years before 1939 became crucial to Labour's conversion to the ideas of the independent public corporation managed by the board of independent experts as the model for public enterprise, and to its decisive rejection of both municipal control and the workers' control idea of the early 1920s. Despite Morrison's defence of the public corporation as achieving 'a

[39] H. Morrison, *Socialization and Transport*, 1933, p.147; PRO, CP 305/291, 21 October 1929.

[40] London Municipal Society, *Memo on the London Traffic Scheme of the Labour-Socialist Government*, November 1929; PRO, MT46/2, memo of 24 November 1929; H. Morrison, *How Greater London is Governed*, 1935, pp.165, 122.

combination of public ownership, public accountability, and business management for public ends', it represented a fundamental retreat in Labour's political programme. Instead of using a strengthened metropolitan government to co-ordinate the development of housing, transport and urban services, advocated in the original vision of 'Home Rule for London', the LPTB reproduced the narrow vision of the Combine. The failure of the movement for a Greater London Authority had spelled the end of the Progressive and Labour dream of municipal socialism in the capital.[41]

[41] Donoughue and Jones, *op. cit.*, pp.116-23, 140-50; Morrison, *Socialization and Transport*, pp.145-6, 149; for a strong contemporary critique of the narrow vision of the LPTB, its divorce from town planning issues, see Robson, *op. cit.*, pp. 333-44.

# *Chapter 7*

# *Localism, the London Labour Party and the LCC between the Wars*

Mark Clapson

The purpose of this essay is to examine the short and long-term significance of the problems in the relationship between the London County Council Labour Group and the Borough Labour Parties, both before and after the London Labour Party took control at County Hall in 1934. The two most important sources of tension here were the Poor Law and Public Assistance, and the nature of executive authority under Herbert Morrison's leadership of the London Labour Party (LLP). Both issues were central to the criticisms of the direction which party policy was taking, and of the nature of Labour's rule from 1934.

## *London's Political Context and Labour's Problems*

The victory of the LLP at the LCC elections of 1934 was an achievement of great political and historical moment. Three years after the national disaster for Labour at the 1931 election, the LLP's resounding defeat of the Tories was a source of inspiration for a dispirited Labour Movement. From holding a mere 15 seats in 1918, the LLP captured 69 in 1934, ousting the Conservative Municipal Reformers (referred to as the Municipal 'Reform' Society by Labour) after 27 years of rule. Labour never lost control of the LCC until the abolition of that institution – a Conservative measure – in 1965.

Herbert Morrison has been identified as the principal engineer of the LLP's success. Of Morrison and the infant LLP a contemporary historian and admirer wrote:

> [this] young man, with the unruly Cockney 'quiff', the pugnacious jaw and the emphatic pointing finger found ample scope for his great resources of energy and organising capacity in the work of helping to create a political

The primary sources for this essay are the London Labour Party Executive Committee Minutes, hereafter abbreviated as 'EC' and followed by the relevant date.

organisation which could cope with the immense tasks which so plainly lay ahead.[1]

These tasks were indeed immense, the product of two major distinguishing characteristics in London's political culture. On one level, a metropolitan and ostensibly unified labour movement had been slow to develop compared to the progress Labour had made in the provinces. The LLP was formed, largely from bodies on the London Trades Council (LTC) in 1914, fourteen years after the National Labour Representation Committee was set up, and eight years after the instigation of the Parliamentary Labour Party. The strange death of Liberal-Progressivism in London was followed by the equally strange slow gestation and birth of a metropolitan Labour Party.[2] Concomitantly, the new party was faced with the difficulty of organizing and mobilizing such a movement within an area of the great scale and diversity of London. Labour historians have emphasized the complex pattern of class division in the capital, which resulted from the vast casual sector of the docks and the myriad of small-scale workshops in the south and east, and the rapid suburbanisation and geographical spread of London consequent upon the growth of the service sector and the increasing number of white-collar and professional workers. This occupational and geographical fragmentation was compounded by the lack of any localized commitment to a religious tradition – Nonconformist or otherwise – and the successive waves of immigration from Europe and Ireland from the 1880s.[3] Until the eve of the First World War, working-class socialism was limited to the largely artisanal Social Democratic Federation, which was located mostly in east London, and, south of the Thames, in Woolwich. The LLP could not become a purely proletarian party because it had to rely on an alliance of artisans, manual workers and middle-class reformers. Printers, dockers, transport workers, black-coated workers and the Fabian socialists were the major constituency of Labour's vote.

Morrison, who became secretary of the party in 1915, was quick to perceive both the possibilities and potential limitations presented by the changing class composition of London to a mass party of labour. His analysis of the 1921 Census clearly illustrates his intention to rely upon working-class areas, and the priority he placed upon the need to win the middle-class vote:

[1] Brian Barker, *Labour in London: A Study in Municipal Achievement*, 1946, p.55. See also Howard Elcock, 'Tradition and Change in Labour Party Politics: The Decline and Fall of the City Boss', *Politics Studies*, 1981, pp.439-47; and B. Donoughue and G.W. Jones, *Herbert Morrison, Portrait of a Politician*, 1973, especially chapters 2, 5, 6, 7, 14, 15 and 16.

[2] For opposing views on this question see J.A. Gillespie, *Economic and Political Change in the East End of London During the 1920s* (Unpublished Ph.D., University of Cambridge, 1983) and Paul Thompson, *Socialists, Liberals and Labour*, 1967.

[3] P. Thompson, 'Liberals, Radicals and Labour in London', *Past and Present*, no.27, 1964, pp.73-101.

> Whole masses of the working-class population are concentrated in certain London Boroughs to such an extent that there are more of them so concentrated than are or will be necessary for Labour's political predominance in those areas. On the other hand if we take such boroughs as Chelsea, Hampstead, Holborn, Kensington, Lewisham, St Marylebone, Stoke Newington, Wandsworth and Westminster (not to mention a number of Parliamentary divisions in divided Boroughs that are otherwise good) we cannot but realise that there are a large number of municipal wards and LCC and Parliamentary Divisions in which the problem of the middle-class voter has simply got to be solved before they can be won by the Labour Party.[4]

Morrison certainly did not take the political allegiance of the working-class for granted, many of whom were Tories 'by conviction or prejudice'. Throughout the inter-war period, he tried not to alienate the property-owning, ratepayer vote. In his writings on local government, Morrison consistently argued that Labour should demonstrate to the electorate its ability to govern with financial rectitude, to prove itself more businesslike yet socially responsible than the Municipal Reformers or the Progressives.[5] Morrison's criticisms of Poplar Council's refusal to levy the LCC rate in the mid 1920s, and his denunciation of the Left, were based in large part on a fear that the respectable middle-class would refrain from voting for a seemingly radical party.

Underlying these psephological considerations was the huge practical problem of co-ordination within the London Labour movement itself. Morrison was forced to negotiate his programme on several fronts. Firstly, he had to deal with the National Executive of the Labour Party, which was often at loggerheads with the Executive of the LLP. For example, Morrison's call for greater self-determination and financial resources for the LLP was repeatedly rebutted by the National Executive.,[6] Secondly, within the Labour movement in London a great number of economic and political interest groups vied to ensure the realization of their sectional aspirations as well as supporting the wider goals of Labour. By 1932, over 190 organizations were affiliated to the LLP, of whom the trades unions were the most important.[7] The London Society of Compositors and especially the TGWU provided continuing support for Morrison throughout the inter-war years. In contrast, the London Trades Council, the parent body to the LLP, grew increasingly critical of its offspring during the 1920s. The most bitter differences between the two were

[4] 'Brain Workers in the Census' (*London Labour Chronicle*, no.96, October 1923, p.8).

[5] See for example, 'What is Economy?' EC 26 September 1922; 'Toryism: The Ratepayers' Enermy', *London Municipal Pamphlets*, 1923; 'What Labour Has Done for London', 1936, pp.12-13.

[6] R. McKibbin, *The Evolution of the Labour Party*, 1974, pp.170-4.

[7] EC 2 February 1932 contains a list of these organizations plus their last annual payment.

highlighted in 1926, when a conference convened by the Trades Council of trade unions, industrial unions, and the co-operative societies supported by East Islington Labour Party, urged the amalgamation of the LLP and the LTC.[8] The proposal collapsed in 1927, due to the lack of enthusiasm of the LTC. This was not surprising, given its sizeable communist membership, and Morrison's condemnation of the General Strike the previous year.

The co-operative societies were also important working-class economic organizations, yet they too proved weak allies. The Royal Arsenal Co-operative Society, a strong source of support for Morrison, was confined to South-East London, and the London Co-operative Society (LCS) which extended over much of the capital was excluded by its rules from direct affiliation to the LLP. Negotiations to secure such affiliation failed in 1926-7, in 1933-4 and again in the late 1930s. It has been suggested that the Communist element within the LCS was the major reason for their unwillingness to join ranks, but the problem went deeper than this. The LCS was fearful that affiliation on Morrison's lines would destroy both its political and financial automony.[9] Effectively, Morrison and the Executive were left to rely on the TGWU as the bedrock of support and finance. This would be wielded by the Executive against the action of organizations within the London Labour movement, especially over the issue of communist affiliation.[10]

The third major problem of co-ordination for the LLP Executive was the relationship of the borough parties both to the Executive itself and to the elected members at County Hall. Local government in London was a two-tier system, consisting of the LCC itself, possessing general powers over the administrative county of London, and the second tier of 28 metropolitan borough councils, established by the London Government Act ten years after the inauguration of the LCC.[11] As the Royal Commission on Local Government in London observed, in 1960, 'the powers given to the metropolitan boroughs were substantially less than those of boroughs elsewhere'.[12] In this context, the town halls of the boroughs operated on a set of localised prerogatives and aspirations which were often in conflict with those of County Hall. For example, poor boroughs such as Poplar in the East End, suffering from heavy unemployment in the 1920s, were forced to levy relatively higher rates to

[8] First proposed EC 2 September 1926. See also EC 7 October 1926, 4 November 1926, 3 February 1927, 3 March 1927.

[9] B. Donoughue and G.W. Jones, *op.cit.* pp.211-12. For details of negotiations between Morrison and the LCS see EC 13 June 1933, 12 July 1934 and 18 January 1939. See also *Co-operative News*, 7 January 1939.

[10] B. Donoughue and G.W. Jones, *op.cit.*, pp.65-6.

[11] *Royal Commission on Local Government in Greater London 1957-60*, p.37, para.138.

[12] *Ibid.*

pay the LCC precepts than wealthy boroughs such as Kensington or Hampstead, where unemployment and the subsequent need to finance it were negligible.

The tension between the wider concerns of County Hall and the narrower focus of borough councils was echoed in internal party politics. The Labour representatives on the LCC were concerned with more generalized London-wide priorities and these often ran counter, or were impervious, to the perceived needs of particular boroughs.

The composition of the LLP Executive itself illustrated the weakness of borough representation. The trades unions, Morrison's hard core of support, had eight representatives, the local Labour Parties seven, the co-operative and socialist societies four, the League of Youth one and the Officers (the chairmen of the committees) held three. Officers were always elected LCC members and, after the victory of the LLP in 1934, they were appointed by the Labour leader to the chairs of LCC Committees. In this way, control of the LCC Labour Group and of the LLP Executive was effectively the same for most of the time. Throughout the later 1920s and the 1930s the officers were staunch supporters of Morrison, and constituted his 'Presidium'. Charles Latham, Isaac Hayward, Lewis Silkin and Donald Daines were the most steadfast in this connection. From the early 1920s, the trajectory of Morrison's plans for a centralized party machine strongly controlled by the Executive posed problems for the borough parties. Consequently, these parties provided the most substantive criticisms of the LCC Labour Group between the wars.

## *The Problem of Borough Politics*

The underlying friction between borough localism and the need for a centralized LLP was always evident to Herbert Morrison. Five years after becoming party secretary he analysed the delicate problem of building up an organization capable of winning the LCC in the following way:

> London local politics present a very peculiar problem. It should be borne in mind that historically London is an aggregation of thirty or more towns, so that while the Metropolis is in a sense one, it is also thirty or more, and it is necessary that the separate entity of each of the localities should be recognised in addition to realising the need for examining the pattern as a whole and maintaining a London organisation to meet that of our opponents.
>
> This points to the need for strong central as well as local organisation, and it is to supply this need that the London Labour Party exists.[13]

As the 1920s wore on, the logic of Morrison's definition developed into a programme for the centralization of the borough parties into one

[13] EC (no specific date, 1920). See also EC 7 June 1928. Morrison wrote 'thirty or more' towns. There were in fact twenty-eight boroughs.

organization under the aegis of the Executive. At the 1928 LLP conference, Morrison and his supporters on the Executive proposed the abolition of the borough parties and their replacement by the LLP as *the* single borough party for London.

The proposal was unsuccessful, as most borough parties felt aggrieved at this attempt to secure greater practical and ideological control over their affairs.[14] Morrison, however, kept up the pressure for their abolition. A postal ballot of the local parties, which he initiated in May 1930, shows the borough and divisional Labour parties were split over the issue of a single party: twenty-six for, twenty-six against, and twenty-three not replying.[15] Of those in favour, a number argued along with the Executive that rationalization of structure would lead to better co-ordination and electoral efficiency. But the direct oppositional responses clearly pointed to a major source of conflict within the party. Central Southwark, for example, turned the principle of the argument against the Executive:

> Borough parties have in the main done their work well while the LLP has been wasteful and inefficient. Closer touch is required but considers that reform is needed not in Borough parties but in the LLP.[16]

Poplar recommended that 'present arrangements' suited them, and Hampstead, one of the more moderate boroughs, politely declined the proposal, fearing that 'local autonomy would be sacrificed'.[17] The need for greater co-ordination within the London labour movement was not in doubt; it was the Executive's increasing disregard for local self-determination which raised the hackles of many dedicated socialists.

Labour representatives in the town halls were fearful that the LCC Labour Group was undermining the borough point of view in policy formulation. A Special Municipal Conference in 1930, almost wholly concerned with the problem of 'Means of Contact' within the labour movement in London, successfully proposed that a consultative committee be set up to increase dialogue between the Labour Parties on the borough councils and the LCC Labour Party. W.H. Green, for the London Labour Mayors' Association, S.W. Jeger (Mayor of Shoreditch) and W.H. Martin (Mayor of Finsbury) defeated the proposal from Charles Latham for greater executive influence within the new body.[18] Yet despite their localist views, Martin, Green and Jeger all became LCC Members from 1928, 1929 and 1931 respectively. Nothing demonstrated more clearly where the power base in London Labour politics was increasingly conceived to be.

14 EC 9 January 1930.
15 EC 8 May 1930.
16 *Ibid.*
17 *Ibid.*
18 EC 12 May 1930.

The opposition to Morrison's plans also reflected a fear that Labour in London was beginning to betray itself by becoming incorporated into the state. It must be remembered that until the 1920s the Labour Party was almost completely a working-class organization.[19] But, given the increasing ideological dominance of Fabianism within the LLP, with its emphasis upon gradual reform, and the professionalization of the upper levels of the party, many socialists were fearful that political and organizational movements were conspiring to subvert the original workerist aims of Labour. The leader of Poplar Council, George Lansbury, derided the 'swarm of young Fabians' moving into the party. Bermondsey and Rotherhithe Labour Party's response to Morrison's plan is understandable in the light of such developments:

> . . . rejects absolutely; views the proposal as a bureaucratic attempt to introduce the capitalist system of rationalisation into labour politics.[20]

In 1934, when Labour at last took control of the LCC, Beatrice Webb wrote with joy in her diary 'The Council returned on 12th March 1934 is completely Fabianised in personnel as well as doctrine . . .'[21]

## *The Poor Law, Public Assistance and the LCC*

As Labour steadily increased its representation at County Hall throughout the 1920s, the 'metropolitan parliament' became more central to debate and conflict within the LLP over the nature and direction of policy, and the administrative aggregation of local government functions. The Poor Law and Public Assistance were the most important issues here, both before and after 1934.

The LLP had been in unanimous agreement with the Minority Report of the 1909 Royal Commission on the Poor Law, that this outmoded and deterrent system of relief should be broken up, arguing that within its prescription 'no policy can be satisfactory'.[22] Opposition to test work and to the means test as a way of assessing relief was universal within Labour's ranks, as was the desire to abolish the mixed workhouse, with its allegedly grudging and undignified treatment of the male and female incumbents. Moreover, the low level of outdoor relief under the Municipal Reformers was repeatedly censured by the LLP.[23]

Before 1929 the responsibility for poor relief lay both with central government (the Poor Law Division of the Ministry of Health) and with local government (the Boards of Guardians in the administrative units

19 R. McKibbin, *op.cit., passim.*
20 EC 8 May 1930. See also G. Lansbury, *My Life*, 1928, p.164.
21 Norman and Jeanne MacKenzie (eds.), *The Diary of Beatrice Webb*, vol.4, 1985, p.330.
22 EC 10 November 1931.
23 B. Barker, *op. cit.* pp.112-33.

called unions). Indoor relief was financed by a common fund based on the rates, but the boroughs were forced to rely upon taxation and borrowing to pay for outdoor relief. However, the poorer the borough, the higher was unemployment, a situation which discriminated heavily in favour of the wealthier boroughs. Here, unemployment was negligible and the need to finance it equally so. The call from progressives and radicals for a more rigorous equalization of the rates by a London-wide scheme to subsidize poor relief in the less wealthy boroughs from the rate base of the richer areas went largely unheeded.

It was against this state of affairs that Poplar's Labour Council rebelled. Since the 1900s, the Labour-controlled Guardians had consistently paid higher levels of relief than elsewhere, but in 1921 the Council 'formally declined to levy rates for the support it was required to give to the Metropolitan Asylums Board, the Metropolitan Police and the London County Council'.[24] The response of the Tory majority on the LCC was to issue a writ against Poplar Council to force them to levy the rates. Due to the debacle which followed, with the imprisonment of Lansbury and many of the councillors, the LCC felt increasingly embarrassed and revoked its legal action.

'Poplarism' was the most famous clash between local and central government between the wars. It also raised in acute form the differences within the Labour Party. Harry Gosling, the leader of the LCC Labour Group, was sympathetic and forceful in the promotion of Poplar's case at County Hall.[25] But Morrison was critical of Poplar's action. This was the most sharply drawn instance of a borough council being out of step with his designs.[26] He sought a middle-way between unilateral borough action over public assistance and the 'reactionary' regime of the Municipal Reform Society. Thus Bermondsey and Poplar's decision in the mid 1920s to pay a minimum wage of £4 to their employees also incurred Morrison's anger.[27]

From 1930 the whole structure of central-local relations with regard to the Poor Law was reformed. The Local Government Act of 1929 transferred the administration of unemployment relief to the local authorities, and left a large measure of room for local government initiatives. Within London, the new public assistance apparatus was comprised of the Public Assistance Committee (PAC) at County Hall, and ninety-nine semi-autonomous district sub-committees and twenty-nine local committees, all within the boroughs. London was 'given power

[24] B.B. Gilbert, *British Social Policy, 1914-1939*, 1973, p.215. In general see pp.214-219 on which much of this account of the Poor Law is based.

[25] N. Branson, *Poplarism, 1919-1925*, 1979, p.54. On Gosling's role, see pp.83-4.

[26] B. Donoughue and G.W. Jones, *op. cit.* pp.45-8; G. Lansbury, *op. cit.* pp.162-9; H. Morrison, *An Autobiography*, 1960, pp.86-8.

[27] H. Morrison, *op. cit.*, 1960, p.89.

genuinely to break up the Poor Law if it chose to do so'.[28]

Both Conservative and Labour groups at County Hall embraced the legislation enthusiastically, seeing in its devolved powers an opportunity for more imaginative schemes of relief. But the slump, and the strict economy measures of the Labour and National Governments from 1931, reduced the money available to local authorities and thwarted these good intentions.[29] The Municipal Reformers reverted to the more stringent practices which had characterized the 1920s. No improvement took place until Labour came to power in 1934.

During this hiatus differences between the LCC Labour Group and the borough parties were largely buried, with one significant exception. A motion by North St Pancras Labour Party, supported by East Lewisham and intended for the 1932 Annual Conference of the LLP, proposed that 'it be an instruction to the LCC Labour Party that only accredited representatives nominated by constituency parties shall, in future, be appointed on area committees of the Public Assistance Committee'. An executive amendment wanted to substitute 'constituency parties' in this wording for 'affiliated organizations or the Executive Committee of the LLP'.[30] Both proposals and amendments failed to be reached by conference, but Morrison promised to consider and report upon the matter. The differences here anticipated the conflicts from 1934 over the status of borough and constituency parties within the Executive's design for a more powerful Public Assistance Committee at County Hall.

During 1933 Labour forced a number of debates in the Council Chamber over this issue. In November for example, the PAC received a letter from Islington Borough Labour Party, which was read out in the Council Chamber, strongly protesting 'against the harsh treatment meted out to applicants in this area for public assistance'. Morrison described the PAC as 'the most scandalously administered Committee of the Council', which 'dodged information and refused the citizens of London the right to know'. Isaac Hayward, calling for a special sub-committee to be set up to administer a more humane policy, accused the Tories of:

> (i) reducing the relief granted to aged persons; (ii) enforcing a continuous reduction in the amounts of out-door relief; (iii) refusing to deal reasonably with the claims for supplementation of unemployment benefit; (iv) unjustly administering the means test; (v) indiscriminately ordering married men on out-door relief to residential training centres; and (vi) taking into account unfairly and improperly the earnings of the other members of the household.

Sir Cyril Cobb, the Chairman of the PAC, refused to meet Labour's

28 B.B. Gilbert, *op. cit.*, pp.229-30. See also G. Gibbon and R. Bell, *A History of the London County Council*, 1939, pp.408-14.

29 B. Barker, *op. cit.*, pp.118-9.

30 EC 6 July 1933.

charges in the Chamber, adding confidently that the 1934 LCC elections would 'settle the question between the majority and the people on the other side. He had not the slightest doubt as to the result'.[31]

On coming to power in 1934, the LLP immediately began to rationalize and humanize the public assistance apparatus. The mixed workhouse was at last abolished, and a standard level of outdoor relief was introduced. This was a fundamental area of a wider programme in which, to use Morrison's rhetoric, the 'stingy economies' of the Municipal Reformers were 'reversed'. In the field of housing for example, both construction and slum clearance were stepped up. During the year 1933-4 the Tories had demolished only 440 houses and rehoused 2,556 people. In 1934-5 Labour demolished 950 unfit dwellings and rehoused 7,601 people. Over 2,000 houses were knocked down in 1935-6 and 12,417 people were given new homes.[32] Education, health and welfare were given greater financial assistance based on small but significant increases in the rates. Moreover, as a symbolic gesture to prove the claim that 'Labour Gets Things Done', Morrison and the new Chairman of the Highways Committee, George Strauss, quickly authorised the demolition of the old Waterloo Bridge and the building of a new river crossing as part of a programme to improve traffic flow in the capital.

The appointment of Charles Latham as Chairman of the Finance Committee, Isaac Hayward as Chairman of the PAC, and Lewis Silkin to the chair of Housing and Public Health, illustrated the Presidium's strength of grip over the key administrative posts at the LCC. Latham's financial orthodoxy was central to Morrison's and Hayward's concern to demonstrate to the electorate Labour's 'care in the dispensation of public funds', especially with regard to public assistance. This meant that improvements in services and the increased expenditure incurred were contained by the insistence upon financial rectitude, an important consideration for the capital's ratepayers, who supplied almost sixty per cent of the LCC's income.[33] The approval of the London electorate was signalled at the 1937 election when, despite Conservative protests at rate levels,[34] Labour increased its majority at County Hall by six seats.

In the wake of this electoral success, borough criticism of the LCC Labour Group appeared fratricidal to Morrison and the Executive, as undermining the basis of centralization within London government upon

[31] Islington Labour party letter in *The Times*, 2 November 1933, p.14, col.d; Hayward and Morrison in *The Times*, 8 November 1933, p.16, col.d.

[32] 'What Labour Has Done for London', *London Municipal Pamphlets*, 1936.

[33] *The London County Council* (annual publication of the LCC), 1938, p.67. The remainder of the LCC's income came from the following sources: 17.01 per cent from 'Receipts in Aid', the charges on Council services; 16.97 per cent from exchequer grants and local taxation; 6.81 per cent from the central exchequer grant.

[34] Municipal Reform Manifesto, 1937, in EC 6 February 1937.

which a successful municipal socialism would ultimately rest.[35] The borough parties, for their part, were fearful that County Hall was wresting too much power for itself and that the pace of reform was too slow. Again, public assistance was central to this debate.

A special sub-committee of PAC was established with Morrison at its helm to consider alterations in the administrative apparatus of unemployment assistance. It aimed to revise the role of the local sub-committees who administered outdoor relief in the boroughs. They possessed discretionary powers over the levels of relief which were largely independent of the PAC at County Hall. Isaac Hayward, as Chairman of the PAC, proposed a new scheme which 'provided for the principle of complete accountability to the Council'.[36] Adjudicating officers were appointed to assess scales of relief, and the number of local sub-committees was cut. The PAC at County Hall assumed new and greater powers than before. Hayward, it should be pointed out, was also the LLP's Chief Whip at County Hall.

The increased levels of outdoor relief were universally welcomed by Labour in London. But the new administrative apparatus met with opposition from a number of Labour parties in the boroughs. In May 1934 North Southwark Labour Party, for example, expressed the worry that public assistance administration would be wholly removed from local sub-committees. An internal circular issued by North Southwark to the other borough parties in the capital was picked up by the press. Hayward pointed to the substance and effect, as he saw it, of North Southwark's complaints:

> I have resolutions from a certain number of local Labour parties expressing concern at newspaper stories to the effect that public assistance administration is to be taken out of the hands of local sub-committees and is to be dealt with entirely by officials. We are having an inspiring but very heavy time at County Hall and I am bound to say that I think it would have been more comradely of our North Southwark friends to have approached me in the first instance before coming to conclusions and circularizing the Labour Party throughout London.[37]

This statement typifies the tactics used by Morrison and subsequently, as party leader, by Hayward. Firstly, they assumed that any criticisms or alternative resolutions should initially be articulated through the Executive before being allowed to gain any momentum of their own. Secondly, North Southwark had highlighted the confusion over the status of the borough sub-committees vis-à-vis officials in the new administration. Hayward argued in reply to North Southwark that there

[35] EC 5 September 1937; 26 May 1934.
[36] EC 25 January 1937.
[37] EC 26 May 1934.

was no intention by himself, as PAC Chairman, nor by Morrison, nor by 'the Labour Party on the Council generally to approve of any scheme whereby applicants for relief would be dealt with entirely by officials'. Two days later, however, Morrison argued that LCC members did not have enough power over local committees, and that officials appointed from the centre were the means to such control:

> Committees outside County Hall will still have to operate; the talk about their complete abolition is nonsense. The real thing is that they will be fewer. The officers must be responsible to the Council, and subject to its direction; there must be no poor person in London without the right of stating a case to and being heard by a properly constituted committee.[38]

Officers were to gain greater power over committees, and members at County Hall were to gain greater power over officers. But the status of borough party influence within these 'properly constituted committees' was diminished, and unclear.

This problem was not confined to public assistance. In relation to education and to hospital and maternity services the threat to local influence was clarified as a result of the conflict between the South East St Pancras Party and the Executive. In September 1934, St Pancras 'condemned the practice of giving Labour members on the London County Council absolute authority in nominating persons to local committees', arguing that in future 'it should be made compulsory for Labour members to consult the Labour Party in the constituency for which they sit *whose collective experience and intimate knowledge of persons qualify them to supply the best people*'. Morrison's reply stated bluntly the Executive prerogative over nomination of officers, arguing further that the LCC Labour Group 'should be free from any obligation to explain why particular people have not been appointed.'[39]

From 1935, a bitter and prolonged row developed between Stepney Borough Council and the LCC Labour Group over the former's policy of taking on casual labour through the employment exchange. Executive objections were two-fold. On the one hand it criticized the costs of such a scheme and, secondly, it was fearful of the alleged dangers such direct political influence over the labour exchange was creating. Morrison was sensitive to the charges of selection and undue political influence 'with regard to appointments to the public service in the East End which have been exploited by Fascists and other opponents of the Party'. This issue came to a head over the giving of Christmas work to the unemployed in December 1936. Stepney Council intended to engage extra labour required at this time by public advertisement in the local press 'and by

[38] 'LCC Public Assistance Administration', memorandum by Morrison, Policy Committee Minutes, 23 May 1934.

[39] Policy Committee Minutes, 25 September 1934. My emphasis.

nomination by members of the council of persons known by them to be in poor circumstances'.[40] Following representations made by Morrison to Stepney Council this latter proposal was dropped. But the Executive exploited its advantage by expelling four councillors who had defended the policy at a particularly uproarious meeting, and by issuing a whip to reverse the whole policy of employing casual workers through the exchange.

In so doing, Morrison succeeded in agitating a number of more moderate councillors within Stepney. Dan Frankel, for example, accused Morrison of having 'difficulty in grasping the matters in dispute' and of prolonging a controversy which was 'having a most disastrous effect on the local situation'. Most important of all, perhaps, was the collective condemnation by Stepney Borough Council of Morrison's actions:

> The crux of the matter is whether the leader of the (LCC) has the power to issue a Whip which is an instruction to reverse a policy approved by the Group repeatedly during two years – such Whip being issued without prior consultation and with a claim for emergency which is quite unjustified . . . nothing we have done calls for apology or is inconsistent with proper administration of our duties as Labour Borough Councillors and we accordingly apply for the immediate withdrawal of our suspension and the reissue of the Labour Whip.[41]

This controversy was not resolved until May 1937, when an executive committee (of Latham, Hayward, Daines and Hinley Atkinson) recommended that the suspension of the four councillors be withdrawn, but that 'undesirable practices' in the arrangements for the employment of labour should be strongly avoided.

The points of conflict between Stepney Council and the LCC Labour Group were clearly articulated by Limehouse Labour Party in their criticisms of Labour members at County Hall. Two years after the LLP had come to power Limehouse argued that 'the policy of the Labour majority on the LCC lags far behind that of the more progressive elements in our movement'. Limehouse objected to the continued policy of sending unemployed men in London to residential colonies or 'training' centres of which the LCC continued to run three, namely Hollesly Bay in Suffolk, Denton in Essex and Belmont, Surrey. For Limehouse Labour Party 'in sending men to such places as Belmont, the LCC Labour majority are acting against the fundamental principles of the Labour movement'.[42]

The second objection from Limehouse, as with Stepney, was based on the loss of local control over the assessment of needs and benefits within the borough. Limehouse criticized the appointment of adjudicating

[40] EC 7 January 1936.
[41] *Ibid.*, and 11 June 1936.
[42] EC 11 June 1937.

officers, 'recruited from the middle classes', in place of the Relief Committees of the boroughs. This development 'militated against the interests of the poor, and cannot easily be justified by a Labour Council'.[43]

Limehouse sought to force these issues to the fore by placing them on a questionnaire which, they argued, should be sent to prospective candidates as a test of their socialist commitment. Consideration of questions as to the desirability or otherwise of sending the unemployed to labour colonies, getting rid of adjudicators and of abolishing temporary and casual labour in the LCC's services would call upon candidates to 'square up' to these issues as a step along the road towards a 'more socialist policy upon the Labour LCC'.[44] This gesture was also an implicit attack upon the process of the selection and adoption of candidates, for whom the LLP Executive was the endorsing authority. Morrison's reply to Limehouse, in the form of a letter, restated the supremacy of the Executive over candidate selection, and forbade candidates from signing the questionnaire.[45] The issue appears to have dropped after this point.

In the event, the responsibilities for unemployed relief of the Public Assistance Committees were swept away in 1937 by Part 2 of Neville Chamberlain's Unemployment Act. However, the central position of poor relief within these political wranglings highlighted the wider significance of the interlocked issues of finance and the redistribution of resources to poorer areas of London. On one level, the most important priorities of the LLP were local finance and the need to respond in some measure to the constraints placed upon it by central government cuts and directives. Hayward's stress upon 'responsibility' in the spending of public funds is explicable in this light, as was Morrison's emphasis upon a 'business like' attitude to the running of LCC services. Within this framework, public assistance administration reflected the cautious ethos of both Westminster and County Hall.

But borough parties were closer and more sensitive to the *local* problems of unemployment and public assistance. They sought, through the local committees, to pursue their own short- and long-term solutions to these problems, for example the recruitment of casual labour through the employment exchange and the payment of more generous levels of relief. From the local point of view, the overbearing influence of the Policy Committee at County Hall and the insistence, often backed up with the expulsion or the threat of it, upon executive authority, underlined the increasing distance between the LCC Labour Group and the borough parties, and a frustrating slowness at the centre to take radical measures to alleviate working-class distress. In short, Labour's rule at County Hall was viewed as increasingly oligarchic, bureaucratic and unresponsive to

[43] *Ibid.*
[44] EC 4 June 1936.
[45] *Ibid.*

the needs and problems of the boroughs. W.H. Green expressed the fear to the 1936 LLP Conference that centralization within London since 1934 had ignored and continued to ignore the aspirations of borough politics:

> Previous decisions of the Conference have been in favour of greater powers for a directly elected central authority for Greater London, but this does not mean necessarily any diminution of the importance of powers of the lesser local authorities. There may be a case for suggesting that some degree of centralization arises from the technological progress of the Community, i.e. in such matters as electricity and transport. *Certainly the Labour Party must not tie itself down to a defence of the parish pump.* If public interest and considerations of economy require centralization of any service, we should not be rigidly conservative as to stand in the way; conversely we should support any justifiable delegation of powers to the Borough Councils.[46]

The source of Green's critical observation, and of the previous conflicts between the LCC Labour Group and the borough parties, was the unlikeliness of any 'delegation of powers' to the borough councils, and the disinclination of the LLP Executive to accommodate local demands within the logic of Morrisonian centralism. A move to increase borough representation on the Executive was put down at the 1936 Conference. But the 1937 LCC elections were to witness the decisive demonstration of Morrison's control within the official Labour movement in London, and the weakness of both the borough parties and the Left at County Hall.

## *The LLP, the Left and the LCC*

The role of the Communist Party and other left organizations in labour politics had long been a major bone of contention between the borough parties and the Executive. The National Conference decision in 1925 to purge Labour of all Communist influence derived further impetus from both the failure of the General Strike in 1926 and the over-riding prerogatives of the London Executive. Battersea Trades Council and Labour Party and South-West Bethnal Green Labour Party were dissolved before the Strike (February 1926) because they refused to recognize the expulsion of Communists. East Lewisham Labour Party, Westminster Labour Party, Holborn Labour Party and Chelsea Trades Council and Labour Party suffered the same fate in September 1926. Hackney Trades Council and Borough Labour Party and North Islington Labour Party were expelled in November of that year.[47]

Perhaps the most bitter affair involving Communist association during the 1930s was the treatment of George Strauss, the LCC member for North Lambeth, after the Council elections of 1937. These were the first

[46] EC 25 November 1936. My emphasis.

[47] EC 4 February 1926; 2 September 1926; 4 November 1926.

since Labour had come to power in London and Morrison was understandably fearful lest Labour lose and the progress of municipal socialism receive a severe setback in the capital. He was thus worried at association with the Communists, and he ridiculed their efforts to 'worm their way into the organization of the Labour Party' by their insistence upon 'what is called united action for the LCC election'.[48] By united action Morrison was referring to the United Front, a communist initiative designed to forge a coalition of working-class parties to fight fascism and the 'reactionary' National Government. It is worth recording Morrison's correspondence with Harry Pollitt, the Secretary of the London Communist Party, in February 1937:

> *Pollitt:* I have great pleasure in sending you copies of the material that we are issuing in connection with the LCC elections. It's good to be alive these days!
>
> *Morrison:* Referring to your letter, it is perhaps well that we should place on record that the publications you enclosed with your letter have been issued without our desire or authority.
>
> I am glad you find it good to be alive. I gather the Tories also find it good that you are alive.[49]

This was an eloquent expression of Morrison's regard for the Communists, and of the views which informed his trouncing of Strauss after the election.

Strauss, whom Morrison had appointed to the chairmanship of the Highways Committee in 1934, had committed the cardinal sin of enlisting Communist support during the 1937 elections, and had publicly declared his support for the United Front by signing its 'Unity Manifesto'. Strauss was re-elected, yet Morrison reacted by removing him from the chair of the Highways Committee, and divesting him of the vice-chairmanship of the Finance Committee. North Lambeth Labour Party 'strongly resented and protested' against Morrison's action, arguing that they betrayed 'narrowness, pettyness and presumption and are a sign of weakness in the movement'.[50] The *Morning Post*, a Tory newspaper, gave qualified approval to Strauss's removal, arguing that 'henceforth everyone knows whose word goes at the LCC and that he who laid the first pick to the fabric of Waterloo Bridge is, as might be expected, no respecter of persons'.[51] In his defence, Strauss pointed to his record of service at the LCC since 1934, and criticized his sacking as a concession to a defeated Conservative opposition:

[48] EC 8 January 1937.

[49] EC 13 February 1937. This exchange is partly reproduced in B. Donoughue and G.W. Jones, *op. cit.*, p.229.

[50] Letter from North Lambeth Labour Party, 25 March 1937. This is held in the collection of manuscripts given to the London School of Economics by B. Donoughue and G.W. Jones, the authors of Morrison's biography.

[51] *Morning Post*, 18 March 1937 (Donoughue and Jones Coll., LSE).

*1a* The London County Hall in 1922

*1b* The Council in Session, County Hall, 1937. Lord Snell in the Chair, G.H. Gater, Clerk to the Council, in front of him

*2a* The Prince and Princess of Wales at the opening of the Totterdown Cottage Estate, Tooting, May 1903

*2b* Millbank Estate, central garden in 1905

*3a* First Prize Garden, Oldbury Road, Watling Estate, Edgware, 1931

*3b* Corbusian slabs, Alton West Estate, Roehampton, in 1958

*3c* Cubicle, Carrington House (single men's lodging-house), Deptford, *c.*1900

*4a* Mrs Dawson and son at their old house, Pender Street, Camberwell, in 1962, before rehousing by LCC

*4b* The Dawsons outside their new home, Marchwood Close, Southampton Estate, 1962

*4c* Dawson bedroom at Pender Street

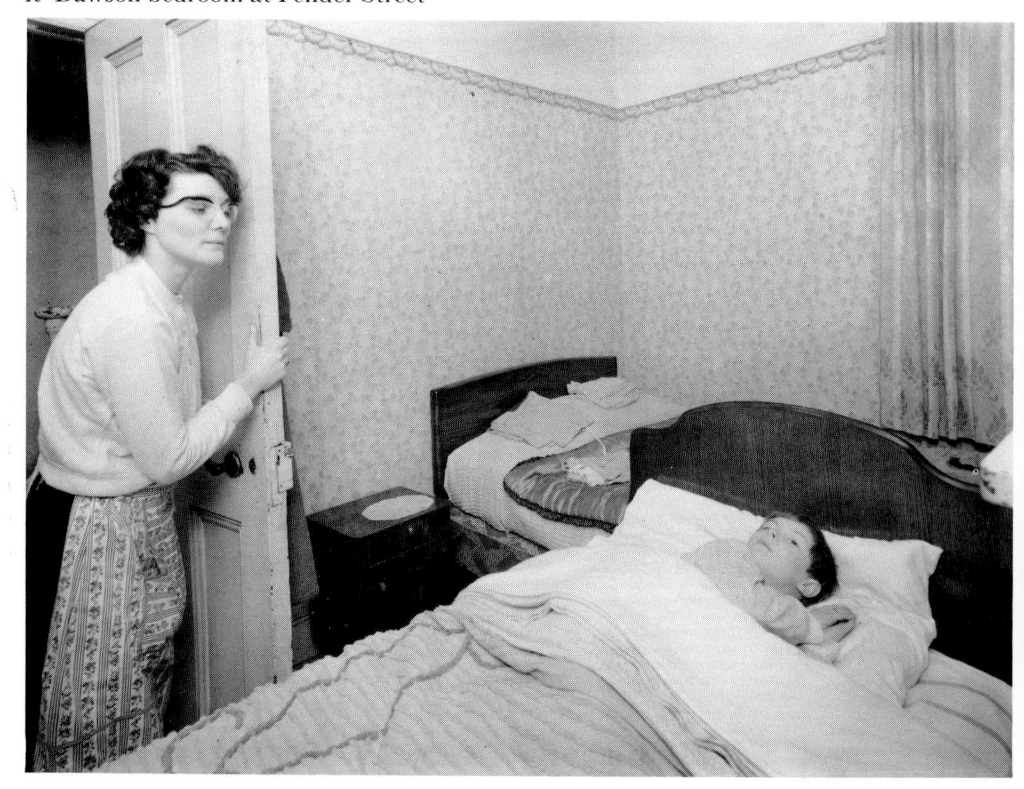

*5a* Dawson lounge at Marchwood Close

*5b* Dawson bedroom at Marchwood Close

*6a* Crawford Street School, Camberwell, drill in hall, 1906: 'legs astride, arms upwards bend'

*6b* Crawford Street School, chemistry laboratory, 1906

*7a* Evacuation of expectant mothers and children, 1943, supervised by LCC clerical officer Dorothy Peirce (*right*)

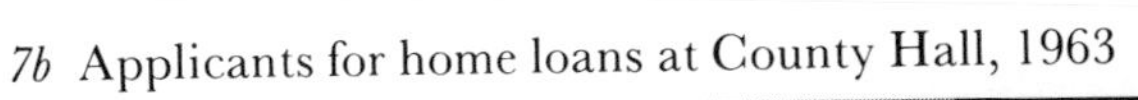

*7b* Applicants for home loans at County Hall, 1963

*8a* Kensington Fire Station in 1905

*8b* 'Dual purpose' fire engine and crew, Fire Brigade Headquarters, Southwark, 1936

*9a* Laying interlacing tramway track, Wandsworth Town, 1906

*9b* Volunteer models ARP uniform for the London Ambulance Service, 1938

*9c* Mr Kucherenko of the Soviet State Committee for Construction Affairs visits Brixton School of Building and shows Michael Johns how to apply mortar, 1955

*9d* A London fireman is measured up for uniform, 1954

*10a* Hammersmith Hospital Laundry, 1936

*10b* Butchers, Supplies Department, Peckham Depot, 1963

*11a* Weights and measures inspector checks milk float, 1953

*11b* Coal officer checks loads in sacks on a wet day, 1929

*12a* Early LCC staff group, 1894

*12b* Interview board, County Hall, 1953

*13a* In a day nursery, Division 9, 1949: a student changes a nappy

*13b* A park keeper steps out, 1960

*13c* LCC temporary restaurant in Stockwell, 1947, with mural of 1943

*14a* Herbert Morrison and Charles Latham inspect members of the Auxiliary Fire Service at the time of the London Fire Brigade's transfer to government control, 1941

*14b* R.W. Gibson, Chairman of the Housing Committee, bemused by a model of Ocean Street Estate, Stepney on the principal floor at County Hall, 1946. Bust of Ivan Maisky, the Russian Ambassador, behind.

*15a* Emma Cons, alderman, 1889-92

*15b* Florence Cayford, Chairman of the Council, in 1960

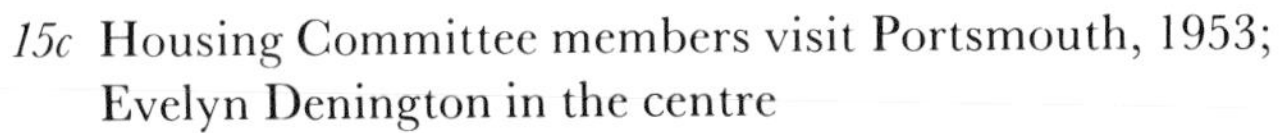

*15c* Housing Committee members visit Portsmouth, 1953; Evelyn Denington in the centre

*16a* Sir Isaac Hayward, Leader of the Council and member since 1927, in 1960

*16b* Laurence Gomme, Clerk to the Council, in about 1910

*16c* Sir George Gater, Clerk to the Council, and boy in 1952

*16d* Francis Sheppard, editor of the *Survey of London* from 1953. 'Job will be finished in 2065', reads the original official caption

> It was made clear that no exception was taken to my work during the past three years and that in part the decision had no relevance to the London County Council administration at all . . . Mr Morrison's action is all the more deplorable because it is a complete surrender to the demand of our opponents during the election that he should throw me overboard – attempts which were treated with the contempt they deserved by the people of London.[52]

Strauss was from a wealthy, upper-middle class background, and it appears that Morrison viewed him as what might be called a 'bourgeois adventurer'. In a letter to Strauss, Morrison invoked his own working class origins to mock the 'well-to-do' Strauss:

> It is better that the relationship between titled well-to-do members of the Party and others who, like myself, are of the working-class, should be a normal relationship of political co-operation, friendship and social equality. This is not always easy, for sometimes an inferiority complex afflicts both well-to-do and poor members of the Party and vitiates their relationship. This afflicts some well-to-do members of the Party so obviously that I suspect them of feeling that they must go further to the Left and talk more about the 'working-class' than anybody else to emphasize the authenticity of their proletarian loyalty.[53]

Resentment works in more than one direction, and the loathing which some borough parties felt towards excessive executive control, and their criticism of the LCC Labour Group, was matched by Morrison's contempt for what he saw as the irresponsible posturing and unrealistic demands of left-wing councils, and of wealthy socialist mavericks such as Strauss. He identified both as alien to the collective commonsense and intrinsic moderation of working-class labour socialism. Morrison saw the LLP under his influence as an expression of these anti-radical attitudes, and its role at County Hall as the institutionalization, and vindication, of gradualism.

The expulsion of Strauss threw into sharp relief the demise of the Left in County Hall by the late 1930s. Morrison's attention was also drawn in 1937 by the unofficial Conference of London Labour Parties, a resuscitation of the ideals of the Constituencies Movement in London.[54] The conference was supported by thirty parties from the capital. As well as calling for a greater representation of Constituency Parties on the National Executive the conference proposed, for London, the establishment of an Association of London Constituency Labour Parties to increase dialogue between these local organizations and, ultimately, to 'provide a means for members of the London and National Executive

52 'Statement by George Strauss, MP, LCC, on his removal from Committee Posts on LCC', March 1937 (Donoughue and Jones Coll., LSE).

53 EC 26 May 1937; see also 14-29 and 31 May 1937.

54 B. Pimlott, *Labour and the Left in the 1930s*, 1987, pp.111-40, on the Constituencies Movement.

Committees to learn the views of Constituency Parties . . .'

Morrison's response was to argue that 'the splendid LCC election victory at last March' was proof that there was no need for any unofficial body within the London labour movement, 'and that the present machinery of Borough and Divisional Labour Parties working in close co-operation with the LLP is highly effective from the point of view of the health and progress of the party'.[55]

It was evident that Morrison, who seven years earlier had been intent on abolishing the framework of borough party politics was now a defender of the status quo against calls for greater dialogue between the LCC Labour Group and the local parties. The decision of the 1937 National Party Conference to vote down the demands of the Constituencies Movement was wielded firmly by the LLP Executive against all subsequent solicitations by local parties. In short, Morrison had won the argument against the Left. More significantly he had brought the borough parties to heel within a political process based upon the priorities and centralized powers of the LCC Labour Group.

## *Conclusion*

Most labour history, organizational and biographical, tends to conclude that Morrison prevailed because he had become so strongly identified with the LLP by the 1930s. As Jim Gillespie has written, Morrison himself pointed to the LLP's rise to power between the wars and broadcast this '[in] terms in which [he] saw his own achievement'.[56] Popular social histories of the inter-war years reiterate this dominant view of Morrison, the LLP and the LCC. Graves and Hodge, for example, write:

> At the London County Council elections of 1934 [Labour's] candidates gained a majority of seats over the Conservative Municipal Reformers. This majority was held for the rest of the period, thanks chiefly to the leadership of Herbert Morrison, the only contemporary Labour leader whose energy made any impression on the general public. The Labour LCC had, on the whole, a good record – especially in matters of slum clearance and rehousing.[57]

The authors add, incorrectly, that 'even the unofficial Left could find little to criticize in its actions'.

Yet for many in London Labour politics, the nature of executive authority and of Labour's rule at the LCC was overbearing and unwieldy. Morrison's reputation as the 'bully of the boroughs' was more than an undeserved sideswipe from those jealous of his influence and power.[58] For

[55] EC 6 July 1937.
[56] J. Gillespie, *op. cit.*, p.365.
[57] R. Graves and A. Hodge, *The Long Weekend*, 1985, pp.331-2.
[58] B. Donoughue and G.W. Jones, *op. cit.*, p.75.

a number of borough parties and spokesmen for a more democratic model, the necessity of centralization need not have meant the denial of effective dialogue with the borough and constituency parties. The result of Morrison's disenchantment with the borough councils as effective mechanisms for the administration of local socialism was a situation within which there existed only a limited space for the collective discussion of political problems.

These contemporary criticisms were early indications of the longer-term legacy of Morrisonian politics at County Hall. Localism as a political force was weakened, and the lineage of centralization in twentieth-century local government was given its own metropolitan version. The inherent problems of borough and local politics were sat upon, not resolved. As Keith Bassett argues, British local government 'has become geared to servicing and maintaining existing central policies rather than aggregating local preferences, formulating local demands, and transmitting them to the centre'.[59] During the 1920s and 30s, these shortcomings were precisely those of which the LCC Labour Group was accused, both in opposition and in power, at County Hall.

[59] K. Bassett, 'Labour and Socialism and Democracy' in M. Boddy and C. Fudge (eds.), *Local Socialism*, 1983, p.84.

# *Chapter 8*

## *Education and Politics: The London Labour Party and Schooling between the Wars*

Malcolm Richardson

When Labour became the majority party at County Hall in 1934, it inherited an education service for London which had already undergone thirty years of continuous evolution and considerably more, if some of the work of the London School Board and the Technical Education Board is taken into account. The LCC Education Department's centralized system of planning and administration, the diverse and comprehensive nature of educational provision and the specialized auxiliary services all underwent significant development under the auspices of the Council's Municipal Reform majority from 1907 to 1934 and particularly under the direction of Robert Blair, the LCC's first Education Officer until his retirement in 1924.

This is the context in which may be assessed the suggestion of R.L. Leonard that one of the London Labour Party's durable achievements was 'the development of the LCC education service, whose reputation was so high that a Conservative government was forced by its own Minister of Education to abandon plans to break it up under the London Government Act'.[1]

It was against the background of the 1918 Education Act's failure in particular that the London Labour Party began to elaborate its educational strategy during the formative years of its development. Its basic approach to the problems of schooling in London was informed by a commitment to work within the legislative framework imposed by central government and to adapt and improve rather than radically recast the administrative apparatus of the LCC and the diverse pattern of London schooling. Labour pursued its main objective of 'equality of educational opportunity' primarily by seeking to widen access to and improve the standards of provision in London's existing system of post-primary education. Only in the latter half of the 1930s did it seriously consider the possibility of more fundamental reform.

[1] R.L. Leonard, 'Morrison's Political Bequest', *New Society*, Jan. 1968, p.6.

### *The LCC and the 1918 Education Act*

The 1918 Education Act consolidated many of the proposals for reform which had been shelved at the outbreak of the First World War. The Act raised the school leaving-age to fourteen. It prescribed a system of compulsory, part-time day continuation schooling up to the age of sixteen for pupils leaving school at fourteen and envisaged a limited expansion of nursery schooling. It also secured a minimum government grant of 50 per cent of all expenditure incurred by local education authorities. This was particularly important for the LCC, which even in 1914 was raising some 70 per cent of its education budget from the rates. Important also was the provision which required local education authorities to prepare ten-year schemes of educational development.

The LCC's scheme was published in July 1920. Sir Cyril Cobb, a leading figure in the Municipal Reform Party who chaired the LCC's Education Committee, claimed that the scheme embodied all the ideals of the 1918 Act, but complained that the Government had failed to provide estimates of the expenditure which would be incurred by local authorities. Adding a cautionary note, Cobb concluded that implementation of the Act depended on the availability of financial resources. The way forward was to ignore 'educational enthusiasts who are out for revolutionary changes' and proceed at a pace which was neither too ambitious nor 'lagging behind popular demand'.[2] Together with the proposals of various teachers' organizations, local borough councils, parents' committees and bodies associated with the London Labour Movement, the LCC's scheme provides an interesting contemporary record of educational aspirations in the metropolis, after they had been heightened by the privations of wartime and by promises of post-war reform.

Within London's system of education, 'the greatest difficulties', admitted the LCC, were to be found in the '80 per cent or so . . . of elementary school children who are left behind . . . after the brighter ones have been drafted into the secondary, trade and central schools'.[3] For these senior elementary pupils – overwhelmingly from working-class backgrounds – housed in the traditional 'three-decker barracks' with their infant, junior and senior departments rising one above the other, schooling was mainly a diet of practical instruction, or 'learning through the hands', with courses in arithmetic, geometry, cookery, laundrywork, handicrafts and gardening, where facilities permitted. Working-class girls in particular, the LCC implied, might be better equipped for their domestic role, if needlework

[2] Sir Cyril Cobb, 'London's Scheme of Education', *The Contemporary Review*, Nov. 1920, pp.652-3.

[3] London County Council, *Scheme of the Local Authority*, 1920, p.64.

courses paid more attention to repairing and adapting clothing.[4]

For those leaving school at fourteen, the Council proposed to establish twenty-two day-continuation schools near employers' premises, where young people up to the age of sixteen would receive general instruction for eight hours a week. Apart from instruction in mathematics, English, history, science, geography and civics, the LCC also envisaged that the schools would cultivate the appropriate norms of social behaviour.

> With shorter hours of labour, one of the great problems is to train young persons to utilize satisfactorily their leisure hours and one of the aims of these schools should be to provide this very important training.[5]

If the senior elementary and the day-continuation schools, and many of the polytechnics and technical institutes were largely the educational repositories of the working class, London's secondary schools remained overwhelmingly the preserve of the fee-paying middle classes. Nearly 75 per cent of their pupils at this time were fee-payers. For those unable to pay, a narrow scholarship ladder enabled some 2,000 or so each year to enter the seventy-odd secondary schools aided or maintained by the LCC. Most scholarship entrants were drawn from the lower-middle class and the skilled working class. For those unable to reach the top rung of the scholarship ladder, some 5,000 pupils annually were selected for a place at one of the Council's fifty-one central schools. Here, from the age of eleven, pupils received a free general education up to the age of fifteen, with a strong industrial or commercial content designed to meet the requirements of local employers. These schools, which were first established by the LCC in 1910, were primarily intended to relieve some of the pressure on secondary school accommodation in London.

The LCC acknowledged that even though many of its secondary schools were seriously overcrowded, especially those south of the Thames, many still admitted fee-payers who were considered unsuitable for a secondary schooling. This resulted in many working-class candidates being excluded and helped to fuel Labour Party demands for more secondary schools and more equitable methods of selection. The LCC defended its system of selection by claiming that if it raised admission standards for its fee-payers, they would merely transfer elsewhere. The result would be the creation of a two-tier secondary system in London, with entry into LCC schools based upon 'intellectual attainment' and entry elsewhere based upon the ability to pay. The Council maintained that this justified its policy of imposing a more rigorous entrance test – the Junior County Scholarship – for pupils whose parents were unable to pay fees, compared with the routine admission test taken by those whose parents were able to 'buy an education'. What the Council most feared

[4] *Ibid.*, p.64.
[5] *Ibid.*, p.98.

was the loss of income from fee-payers, the loss of qualified teaching staff and an outcry from middle-class parents whose children failed a more rigorous entrance examination. It therefore preferred to maintain what was in effect its own two-tier system of selection. Pupils from working-class backgrounds also faced other obstacles. Although the LCC planned its level of secondary provision on the basis of ten places per thousand of the population (a target set in 1909), there were in practice enormous variations across London. The level of admissions varied from an average of 2.7 places per thousand in the six poorest inner London boroughs of Bermondsey, Bethnal Green, Poplar, Shoreditch, Southwark and Stepney, to 15.7 and 18.8 respectively in predominantly middle-class Wandsworth and Lewisham. Moreover, the scheme of 1920 envisaged only a marginal increase in secondary accommodation, from 37,087 to 41,226 places. This was little more than half the extra accommodation which was required to meet its target of ten places per thousand of the population (the equivalent of 45,000 places).

The class inequalities, highlighted by the geographical division of educational opportunity, the narrowness of the scholarship ladder, the injustices of the fee-paying system and the inferior status of the senior elementary and central schools, were to be the main concerns of the London Labour Party's educational strategy between the wars.

### *An 'Education Charter for London'*

In October 1919 a joint committee was formed, which included representatives of the Co-operative Union, the London Labour Party, the London Trades Council and the Workers' Educational Association (WEA). Its objective was to secure 'the best administration in London of the permissive clauses of the Education Act 1918' and on this basis to organize a conference 'to formulate ... the workers' considered judgement on what the new London education scheme must provide'.[6]

The conference met on 13 December 1919. Nearly 500 delegates from trade unions, co-operative bodies, teachers' organizations, parents' committees, local Labour Parties and the WEA endorsed an eleven-point 'Education Charter for the Metropolis' which was later submitted to the LCC. The 'Charter', which was closely modelled on the programme of the WEA, essentially sought an expansion of educational opportunities by widening educational access and improving standards of provision. Its main significance was that it embodied a series of concrete objectives, most of which were pursued by the London Labour Party as it sought to highlight particular educational concerns or press certain educational objectives at the LCC. The 'Charter' demanded more open-air nursery

[6] *The Highway*, Nov. 1919, p.30 and Dec. 1919, p.51.

schools, within easy access of homes of children, the raising of the school-leaving age to fifteen as soon as possible, and a reduction in the size of classes in elementary schools to forty and within a reasonable period to twenty. The 'joint committee' pointed out that the LCC's own figures showed that 73 per cent of elementary classes contained more than forty pupils. Criticism of the levels of secondary provision and the different admission tests imposed on fee-payers and scholarship entrants was coupled with a demand for free secondary schooling with adequate maintenance grants for 'all capable of benefiting thereby'. Whilst this effectively demanded the abolition of fee-paying in the LCC system, it also endorsed the principle of secondary selection and by implication, the claims of those such as Cyril Burt, the Council's educational psychologist, that 'capacity to benefit' was something which could be objectively ascertained.

For those leaving school at fourteen, the 'Charter' called for free continuation schools to prepare young people for the 'rights and responsibilities of citizenship'. The notion of 'citizenship' stressed the ideals of social harmony and individual responsibility and was part of a shared discourse on some of the basic principles of social organization, between labourism and progressive liberalism.

### *The 'Economy Campaign' and the LCC*

Demands for government economies surfaced at the end of the short, inflationary post-war boom, during 1920 and 1921. A lurid 'Anti-Waste' campaign against alleged 'squander-mania' was promoted in sections of the press such as *The Daily Mail*. As a result the government appointed a committee of business representatives under Sir Eric Geddes, to examine its expenditure programme. The Geddes Committee recommended cuts of £75 million in the budget estimates for 1922, including some £18 million from the education budget, provisionally estimated at £50 million. The Committee also recommended cutting the salaries of teachers by 10 per cent; excluding children below the age of six from schooling; increasing the size of elementary classes; and reducing Exchequer grants to local education authorities.[7]

Leading the 'anti-waste' campaign in London were representatives of the Municipal Reform Party and its metropolitan umbrella, the London Municipal Society. Through a series of meetings and propaganda on the themes of 'high rates' and 'government waste' the society demanded 'economy' in order to reduce the rates. Parliamentary protection for the local 'Ratepayer' was to be enforced by pruning the programmes of the Board of Education and the Ministry of Health in particular.[8]

[7] B. Simon, *The Politics of Educational Reform, 1920-1940*, 1974, pp.37-58.
[8] *The Times*, 20 Jan. 1921, p.7 and 10 Feb. 1921, p.12.

A year before the publication of the Geddes proposals, the LCC's scheme of 1920, and most of the proposals for reform in the 1918 Education Act, were pushed aside in January 1921 when the Board of Education issued Circular 1190. This effectively suspended government funding on all but the most urgent local education authority projects. Taking this as their cue, supporters of the 'anti-waste' campaign within the Municipal Reform Party at the LCC, such as Canon H.J. Swallow and J.M. Gatti, pressed for economies. The Council quickly passed a resolution suspending all educational expenditure financed from the rates, unless it qualified for a 50 per cent Board of Education grant. Susan Lawrence, a Labour member of the Education Committee, claimed that this decision was a signal to the government that the Municipal Reformers at the LCC would dutifully obey all its demands for economy.[9]

During the next eighteen months, despite considerable opposition from within the Municipal Reform Party, the Council introduced a programme of economies. Amongst the most substantial measures were a ban on married women teachers (which was not lifted until July 1935); an increase in secondary school fees; the abolition of compulsory continuation schooling; a 50 per cent cut in the school meals budget; and an attempt to appoint some 300 unqualified teaching staff in the infants departments of elementary schools.

### *Teachers', Labour and Parents' Committees*

Opposition to educational 'economy' quickly manifested itself in the electoral defeat of government candidates, as in the Camberwell North parliamentary by-election in February 1922, when Labour's Charles Ammon overturned a comfortable Conservative majority. Especially significant was the translation of some of this opposition into growing support for the Labour Party amongst sections of the teaching profession and attempts to mobilize parental support through the formation of local parents' committees.

In the forefront of this activity in London were members of the National Union of Women Teachers (NUWT). Parents' committees emerged as local pressure groups formed to agitate against demands for 'educational economy'. They were primarily intended to 'organize the ratepayer as a parent' in order to foster greater parental interest in educational issues and pressure local authorities by 'challenging every piece of foolish and stupid economy and encouraging every piece of wise educational expenditure'.[10] During 1922 more committees were established at parents' meetings organized by local branches of the NUWT to protest

[9] Susan Lawrence, *London Education*, 1923, p.5.
[10] A. Greenwood, *Report of 9th Annual Conference of Educational Associations*, 1921, p.53.

against the proposals of the Geddes Committee and the decision of the LCC to hire unqualified teachers. The NUWT claimed that many parents were dissatisfied with the LCC's education policy and urged the formation of parents' committees (sometimes called Parents' Unions, or Guilds) in connection with every LCC school by the time of the 1925 LCC elections.[11] Typical was a 'well attended enthusiastic meeting of parents' organized by Battersea NUWT at the Tennyson Street LCC school on 16 March 1922. After passing a resolution of protest against 'the cutting down of the children's education', a Tennyson Street Parents' Union was formed to organize monthly meetings to 'watch over the educational interests of the children'.[12]

Although the campaign against the appointment of unqualified teachers had some local successes, the effectiveness of parents' committees as an organized pressure group was limited and depended much upon the initiatives taken by other organizations, such as the NUWT and the London Labour Party. Despite the involvement of some Labour Party members in Battersea and Poplar in particular, the London Labour Party gave little positive encouragement to this type of activity and preferred to channel its protests through its elected representatives and allied organizations.

Teachers were one group of 'middle class professionals' whom Herbert Morrison, in particular, was anxious to enlist in support of the Labour Party's LCC ambitions. Criticizing what he regarded as the teachers' outmoded political attitudes and writing in the context of moves early in 1923 to establish a Teachers' Labour League, Morrison invited teachers who were Labour supporters, to work to secure the affiliation of the teachers' organizations to the London Labour Party and to ensure that at the 1925 LCC elections, 'no teachers' candidates . . . run under any auspices other than those of the Labour Party'.[13] During the November 1922 general election the NUWT had urged its members in London to concentrate all their energies on securing the return of Labour and Liberal candidates to Parliament. The attitude of the NUWT at this time appeared more favourable to Labour than the official doctrine of 'professional neutrality' espoused by the London Teachers Association (LTA), by far the largest of the London teachers' organizations. This doctrine had frustrated attempts during and after the First World War to secure the LTA's affiliation to the London Labour Party.

Affiliation of the teaching unions to the Labour Party was also one of the objectives of the Teachers' Labour League, which was formed as a national organization in London in May 1923. Its basic objectives were to

[11] *Woman Teacher*, 24 November 1922.
[12] *South Western Star*, 17 March 1921.
[13] *London Labour Chronicle*, April 1923, p.3.

mobilize 'public opinion' on educational questions and secure Labour representation on governing bodies and in Parliament. Membership was diverse and local branches were quickly established in a number of districts, including Lewisham, Hackney, Kennington and in West London. Amongst the fifty or so members of the League's Hackney branch were the secretary of the local Trades Council (A. Duncan), a founder member of Hackney North Labour Party (Florence Du Vergier), the Principal of Clapton Girls' Grammar School (Mary O'Brien Harris) and Communist Party member Marjorie Pollitt, who in 1926 was dismissed from her teaching post by the LCC because of her political activities in the General Strike. The branch combined social activities and work in the teaching unions with public meetings, where for example Mary O'Brien Harris outlined her work on individual study programmes which were based upon the ideas of Montessori.[14]

Although the League was affiliated to the London Labour Party, it made little or no attempt to secure support for its ideas at the Party's annual conference, preferring instead to concentrate on activities within the National Union of Teachers (NUT) and the annual conference of the Labour Party, where in 1925 and 1926 it secured considerable support for its proposals to counter 'anti-working class bias' in the classroom.[15] The League's activity within the Labour Party was shortlived. Its increasingly militant political orientation made it a likely candidate for the purge of 'Communist-influenced' bodies from the Labour Party which was conducted in the mid 1920s and it was expelled, along with seven local Labour Parties, from the London Labour Party in 1927. Thereafter its influence dwindled as it followed the sectarian turns of 'Third Period' Stalinism from the late 1920s.

In the same year (1927) a minority of members opposed to the League's political orientation seceded to form the National Association of Labour Teachers (NALT), one of whose objectives was to develop an educational policy for the Labour Party. Two of its founder members were Florence Du Vergier and Mary O'Brien Harris. Although the NALT quickly established contact with the London Labour Party it was not until 1934 that it formally affiliated and began seeking support for its ideas within the Party and at the LCC. In the meantime it concentrated on building up its support within the NUT in particular and developing its ideas for an alternative system of 'post-primary' or secondary schooling, based upon the 'multilateral' concepts current in progressive educational discourse since the mid 1920s.[16]

[14] Mary O'Brien Harris, *Towards Freedom: An Experiment in Education*, 1923.

[15] R. Barker, *Education and Politics, 1900-1951. A Study of the Labour Party*, 1972, pp.148-150.

[16] J.D. Burgevin, 'Politics and Education: A Case Study of a Pressure Group, the NALT 1927-1951', Ph.D., Syracuse University, 1969.

## *The Hadow Report and After, 1926-1934*

The NALT's ideas, first published in 1930, as *Education: A Policy* were developed partly through a critique of the 1926 Hadow Report (*The Education of the Adolescent*). The Hadow Report set out a basic framework for Board of Education policy during the remainder of the inter-war period and beyond, culminating in the 1944 Education Act. Its recommendations included raising the school leaving-age to fifteen within six years and the provision of some form of post-primary schooling for all pupils over the age of eleven-plus in different types of secondary school, all equipped to the same standards.

The Hadow Report was discussed by the LCC Education Committee on 2 November 1927. A report from the General Purposes Sub-Committee drawn up by the Education Officer, G.H. Gater, claimed that LCC policy was already in line with Hadow's recommendations, although it admitted that the extent to which it had been able to implement its policy fell far short of the ideal recommended in the Hadow Report. Whilst the Council planned a further expansion of its selective secondary and central schools, the report stated that it had so far been unable to find a satisfactory solution to the long-standing problem, mentioned in the Council's scheme of 1920, of making suitable provision for the majority of pupils over the age of eleven who remained in the elementary schools. The basic tenor of the report was that further development of the Council's post-primary provision along the lines proposed by Hadow would continue to be constrained by considerable financial and administrative difficulties. This response was echoed by a majority of the Education Committee. Whilst the Committee endorsed some of Hadow's proposals on curriculum development and methods of selection at eleven-plus, it rejected as too costly the proposal that there should be parity in the levels of staffing and equipment between the different types of secondary school. It also agreed not to advance any proposal for raising the school leaving-age, pointing out the administrative difficulties and financial costs involved. The Committee sought to justify its position by citing a letter from the President of the Board of Education, Eustace Percy, to the Hadow Committee. In this Percy had stated that the Board had no immediate intention of introducing legislation on a matter which was entirely at the discretion of local education authorities under powers conferred on them by the 1921 Education Act. Attempts by the Committee's Labour members to incorporate some of Hadow's recommendations into the report were unsuccessful. The Committee rejected Labour amendments calling for the statutory leaving-age to be raised to fifteen with maintenance allowances and for parity of conditions between different types of post-primary school.[17]

The school leaving-age and the expansion of secondary schooling were the two major issues at the centre of Labour's concerns and provided the main focus for its criticisms of the policy of the Municipal Reform Party in the wake of the Hadow Report. In a comparative survey based largely upon Kenneth Lindsay's influential *Social Progress and Educational Waste*, published in 1926, Barbara Drake (a co-opted member of the Education Committee) claimed that the lower levels of secondary provision in London compared with other parts of England and Wales meant that its elementary school children were at a relative disadvantage:

> The elementary school child has in London about four-fifths the chance of a secondary education that he has in the country as a whole; a little more than one-quarter the chance that he has in Bradford, about one-third the chance that he has in Halifax; or if we come nearer home, rather more than one-third the chance that he has in Southend-on-Sea; rather less than half the chance he has in suburban Middlesex.[18]

Bradford, with its extensive system of 'free places' was at this time second only to Wallasey in having the highest level of secondary provision (19.3 secondary pupils per thousand of the population, compared with an average over England and Wales of 9.0 and only 7.6 in London). Moreover, claimed Drake, in 1925 the LCC actually awarded fewer junior county scholarships than it did twenty years previously, in 1905 (1,684 compared with 2,167).

Such criticisms increased, particularly after the election of the second Labour Government in June 1929, as members of the London Labour Party sought to highlight the injustices of the LCC's fee-paying system and the Council's negative response to demands to raise the school-leaving age. For example, when Charles Trevelyan, the new President of the Board of Education, introduced a Bill in December 1929 to raise the leaving-age to fifteen by 1 April 1931, with means-tested maintenance allowances, the LCC's Education Committee reaffirmed its existing policy, concluding that the measure could not be implemented in the time allowed.[19] This was accompanied by an assurance from Sir John Gilbert, who chaired the Committee, that a majority of the Municipal Reform Party were not opposed to raising the leaving-age. Marshall Jackman (Labour member for Hackney South and a member of the NALT) challenged the Committee's conclusion. A falling birth-rate and an exodus from inner London had, he claimed, created some 80,000 surplus places in the elementary schools. Moreover the LCC's own statistics

[17] LCC Minutes of Education Committee, 2 November 1927, pp.610-2; *London Teacher*, 11 November 1927, p.500.

[18] Barbara Drake, 'London Education', *London News*, August 1927, p.2.

[19] *London News*, January 1931, p.1.

indicated that even in 1932, when the full effect of raising the leaving-age would be felt, the number of extra pupils would not exceed the current roll of 620,000 by more than 17,000 and would decline thereafter. Therefore, concluded Jackman, the Government's proposals were entirely practical and the Council would be able to meet the extra demand by using the surplus accommodation with some temporary adjustments.

The London Labour Party also emphasized its policy of free secondary schooling as a way of increasing the numbers entering London's grammar schools. In July 1930 Labour members of the Education Committee introduced a motion which recommended that the Council abolish fees in its maintained secondary schools. The motion was rejected and in the following March the Party fought the LCC election on a manifesto which proclaimed its meritocratic belief that 'a child's natural ability and not its parents' purse should determine the extent of its education'.[20]

Although Labour continually criticized the Municipal Reform Party's lack of commitment to educational progress, by 1931 a considerable amount of reorganization and development had in fact taken place, largely under the impetus of the Council's three-year programmes which began in 1925. The provision of twenty-five new elementary schools and the modernization of some twenty-three others meant that overcrowding in elementary classes had been significantly reduced and facilities for handicraft and domestic instruction somewhat improved. Secondary provision had also expanded with the construction of twelve new secondary schools, the modernization of twenty-five others and a modest increase in the number of junior county scholarships. Other developments included two new nursery schools, five new open-air schools and more provision for adult education.

Not for the first time however these developments were threatened by another round of economy heralded by the publication of the May Report in July 1931 and the collapse of the Labour Government the following month, when the Cabinet split on the issue of cutting the dole. Circular 1421, issued by the Board of Education in September 1932, translated May's demand for cuts in the Government's education estimates into a directive to raise secondary school fees in line with parents' 'ability to pay'. The London Labour Party protested against the 'meanness and stupidity' of the measures, adding its voice to the largest number of protests received by the Board of Education on any issue in the inter-war period.[20] But the protests had little immediate effect. Further economy measures followed, including a ten per cent cut in teachers' salaries. The LCC cut its education budget by £1.5 millions at the same time as the Government reduced its grant by £1.7 millions. The inevitable results

[20] Simon, *op. cit.*, p.335 (Appendix 1); London Labour Party, Executive Committee Minutes, October 1931-October 1932, Folio 5199.

included reductions in the level of scholarship grants and school maintenance, postponement of new school building and increased secondary school fees. Even the Conservative press grew alarmed when the LCC abolished school prizes.

The unpopular legacy of these measures and the cuts in the scales of unemployment relief contributed substantially to Labour's LCC election victory in March 1934.

### *Extending the Educational Ladder: Labour's Policy at the LCC*

The 1934 LCC election inaugurated an unbroken succession of Labour majorities at County Hall. The Party's 1934 election manifesto combined a vigorous condemnation of Municipal Reform stewardship with a vague programmatic statement of principles. But Labour promised a more efficient management of LCC affairs, rather than any radical reform. Administrative efficiency and a 'rigorous control of the Council's financial services' would, the Party claimed, help to secure 'value for money' for the 'Ratepayer', without impairing Council services.[21] As far as education was concerned, Herbert Morrison promised an expansion of educational opportunities. Better administration and improved school meals, medical and other services, would reduce the effects of poverty and help to create an education system 'designed to produce citizens with free upright minds, capable of thinking for themselves'.[22]

General statements of principles however and criticism of the record of the Municipal Reformers could not be a substitute for Labour's lack of a detailed programme of educational priorities and objectives. Morrison had already highlighted the problem when, in January 1933, he complained to his Executive Committee that the Party possessed no clear educational policy for London.

On Morrison's advice, an Education Research Group was established under R.H. Tawney (one of the Labour Party's leading educationists and Professor of Economic History at London University) to examine the problems of London education and 'the measures necessary for their solution'.[23] With such a wide brief it was hardly surprising that the Research Group was unable to complete its work in time for the 1934 LCC elections as intended. In fact, it only succeeded in issuing a rather anodyne report, in July 1935, in response to allegations made at the London Labour Party's 1934 annual conference, that text-books in use in LCC schools contained 'militaristic, patriotic and capitalist propaganda'.[24]

[21] *London News*, February 1934, p.1.
[22] *The Star*, 7 March 1934; *London News*, February 1934, p.1.
[23] London Labour Party, Executive Committee Report, 1932-33, p.11.
[24] *Ibid*, Executive Committee Report, 1934-35, pp.22-3.

The real significance of the Research Group lay in its membership, which spanned three influential bodies concerned with education policy: the NALT (G.S.M. Ellis and W.H. Spikes), the Labour Party's Advisory Committee on Education (R.H. Tawney, Barbara Drake and Hugh Franklin) and the LCC Education Committee (Freda Corbet, Agnes Dawson, Eveline Lowe, in addition to Tawney, Drake and Franklin). This cross-membership helped the advocates of 'multilateral schools' in their successful endeavour to secure the LCC's endorsement of some of their proposals in 1935.

Whilst the London Labour Party lacked a detailed educational prospectus at the time of the 1934 election, some idea of its priorities can be gleaned from the synopsis of a lecture entitled 'Schools and Scholars: The Right to Knowledge' which was one of a series of Party lectures on 'Planning London for Socialism' given by its LCC representatives during the winter of 1933-4. This defined the Party's general objective as 'better and extended equal educational opportunity for all' irrespective of parental income, based upon a greater variety of post-primary provision. This objective was to be implemented by making use of the opportunity afforded by falling school rolls to decrease class sizes; extending the school meals and medical services; providing more nursery schools; increasing the number of scholarships and extending adult education.

The London Labour Party's annual conference also began to show a much greater interest in the practical details of educational reform. No less than twenty-eight motions on the topic appeared on the agenda of the half-dozen conferences from 1934 to 1939, compared with a mere eight during the period 1918-34. Most of these were concerned with four basic issues: nursery provision; nutritional standards; staffing and facilities; and the structure of post-primary provision. Many were carried despite frequent opposition from the Party's Executive Committee, which was largely filled with nominees sympathetic to Morrison's cautious leadership at County Hall.

Conference requests for more nursery provision, in 1935 and 1936, were rejected by the Party leadership at the LCC on financial grounds. Despite the Party's long-standing commitment, Morrison in particular queried whether children under the age of five should attend school at all, other than on social grounds. Other Conference requests, for free school meals for children whose parents were on low incomes and for the provision of milk, encountered similar obstacles. It was largely due to Barbara Drake's persistent advocacy that a very limited scheme for the provision of milk during school holidays was introduced in 1937 for those with a doctor's recommendation. In practice, the Conference exercised little direction over the policy pursued by the Party at the LCC. This was partly because the latter functioned as a relatively autonomous organization under the aegis of a Policy Committee, composed of the Party's LCC leadership and the chairmen of council committees. The Policy Committee arrogated to itself most of the crucial decisions affecting Party policy in committees and was rarely challenged. Another factor was the considerable, often decisive, sway exercised by the Education Officer, E.M. Rich (a protégé of Robert Blair) and other leading LCC officials, working in harness with the committee chairmen.

The general direction of education policy at County Hall, is evident in the three-year education programme for 1935-8, which was adopted by the Council in February 1935. Introduced with 'due regard to economy', the Triennial Programme had two main objectives: to increase the level of secondary school provision and to secure improvements in the standard of elementary schooling. It proposed increases in the number of junior county scholarships from 1,750 to 2,550 and in the number of supplementary scholarships, from 450 to 500. Eveline Lowe, who chaired the Education Committee, claimed that the increases would produce an extra 6,800 scholarship places by 1942-3. The extra scholarships were to be complemented by building two new maintained secondary schools in South East London, together with major improvements at five maintained and sixteen aided secondary schools. Elementary provision would be improved by building one new school and modernizing some thirty others. Together with extra teaching staff these improvements would mean, according to Lowe, that within a decade London's elementary schools would stand comparison with any elsewhere in the country. The significant amount of building and reconstruction work was reflected in the capital costs which, it was estimated, would quadruple to about a million pounds in the first year of implementation.

Generally, the programme was favourably received. *The Times Educational Supplement* commented that the proposals did not depart from established principles and were unlikely to arouse much criticism. The London Teachers Association welcomed the plans, but criticized the absence of proposals to raise the school leaving-age and improve the standards of central schools. Some criticisms were also made by Municipal Reformers who feared that increasing the number of scholarship places would 'lower academic standards'. Others, such as W.H. Webbe, the Party Leader, praised the programme's modest objectives as a 'glorious example of socialist self-denial'.[25]

### *Labour and the School Leaving-Age*

Although the London Teachers Association criticized the absence of proposals to raise the leaving-age, the Council had already made an unsuccessful attempt to deal with the issue during 1934.

Following requests from the Workers' Educational Association and the

[25] *London Teacher*, 8 February 1935, p.67.

Education Committee of East Ham Borough Council, the LCC convened a conference of representatives from neighbouring local education authorities with a view to making a joint representation to urge the government to raise the leaving age to fifteen. Although local authorities had the power to raise the leaving-age under by-law, the LCC Education Committee concluded that the best way to ensure uniformity in an area such as Greater London, would be for the government to introduce national legislation.

At the conference on 29 June, the Council was represented by Eveline Lowe, Herbert Morrison and R.H. Tawney, now a co-opted Labour member of the Education Committee. Tawney introduced a motion urging the Government to introduce legislation to raise the leaving-age to fifteen from April 1935. During the ensuing debate, representatives from the county councils of Essex, Surrey and Kent, in particular, stated that whilst they were not opposed in principle to the idea, lack of suitable school accommodation in their areas made the proposed time-scale impractical. As a compromise, Morrison proposed that the legislation should instead become operable at the earliest possible date. Even though the motion was carried in this amended form, over half the representatives (mainly from the outermost authorities) abstained. The outcome simply reaffirmed a principle for which there was already widespread support, but effectively left the question of implementation in the Government's hands. There the matter rested until February 1936, when the National Government introduced a Bill to raise the leaving-age to fifteen from September 1939. The Bill became law in July 1936, but was rendered irrelevant by the outbreak of war.

### *The London Labour Party and the 'Multilateral School'*

On 25 July 1934 the Council requested the Education Committee to report on all aspects of post-primary provision in London. The task was delegated to a special Joint Section composed of sixteen members of the Elementary and Higher Education Sub-Committees, under Hugh Franklin, the latter's Vice-Chairman. Its twelve Labour members included several leading advocates of the multilateral school. Hugh Franklin and Barbara Drake, had been members of the Labour Party's Advisory Committee on Education, which in a memorandum of 1929 to Charles Trevelyan, the Labour President of the Board of Education, had advocated a post-primary system based upon the multilateral school.[26] Two other members, T.H. Jones and Mary O'Brien Harris, were members of the NALT, and along with Franklin, were in regular contact with another NALT member, W.H. Spikes, a physics teacher at Brockley

[26] Simon, *op. cit.*, p.154.

Grammar School. Spikes was the main author of the NALT's *Education: A Policy*, which advocated a system of multilateral schooling 'under which all children of a given age would attend the same Secondary School, finding within it varying courses to suit their individual needs, but doing much of the work in common and enjoying a common social life within the school'.[27]

NALT's concept of 'multilateralism' was derived from French and Austrian examples, particularly the French *école unique*, and modified on the basis of North American experience and the work of Mary O'Brien Harris on individual learning programmes.[28] The relative merits and practical details of what were similar proposals to those outlined in *Education: A Policy* were discussed by the Joint Section over a period of eight months, before it presented a final report to the Education Committee in May 1935. An interim report presented in January surveyed existing arrangements. Considerable differences arose between staunch defenders of the existing system, such as E.M. Rich, the Education Officer, and critics such as Franklin. These differences were most clearly expressed in two particular reports: one from Rich advocating the retention of the current system and the other from Franklin, advocating a unified system. The orthodox views of Rich were encapsulated in a number of terse paragraphs. Typical was the suggestion that 'the great majority of London's children are destined to pursue occupations which will make little demand on specialized gifts, [therefore] to give a more expensive form of education . . . to more than a proportion of London children would be a misuse of the educational system'. Consequently it was only necessary to devote expensive resources to relatively few of London's schools whilst ensuring that 'those of less capacity should become aware of their own limitations, as a spur to greater effort and as an understanding of the conditions in which they are likely to enter adult life'.[29] In other words, the type of post-primary education children received should be determined directly by the needs of the labour market. For the great majority, schooling would be a conditioning process designed to reconcile 'the less able' to their subordinate role in the economic and social order – a process of 'learning to labour'.

Franklin's advocacy of a unified system of post-primary provision was based largely upon the proposition that selection at eleven-plus was an unreliable indicator of future potential, as the Hadow Report had admitted. Since it was hazardous to forecast at the age of eleven how a

[27] National Association of Labour Teachers, *Education: A Policy*, 1930, p.2.

[28] *Times Educational Supplement*, 8 March 1947 (letter from W.H. Spikes).

[29] Greater London Record Office, Minutes of Joint Section of Elementary and Higher Education Sub-Committee, 17 January 1935 (Enclosure F: Memorandum of E.M. Rich, pp.1-2).

pupil was likely to develop, it was difficult to justify 'an almost final cleavage' at that age 'into separate and almost immutable strata'.[30] Another memorandum from Franklin outlined the salient features of a multilateral system, which he claimed would end the injustices of selection at eleven-plus. In London it would be possible, suggested Franklin, to merge grammar, central, senior elementary and technical (trade) schools into a unified multilateral system under a single regulatory control.

Admission to each school would be automatic and non-selective; with a parallel five-class entry, thirty pupils in a class and a minimum course length of five years, to produce a total roll of between 800 and 900 pupils. This was substantially less than the 1,200 to 2,000 eventually proposed for the LCC's system of comprehensive high schools in its London School Plan (1947). For the first three years, up to the age of fourteen, all pupils would receive a common schooling, based upon a general curriculum which would include English, history, geography, mathematics, science, handicrafts, art, civics and, possibly a foreign language. 'Subject sets' however, would be formed in some subjects, embracing children of more or less 'equal ability'. During this diagnostic period, according to Franklin, with the aid of the 'subject sets', a 'child's natural aptitude and bias will reveal itself gradually . . . so that the able and less able children will find their own levels by a perfectly natural process'.[31] At the age of fourteen-plus, the five parallel classes whilst maintaining a common core curriculum, would be regrouped into courses with different types of 'bias', (e.g. literary, mathematical-scientific, commercial, technical and artistic) up to the age of sixteen-plus. All vocational training would be undertaken after the age of sixteen and competitive external examinations would be replaced by a nationally recognized LCC Leaving Certificate based upon assessment and a pupil's school record.

Under the multilateral system 'selection by differentiation' would take place over a three-year period instead of once and for all at eleven-plus. Making selection a gradual diagnostic process within a common system of schooling would, Franklin stated, avoid the problems of selection at eleven-plus and mitigate the social divisions perpetuated by maintaining different types of secondary school.

The Joint Section's final report which was endorsed by the Council in June 1935 advocated a multilateral system for London, but made no specific recommendations because of legislative and other implications, such as cost. Although the Joint Section was requested to investigate these in more detail, no further reports were presented, partly because its remit lapsed with the 1937 LCC elections.

[30] *Ibid.* (Enclosure G: Memorandum of H. Franklin, pp.1-2).
[31] *Ibid*, 18 March 1935 (Enclosure J: Memorandum of H. Franking, pp.2-3).

The NALT now pursued the matter at the London Labour Party's 1937 and 1938 Annual Conferences. In 1937 motions from the NALT and Hackney Central Labour Party both included requests for the unification of post-primary education in London. Neither was debated because of lack of time. It was clear however that there was also important opposition to the NALT's proposals within the Party leadership. In a memorandum to the Party's Executive Committee, Morrison objected that 'there is a good deal of matter in these motions which really cannot be carried through . . . for financial and other reasons'.[32] Undeterred, the NALT pursued the issue again at the 1938 Conference and for the first time called for a 'reconsideration of the whole structure of post-primary education with a view to the substitution of a unified system of multilateral schools which would provide equality of opportunity for all children'.[33]

During the previous twelve months, members of NALT, such as Evelyn Denington (its Secretary), Cecil Denington, W.H. Spikes and Margaret Davies, had mounted an intensive campaign to mobilize support, using leaflets, writing to the local press and addressing numerous trade union and Labour Party branches throughout London.[34] Their efforts paid off. Despite strong opposition from the Party's Executive and Morrison in particular, the NALT's motion, which was proposed by Evelyn Denington, was carried overwhelmingly.

One of the arguments used by the Executive against the motion, was that the large size of the proposed schools would make it 'very difficult to maintain that personal touch between head teacher and pupils . . . which is so vital a factor in a living organization such as a school'.[35] Ironically this was to become one of the main objections levelled by critics of the LCC's post-war plans for a system of much larger comprehensive high schools which the Labour leadership at County Hall sought firmly to rebut.

The Conference resolution was referred to the Labour Party's Educational Advisory Committee; in June 1939 the Committee issued a memorandum which suggested that whilst wholesale change to a multilateral system would not be possible under the current Conservative government, the LCC could begin to introduce such schools in new housing development areas. This, it optimistically concluded, would help to prepare the ground for a national policy under a future Labour administration.[36]

However, when a Labour Government was elected in July 1945, it

[32] London Labour Party, Executive Committee Minutes, 14 October 1937.

[33] London Labour Party, Executive Committee Report, 1937-8 (Motion 35).

[34] Burgevin, *op. cit.*

[35] London Labour Party, Executive Committee Minutes, 17 November 1938, Report by Secretary.

[36] Barker, *op. cit.*, pp.73-4.

embraced not a multilateral system but a modification of the pre-war pattern based upon a tripartite structure of grammar, technical and secondary modern schools cloaked in the democratic colours of the 1944 Education Act. It was in the context of the continuation of selective secondary schooling therefore that in 1947 the LCC adopted proposals for the reorganization of post-primary provision in London, including the development of a system of comprehensive high schools.

The inter-war period profoundly affected the London Labour Party's approach to the problems of educational reform. The failure of the 1918 Education Act and the incremental progress of educational development under successive governments encouraged a cautious outlook which saw only limited possibilities for reform. Consequently the Party tended to focus its concerns on some of the most pressing problems, such as the school-leaving age, inadequate facilities, oversize classes and the fee-paying system. The Party's objective of seeking to secure greater 'equality of educational opportunity' was defined in meritocratic terms, rather than in the more egalitarian forms proposed by the NALT. The tensions and ambiguities within and between these different approaches remained unresolved in the post-war period. They have remained an important factor in the post-war development of schooling in London.

## *Chapter 9*

# *Working for London's Fire Brigade, 1889-1939*

Terry Segars

Under the London County Council, the fire brigade in London failed to make a decisive break with the traditions it inherited from its predecessor under the Metropolitan Board of Works, the Metropolitan Fire Brigade. As a result, the brigade was relatively backward by almost any measure that could be applied, until after the Second World War.

Despite this failure the brigade is worthy of study for reasons that are both particular to London and to the British fire service in general. The brigade dominated the service nationally in terms of size and prestige, and the Council was the only local authority in the country which had a statutory duty to provide a fire brigade. The public admired the firemen – 'worshipped' and 'adored' them in fact, according to the press on occasions.

Many of the MFB's traditions persisted under the LCC, including the policy of recruiting only sailors as officers or firemen, the tardy introduction of new technology and equipment, and the restricted involvement of elected members in monitoring the brigade. The LCC also attempted to maintain the master-and-servant relationship of the MBW era within the brigade, well beyond the time when it was practical to do so. The Council seemed content to follow its chief officers whose overriding concerns appeared to be the brass-bound aura of the brigade and the maintenance of discipline, rather than its effectiveness as a fire-fighting force. This attitude inevitably spilled over into labour relations policies and even when trade union recognition was conceded, it was carefully controlled.

The fire brigade differed from many of the other services provided by the Council, in that up until 1920 the workforce was required to live over or around the work place in tied housing. This requirement pulled into the employer's influence the men's wives and families. The brigade's expectations of the wives' role were almost as precise and demanding as those it had of its men.

Another feature of the persistence of the brigade's traditions was the continuity of policies right up until the Second World War, regardless of who was in control of the Council – Progressives, Municipal Reformers or the Labour Party. It is the Labour Party's willingness to carry on with traditional policies that is most surprising. Labour claimed to be willing to break with tradition in order to bring about improvements for the benefit of working people. But this was not the firemen's experience, as far as their conditions of service were concerned.

### *The Board of Works' Brigade*

The Metropolitan Board of Works took over responsibility for the fire brigade from the insurance companies in the wake of a massive wharf and warehouse fire at Tooley Street in September 1861. The fire enabled the companies to convince the Government that fire protection was a much wider responsibility than they should be expected to bear. As often happened in fire service history, a major fire provided the cruellest evidence of the need for change. James Braidwood, the brigade's chief officer, lost his life at the fire when a wall collapsed upon him, and the insurance companies had to pay out over £1.5 million in claims.

Responsibility for fire protection passed to the MBW on 1 January 1866. The Government insisted that the Metropolitan Fire Brigade be run for much less than the new Chief Fire Officer, Captain Eyre Massey Shaw, believed was necessary. The companies maintained their influence over the brigade as it was financed jointly by them, the Government and the MBW. But the insurance companies contributed less than half of what they had paid out annually when the brigade had been under their direct jurisdiction.

The companies thus retained what was effectively a veto over any developments or improvements in the brigade. They certainly exercised their influence, objecting, for instance, when the Board took on the responsibility for the saving of life from fire. This work had hitherto been carried out by a charity, the Royal Society for the Preservation of Life from Fire. The companies also used their political influence to block any legislation that the Board of Works promoted which was designed to increase the funds of the MFB. The Board reported that 'members of the House of Commons who support the companies' views have hitherto always blocked the Board's bills . . .'[1]

The brigade in London was underfinanced throughout the period of its existence under both the MBW and its former owners. This had disastrous consequences for firemen and the public alike. Coroners occasionally criticized the brigade's inadequacies when conducting inquests on fire victims who, it was thought, would have had a better chance of surviving had the brigade been more efficient or simply more readily available. The Board even tried to use these criticisms to lobby for

[1] Greater London Record Office (GLRO), Metropolitan Board of Works (MBW) Annual Report, 1888

more money. After a fatal fire in October 1888 in fashionable Wigmore Street, the Middlesex Coroner said quite bluntly that the brigade was under strength.[2] Equally bluntly, the Board agreed with the coroner and drew his comments to the attention of the Home Secretary. It was pointed out that the MBW could do nothing to counter the unsatisfactory situation because of the financial restrictions imposed upon it.

Braidwood's death at Tooley Street represented only the tip of the iceberg of hazards which rank and file London firemen were facing from day to day. The simple necessity for more men, machinery and fire stations was widely recognized.

### *Resistance to Change*

These financial restrictions had long prevented the introduction of new machinery. Steam-driven fire pumps, for instance, had become available from the 1830s and, although there were problems with the supply of sufficient water, private brigades, notably the brigade run by Frederick Hodges from his gin factory in Lambeth, made much use of them. A steam-driven pump could produce a water jet 150 feet high and pump up to 500 gallons of water a minute, while the manual fire engines that Braidwood had clung on to needed at least thirty men working levers alongside the machine to produce anything like a comparable performance. Much is made of the conservatism of Braidwood and his men by fire service historians in order to account for the rejection of steamers by the brigade. Sally Holloway claims that the 'men were said to be so hostile to the [steam] engine that its hose was cut and everything possible done to sabotage it'.[3] Nevertheless, together with the water problem, these objections served the insurance companies well in keeping down the capital cost of the brigade. That the fire losses were higher than they need have been would not have worried the companies too much. Losses could be recouped through higher premiums and new business; an expensive fire was the best possible publicity for companies wishing to promote the virtues of fire insurance.

Captain Shaw certainly improved matters in the early days of the MFB after 1866, quickly extending the use of steamers within the brigade, increasing the manpower and fire stations to cover the 117 square miles of the MBW area instead of the ten square miles of the City and Central London that the previous brigade had protected. Even so, modernization could not outstrip the finances available. As late as 1884 the Metropolitan Brigade was still installing manual engines in new stations, although many private and public brigades had long abandoned them in favour of

[2] GLRO, MBW 962.

[3] Sally Holloway, *London's Noble Fire Brigades 1833-1904*, 1973, pp.20-1.

steam.[4] Even in the 1890 edition of his book, *Fire Protection*, Shaw devoted considerable space to manual fire engines.[5]

Under the LCC Shaw was able to start a development programme. Firemen's conditions of service were improved: pay was increased by ten per cent in 1891 (though the next increase did not occur until 1907); rents were reduced and accommodation improved; a pension scheme was established providing two-thirds of pay and allowances after twenty-eight years' service; leave was granted for all ranks of one week a year plus twenty-six days (one day off in fourteen). Time off had been haphazard under the MBW, depending on the availability of manpower. These improvements for the lower ranks were counterbalanced by reductions in the salaries of the most highly paid officers. The Chief Fire Officer's pay was reduced from the £1,200 per annum that Shaw had been paid, when the Council first took over, to £800.

In its first five years under the LCC, the brigade also expanded. Staff increased by 134 (plus nineteen per cent), the bulk of these being firemen, and one new station was built while others were rebuilt or refurbished. Despite these early initiatives, a tragic workshop fire of 1902 in Queen Victoria Street in which nine people died showed the true size of the brigade to be far removed from the extravagant claims sometimes made for it.

Yet Shaw and his immediate successors made no great impact on modernizing the brigade's equipment. If anything advances became less likely following a change in Council policy in the 1890s to recruiting as principal fire officers men who had no previous experience of the workings of the fire service. Following the Queen Victoria Street fire the brigade was subject to considerable public criticism. The inquest jury absolved the brigade of any negligence, though with the qualification 'considering the appliances at their disposal'. But newspapers commented upon the reluctance to introduce new equipment and ideas into the brigade. Much of the blame for this conservatism was said to be due to Commander Wells, the Chief Officer. A book published shortly after the fire, *The Decay of London's Fire Brigade*, heaped the blame upon Wells, describing him as 'a champion opponent of reform'.[6] The anonymous author, 'Phoenix', complained that 'Our firemen today are asked to cope with twentieth-century perils with nineteenth-century machinery',[7] and went on to point to the superior equipment and procedures in use in other British brigades and on the Continent. For instance the pumping capacity of London's fire engines was 450 gallons per minute, while Liverpool had one that could pump 1,800 gallons per minute. There appeared to be no other British

[4] *Ibid.*, p.140.
[5] Captain Eyre M. Shaw, C.B., *Fire Protection*, pp.62-95.
[6] 'Phoenix', *The Decay of London's Fire Brigade*, 1902, p.50.
[7] *Ibid.*, p.7.

brigade that used a pump with as limited a capacity as those in London. Wells may have still been experiencing problems with the water supply, but if so, he did not say so. Instead he complacently defended his policy, stating, 'A 450-gallon engine is as much as I want'.[8]

It was not only the pumps that concerned 'Phoenix': the escape ladders had proved too short to reach all those trapped at the Queen Victoria Street fire while there were longer alternatives available and in use on the Continent; hook ladders to augment escape ladders were not suitable for London, Wells told the coroner; and chemical engines which used carbonic gas to force water through the fire hoses and were got to work very quickly by the brigades on the Continent, had also been rejected for use in London.[9]

Perhaps the most serious criticism concerned deaths in fire. While 'the polish of the men's brass helmets has improved', claimed 'Phoenix', 'the death rate from fire has increased'.[10] In the four years 1892-5 deaths from fire in London were 319, while in the four years 1898-1901 the figure was 388, an increase of more than one fifth.[11] In the year after Shaw resigned, 1892, there were sixty-four deaths in fire in London, and in the year before the Queen Victoria Street fire, 1901, there had been ninety-seven fire deaths; an increase of over a third in less than ten years.[12] 'Phoenix' largely exempted the members of the Council from criticism, but pointed out that a plan for expansion in the brigade had been rejected in 1894. The Council had to rely on their chief fire officers; previous chief officers had developed the brigade, whereas Wells had resisted innovation, closed the small sub-stations and replaced the hand escapes with horse-drawn ones; it was this that had sent the death rate up, 'out of all proportion to the population . . .'[13] What this meant in comparison with other major British cities was shown in dramatic fashion by a chart that projected fire deaths on the scale experienced in London with the actual fatalities.[14]

| | *Actual Number of Deaths from Fire in 1901* | *London in Proportion would have had* |
|---|---|---|
| *London* | 97 | |
| Belfast | 1 | 14 |
| Glasgow | 4 | 24 |
| Edinburgh | 2 | 28 |
| Aberdeen | 1 | 31 |
| Birmingham | 6 | 53 |
| Bristol | 4 | 64 |

[8] *Ibid.*, p.26.
[9] *Ibid.*, p.16.
[10] *Ibid.*, p.19
[11] *Ibid.*, p.28.
[12] *Ibid.*, p.28.
[13] *Ibid.*, p.50.
[14] *Ibid.*, p.29.

'Phoenix' tried to show how the brigade had become less efficient by comparing fatalities under Wells with those of his predecessors, but in doing so the case against Wells was overstated. If the calculation of fire deaths had been based upon 1893, when eighty-two lives had been lost, rather than 1892, when the figure was sixty-four, then the rate of increase would have been only half that portrayed by 'Phoenix'.

### *Sailors Only: Officers and Men*

The problems highlighted by the Queen Victoria Street fire were reinforced by the brigade's recruitment policies under the LCC. The recruitment of former sailors as firemen was a well-established tradition by the time the LCC took over. Braidwood had introduced the practice and a naval background became a prerequisite for employment as a fireman under the MBW. He argued that the life at sea was the best possible background for the fire service.

Shaw continued with this policy, arguing:

> The sailor has learnt discipline, and is so strong and handy at climbing and other quick work, that he can be made available for the general work within two or three months, and I defy anyone to do that with any other class of men.[15]

Charles Booth found that some men only went to sea in order to qualify to join the brigade.[16]

The famous Captain Shaw had had an army background, followed by command of the police and fire service in Belfast. He had been recruited by the London insurance companies to take charge of the brigade on Braidwood's death. The MBW, having inherited the autocratic Shaw with the brigade, allowed him to run it practically as a private fiefdom, but when the less complacent LCC took over in 1889 differences rapidly came to a head and Shaw resigned suddenly in June 1891.

Shaw's successor, Captain Simonds, was an engineer with experience of fire-fighting in London. Following allegations of minor corruption and a sense that discipline in the brigade had deteriorated, Simonds was dismissed in 1895. With the object of restoring disciplinary standards, the LCC appointed as chief officer Commander Wells, a career naval officer. When Wells resigned in 1903 following the criticism of the brigade's performance at Queen Victoria Street, he was replaced as Chief Fire Officer by another naval officer and gentleman, Captain Hamilton. When Hamilton departed five years later, *The Fireman* had this to say: 'He knew nothing about fire-fighting when he took over the command of the London Fire Brigade and that knowledge, in this respect, had not greatly

[15] PP 1867, X, 471, Select Committee on Fire Protection, p.214.

[16] London School of Economics, Booth Manuscripts, B147, p.2.

increased when he left'.[17]

Under Wells's leadership, direct entry from the naval service became a near-exclusive route into the brigade, for officers and men alike. This policy was by no means universally popular. In 1899 *The Municipal Journal and London* reported, 'Some astonishment has been expressed that an outsider and an ex-naval officer, with no experience of fire brigade work, has been appointed third officer of the London Fire Brigade'.[18] Later in the same year, a report from the Fire Brigade Committee was accepted agreeing that the seamen-only rule was undesirable. John Burns, a leading Progressive member, favoured

> open competition in the interests of the efficiency of the Brigade. Londoners of whatever calling should have an equal chance with any others provided they were fit for the work. He pointed out that restricting employment to seamen led to favouritism. Bricklayers, scaffolders, and others engaged in the building trade had special qualifications on account of their knowledge of the internal arrangements of buildings. He did not plead, however, for preference for any trade, but argued that a ring fence should not be created in London labour by the exclusive employment of seamen.[19]

Despite fierce opposition from the Chief Fire Officer, the 'sailors only' rule was abandoned, but it proved to be a hollow victory. The *Notebook on the London Fire Brigade* shows that in 1905 only ninety-four men out of the establishment of 1,351 did not have a seafaring background.[20] While that may have been too soon after the policy change to reflect the intended wider recruiting base, in 1925 an official publication still claimed that, 'Most of the Brigade's recruits are seamen either from the Royal Navy or the Merchant Service'.[21] And when John Horner joined the brigade in 1934 he and his fellow recruits mirrored those employed by Braidwood a century before:

> My drill class, I remember it well, they had got their full naval service in. You know, the recruiting age of the London Fire Brigade was arranged . . . the maximum age of recruitment was thirty-one, so that a man could do boy service in the navy and be thirty-one when he came out of the navy with his full time, and join the London Fire Brigade.[22]

The formal abolition of the 'sailors only' rule applied to senior officers as well. Major C.C.B. Morris, who became chief officer in 1933, was appointed an assistant divisional officer in the brigade in 1908, having previously served on the Great Eastern Railway as engineer in charge of

[17] Holloway, *op. cit.*, p.158.
[18] *The Municipal Journal and London*, 9 February 1899.
[19] *Ibid.*, 14 July 1899.
[20] *Notebook on the London Fire Brigade*, 1905.
[21] *The London Fire Brigade*, 1925, p.7.
[22] John Horner, taped interview, 8 July 1975.

the motor department.[23] Morris's expertise with motors would have made him a particularly valuable recruit at a time when the brigade was starting to change over to petrol-driven fire engines and no doubt was a factor in his elevation to second in command of the brigade in a little over ten years. But Morris was the exception rather than the rule, and a naval career remained the most common background for senior officers. Commander Aylmer Firebrace was more typical. He had applied for the post of Chief Fire Officer in 1919 while still second in command at the Royal Navy Gunnery School. Although unsuccessful, he was nevertheless appointed as a senior officer and was sent to Fire Brigade Headquarters in Southwark to do drills with the recruit firemen. He followed Morris as chief officer in 1938.[24]

Although after the early 1900s it could not be claimed that the entire workforce were ex-sailors, the full-blown ethos of navy life long continued to dominate the brigade. For the senior officers there were batmen and chauffeurs; for the men, wooden sea chests in which to keep their uniforms, round sailor-style hats, seamen's jumpers and mess clubs to organize their meals. Horner remembers being sent as a new recruit – the junior buck – to wash the floors at the house of one of the senior officers, Mr Kerr, at the back of the Southwark Headquarters. He told his station officer, 'I think there's a mistake sir . . . the cook wants me to scrub the nursery, the kitchen . . .' 'That's right,' replied the station officer, 'junior buck, Thursday day duty, junior buck, Mr Kerr's house.' Every Thursday morning while Horner was at the Southwark Headquarters he had the same argument and never did scrub Mr Kerr's kitchen.[25]

One of the most damaging effects of maintaining a brigade like this was the hostility to change of any sort on the part of the members of the brigade, and worse still, an organization that could not accommodate change. The most senior managers, the principal officers, never learnt anything about the fire service until they were given significant responsibilities within it; whether they were ever more than figureheads seems doubtful. The comment about Captain Hamilton's abilities above suggests not. Cyril Demarne, a fireman in the West Ham brigade before the Second World War and its Chief Fire Officer after the war, testified to the competence of the principal officers as administrators and organizers, but on the subject of fire-fighting added: 'No principal officer . . . was ever allowed to poke his nose in at a fire. He could make general suggestions but if he dared say . . . put a pump over there, they would tell him in fireman's language where he could go!'[26] This account is in marked contrast to the well-ordered official version given by Major Morris:

23 *London Town*, 1933, p.181.
24 Commander Sir Aylmer Firebrace, *Fire Service Memories*, 1949, p.16.
25 John Horner, interview.
26 Cyril Demarne, taped interview, 24 May 1981.

As the Principal Officers arrive they first go to the Superintendent and obtain from him the details, afterwards taking up their positions on different sides of the fire. If they want immediate assistance of any kind – say, further branches – the message goes to the Superintendent, who invariably has some appliances and men 'up his sleeve'... Owing to a complete de-centralization of orders the Senior Officer in charge is free to keep an eye on the general situation, only sending a message to the Superintendent if he requires a major alteration, e.g. a further reserve of appliances.[27]

### *Fire Service Trade Unionism*

From its inception the LCC was resistant to demands for trade union representation. This policy was applied rigorously in the most conservative of the Council's departments, the fire brigade. Its blue collar workers, including firemen, were at first merely allowed to petition for improvements in conditions. In the early years, as services expanded, the LCC found itself 'fielding petitions from an enormous and disparate range of manual workers, including road sweepers, sewerage workers, hospital porters, laundrymen, dustmen, gardeners, caretakers in cemeteries, lunatic asylums, children's homes, etc'.[28] Petitioning was by no means always successful and was risky to organize, with increments in pay or promotion under threat for anyone who presented a petition at the wrong time or too forcefully. Shaw had rejected a petition on pay that pilots on the fire floats put forward late in 1889, soon after the London dockworkers had won the 'dockers' tanner' and recognition for their union, because he thought the men were trying to capitalize on the dockers' success. He said that if the men's application was granted, 'the natural inference would be that the County Council was intimidated and had yielded in order to prevent a strike'.[29] The men apologized and withdrew the petition. An extract from a letter to the Progressive weekly, *The Municipal Journal and London*, shows how weak the men were when putting forward such petitions, something they did more than once and without success, in the 1890s:

After several attempts within the past few years to bring our grievances before the Fire Brigade Committee we have failed . . . I helped bring about our petition to the Council a little more than two years ago. Some of us believe that that petition was never seen by the Fire Brigade Committee. But we will now take the opportunity to ask the members of the Fire Brigade Committee to kindly listen to our earnest appeal, to consider our long, continuous and monotonous hours of duty. There is no man in the brigade believes that it is

[27] Major C.C.B. Morris, *Fire*, 1939, p.53.
[28] Ellen Leopold, *In the Service of London*, 1985, p.45.
[29] GLRO, FB/STA/1/1.

our chief's wish that we should work these long hours, as we have proved him to be a gentleman and an efficient officer in the work he has charge of.[30]

The letter, which was unsigned, pointed out how Commander Wells, the chief officer who had succeeded Captain Simonds in 1896, had already 'much reduced the petty tyranny that [they] were subjected to by . . . officers'. It was most unusual for the firemen to make such an appeal public in this way and suggests a strong feeling of frustration among them, but the writer was circumspect enough to make flattering remarks about Wells throughout the letter.

The question of the hours firemen worked had been a contentious one since the MBW's time. It was another problem which stemmed from the financial straitjacket within which the brigade had to be run: more men would have meant more money. Shaw explained in 1876 that the men worked a system of continuous duty and succinctly described what that meant. 'Our men are like sailors on board a ship; they are either at work or ready for work . . . [they] have no time at all off duty, except by permission'.[31] A fireman from Holloway reported: 'As regards excessive duties, I have to state that in one case I have done 74 hours, and even more, without having my boots off my feet . . .'[32] Another at Blackheath could remember working ninety-two successive hours. This was a time when workers in industry were working between fifty-four and fifty-six and a half hours a week and those in regular work had their ten-hour day reduced to one of nine hours.[33] It was a situation that continued under the LCC. Harry Price, a coachman at the Kings Road fire station for a few years before the First World War, remembered that the continuous duty was one of the reasons he left the brigade and went on the buses. 'The reason why I didn't stay that length of time was that you only got one day off in fifteen'.[34] In between the days off there was an informal procedure whereby the men could 'book gone' for fifty-nine minutes, though they could only do that if there was someone to cover for them.

Firemen did not benefit when the LCC adopted a fair wages resolution in 1889. This mainly assisted those working on building contracts for the Council. Nor at that time had the men broken sufficiently from their own traditions of service to consider joining the new general unions formed during the trade boom of 1889-91, when trade union membership more than doubled.

The continuing uncertainty associated with petitioning and indifferent chances of success, together with the oppressive conditions of service and

[30] *The Municipal Journal and London*, 24 February 1899.
[31] PP 1876, XI, 371, Select Committee on the Metropolitan Fire Brigade, p.24.
[32] *Ibid.*, p.48.
[33] M.A. Bienefeld, *Working Hours in British Industry*, 1972, p.106.
[34] Harry Price, taped interview, 27 November 1976.

low living standards that the firemen and their families had to endure, was encouragement enough for them to start to join trade unions during the next general growth in trade union membership, from 1905 onwards. Firemen joined general unions like the Municipal Employees Association (MEA), the Workers Union or the Amalgamated Society of Gas, Municipal and General Workers. A dispute among the leaders of the MEA in 1907 led to the London firemen's branch of the MEA transferring *en masse* into the National Union of Corporation Workers. Nearly half the London firemen, 490 in all out of a total strength of 1,085 for admissible ranks, were members of the Corporation Workers. This was a high percentage considering the hostility of both councillors and officers to trades unionism within the brigade. It is less surprising to find this opposition among the senior officers of the brigade who had been brought up on naval discipline, than among the councillors, since trade unions were recognized for other of the Council's manual workers. By contrast, there was a strong similarity in the attitude the Council adopted to both firemen and the more senior white-collar staff. And eventually similar solutions were imposed on both groups.

The LCC's Fire Brigade Committee was undoubtedly reacting to the growth of trade unionism among firemen when, in 1906, it laid down that firemen wanting to raise anything with the Council or Fire Brigade Committee should do so through the chief officer. 'Any infraction of this rule will be held to be a serious breach of discipline involving dismissal'.[35] This attempt to reinforce the system of petitioning and opposition to trade unions in London was markedly different to attitudes in brigades elsewhere before the First World War. In the Manchester brigade, for instance, the Chief Fire Officer had told the union:

> Any man desirous of joining the MEA is at liberty to do so and the delegate has permission to visit the station and address the men out of working hours.[36]

### *Stopping the Union*

While warning all fire brigade recruits in 1913 that 'any connection with any outside trade union cannot in any circumstances be allowed',[37] the Council attempted to head off the enthusiasm for trade union membership among firemen by offering to set up a Staff Committee to take up issues on the men's behalf. Although the committee would have been elected by ballot of the men, it would have been paid for by the LCC and not been the independent trade union that the men wanted. Not surprisingly they

[35] GLRO, CL/FB/1/153, Report by Chief Fire Officer to LCC Fire Brigade Committee, 26 November 1913.

[36] National Museum of Labour History, NUPE records.

[37] GLRO, CL/FB/1/153.

rejected the plan.

During the First World War the Council maintained its hostility to the firemen's trade union. This was out of step with events outside the fire service where, because of the demands on the munitions industry and the effect these had on other trades, employers were obliged to extend recognition of trade unions to areas in which the unions had often not even existed before the war. When the Corporation Workers formed a special firemen's branch to cater for a growing membership early in 1914, 'Out of 1,300 firemen in London, 1,100 were members of the Union'.[38] Their demand for recognition was made more urgent during the war by the sharp increases in prices. Wages generally failed to keep up with price increases in the period, but firemen fell further behind than most. Unskilled and semi-skilled workers benefited most from the wartime trade union boom; relative to these workers, firemen slipped behind in the pay league. Before the war firemen's pay had been midway between that of labourers and mechanics but by April 1918 the Chief Fire Officer, Lieutenant Commander Sladen, reported that firemen were 'considerably below both grades of workers'. He went on to illustrate how firemen's pay had fallen behind:

> women tramway conductors after one year in the Council's service are actually higher at 54s 3d a week including war wage, the minimum wage of a fireman being 45s including war wage.[39]

Sladen had always been more alive to the difficulties that the strong trade union membership among firemen posed for the Council. He told his colleague, the Chief Constable:

> There are indications that unless some more definite understanding as to the practice of the Council [is given] some serious disciplinary difficulties will arise.[40]

He thought that the war wage should be reconsidered every six months.

A strike threat by the London firemen hard on the heels of the policemen's strike in September 1918, just as the war was ending, led to an award by Lord Askwith, the Government's Chief Industrial Conciliator, which conceded recognition to a firemen's trade union with a non-fireman as 'Spokesman'. It was not however to be any union of the men's choosing, but an entirely separate trade union for London firemen only, completely isolated from the general council workers' unions with which they had previously been involved. This arrangement was out of step with developments among other LCC manual workers at this time. From the time that a Fair Wages Resolution was adopted in 1889 there had been

[38] *West London Observer*, 26 June 1914.
[39] GLRO, FB/STA/1/6, 29 April 1918.
[40] GLRO, FB/STA/1/6, 8 November 1917.

implicit acceptance of the building trades unions by the Council. The national unions representing the permanent manual grades won acceptance when, as a result of the Whitley Committee's recommendations in the summer of 1918, National Joint Industrial Councils were set up to cover local authority workers in non-trading services.[41] The fire brigades were not among these services and the firemen accepted the restrictions imposed by the Askwith award, forming their own Representative Body and breaking away from the Corporation Workers in the process. Even this settlement went too far for the Chief Officer, Lieutenant Commander Sladen, who resigned soon afterwards. The LCC insisted upon this arrangement right up until the end of the Second World War, even though the Representative Body joined forces with a more broadly based Firemen's Trade Union (later to become the Fire Brigades Union) in the early 1920s.

The new machinery for London firemen's negotiations most closely resembled that accepted by the Council's white collar staff. The relationship between their Staff Association and NALGO had been broken when the Council had decided in 1915 to 'exclude persons who were not themselves members of the staff from representing administrative staff . . . in negotiations with the Council'.[42]

The Council would only recognize the firemen's Representative Body, not their union, and rejected all efforts to get them to move away from the Askwith Award. Within three years of the award an application by Station Officers to be allowed to be part of the Representative Body, was rejected by the Council, even though it was claimed that sixty-two of the seventy-nine station officers were already members of the FTU.[43] A few years later, in 1930, the sub-officers asked to be allowed to break away from the Representative Body and form their own Staff Committee. The Council also rejected this request, insisting upon close adherence to the Askwith Award.

John Horner, the Fire Brigades Union's General Secretary from 1939 to 1964 and an ex-London fireman, had the dual role of 'Spokesman' as well, and remembers how pedantic the LCC were about the separation of the two organizations:

> I had to be very careful how I addressed myself to the London County Council. I had to be known and speak as the Spokesman of the Representative Body and not as the Union Secretary. And if I spoke as the Union Secretary I was called to order . . . If I wrote by mischance on union notepaper, it would be sent back and wouldn't be accepted.[44]

[41] Bernard Dix and Stephen Williams, *Serving the Public – Building the Union*, 1987, p.180.

[42] Susan Pennybacker, *The 'Labour Question' and the LCC , 1889-1919*, Ph.D. Thesis, Cambridge University, 1984, p.289.

[43] GLRO, CL/FB/1/153, Report by Chief Fire Officer to LCC Fire Brigade Committee, 1 December 1921.

[44] John Horner, interview.

### *Tied Housing and the Service Tradition*

The long hours that the men worked before the First World War mirrored what they had been used to while at sea; they were always on call, always ready to serve the master. This control extended beyond the fireman. In order to work virtually continuous duty the men had to live over or around the station in tied housing with the result that the firemen's wives and families were also conditioned by the regime: constant availability and respectability were watch-words for the whole family. A man could never claim any real independence if he was always at his master's beck and call, and even less so if the same pressures were also felt by his wife and children. The standard of accommodation varied between stations as well as between ranks: in 1889 a superintendent was allowed four rooms rent free; an engineer three rooms rent free; both first and second class married firemen paid two shillings and sixpence a week for two rooms; while a fireman in single-men's quarters paid a rental of one shilling a week.[45]

Jim Bradley, the leader of the London men's trade union, never served in the brigade but had been born and brought up on a fire station and had first-hand experience of its effect on family life. In 1920 he told a Parliamentary Committee into fire service pay and hours that the men did not want to live around the fire stations:

> all the time they are there they are under discipline, and the wives are under discipline. If you take a woman into a London fire station . . . it is practically condemning her to penal servitude from the time she enters the station until she leaves . . . The man cannot hold the baby while the wife goes out and does a bit of shopping because he never knows when the bells are going down, or he may be called to the other end of the district perhaps to put in a fire-alarm glass . . . She can never go out with her husband except at the particular time he is on leave. A woman's life in the fire brigade is not altogether honey.[46]

The brigade's officers used their power to allocate housing as a disciplinary measure, moving anyone giving problems to less desirable quarters. Sladen, the former chief officer, told the 1920 Committee, 'If there were discordant elements in the stations, it was generally easy, with the help of judicious removals, to dissipate trouble'.[47] Bradley had told the Committee of a man moved from the Kingsland Road station to one in Millwall. 'When he got there he had to sell half his home because he had not got room to put his furniture in'.[48]

[45] *Notebook on the London Fire Brigade*, 1908, p.18.

[46] PP 1920 (Cmd.876), XXI, 505, Minutes of Evidence taken before the Committee on the Hours, Pay and Conditions of Service of Firemen in Professional Fire Brigades in Great Britain (Middlebrook Committee), QQ. 176 & 188.

[47] *Ibid.*, Q.324.

[48] *Ibid.*, Q.206.

From these examples it can be seen why it was that one of the most important early victories that the men won through their newly recognized trade union in 1920 was a cut in hours to seventy-two a week. The manpower was split into two platoons and one platoon was off-duty while the other was working. The Council, which was having difficulty providing sufficient suitable accommodation, rescinded the requirement for firemen to live on fire station premises, and a weekly rent allowance of 8s 6d was introduced for men who had completed their probationary year. While it was probably viewed by some as a mixed blessing because of the shortage of housing, tied housing was phased out for the lower ranks. In a major step forward the employer's influence over the men and their families for twenty-four hours a day was broken.

### *Relations with Labour*

Despite the firemen's conservative background, the necessity for political activity had always been accepted within their trade union organization. The most prominent of their early leaders, Jim Bradley, had been a member of the Social Democratic Federation and was a founder member of the Bethnal Green Labour Party. Throughout his years of trade union activity in the MEA, as Secretary of the firemen's branch of the Corporation Workers and Spokesman of the Representative Body, he maintained left-wing views. In 1922, soon after the merger with the FTU, a political fund was set up and the union affiliated to the Labour Party; the union soon began to sponsor Labour candidates in Council elections.

It is not without significance then, that the period John Horner refers to above was that of the Labour-controlled LCC under Herbert Morrison and his successors. Morrison's relations with the union were as bad as those of any of his predecessors and dated from his early years as Secretary of the London Labour Party in the 1920s, when he was leading the battle within the Labour Party against communist activity inside it. The Communist Party wanted to affiliate to the Labour Party in the way that some socialist societies were allowed. Morrison opposed this and membership of both parties by individuals. He also blamed the Communists and their allies for Labour's election defeats. After the 1925 LCC election, for instance, he wrote in the London Labour Party's newspaper, *London News*, of the tragedy that:

> the almost solidly working class division of South West Bethnal Green should remain a lonely spot in the 'all red' East-end of London, a constituency still retained by the anti-Labour forces . . . so long as its development is restricted by the little Communist group which appears to be left in control of things, it is probable that the anti-Labour forces will continue to rejoice . . .[49]

[49] *London News*, April 1925.

After the 1925 Labour Party Conference had decided there should be no CP affiliation, joint CP/LP candidates or individual CP members of the Party, the Communists started to run their own candidates in Council elections and also to support Labour candidates who had been nominated by local Labour Parties which had been disaffiliated over this issue. The Communist Party also set up the National Left Wing Movement to work within the Labour Party and get the proscriptions reversed. Jim Bradley, the London firemen's Spokesman and Secretary of the Firemen's Trade Union, became a member of the Left Wing Movement's Advisory Council.

Along with Minnie Birch, a Communist Party activist and member of the Workers' Union, Bradley stood in Bethnal Green as one of the unofficial candidates in the LCC elections of 1928. At first the FTU gave him its backing, but that was withdrawn after a meeting with Morrison. Bradley only polled 1,238 votes, not enough to have been accused by Morrison of having let in the Liberals. There was a fierce row after the election because Labour Party posters had been defaced by Bradley's supporters. The official candidates had been members of the Transport and General Workers Union and Bradley was obliged to send a humble apology to Ernest Bevin, the General Secretary. At the FTU Conference later that year the President assured delegates that 'Associations with all bodies not recognized by the National Labour Party and Trades Union Congress have now definitely ceased . . .'[50]

When Labour finally won control of the LCC in 1934, the firemen expected to be able to get some reduction in their seventy-two hour working week; they wanted a forty-eight hour week. However, Labour's plan for the London Fire Brigade was constructed on Morrisonian, cost-effective lines with very little scope for improvements in firemen's conditions of service. A large fire at Rum Quay in the West India Docks in April 1933 had shown up the lack of pumping appliances; sixty of the brigade's sixty-nine pumps had been in use, leaving the rest of London with inadequate fire cover. It was another area in which London lagged behind other brigades, which had dual-purpose appliances that both transported an escape ladder and had a pumping capacity. Single-purpose appliances were a hang-over from the days of horse-drawn fire engines. Motor vehicles made possible a combined function; the West Ham brigade for instance, had used these sort of appliances, pump escapes as they were called, since at least the early 1920s. The main feature of Labour's plan provided for the purchase of a number of ready-made pump escapes and the conversion of a number of existing escape vans to pump escapes. Although there was a tiny increase in the manpower establishment, the whole scheme, it was claimed, gave a net

[50] Fireman's Trade Union, *Ninth Annual Report*, 1927, p.6.

saving of £50,000 a year.[51]

The London Trades Council backed the firemen, declaring, 'The present seventy-two hours per week worked by these employees is, in the opinion of the Council, excessive, and contrary to established trade union practice'. This stung Morrison into making a lengthy reply in Labour's *London News*.[52] He claimed that no fire brigade in the country worked less than seventy-two hours a week and many still worked a continuous duty system. The LCC, he said, was simply abiding by earlier awards of the Industrial Court against reductions in hours. Yet the LCC Labour Group had supported the men's claim for the forty-eight hour week when they had taken the Municipal Reform-controlled LCC to the Industrial Court in 1932 and 1933. Morrison rejected the Trades Council's claim that there was any trade union principle involved. He alleged that the men spent much of the night duty resting on trestles, not actually working, and pointed to improvements in conditions that the fireman had already had, with restoration of half of certain pay cuts caused by the financial crisis of 1931 and increased rent allowances. The £200,000 which the reduction in hours would cost could not be justified, he said.

Percy Kingdom, Bradley's succesor as 'Spokesman', wrote to the *London News* in reply to some of these points. While no brigade in the country worked the forty-eight hour week, he said, many of the smaller brigades looked to London to set the pace when it came to conditions; if it was not conceded in London, it would not be conceded anywhere. Kingdom claimed that Morrison had dealt with the hours question in the same way that his predecessors in the Municipal Reform Party had done; they too had claimed it would cost too much and it was not the right time for such a concession. As for the rent allowance increase, the union had claimed four shillings a week and been given one shilling and sixpence, while the allowances for new entrants had been cut by two shillings and sixpence. At least the Moderates had consulted the Representative Body over new rates for recruits. Finally, Kingdom voiced the unease that many trade union activists must have felt over Morrison's attitudes. Trade unionists were bewildered, he said:

> at the lengths to which Mr. Morrison has gone in his endeavour to justify his position and the views he puts forward to counteract a claim that is fully in accord with the spirit and policy of the Trade Union and Labour Movement. His very precise though narrow presentation of the fact as regards firemen's hours of duty has caused keen resentment among firemen both in London and elsewhere, and cannot surely have been of any moral or material value to the Movement of which he is a member.[53]

[51] *London News*, April 1935.
[52] *Ibid.*, March 1935.
[53] *Ibid.*, June 1935.

Firemen made no real progress on the hours question until the eve of the Second World War, when Morrison promised to implement a sixty-hour week on 1 January 1940. But that agreement was never introduced, because with the onset of the war the men went on to continuous duty. When the sixty-hour week finally did come in, it was in 1946 as part of a national package of pay and conditions.

The Council did not fully recognize the Fire Brigades Union until 1945, and then only because it had established itself as a major force within the National Fire Service in the course of the war and any attempt by the LCC to maintain the pre-war farce of partial recognition would have been laughable. When the Attlee Government denationalized the service in 1947 national bargaining machinery was set up to deal with pay and conditions, while the Home Office monitored the operational aspects of the service through a series of technical committees. The Fire Brigades Union was the most prominent body representing firemen on all these new institutions. Wide-ranging changes that had taken place within the fire service during the war militated against the parochialism of separate fire brigades operating in isolation from each other, whether it was for conditions of service or working practices. There was certainly no place in this post-war world for a special union for London firemen alone.

### *Conclusion*

This essay has been based on the premise that for the first fifty years the LCC's fire brigade failed to develop and play a progressive role in either the capital or the British fire service as a whole.

These failures were rooted in the LCC's inability and in some cases, unwillingness, to break with the tradition of the fire service inherited from the much ridiculed Metropolitan Board of Works. On the question of recruitment we have seen how the Council compounded the already restrictive MBW policy of employing only former sailors, by extending the practice to senior officers.

It is in the nature of emergency services for major incidents to reveal shortcomings. However, the disturbing consistency of the brigade's technical backwardness, as shown in the fires at Queen Victoria Street fire in 1902 and thirty years later at Rum Quay, suggest there were more than occasional lapses. The Council had to rely on its senior fire officers for technical advice about the brigade, but the Council's policy of employing officers who had only the most limited knowledge of firefighting was never likely to lead to sound technical innovation. The policy led instead to undue emphasis by chief officers on the problems of running a disciplined service and an almost fantasy world of the fire station as a ship on land.

Neither the Council nor its senior fire officers were able to prevent the establishment within the brigade of a firemen's trade union. However, they did manage to inhibit the radicalising potential of even this by insisting on a 'London only' solution to the dispute; in so doing they significantly delayed the development of fire service trade unionism in the rest of the country.

If there was a broad continuity over the fifty years in the way the chief fire officers ran the brigade, that is less surprising than the fact that the Council was run by all shades of political party over the period. Socialists and trade unionists expected much from the Labour Council of 1934. But while Morrison was prepared to support plans for improvements in machines and equipment, he proved no different to his predecessors on the subjects of trade union recognition and conditions of service.

Before the Second World War the London Fire Brigade was pre-eminent among brigades in the British fire service. A close inspection suggests that this position relied more on its size and prestige as the guardian of the capital than it did on its efficiency and progressive traditions.

# *Chapter 10*

## *The LCC Hospital Service*

John Sheldrake

On 27 March 1929, Neville Chamberlain's Local Government Bill received the Royal Assent and signalled the break up of the Poor Law. The new Act had 'a long and varied ancestry'.[1] Its provisions went back to the majority report of the Royal Commission on the Poor Law of 1909 and the report of the sub-committee on local government prepared under the chairmanship of Sir Donald Maclean in 1918. Chamberlain's legislation abolished the Boards of Guardians and transferred their responsibilities to the councils of the counties and county boroughs from 1 April 1930.[2] In terms of the treatment of the sick, this change meant that what had been 'previously regarded as a matter for charitable institutions (or) relieving the destitute poor was now seen as one of the functions of a public health authority'.[3]

Under the 1929 Act each local authority was free to make its own arrangements concerning the proportion of its hospital accommodation retained for Poor Law purposes and the proportion operated as part of its general public health services.[4] During April 1929 the Ministry of Health issued circulars to the local authorities requesting the formulation of administrative schemes for the assumption of Poor Law functions.[5] Of 145 schemes, two thirds had received ministerial approval by the end of October 1929 and the remainder by January 1930.[6]

Although the Ministry of Health exhorted the local authorities to make the greatest possible use of their new health powers, the initial results were disappointing. The counties and county boroughs were reluctant to assume new obligations 'in the face of a world financial crisis and mounting unemployment'.[7] Their reluctance persisted: only in the three years before the outbreak of the Second World War did English local

[1] C. Mowat, *Britain Between the Wars, 1918-1940*, 1983, p.340.
[2] Cmnd. 3667, *Eleventh Annual Report of the Ministry of Health*, 1929-30, p.179.
[3] G. Gibbon and R. Bell, *History of the London County Council, 1889-1939*, 1939, p.320.
[4] B. Abel-Smith, *The Hospitals, 1800-1948*, 1964, p.368.
[5] B. Gilbert, *British Social Policy, 1914-1939*, 1970, p.232.
[6] Cmnd. 3667 (see n. 2).
[7] Gilbert, *op. cit.*, p.233.

authorities provide more hospital accommodation under their public health powers than under their Poor Law powers. Even as late as 1945 the Ministry of Health was complaining that in many areas 'little or nothing had been done to develop municipal hospital services'.[8]

The London County Council was by far the most active local authority. By 1939 it provided almost three-fifths of the total English municipal general hospital accommodation. But though the LCC hospital service has been described as 'probably the finest municipal hospital service in the world',[9] its achievements were more in the realm of reorganization, rationalization and administration than in a massive programme of new hospital building. Although some £3 million were spent on the improvement of hospitals between 1930 and 1939, only one new hospital was planned. Indeed, owing to rationalization, by 1939 the number of available beds in London's municipal hospitals had declined rather than grown since the LCC took over the service.

### *Reorganization in London*

In 1930, London already possessed the basis of a municipal hospital service. Under the Metropolitan Poor Act of 1867, a Metropolitan Common Poor Fund had been established to pool the resources of the London poor law unions and parishes. The Metropolitan Asylums Board (MAB) had been set up to build and maintain isolation hospitals for infectious cases, infirmaries for non-infectious cases, asylums for the mentally ill and dispensaries for patients who did not require in-treatment.[10] The hospitals of the MAB were, in the main, special hospitals for the treatment of infectious diseases and tuberculosis. They also included some children's institutions. The fact that the MAB's hospitals were well equipped and organized with reference to London as a whole, substantially eased the LCC's task in establishing a co-ordinated hospital service.[11] As Gibbon and Bell observe 'the excellence of the organization of these hospitals and high standard of planning and equipment were of great advantage to the Council'.[12]

When the LCC assumed responsibility for the functions of the twenty-five Metropolitan Boards of Guardians and the MAB, a huge expansion took place in the Council's public health work. The LCC's responsibilities became 'onerous and to a considerable extent dissimilar from the duties

[8] A. Gray and A. Topping, *Hospital Survey: The Hospital Services of London and the Surrounding Area*, 1945, p.6.

[9] W. Jackson, *Achievement: A Short History of the London County Council*, 1965, p.25.

[10] M. Bruce, *The Coming of the Welfare State*, 1961, p.102.

[11] Cmnd. 4372, *Fourteenth Annual Report of the Ministry of Health*, 1932-3, p.34.

[12] *Ibid.*, p.337.

hitherto discharged'.[13] These duties had been limited to the operation of the school medical service and schemes for dealing with mental health, tuberculosis and venereal disease. In order to meet its increased responsibilities the Council reconstituted its Public Health Committee and redesignated it as the Central Public Health Committee. Section 14 of the 1929 Act enabled the Council to co-opt individuals to this committee, thereby gaining experienced former members of the London Boards of Guardians and the MAB. During the debate on the Local Government Bill in the House of Commons, the Labour Party had opposed such co-options on the basis that they would make it 'possible for reactionary Guardians to continue to work in Poor Law administration'.[14] Ironically, Dr. Somerville Hastings (perhaps the best informed LCC Labour member on matters of public health and for many years Chairman of the Hospital and Medical Services Committee) made his initial appearance on the Central Public Health Committee as a result of co-option.

In the months prior to the transfer of the services, the Council's Public Health Department, under the forceful leadership of Sir Frederick Menzies, the Medical Officer of Health, was substantially enlarged and redesigned. From 1 October 1929, the Department was organized in three branches:[15]

(i) General Hospital, including district medical work, and concerned largely with the institutions transferred from the Poor Law Guardians;
(ii) Special Hospital, including control of acute infectious diseases and concerned largely with the work previously discharged by the MAB;
(iii) General Public Health, including housing and the school medical service.

The powers of the Public Health Committee were transferred to the Central Public Health Committee on 1 April 1930.[16] On the transfer of functions, the poor law institutions were divided into two groups. The administration of those used primarily for the sick was entrusted to the Central Public Health Committee, whilst the management of the remaining institutions passed to the Public Assistance Committee. The services taken over in 1930 included seventy-six hospitals and institutions containing amost 42,000 beds (see Table 9) and a staff of 20,000 together with the ambulance services of the Boards of Guardians and the MAB. The Council was confronted with the task of assimilating these services and achieving their reconstruction, as far as possible, as public health services.

[13] LCC Annual Report, 1929, vol. I.
[14] Abel-Smith, *op. cit.*, p.362.
[15] LCC Annual Report, 1929, vol. III.
[16] The Central Public Health Committee became the Hospital and Medical Services Committee in March 1934.

### *Relations with the Voluntary Hospitals*

The Ministry of Health's desire was that 'an effective municipal hospital service for London' might 'take its proper place beside the voluntary hospitals'.[17] London possessed a substantial number of voluntary hospitals and these were 'the main repositories of medical aid in London'.[18] In 1932 these voluntary hospitals contained a total of 14,000 beds.[19] Section 13 of the 1929 Act required the local authorities to consult representative bodies of both the voluntary hospitals and their medical and surgical staff as to the 'hospital accommodation to be provided and . . . the purpose for which it would be used'.[20] Early in 1930, the LCC approved a scheme of voluntary hospital representation submitted by a joint committee representing the King Edward's Hospital Fund for London, the Conference of Teaching Hospitals and the London Regional Committee of the British Hospitals Association. The scheme established a committee of forty representatives, the London Voluntary Hospital Committee, which met the Council's representative for the first time on 30 May 1930. Relations between the two sides were sometimes strained and the degree of co-operation limited. However, an early result of the meetings with the London Voluntary Hospital Committee was the production of a joint survey of the muncipal and voluntary medical and surgical services in London to be used as a basis for future planning. A further initiative concerned medical teaching and it was in this sphere that the most important collaboration between the LCC and the voluntary hospitals developed. Early in 1933, a scheme was inaugurated for the association of the Council's general hospitals with the medical schools of the eighteen voluntary hospitals. This enabled the facilities of the general hospitals to be made available for the teaching of undergraduates.

In terms of advanced medical education, the Council collaborated with the Ministry of Health and the University of London in establishing the post-graduate medical school at Hammersmith Hospital which was opened by George V in May 1935. The Council made itself responsible for the necessary building and engineering works and also provided half of the £200,000 required to finance the development.[21]

[17] Cmnd. 4978, *Sixteenth Annual Report of the Ministry of Health*, 1934-5, p.58.
[18] Gibbon and Bell, *op. cit.*, p.11.
[19] Abel-Smith, *op. cit.* p.372.
[20] Cmnd. 3936, *Twelfth Annual Report of the Ministry of Health*, 1930-1, p.57.
[21] Cmnd. 4978 (see n. 17), p.65.

## *The Hospital Service*

Of the total hospital accommodation transferred to the Council, twenty-nine Poor Law hospitals containing 18,000 beds, and two colonies for sane epileptics containing 800 beds, were assigned to the General Hospitals section. Additionally, the same section became responsible for twelve public assistance institutions of a 'mixed' type (containing both sick and healthy inmates) with some 9,500 beds. All these hospitals and institutions, with the exception of one colony for sane epileptics transferred from the MAB, had previously been administered by the Boards of Guardians. Having been established at various dates by numerous authorities acting independently of each other for the service of their respective districts, they represented a complex problem in terms of developing a co-ordinated and uniform municipal hospital service. The hospitals varied in size from 220 to 1,500 beds and, whilst some were relatively modern, well-equipped buildings the majority were antiquated both in design and equipment.[22] Further, there was no uniformity of staffing or service conditions. The hospitals and institutions, taken together, provided for a wide variety of clients including those suffering from acute medical or surgical conditions, those suffering from diseases for which provision under other than Poor Law powers existed (such as tuberculosis and venereal disease), maternity patients, chronic sick and the infirm. In the institutions there were a significant proportion of individuals who were physically healthy but destitute.

In total the Council took responsibility for twenty-six public assistance 'mixed' institutions, as distinguished from hospitals. The twelve institutions mentioned above were placed under the direction of the Central Public Health Committee, whilst the remainder came under the auspices of the Public Assistance Committee. The 'mixed' institutions contained roughly 22,000 beds and a 'sick' population only slightly greater than the 'healthy'. The relocation of sick people from the public assistance institutions to public health establishments and vice versa proved difficult and a number of healthy people were still in public health institutions in 1939.[23]

The process of breaking up the Poor Law was advanced by the Council's use of their statutory powers under the 1929 Act to 'appropriate' as much as possible of the accommodation inherited from the Boards of Guardians for use as general hospitals.[24] All but one of the twenty-nine hospitals mentioned above had been 'appropriated' by 1 April 1931. The

[22] *Ibid.*, p.56.
[23] Gibbon and Bell, *op. cit.*, p.325.
[24] Cmnd. 3936 (see n. 20), p.50.

purpose of 'appropriation' was to give the hospital concerned the status of a hospital for the general service of the public, thereby enabling patients to be admitted simply as sick persons rather than as recipients of poor relief. The 'appropriations' were therefore a significant step in promoting the development of the former poor law hospital services into an integrated municipal hospital service.

For the first time, the former poor law hospitals and institutions providing for the sick had to be considered as a whole. Accordingly, during 1929 and 1930, all of these hospitals and institutions were surveyed and their needs reviewed. The age, design and equipment of the premises varied greatly. Particularly in winter months, some districts suffered a shortage of beds and there was a general shortage of convalescent accommodation. As a result of the survey, it became the Council's immediate policy to do five things:[25]

(i) Establish a satisfactory standard of accommodation and equipment. (This was a matter of urgency as some hospitals contained wards with unplastered walls and broken floors. Further, very few of the hospitals had modern arrangements for operations and many lacked adequate X-ray, dental and pathological departments.)

(ii) Furnish every hospital with efficient and modern plant and machinery. (In many of the hospitals, the boiler-houses, engine rooms, kitchens and laundries were inefficient or obsolete.)

(iii) Provide proper accommodation for special categories of patient. (In particular it was planned to improve conditions for maternity cases and patients suffering from mental problems and venereal disease.)

(iv) Adapt the former mixed institutions to deal specifically with cases of chronic illness. (This decision meant that the Council, 'more from chance than conscious design',[26] perpetuated the distinction of separate hospitals for the acute and chronic sick.)

(v) Provide more accommodation for those patients suffering from acute illness.

The problem of convalescent accommodation for men was partly mitigated by the opening of Queen Mary's Hospital, Sidcup. This former military hospital was reconditioned and opened in July 1930 to provide 500 beds. The problem of convalescent accommodation for women was eased when the General Hospitals Department obtained the Tooting Home. This former poor law institution was reconditioned and reopened, at the end of 1930, as a hospital for female convalescents and female chronic sick under the name of St. Benedict's Hospital. St. Benedict's was 'appropriated' in April 1932 and it was in its grounds that the Council's planned 600-bed hospital was eventually constructed. By the end of 1934, a further 447 beds had been provided by new construction at five hospitals

[25] Gibbon and Bell, *op. cit.*, p.325.
[26] Abel-Smith, *op. cit.*, p.373.

(providing a total of 1,267 beds including Queen Mary's and St. Benedict's). By reconditioning, at three institutions and two hospitals, wards previously unsuitable for sick patients had been converted to provide a further 556 beds.

The Council's programme of improvements embraced both patient comfort and standards of medical provision. As part of this programme the Council addressed itself to the question of ward size and the amount of space provided for each bed. Standards in the Poor Law hospitals had been generally low – wards being too narrow and the space between beds inadequate, resulting in overcrowding. In 1935 the Council decided that wards should be twenty-six feet wide and that wall space for each bed should be eight feet in acute wards and seven feet in chronic wards – a substantial advance in terms of the patients' comfort.

In the care of the mentally ill, the Council decided to concentrate all cases in six large units (three on each side of the Thames) each unit being provided with a specialist consultant and trained psychiatric social worker. These units replaced the twenty-one small observation units of the Poor Law hospitals which had been spread throughout the service and lacked specialist consultants.

Regarding other specialized services, the LCC established units for plastic surgery, thoracic surgery, treatment of thyroid ailments, urological diseases, rheumatoid arthritis, cardio-vascular diseases and X-ray and radium therapy. In conjunction with these units they 'obtained the services of distinguished consultants, including Lord Dawson of Penn, Sir Harold Gillies, Sir Thomas Dunhill, Sir Comyns Berkeley and Sir Leonard Hill'.[27]

The Council made rapid advances in maternity provision. As regards maternity beds, by 1934 new departments had been created at two hospitals and old departments replaced by modern ones in two others. Seventeen new labour rooms had been created at various hospitals and ten new ante-natal departments established. By the end of 1934 the number of maternity beds provided as part of the general hospital service amounted to 723, whilst ante-natal clinics were provided as twenty-four hospitals. Tables 7 and 8 illustrate the rapid growth of this work.

It has already been noted that the special hospitals transferred from the Metropolitan Asylums Board did not pose the same problems as the general hospitals. Provided and administered under a single authority, they already conformed to the requirements of a strategic, integrated service. Indeed the special hospitals, many of which were far beyond the LCC's boundaries, remained substantially a separate entity providing care for very different patients than those of the general hospitals. The hospitals of the MAB might well have continued to operate under an

[27] Gibbon and Bell, *op. cit.*, p.328.

[28] Cmnd. 4978 (see n. 17), p.56.

Table 7

*Ante-Natal Clinics*[28]

Total Attendances

| | |
|---|---|
| *1931* | 36,198 |
| *1932* | 48,618 |
| *1933* | 57,887 |
| *1934* | 73,142 |

Table 8

*Births in General Hospitals and Institutions*[29]

| | *Live and Still Births* | *Total % of Births in London* |
|---|---|---|
| *1931* | 10,191 | 15.0 |
| *1932* | 11,425 | 17.8 |
| *1933* | 11,917 | 20.3 |
| *1934* | 13,253 | 23.2 |

independent organization but for constitutional problems and the LCC's declared willingness to undertake their administration.[30]

*The Ambulance Service*

Prior to 1930 the LCC, the MAB and the Metropolitan Boards of Guardians all provided ambulance services of various kinds. The Council's service was primarily an accident service used for transporting accident cases to hospital. It also dealt with emergency cases occurring at home. The ambulances of the MAB were mainly used to transport patients to and from the Board's fever and other special hospitals. The Board's ambulances were made available for private cases, on the payment of charges, and also undertook work for the other authorities. The Board also provided river ambulance steamers to service their smallpox hospitals. The Guardians' ambulance service transported

[29] *Ibid.*, p.61.
[30] A. Powell, *The Metropolitan Asylums Board and its Work, 1867-1930*, 1930, p.97.

patients to and from the various Poor Law hospitals and institutions. The voluntary hospitals generally hired vehicles from the MAB, although a very few did operate ambulances of their own. In total the MAB possessed 107 ambulances in London, the LCC twenty-one, and the Guardians twenty-six (of which sixteen were obsolete).[31]

When the functions of the MAB and the Boards of Guardians were transferred to the Council, the three services were reorganized and placed under a central administration. The Council's ambulance service became the Accident Section of the London Ambulance Service, while the MAB's service formed the General Ambulance Section. The thirty effective vehicles inherited from the Guardians were incorporated into the General Ambulance Section. A headquarters for the whole service was established at Victoria Embankment. This was transferred to County Hall in October 1932. Some idea of the scope of the London Ambulance Service may be gathered from the fact that the Accident Section received almost 45,000 calls during 1934, whilst the General Ambulance Section carried over 300,000 people during that year. The total mileage for the year was in excess of two million miles.[32]

By 1939 the LCC ambulance service possessed a fleet of 165 ambulances and twenty ambulance buses. The latter vehicles were used for carrying convalescent patients, many of them children, to homes at the seaside or in the country. A network of ambulance stations had been established throughout the capital on such a basis that no part of the city was more than two miles from a station. A twenty-four hour service was in operation and any call could be answered, on average, within six and a half minutes. In total the ambulance service employed 400 staff.[33]

## *Conclusions*

During the period 1929 to 1939 the LCC became the 'greatest Local Health Authority in the Empire'[34] and even the Council's critics described the progress made in the development of its hospital service as 'remarkable'.[35] Nevertheless, although London possessed the basis of 'a comprehensive general public hospital service' areas of difficulty remained.[36] Thus whilst London had sufficient total hospital accommodation to meet its requirements, the hospitals were badly sited as regards the needs of patients. The historic voluntary hospitals were largely concentrated in central London. Many of the special hospitals

[31] Cmnd. 4978 (see n. 17), p.56.
[32] *Ibid.*, p.78.
[33] Gibbon and Bell, *op. cit.*, p.342.
[34] Sir G. Newman, *The Building of a Nation's Health*, 1939, p.182.
[35] Gray and Topping, *op. cit.*, p.54.
[36] PEP, *Report on the British Health Services*, 1937, p.17.

formerly adminstered by the MAB had been constructed far beyond the LCC's administrative area. Both the voluntary hospitals and the former hospitals of the MAB drew a large proportion of their patients from outside the LCC area. Above all, there was the difficulty of reconciling the operation of two parallel services, municipal and voluntary. As Gray and Topping noted, 'there is little doubt that, in spite of the general good relations, obtaining co-operation between the municipal and voluntary hospitals . . . has not been as close as it might have been, to the detriment of the service and consequently of the Londoner'.[37] Thus, although the LCC hospital service was able to take its place beside the voluntary hospitals, the persistence of the two services undoubtedly placed a limit on the possibility of achieving a fully integrated hospital service for London. In the event the problem was soon overtaken by the onset of the Second World War, the creation of the Emergency Medical Service and the process of regionalization subsequently conducted under the auspices of the National Health Service.[38]

In considering the LCC's hospital service it is possible to speculate that the future of health provision in Britain might have taken an entirely different course from the national system which actually developed. Public aspirations for ever improving health care grew rapidly after 1929 and soon rendered the thinking embodied in the 1929 Act substantially outdated. The financial difficulties encountered by the voluntary hospitals and the inefficiencies which emanated from the existence of two parallel services brought demands for a comprehensive service. The notion of creating such a service under the auspices of the local authorities raised, for the consultants of the voluntary hospitals, the spectre of control by the local medical officers of health. In the event, the national system preserved the status of the consultants and the integrity of the voluntary hospitals at the expense of local control.

[37] Gray and Topping, *op. cit.*, p.53.

[38] *Hospitals and the State: Background and Blueprint 1*, The Acton Society Trust, 1955, p.15.

Table 9

*1. Hospitals Transferred from the Metropolitan Asylums Board*

| | Number | Number of Beds |
|---|---|---|
| Infectious diseases (fever and smallpox) hospitals | 14 | 8,700 |
| Tuberculosis hospitals and sanatoria | 9 | 2,057 |
| Special children's hospitals | 5 | 2,400 |
| Hospitals for special diseases (eg VD) | 3 | 132 |
| Epileptic colonies | 2 | 705 |
| Total | 33 | 13,994 |

*2. Hospitals and Institutions Transferred from Boards of Guardians*

| | Number | Number of Beds |
|---|---|---|
| General hospitals | 28 | 17,350 |
| Institutions allocated as hospitals | 12 | 9,620 |
| Children's infirmary and nursery | 1 | 200 |
| Total | 41 | 27,170* |

* Plus 820 when the Council bought Queen Mary's, Sidcup and took over St. Benedict's Hospital.

SOURCE: LCC Annual Report 1930.

# *Chapter 11*

## *LCC Restaurants and the Decline of Municipal Enterprise*

Ellen Leopold

The LCC came late to municipal trading. It was municipal corporations like Birmingham and Sheffield which, beginning in 1848, pioneered the public sector ownership and provision of utilities like water, gas and electricity. London, by contrast, failed repeatedly to gain parliamentary approval to purchase water or electricity companies from the very powerful vested interests which controlled utilities in the capital. As a result, it missed out entirely on the first wave of municipalization. This concentrated on the takeover of what were considered 'natural' monopolies, that is, services which benefited from the advantages of centralized ownership and supply.

Once municipal corporations had proved their competence and efficiency in the running of utilities, they extended their entrepreneurial role by intervening in markets in direct competition with private enterprise. Bradford, for example, set up and operated a wool conditioning house, Sheffield a printing plant and St Helens a milk depot. With the widening of the economic role of public corporations came the rise of a more coherent political philosophy concerning the broader implications of public sector intervention. The LCC Progressives were directly involved in this change which effectively transformed the discussion of municipal trading into a debate on municipal socialism. Their articulate and sustained espousal of the public ownership and control of many sections of the economy made the activities of their own Council very visible and very vulnerable.

The LCC Civic Restaurant service was the last casualty in a long LCC tradition which viewed direct competition with the market as a means of improving the quality of services provided to Londoners (as well as the quality of employment offered within the service itself). That tradition began shortly after the establishment of the LCC itself, with the setting up of the country's first direct labour organization which acted in direct competition with (and as a brake on the excesses of) private building contractors. It continued into the early twentieth century with the short-lived subsidized steamship services on the River Thames. The LCC Restaurant service, providing thousands of cheap and healthy meals daily at hundreds of outlets scattered across London, represents the LCC's last major battle with competing private sector interests. The closure of the service in 1954 signifies the failure to establish a tradition of active public intervention in the local economy as the norm for local authorities.

## *The Underlying Failure of Policy*

At the end of the First World War and later (in 1930 and 1939), attempts were made to introduce a general enabling bill granting local authorities the power to trade directly with the public (only the bill in 1930 got to a Second Reading). These bills were in effect designed to liberate local authorities from financial control by central government, by empowering them to determine their own trading activities without recourse to Parliament for special legislation to sanction each new project.

Supporters of this kind of legislation envisaged a radical extension of local authority powers:

> A young person today lives in a municipal house, and he washes himself – or I hope he does – in municipal water. He rides on a municipal tram or omnibus, and I have no doubt that before long he will be riding in a municipal aeroplane. He walks on a municipal road; he is educated in a municipal school. He reads in a municipal library and he has his sport on a municipal recreation ground. When he is ill he is doctored and nursed in a municipal hospital and when he dies he is buried in a municipal cemetery. But I hope he does not anticipate that event.[1]

Those fearing the menace of unbridled municipal socialism that this picture conjured up concentrated their opposition upon attacks on the financial liabilities that such a far-reaching programme would incur. And their arguments were put most persuasively and most volubly by potentially competing private sector interests. Should the ratepayer be asked to subsidize potential or actual loss-making activities when competing private sector operations worked in a harsher climate which sent inefficient or unprofitable firms to the wall? More particularly, should the local trader be asked to subsidize his own competition through the rates?

These arguments were most likely to evoke a sympathetic response when the traders were small, very local and very visible and when consumers paid a direct charge in exchange for an immediately tangible service (e.g. a film, a meal or a bus ride). When private interests and the nature of trading were both less immediately visible, as with the 'consumption' of roads or, one step further removed, the 'consumption' of materials or machinery purchased from private suppliers for the

[1] *Parliamentary Debates*, 14 February 1930, cols.804-5. The Second Reading of the Local Authorities Enabling Bill was moved by John McShane, the first Labour MP for Walsall, elected in 1929.

construction and maintenance of those roads, the interest or awareness of the public in municipal expenditure was far less marked. Suspected price rings in operation in the supply of some standard materials (like bricks) often escaped notice, while complaints about the damage to competition caused by subsidized direct labour organizations claimed considerable media attention. In general, the more embedded within the core of local authority structures, the more easily expenditure evaded direct scrutiny from the ratepayer. This created conditions which were often more favourable to the internal expansion of local authority bureaucracies than to the expansion of direct services they were set up to adminster.

The visibility of direct trading with the public and the controversy it aroused made a more explicit debate about financial accountability in the public sector essential. Yet this debate did not occur. Labour supporters of municipal enterprise remained muddled on the question of profitability. Many argued that municipal control, by its superior organization and economies of scale, would inevitably give rise to efficient and profitable operations: the problem then became what to do with the working surpluses rather than how to address the need for continuing subsidy. Others shunned the financial arguments entirely and concentrated instead on the obvious advantages for social welfare to be gained by the collective provision of, for instance, milk and bread, which would at the very least eliminate corrupt traders dealing in adulterated substances. In the end, they shirked the difficult but necessary tasks of defining a new set of financial objectives to govern the provision of municipal services and identifying those services to which they would be applied.

There was also a more profound evasion of the issue of selective state support. The universal provisions of marketed municipal services would challenge the more traditional paternalism of the state, which had restricted its involvement to those in need and unable to provide for themselves rather than to all comers indiscriminately. The role of attending to the poorer elements of society which left the operation of most markets untouched could find qualified support amongst enlightened entrepreneurs. But offering services more democratically and more competitively was a direct threat to the established order and opened up unwanted – and unresolved – debate on the appropriate demarcation between public and private sector spheres of activity and influence, and between central and local government.

The failure to address these issues explicitly and to produce an alternative model for state intervention left municipal services perpetually vulnerable to models imported from the private sector. More particularly, local authority services were often shackled to financial accounting practices based on commercial enterprises which bore little resemblance to publicly-run operations. In the long run manipulation of these practices became the primary mechanism by which central government imposed restraints on the post-war activities of many local authorities. Over time they often acquired additional restrictive characteristics which would have strangled all but the toughest commercial operations. Rigid principles inflexibly applied would, it was hoped, guarantee financial rectitude in those areas of municipal spending which were most visible to the ratepayer.

These restrictions amounted to a failure of nerve, an inability to espouse and defend a radically different approach to the provision of services. The compromise framework for municipal enterprise that resulted from this unresolved mix of public and private sector objectives carried the seeds of its own destruction. The case of the LCC provides a vivid illustration.

### *Evolution of the LCC Service: the Stimulus of War*

The LCC was the only county council designated by the Civic Restaurants Act of 1947 to continue in the post-war period as a civic restaurant authority. This was, in part, recognition of the Council's impressive wartime contribution to communal feeding, involving the supply and distribution of food over a vast geographical area. From very early on, the LCC had demonstrated a remarkable capacity for efficient large-scale planning in this field. In April 1939 LCC officers met with representatives from the Ministry of Health to address some of the problems of emergency food and shelter that a direct attack on London would create. Within one month of the meeting, the LCC produced a scheme for forty-three 'first-line' feeding centres to cater for 150,000 people at twenty-four hours notice.[2]

When Lord Woolton, Minister of Food, approached the LCC to provide hot food for Londoners after the first air attacks on London in 1940, the Council was able to respond quickly by tapping into a pre-existing decentralized supplies and stores network. The LCC already provided a wide range of catering services in fulfilment of its social welfare responsibilities (serving meals to clients of all ages from babies to the elderly in residential homes). Wartime demands were able to exploit both the centralized expertise that co-ordinated these operations and the bulk purchasing system it had built up over three decades. They were also able to draw upon the divisional structure established by the LCC for the local administration of its education service.

Because of its accumulated experience and its pre-existing infrastructure, the LCC was able to respond quickly to demand. Starting from a field kitchen in the Isle of Dogs on 15 September 1940, the Council was operating twenty-seven feeding centres two weeks later and almost double this number by the beginning of October. The service, which

[2] R. Titmuss, *Problems of Social Policy*, 1950, p.51.

began as 'cash and carry', filling containers brought along to the kitchens, soon opened dining facilities for those who brought along their own cutlery and crockery and finally offered proper cafeteria catering from increasingly restaurant-like accommodation in a mushrooming number of centres, which reached a peak at 242 in May 1943. The Leader of the Council, Lord Latham, generated publicity for the new patriotically-labelled 'British Restaurants' through radio broadcasts, urging Londoners to locate the one nearest them from lists supplied to town halls and Citizens Advice Bureaux.

From the very beginning, the Ministry had insisted that although the meals service was intended to reach the poorest of Londoners, it was not to be means-tested.[3] The assignment of the Londoners' Meals Service to an Inter-departmental Committee within the LCC rather than to its Public Assistance Committee reflects this broader base. To create a universal service, everyone was expected to pay cash for meals. Prices were set as low as possible and were originally based on the cost of raw food with only a small proportion added on to cover the cost of fuel. This produced a main meal of meat, two vegetables and a sweet for 9d or 10d. Overheads (salaries of staff, cost of equipment, administrative charges, etc.) were disregarded at first. But as demand grew and the war continued and the Council's awareness of the real financial costs incurred by the service increased, the formula for setting the price of meals was changed to incorporate more of the invisible cost elements. The original mark-up of 25% on the cost of raw food was, in March 1941, raised to 66%. This still left the price of a meal well within the grasp of most Londoners and well below that charged by those restaurants and cafés which managed to stay open.

Because the meals centres were so widely dispersed across the County of London, they were able to play an important role in sustaining local communities throughout the war. The greater the number of restaurants, the shorter the distances between them and the schools, old people's homes, community and rest centres which they served. They also provided essential support to the local economy: up to 60% of the food in LCC restaurants was purchased in local shops, which helped to compensate for the loss of trade caused by wartime conditions.

In May 1943, the Board of Education issued a circular asking local authorities to arrange for an expansion in their provision of school meals to cover up to three quarters of the school roll. With just a quarter of the LCC school roll taking school meals in July 1943, the expansion required was considerable. The LCC's Chief Meals Officer, believing it unnecessary and indeed wrong to set up a separate organization to offer school children a midday meal, decided to extend the capacity of their meals centres and restaurants to meet the additional demand, making

[3] GLRO, Correspondence with Ministry of Food, 12 September 1940.

arrangements for the transport of thousands of school meals daily from restaurant kitchens to school premises as well as serving meals directly to children in the restaurants.

The provision of specially designed meals for school children containing 1,000 calories with additional protein and fat, prompted concern from the Home Office about the lack of comparable facilities for young people between fourteen and eighteen. This led to the introduction in 1943 of a one-shilling voucher for young civil servants which could be exchanged for a main meal in an LCC civic restaurant. The success of the scheme led to an avalanche of similar requests from other government departments followed by private companies, each of which made special arrangements with individual LCC restaurants to cater to all overflow staff needs, not just those of young people. In this way, the LCC served as the catalyst for the development of what became the Luncheon Voucher Scheme.

The LCC also provided a significantly greater proportion of its meals to old people than did other local authorities engaged in communal feeding. An estimated 14.5% of diners in London restaurants were over sixty years old compared with just 1.6% in Birmingham.[4] This reflected the significant role played by voluntary organizations working together with the LCC to meet the additional difficulties faced by the elderly and infirm during the war in shopping for and preparing meals. Responsibilities were shared: meals prepared in LCC restaurants were delivered by volunteers to community centres, dining halls or directly to homes, encouraging the development of 'Meals on Wheels' schemes across London.

Neither of these services to the young or the old was ever expected to generate profits. Nevertheless the shared use of restaurants by a variety of social services did reduce their running costs. They also helped to encourage much wider acceptance of civic responsibility for the feeding and nutrition of the adult population more generally, as part of the LCC's broader obligations to promote public health and welfare.

Radical changes in the popular conception of a healthy diet were promoted through the civic restaurants. Meatless dishes were introduced out of necessity but were very gradually accepted as a satisfactory alternative. Raw vegetables were introduced as a substitute for scarce fresh fruit to increase the amounts of Vitamin C in the diet, particularly in school meals. The realization that Vitamin C was highly perishable, when food was kept for long periods in hot containers or plates, led to the reduction of cooking times, the restriction of distances from kitchen to school and to the practice of serving meals directly from 'pot to plate'. In passing on these dietary benefits to all its customers, the restaurants played an important educational role, offering the carrot without the stick

[4] National Council of Social Service, *The British Restaurant*, 1946.

and so minimizing the sense of paternalistic intervention that so often accompanied state support for social services. For its public clientele at least, consumption in civic restaurants remained entirely voluntary.

### *The Post-War Decline*

The passage of the Civic Restaurants Act in 1947 appeared not just to confer the nation's retrospective approval on the wartime work of the British Restaurants but to recognize the potential contribution that co-ordinated planning for large-scale communal feeding might make in peacetime. The legislation paved the way for authorities to move out of the church halls, shops and schools requisitioned for emergency use in wartime and into premises specifically designed or adapted for restaurant use. Sloughing off the inheritance of wartime scarcity and adhoc-ery would, it was hoped, set the municipal restaurant on a completely new footing, freeing it from earlier associations with public assistance and privation. In this guise the legislation appears as an attempt to promote a democratic service, carrying over into peacetime some of the egalitarian spirit used to fuel wartime patriotism.

Yet paradoxically the terms prescribed by the Act, under which the transition from a temporary to a permanent operation was to take place, doomed the post-war municipal restaurant to failure by transforming communal feeding from a genuine municipal service to a commercially based operation.

Though the wartime meals service had always been expected to operate on a largely self-supporting basis, the Ministry of Food did agree 'to reimburse any approved operating deficiency in the event of a loss being unavoidably incurred'. While there was not always agreement on which expenses were avoidable, the promise of central support acted as an inducement to local authorities who might otherwise have been unwilling to undertake the necessary investment in the planning and implementing of communal feeding schemes. The 1947 legislation not only removed this safety net but at the same time prohibited local authorities from subsidizing their own schemes. The need to become and to remain financially self-supporting was now to take precedence over considerations of policy. Newly established as independent offshore operations, civic restaurants were cut loose both from the financial lifeline of the administering authority and from inclusion in the further development of its social policy.

That this shift in perspective was ushered in by a Labour government with a sizeable majority reflects the longer term failure of the Labour Party to address the contradictions posed by municipal trading and to confront the unspoken prejudices surrounding any extension of local authority powers in this area.

The linked provision of meals for the elderly and school lunches with meals sold directly to the public might have enhanced the future prospects of civic restaurants by strengthening their incipient role as part of the social infrastructure. This was encouraged by other pieces of post-war legislation like the National Assistance Act of 1948, which allowed the LCC to subsidize the costs of hot meals to the elderly by a grant from its Welfare Committee. Similarly, the 1944 Education Act not only empowered education authorities to provide school meals: it also encouraged an expansion in the number of young adults pursuing further education through evening study after work. To support this trend civic restaurants were expected to provide an essential source of inexpensive well-cooked meals for which there was no affordable alternative.

The Civic Restaurant Act did not however encourage experiments of this kind which intensified the use of existing resources, increasing the efficiency of the operation as it increased the variety of customer. Instead the new legislation inhibited these developments by creating separate classes of customers subject to separate accounts. This undermined the essential democracy of the service, driving a wedge between its subsidized users (the elderly and school children whom the LCC Welfare and Education Committees could support on an open-ended unit cost basis) and the general public (who were to pay for themselves on a cost-plus basis).

Disqualifying from public subsidy a clientele which in practice consisted primarily of low-wage workers was just the first step in what turned out to be the progressive disengagement of local authorities from active involvement in food policy as it related to health issues. This withdrawal marked the failure of the state to seize the opportunity thrown up by the war to link a commitment to the promotion of a healthy population through healthier eating habits with its new commitment to the treatment of illness through the establishment of the National Health Service. The NHS was set up in 1947; the Ministry of Food disappeared in 1955.

The Civic Restaurant Act embodied the shortsightedness of a narrow formulaic solution to complex social objectives. Substituting the need for profitability for the need to provide a decent low-cost meal implicitly restored the market mechanism as the appropriate means for distributing resources. This had a devastating effect on the LCC's ability to redress some of the imbalances between wealthy and poor residents – and areas – of London.

Every investment made by the Council benefited some groups of Londoners more than others. Beneficiaries ranged from Council tenants housed on new LCC estates to owners of commercial property adjacent to road improvement schemes carried out by the Council. The distributional impact of investment had been well understood since the early days of the LCC, when the Progressives attempted to appropriate (for Council use elsewhere) the anticipated gains in property development value which would be directly attributable to the LCC-financed Kingsway-Aldwych Improvement Scheme.

In a 1946 discussion of the future of British Restaurants still operating under emergency wartime powers, Lord Latham, as Leader of the Council, had argued that control of the Meals Service should be granted to the LCC rather than to individual metropolitan boroughs precisely to enable the larger authority to use the surplus from the more successful restaurants to subsidize the less successful ones. In addition, the strategic authority would be able to override the objections of some more conservative borough councils to the location of civic restaurants within their borders, thereby addressing the needs of those on lower incomes working and/or living within wealthier areas.

On the whole, civic restaurants with higher turnovers tended to be those in more middle-class districts, where incomes – and rates – would also tend to be higher. In such districts more people would be able to afford to eat out. While the overheads would be largely the same in restaurants of similar size in different districts of London, the volume of trade would be relatively higher in the more prosperous areas. A comparison of the costs of thirty communal restaurants carried out in London in 1943 revealed that of fifteen restaurants which did not show profits (all of comparable seating capacity), nine were located in working-class but only two in middle-class residential districts. The progressive running down and closure of the commercially less successful restaurants was therefore bound to punish those on the lowest incomes most severely.

The terms of the new legislation stipulated that if, after an initial period of two years, the restaurant service ran at a loss for three consecutive years, in the absence of convincing arguments pointing to a likely change in the established trend, the Minister of Food had the power to close the service down. This imposed an impossible burden on the LCC service. It already operated with considerable economic disadvantages, many of which enhanced its value as a public service. First, it paid its staff at wage rates roughly 20% higher than those paid by commercial establishments, making wages and salaries about 30% of turnover (compared with about 25% in commercial operations). Secondly, it priced its meals lower than those obtaining in nearby restaurants, reducing its turnover for a given volume of trade. Thirdly, administrative costs were higher because of the need for co-ordination and record-keeping on a vast scale and the overhead costs of employer contributions to pensions, holiday and sickness pay. All these additional costs resulted from policy decisions which could no longer be sustained in the context of the new regulations. The inexorable drive for profitability systematically undermined the advantages in quality of service and employment introduced by the Council.

In addition, the LCC faced inflated post-war rents and maintenance and adaptation costs for property which was often in poor condition and unsuitable for restaurant use. It also had to cope with a continuing downward trend in post-war demand for commercial catering of all kinds, as more companies opened canteens for their own staff, women previously engaged in war production returned to the home and more non-rationed foods became generally available to suburban as well as inner urban shoppers. Moreover, the lifting of restrictions on building activity in 1953 enabled proprietors to repair war-damaged local cafés and restaurants and to reopen for business.

One of the most important contributors to a decline in turnover was the progressive fall in demand for school meals, as more schools opened or reopened their own kitchens. The volume of business provided by the school meals trade had helped considerably to defray the high level of administrative costs borne by civic restaurants, which now proceeded to rise. But behind the wholesale hiving-off of school meals lay a drive for economy and control initiated by the Ministry of Education. In 1950 the Minister complained that wages paid for operative staff in civic restaurants were too high and asked the Council to revise them. He also encouraged a reallocation of school meals from civic restaurants to central or school kitchens wherever possible on the grounds that overheads were lower in the latter. In fact overheads were lower because they were subsidized: unit costs charged for central or school kitchen meals did not include a charge for rent or capital costs.

The LCC Restaurant and Catering Department faced a further obstacle in their efforts to establish meals services in those areas that most needed them. The geographical distribution of restaurants and kitchens had to some extent been determined by civil defence planning which had located billetting areas in an 'S' plan ranged over the north-west and south-west sides of London to cope with the evacuation of population from the South Coast towns into London in the event of an invasion. This led to a relative over-supply of emergency restaurants in the western half of London and a relative vacuum in the more heavily bombed east.

The Ministry of Food had agreed on a total of about 150 licences for the LCC restaurant service. This was the number of premises the LCC had taken over from the Ministry upon the enactment of the 1947 legislation. LCC officers hoped to correct the imbalance between east and west within this total by allowing some of the wartime meals centres established in requisitioned premises in the west to be restored to their original use while opening new restaurants in poorly served areas in the East End. But the Ministry of Health (which had to approve Ministry of Food decisions) was unwilling to allow replacement on a 'service' basis, insisting in the name of 'fair play' that terms applying to private caterers seeking building licences to repair or replace damaged property apply equally to the entire LCC service. Since applications for alternative development from commercial caterers were only considered for replacement property within the immediate vicinity of the original restaurant site, similar restrictions were applied to the LCC service, despite repeated protests. This meant that the LCC was also barred from investing in existing commercial establishments which could have produced immediate income to help offset the heavier costs (and delayed productivity) of investment in the adaptation or alteration of replacement premises.

In this way the entirely unrelated objectives of civil defence planning were allowed to determine the distribution pattern of the post-war restaurant service, effectively reinforcing existing disparities between the two sides of London. Thwarted from setting up new restaurants where it chose to, and forced to keep itself out of the red, the LCC embarked on a two-pronged campaign to renew the service, closing those restaurants in gravest financial difficulties while simultaneously opening new ones in areas of perceived need which both met Ministry requirements and might be expected to pay their own way. Many of these post-war developments were enthusiastically received by local Trades Councils and Trade Unions. So, for example, the Lewisham No. 1 Branch of the Amalgamated Engineering Union congratulated the LCC Civic Restaurant Committee for 'its decision to go ahead with the opening of an LCC restaurant in Catford' (replacing two meals centres) 'which catered for hundreds of low income people'.[5]

At the same time, the Committee received petitions from regular users protesting at the closure of many other restaurants: 800 'regular users' fought to keep open the Fishmongers' Hall Restaurant, London Bridge. Defenders of the threatened Moatside Restaurant, argued that it was 'the only reasonably priced restaurant in the neighbourhood and its closing will cause grave hardship'. Customers of the Chilton Restaurant made an unusual offer: 'If the restaurant runs at a loss, we would willingly bear with an increase in charges rather than be forced to transfer our custom to another establishment'. Most of these protests were to little avail: in the period 1949-50 the LCC opened twelve but closed sixteen restaurants. Though still in 1950 operating more than a hundred civic restaurants (a quarter of the national total), over the following year the pace of closure increased: between April 1950 and April 1951, the Restaurant and Catering Committee opened seven but closed thirty-four restaurants, leaving it with seventy-eight still operating.

In 1952 the District Auditor, pursuing a tactic that has recently become more familiar, decided to challenge the LCC's restaurant accounts in such a way as to transform an annual surplus to an annual deficit. There was no question of the Council's having used illicit practices. It was simply accused of overcharging for school meals, thereby increasing the internal transfer payment from the Education to the Restaurant and Catering Committee and of carrying forward surpluses from earlier years, which

[5] *The Kentish Mercury*, 4 April 1950.

the District Auditor now disallowed. In effect the District Auditor had been able to supplant the LCC's pricing mechanism with his own in much the same way that a more recent Conservative government has been able to set the level of rate that a local authority can legitimately impose or determine the level of return that a direct labour organization must make on its turnover. The change the District Auditor made to the accounts on paper (purely a notional change involving no charge to the rates) was nonetheless sufficient to make a big splash in the press and helped to keep opposition to the restaurant service alive and confined to purely financial arguments.

Though open to the general public and often attracting a wide cross-section of the population, the LCC restaurants tended to be associated from the beginning with the more modest end of the catering spectrum. For LCC Tory Opposition leader Henry Brooke, the civic restaurant was 'a rough and ready place for poorer people'. This reinforced a common view of them as glorified soup kitchens, which fitted in with more or less accepted views of the LCC's social welfare role. The more the Council deviated from this role by extending the scope of municipal restaurants and by moving them up-market in an attempt to raise the level of turnover, the more conflict it generated. When the Council opened the Ramillies Restaurant in Oxford Street with uniformed waitresses, flowers, ornamental lighting and licensed to sell drinks with meals, it met with a barrage of criticism from several local trade associations. Some decried the wasteful expenditure involved in raising the level of amenities provided. Others followed the line of the Westminster Chamber of Commerce which protested in a letter to the Council that:

> the opening of a civic restaurant in any area immediately lowers its tone. Oxford Street was, at one time, one of the finest shopping streets in London . . . The setting up of a civic restaurant . . . would be a retrogressive step much to be deplored.

Behind both types of criticism lay an assumption that civic restaurants were designed to cater for a type of clientele in a context that was incompatible with the middle-class prosperity of a major shopping precinct. Location in Oxford Street was, therefore, a violation of their perceived notions of local authority undertakings; the LCC was now trading in an area that was hitherto off limits.

Equally vociferous were the countervailing voices of local Trades Councils raised in support of the new scheme. The Knightsbridge and Pimlico Branch of Shop, Distributive and Allied Workers welcomed:

> the proposal of the LCC to open a civic restaurant in Oxford St. It believes this will meet a long felt need for a restaurant providing meals at reasonable prices for workers in these parts which is in no way met by luxury and semi-luxury restaurants in this area.

In the end, the Ramillies Restaurant which was opened in August 1949 by the Minister of Works and hailed as 'a people's restaurant' by the *Daily Herald*, failed to pull in the turnover so desperately needed. Faced with the decline in demand that plagued all catering establishments in the early 1950s, it closed its doors just two years later. If the Council had been empowered to carry the losses until trade picked up in the mid-fifties, the history of civic restaurants might have been very different. In the event the Minister of Food took the decision in August 1954 to close down the entire service. The LCC, in response, asked him to exercise his power under the Civic Restaurants Act to allow the Council to continue operating eleven restaurants which were running at a profit and likely to continue to do so and which were not in requisitioned premises. The Minister, by his refusal, in effect swept away the criteria by which the rest of the service had been damned, thereby 'denying to the ratepayers of London the opportunity of enjoying a continuation of this service with every prospect of a profit' (as the Chairman of the Supplies Committee had argued in a letter to the *South London Press*).

The closure of the LCC's restaurant service created hardship for those on the lowest incomes (shop assistants and black-coated workers), who were least likely to be able to afford the cost of meals in new or reopened cafés or to be accommodated by the expansion in industrial or company canteens. One of the groups benefiting from the latter development was the largely white-collar LCC staff enjoying the benefits of the County Hall Restaurant Service. County Hall restaurants already received considerable subsidies from the Council, subsidies that were disallowed for its Civic Restaurant service. They were not charged for rent, rates, central heating or water. Yet despite this support, they had run an annual deficit from 1946, with every meal more heavily subsidized by the ratepayer than any meal in a civic restaurant had ever been.

In 1952, after the District Auditor had imposed further constraints on the accounting practices of the LCC restaurants, the Council followed the Treasury in agreeing to increase assistance to its own non-industrial canteens. It duly relieved the County Hall restaurants of further running costs including the cost of maintaining, lighting and cleaning the accommodation and the costs of replacing and maintaining heavy equipment and furniture. It also agreed an additional sum to carry out redecoration.

So, five years after the passage of the Civic Restaurants Act, the LCC, having attempted to raise the standard of living of the less privileged groups of Londoners through the provision of a democratic local meals service, found itself in the position of having contributed to an increase in just those inequalities it had hoped to moderate. Forced by the terms of the legislation to adopt the narrowest of cost-accounting criteria, it was led to abandon its direct support of a much needed local service just as it increased the scale of comfort subsidized by the ratepayer for its own administrative elite in County Hall. The pettiness of this short-sighted view was put eloquently by Norman Prichard, Chairman of the Supplies Committee, upon closure of the Restaurant Service:

> The net loss of £71,000 (not allowing for £60,000 income tax and profits tax paid to HM Government) is equivalent to less than 1/20 of a penny rate annually over the period during which the service has continued . . . The truth is . . . that for a net loss to public funds of only £11,000 on a turnover of nearly £6,000,000, Londoners enjoyed 70,000,000 good and cheap meals; a much valued service was rendered to many thousands of old folk which the voluntary agencies will find it hard to replace without increased public and private expenditure; and 20,000,000 meals were provided for school children without a penny profit, at a time when it would have been very costly, if not impossible, to provide them from any other source. This, I submit, is a fine record, of which any undertaking might be proud, and the mass of Londoners will, I am sure, share my own deep regret that by the action of the Minister, the Council has been forced to close it down.[6]

In retrospect, the LCC restaurants spawned by the 1947 Act appear primarily to have served the transitional needs of public catering between war and peacetime. The wartime service had itself contributed to the creation of a new demand for meals outside the home. The dispersal of families caused by evacuation and the high proportion of female employment in war production removed many women from the kitchen, creating the need for an acceptable substitute. The LCC restaurants together with the new industrial and company canteens met this demand and in the process accustomed many workers to taking a midday meal near their place of work rather than returning home. The LCC restaurants helped to turn this into a habit which survived into the post-war period, creating a market to be exploited and developed by private caterers after 1954.

The immediate post-war period imposed hugely inflated costs on the LCC restaurant service in the form of high rents, wages and property values. Because the scarcity of skilled labour and materials continued into the late 1940s and early 1950s, building work was limited by central government to projects deemed to be essential during the early years of restricted supply. Paradoxically the failure of many commercial establishments to be granted building licences, before restrictions were lifted in 1953, allowed them to escape the period of uncertain demand and high financial risks which proved the undoing of the LCC restaurants.

Although granted licences for renovation and repair denied to private caterers, the LCC service was restrained by the 1947 Act from making the kind of investment decisions and taking the kind of risks which were open to commercial operations. First hemmed in by the legislation, the LCC

[6] *LCC Minutes*, 2 November 1954, p.577.

Restaurant Service then fell prey to the change in national government in 1951. The new Conservative government was more likely to give a sympathetic hearing to the continuing complaints of competing private sector interests. Not surprisingly, the financial performance of the LCC Restaurant Service became one of the main issues in the LCC election campaign in the following year.

In stripping away the captive markets from the restaurants (like school meals which were reassigned to Education), central government put direct catering to the public increasingly at risk. This was precisely the area of service that constituted a radical extension of municipal trading, offering, as it did, a service to all comers on an equal basis. A democratic municipal service of this type posed a threat to the more acceptable provision of social services (including school meals) based on selective means-testing. Ultimately, the civic restaurant disappeared because it failed to disturb the deep-seated requirement that local government maintain a clear physical and financial separation between the recipients of public assistance and the public at large. The temporary blurring of this distinction was only tolerable in wartime, when enemy action rather than class society determined the distribution of emergency need.

## *Chapter 12*

# *'Spread The People': The LCC's Dispersal Policy, 1889-1965*

Andrew Saint

For most of its seventy-six-year span, the London County Council presided over a falling population. The growth of the County of London slowed during the LCC's first decade, peaked at 4½ millions in the 1900s, and then reversed into a quickening decline until by 1961 the figure had fallen below 3¼ millions.[1] Most of this reduction took place naturally, as people and businesses alike found life on the outskirts of London or elsewhere more amenable than in the city centre. Yet for the whole of its existence the LCC itself, irrespective of the party in power, also encouraged and promoted the process of 'decentralization' or 'dispersal'. The consistency of its efforts outweighed the spasmodic enthusiasm and initiatives of central government or the metropolitan boroughs. The LCC, in other words, was the key political institution in abetting the dispersal of Londoners. The impact of this population policy upon London as a city and upon the lives of hundreds of thousands of its citizens can hardly be quantified. It was certainly colossal.

In terms of institutional power-politics, the whole process now appears curious. For what the LCC effectively did by planning for a lower population in the centre of the capital was to weaken its own power-base. In the long run, every person taken out of the administrative County of London diminished its authority and influence. And in the twenty-year period after the Second World War when the business of dispersal was at its height, a Labour LCC was helping to pluck from its area those very working-class Londoners on whom it most relied for support. It is rare, to say the least, for a successful political body to be so seemingly blind to its long-term interests.

In reality the contradiction was once less apparent, if it was apparent at all. From the time of the Ullswater Commission in 1923 to the creation of a Greater London Council in 1965, the dream of the larger county or region of London which would one day come into its administrative own could persuade many LCC members and officers that citizens uprooted

[1] *London Statistics*, new series vol.7, 1965, p.19; *The London Encyclopaedia*, ed. Ben Weinreb and Christopher Hibbert, 1983, p.614.

from the slums and guided to surrounding counties were sent, as it were, on loan, to be one day reunited with the mother-county once a proper regional government had been established. Likewise there were those – more perhaps on the right than on the left of the political fence – who interpreted the thousands of working-class Londoners dispatched to the new and expanded towns of the 1950s as shock troops who might convert the countryside to socialism, rather than as refugees who left their old haunts vulnerable to middle-class infiltration.

But the saga of dispersal and the LCC's role in it make scant sense if the Council is conceived as an independent, monolithic body, alert only to its own interests and those of its population. As other essays in this book show, the LCC was a more fragile body than some have supposed, sandwiched between upper and lower tiers of government and secure only in the administrative certainties of the moment. A coalition of interests, it was weakly linked with its constituents and electors and therefore always susceptible to outside pressures. Continuities in LCC policy derived less from regular manifestations of electoral feeling than from the strength of certain trends in national ideology – aided, no doubt, by administrative momentum. The LCC's long commitment to dispersal highlights the persistence among all British political parties of the puritan distaste for cities and urban life, a habit of mind manifest well before the Council was set up and still vigorous when it gave way to the GLC in 1965.

The LCC, then, was not of itself the vanguard for diminishing and cleansing the 'great wen' of London. But for the first half of the twentieth century, it offered to those who belonged to this vanguard the most practical vehicle for carrying that intention through. The New Towns programme which became official national wisdom for the third quarter of the century then built upon the record of the LCC and relied in great measure on that body's support and experience. How that support and experience were amassed and then deployed forms the burden of this essay.

## *Early Efforts: A Transport Policy for Dispersal*

The publication in 1898 of Ebenezer Howard's *Tomorrow: A Peaceful Path to Real Reform* is often taken as a turning point in British planning history. Directly from Howard stemmed the beginnings of the Garden City Association (later the Town Planning Association) and the foundation of Letchworth (1903) and Welwyn Garden City (1919) – prototypes of the self-sufficient, low-density community, conceived in dialectical opposition to the city, planned without municipal aid, and yet the precursors of the later New Towns.[2] Without Howard's blueprint for

[2] C.B. Purdom's *The Building of Satellite Towns*, 1948 ed., still offers the richest account of Ebenezer Howard, Letchworth and Welwyn Garden City.

curtailing the growth of London and the practical shape that it took, the pattern of dispersal from London after 1945 would have been quite different.

Yet Howard's book did not appear in a vacuum. So familiar was its moral drift, its small-town utopianism, even its Henry Georgeite ideas on tenure, that Bernard Shaw felt able to dismiss it as 'the same old vision'.[3] The notion of dispersing the population of London was then far from new. It appealed to many Victorian reformers, branded by the shock of urban industrialization, the proximity of the slum, and the terror of disease – physiological, political and spiritual. As early as 1821, William Cobbett had proposed that 'the dispersion of the wen is the only real difficulty that I see in settling the affairs of the nation and restoring it to a happy state. But dispersed it *must* be . . .'[4]

The LCC was born at the end of the 1880s in a climate of intensifying calls for dispersal. Practical action, in so far as there had been any, had centred upon slum-clearance and improvements in transport rather than housing or relocating jobs. But these proved feeble tools: clearance intensified overcrowding, and some critics already argued that roads and railways in themselves did the same. The only incentive that had been brought to bear to encourage dispersal was the subsidizing of trains. This had begun in a very small, piecemeal way in the 1860s as a means of wringing concessions out of railway companies when they wanted to tear down houses for lines and stations in inner London. It first yielded tangible results in the next decade when the Great Eastern Railway was persuaded to run substantial numbers of 'workmen's trains'.[5] The Cheap Trains Act of 1883, which followed on from debate on the Artizans' and Labourers' Dwellings Improvement Bill the year before, marked the start of a consistent dispersal policy for London. Puny though it was, it embodied the idea that working-class housing could only be successfully established in the outer suburbs of London if supported by a system of adequate transport with subsidized fares. The same conclusion was reached by the Royal Commission on the Housing of the Working Classes in 1884-5 when it stated that 'workmen's fares should not be greater than the difference between rents of working-class homes in London and the suburbs'.[6]

This premise of an integrated housing and transport policy, with

[3] Dan H. Laurence (ed.), *Bernard Shaw, Collected Letters, 1898-1910*, 1980, p.103. See also pp.118-9 for Shaw on Howard, 'The Garden City Geyser'.

[4] William Cobbett, *Rural Rides*, 4 December 1821 (Everyman Edition, 1912, vol.1, p.43).

[5] H.J. Dyos, 'Workmen's Fares in South London', reprinted from *Journal of Transport History*, 1, 1953, in D. Cannadine and D. Reeder, *Exploring the Urban Past: Essays in Urban History by H.J. Dyos*, 1982, pp.87-100; T.C. Barker and Michael Robbins, *A History of London Transport*, vol.1, 1975 edn., pp.54-6, 116, 173-4, 215-20.

[6] Quoted in Dyos, *op. cit.*, p.97.

incentives for working-class families to move away from the centre, is fundamental for an understanding of the LCC Progressives' housing policy in the 1890s. During these years, there was no serious argument but that central London was too big and too dense for health, comfort and civilization. The Progressives therefore began to fumble their way towards a concerted municipal policy for dispersal. Following previous leads and armed with the superior information-gathering powers of its Statistical Department under Laurence Gomme and, later, Edgar Harper, the LCC promoted a series of enquiries in 1892, 1897, 1898 and 1902 into the expanding but geographically uneven provision of workmen's trains, including a survey of organized labour and its experience of the trains.[7] These enquiries had no direct legislative outcome. But they helped establish a clearer relationship between fare-structure and housing as part of the emerging discipline of English urban planning. They probably also prodded the railway companies to run more cheap trains at more convenient hours.

It was with dispersal also in mind that the LCC Progressives resolved to purchase tramways. Having first decided in principle to do so in 1891, the second, more radical Progressive administration endorsed the decision in 1894-5.[8] Bad labour conditions on the trams, the greed and inefficiency of the private companies which ran them, and a general enthusiasm for municipal enterprise played some part in these decisions. But for most Progressives, the main social motive was to do with working-class housing and transport. Since they could not influence the location of jobs to any great extent, they wished to safeguard means of cheap transport to existing locations and thus reduce overcrowding in the centre. The philosophy was not to provide a general subsidy out of the rates for any tramways which they might take over, but merely to issue subsidized workmen's tickets for a certain number of trams, as the railways had done, and to pay for the difference out of the profits on the line. This indeed was how LCC tramways were to work for many years after they came into operation from 1898.

Another plank of early Progressive social policy was for the LCC to build housing itself, a decision taken in 1892 when the Progressives were first returned with a clear majority. The attention paid to the Council's earliest ventures in municipal housing, notably the great Boundary Street project at Bethnal Green (1893-1900), has obscured the fact that many housing reformers felt them to be a failure. The obstacles encountered in these schemes were colossal.[9] For the most part, they were built either on awkward slum-cleared sites which the LCC had inherited from the

[7] *Ibid.*, pp.94-8.
[8] Barker and Robbins, *op. cit.*, vol.1, 1975 edn., pp.267-70, and vol.2, 1974, pp.22-30.
[9] Anthony S. Wohl, *The Eternal Slum*, 1977, pp.260-73; Susan Beattie, *A Revolution in London Housing*, 1980, pp.53-4.

Metropolitan Board of Works or, like Boundary Street, in the place of further slums which health officials insisted that the Council tackle immediately. The philanthropic housing companies had increasingly been refusing to build on such expensive sites, so the LCC was pressed into doing the job itself. But progress proved dispiritingly slow, while successive governments showed no mercy in relaxing the stiff loan conditions for housing finance. The costs of compulsory purchase, clearance and debt-servicing plus the durable quality of the new buildings forced the LCC to charge high rents for its flats – rents only just within the reach of the respectable artisan, let alone those in casual employment or those evicted when the sites were cleared. To many minds, the type of 'high-rise' flat represented by Boundary Street amounted to little more than barrack blocks previously built by the housing companies of the 1870s and '80s, perhaps with slightly better architecture. They did not begin to solve the problem of overcrowding.

All this persuaded the Progressives to review their housing policy when they were returned to the LCC with their second clear majority in 1898. They quickly came to two decisions: to switch from slum-clearance to housing for need, the looser category introduced under the Housing Act of 1890; and to concentrate as far as they could on suburban rather than central housing – in other words, to promote dispersal by building housing as well as subsidizing fares.[10] But the LCC had no clear powers to build outside the County of London, while within it there were fewer and fewer sites available for substantial suburban development. One was soon secured: Totterdown Fields at Tooting, the earliest of four 'cottage' estates started in outer London by the LCC before the First World War. To service Totterdown Fields and future estates in South London, the Progressives in 1898 exercised their option to take over the management of the South London Tramways Company and began to electrify the line to provide a fast, cheap link with the centres of employment. This was the first step in establishing the LCC tramways network.[11] But if integrating housing and transport in this way was to have any broad success, the Council had to get parliamentary sanction to build outside its own boundaries. Thus was promoted what became the Housing of the Working Classes Act, 1900.

### *Politics and the Progress of the Cottage Estates*

The 1890 Housing Act, on which municipal housing was first based, had been largely a consolidating measure that prompted only short

[10] LCC Minutes of Proceedings, 29 November 1898, pp.1434-40 and 6 December 1898, pp.1457-9.

[11] Barker and Robbins, *op. cit.* vol.1, p.264; vol.2, pp.7-8, 91-2, 98.

parliamentary debate. But the 1900 bill, though narrow in scope, afforded Parliament a first chance to consider what municipal housing amounted to and so was thoroughly discussed. The LCC's controversial policies and record dominated the debate.[12] Yet the measure was brought forward by the Conservative Government. Some few speakers like the Finsbury MP, H.C. Richards, argued that the LCC had simply made a bad job of its block dwellings and had no business to decant his constituents ten to twelve miles out in the country: 'We must deal with London as we find it, and the working man asks that he shall be allowed to live near the work in which he is engaged'. The one London 'working man' to give his views, Will Steadman, MP and LCC Progressive member for Stepney, took an equivocal line. The only answer, he thought, was a fresh housing bill with new terms for finance and compensation; in other words, working people preferred inner-city housing if it could be secured for low enough rents. But most members, Conservative and Liberals alike, accepted the arguments for dispersal with, if anything, the Tories keener. 'Clearly it is the business of the local authority to get the people out of the crowded area into the country,' asserted T.W. Russell, Secretary of the Local Government Board. Summing up, A.J. Balfour pressed the issue into the realms of motorway idealism. 'I sometimes dream . . .', he mused, 'that in addition to railways and tramways, we may see great highways constructed for rapid motor traffic, and confined to motor traffic, which would have the immense advantage . . . of taking the workman from door to door, which no tramway or railway could do.' And so the bill passed.

Dispersal therefore commanded all-party support at the turn of the century, with few dissenters. So the LCC was able to proceed uncontroversially with its first suburban estates: Totterdown Fields and Old Oak within the County of London, Norbury and White Hart Lane just outside. They were slow to realize, at least as slow as the urban clearance schemes which had preceded them. Yet the LCC was quick to represent them as a success before the Royal Commission on London Traffic, the other occasion in this period when the practical issues of dispersal as opposed to its moral desirability were thoroughly gone into. A bevy of LCC witnesses appearing before this body in 1903 argued – prematurely, considering how little had then been built – that their suburban estates were a model of happiness and financial self-sufficiency, compared to the big block dwellings like the Bourne Estate in Clerkenwell which they still felt obliged to build in modest numbers for people who needed to live near their work. 'Anyone would prefer living in a little cottage with a nice little garden with healthy surroundings, to living in a block dwelling five or six stories high,' claimed the LCC's Housing

[12] Parliamentary Debates, 4th series, vol.82, 10 May 1900, cols. 1260-1349; vol.83, 17 May 1900, cols. 427-579.

Manager, S.G. Burgess.[13] Edgar Harper produced statistics to show how cheap suburban development could be so long as fares were subsidised, and hinted at modest evidence for the beginnings of a voluntary dispersal of London industry. Riley, the LCC Architect, claimed that Totterdown Fields was self-supporting, and regretted that those displaced by the Council's Kingsway and Aldwych improvements were to be rehoused centrally rather than on suburban cottage estates.

These views were accepted lock, stock and barrel by the Commissioners. Block dwellings, they reported, led to 'a great waste of public money and a still crowded population per acre', suburban estates to 'no loss of money at all and a population housed in healthy surroundings ... In order to relieve overcrowding, means must be provided for taking the population into and out of London, not in one or two directions, but in many directions, at rapid speed, frequent intervals and cheap rates.'[14] Effectively they accepted that it was easier to subsidize 'carriage' rather than 'rent'. What they did not face was that in many cases there were no existing transport subsidies or inadequate ones, because the cheap fares came not from direct government or municipal grants but mostly from piecemeal concessions wrung out of the railway companies. Where there were no guarantees of cheap transport, as with the grand suburb for 40,000 then planned by the LCC at White Hart Lane, Tottenham, Burgess had had to concede lamely that the development would do nothing much for the poor but would at least relieve the centre.

Had the LCC's early cottage estates been objectively investigated a decade later, such ringing claims could hardly have been made for the success of early municipal dispersal policy. By 1914 the 1,250-odd cottages of Totterdown Fields had been completed and let. But Norbury in Croydon was only half built and was as much tenanted by local people as by inner Londoners. White Hart Lane had failed to get the direct tube link hoped for in 1903 and had been cut back drastically in size, despite a private donation to encourage East Enders to move out to it; Old Oak was hardly off the mark. These setbacks were partly attributable to the advent of the economy-minded LCC Moderate (or Municipal Reform) administration in 1907. Conservatives as they basically were, the Moderates were by no means opposed to dispersal. As their record on the LCC over the next twenty-seven years was to prove, they were much more hostile to block dwellings, which virtually disappeared from LCC housing programmes until 1926. But they questioned whether the LCC ought itself to intervene so actively in promoting dispersal, and particularly in providing infrastructure and services on the cottage estates to the

[13] PP 1906, XL, Minutes of Evidence to Royal Commission on London Traffic, 10 July 1903, col. 5863. Harper's interesting evidence is at cols. 4619ff.; Riley's at cols. 6886ff.

[14] PP 1905, XXX, Report of Royal Commission on London Traffic, paras. 13-17.

standard upheld by the Progressives. The Moderates therefore postponed or cancelled the purchase of further suburban sites, tried in vain to sell portions of the sites already acquired (principally at White Hart Lane, where the Liberal Government blocked the manoeuvre), reduced the size of the houses to be built, and left out of the developments some of the community buildings and open space once planned for them.[15] At one time the Moderates contemplated mixing the classes on the cottage estates, but this came to nothing. In this way, the model of the LCC cottage or 'out-county' estate established before the First World War provided a minimum of small, single-class dwellings, linked to the centres of employment in London by reasonable, part-subsidized transport. There were schools and churches but few shops and, inevitably, no pubs. These estates became the prototype not just for the later suburban estates which the LCC built over the next forty years, but also for the kind of suburban development undertaken under the national Housing Act of 1919, the Addison Act. More than Hampstead Garden Suburb or Letchworth, the LCC's cottage estates furnished an economical model for healthy working-class housing away from the city centres.

Since the Moderates favoured dispersal but were dubious about the LCC's role in promoting it, they looked to other agencies to do so. The alternative during their early years in power seemed to be garden cities, which the Moderates explicitly endorsed in their election campaign of 1907,[16] At this time, the garden-city movement had matured from the pipedream it appeared to be when the LCC first contemplated building in the suburbs. Letchworth was at the peak of its promise in 1907, and the clever planning of its streets and houses under the guidance of Raymond Unwin was beginning to influence the LCC's own cottage estates. It seemed to be attracting industry as well, which offered the prospect of taking ordinary working people out of London as well as mere middle-class idealists. Letchworth was soon to lose momentum, but in the years before 1914 it generated in its wake a rash of garden suburbs (though no self-sufficient garden cities) and a burst of enthusiasm for town-planning.

There were various links between the LCC and the garden-city movement. Ebenezer Howard had worked for a time as a shorthand reporter at LCC meetings. Several active LCC Members belonged to the Garden City Association, including John Benn, Lord Carrington, W.H. Dickinson, Lord Meath and a close contact of Howard's, the Revd. Fleming Williams. One member, T.H.W. Idris of St. Pancras, moved a portion of his mineral-water concern from Camden Town to Letchworth

[15] Robert Thorne, 'The White Hart Lane Estate: An LCC Venture in Suburban Development', *London Journal*, vol.12, no.1, 1986, pp.85-8.

[16] London Municipal Society, *Houses for the People*, pamphlet of 1906 (Guildhall Library store, 612.3).

as an earnest of faith in dispersal.[17] Most of these men were middle-class Progressives, and some were single-taxers or radical religionists of the kind always attracted by experiments in community living. But some were Conservatives as well. The most interesting was Captain G.S.C. Swinton, who claimed in 1912 to have 'graduated in the school of Garden Cities' and to have 'sat at the feet of Mr. Howard for eleven years'.[18] Swinton was something of a practical planner; indeed he relinquished the Chair of the LCC on being appointed to the three-man commission for planning New Delhi in 1912. But he was also secretary of the London Municipal Society and probably the person most responsible for persuading the Municipal Reformers to endorse garden cities. In 1910 Swinton published a pamphlet under the LMS's auspices entitled *Spread The People*, which echoed and elaborated upon the sentiments expressed by Balfour a decade before.[19] The congestion of cities, he argued, was 'bad for trade and bad for the physique of the race'. Railways had done nothing to help disperse the population, so the state should invest in roads, principally a royal road or 'wayleave' drilled through the centre of every large town and stretching from the Channel to the Grampians. A 'land-way' through London 'of the width of the Thames' would give quick access to the depopulated countryside, encourage the erection of factories and houses on cheap land and promote the dispersal of the working classes, claimed Swinton. 'In the city they are an encumbrance. In an open land they can be left to look after themselves, they can scrape along somehow without harming anybody. Where the people mass together they become a danger.'

Swinton's eccentric scheme can never have commanded much practical support. But the tone of his remarks helps to explain why dispersal went on appealing to Conservatives before and after the First World War. In the aftermath of war and with the examples of Russia and Germany to hand, the appeasement and dispersal of the urban working classes became objectives of national housing policy. The post-war housing strategy of the LCC Municipal Reformers fell in with the dictates of this national policy from 1919 and the twists and turns of housing subsidy. Always keener to lower the rates than to embark upon new municipal ventures, they rarely showed overt enthusiasm for building council housing. But, backed by the LCC's housing and planning bureaucracy which had learnt how to build and manage suburban estates and expected to do more, they set dutifully about what they saw as a national responsibility. The attitudes of Cecil Levita, a long-serving Chairman of the LCC Housing Committee, were typical. 'It was generally

[17] Purdom, *op. cit.*, pp.28, 148, 169, 489.

[18] *Garden Cities and Town Planning*, vol. 11, 1912, pp.75, 76.

[19] G.S.C. Swinton, *Spread the People*, London Municipal Society pamphlet, [1910] (Greater London Record Office, P27.5).

understood his task was to slow down housing expenditure. He can be said to have come to curse and remained to bless. He was a soldier and had very much the military manner. But like everyone who has been brought up against the reality of the housing shortage, he soon became a convert and brought considerable drive into the work.'[20]

In this way a series of suburban LCC cottage estates sprang into existence in outer London, larger by far than the pre-war estates but no less barren of facilities: St. Helier, Watling, Downham, Bellingham, Mottingham and, above all, Becontree. These developments set a standard for decent working-class housing in the Greater London area on a scale never achieved before. But as communities they were a nullity – suburban commuting ghettoes without the vitality or companionship of the inner city, as Ruth Glass's study of Watling was the first to show objectively in 1939.[21] The underlying reason for their inadequacy was the Municipal Reformers' unwillingness to grasp the nettle of industrial location. Between the wars outer London, prospering as much of the rest of the country was not, acquired a hefty addition of manufacturing and other forms of employment. The LCC, having botched its first battle for increased boundaries in 1923, also failed to influence industrial location by any alternative means. This was most manifest in the case of Becontree, planned by the Municipal Reformers in the first flush of post-war optimism not as a mere suburban estate but as a great municipal garden city which would put rivals like Manchester's Wythenshawe to shame. The result was a travesty of expectations, a vast dormitory desert with little pockets of employment, rescued from disaster only by the arrival of Fords at Dagenham in 1931.[22] The Becontree debacle was a gift to LCC Labour propagandists in the years before they won power in 1934, as they sought to excoriate the Municipal Reformers for slackness and lack of vision in housing and planning policy.

### *Labour, Morrison and the Green Belt*

Yet Labour too believed in dispersal. It was the Labour Party which was to set the seal on the policy by translating it into an urgent national strategy after 1945 and helping to decant hundreds of thousands of Londoners out of their city in the following twenty years. Labour's record on the issue is so important that it merits examining in greater detail.

Early socialists appear to have been divided on the issue of dispersal. Middle-class Fabians, sanitary reformers, clerics, puritans, co-operators, single-taxers and simple-lifers, all of whom found a place among early

[20] Sir Percy Harris, *Forty Years In and Out of Parliament*, [1946], p.82.

[21] Ruth Durant (later Ruth Glass), *Watling, A Survey of Social Life on a New Housing Estate*, 1939.

[22] William A. Robson, *The Goverment and Misgovernment of London*, 1939, pp.431-7.

LCC Progressives, tended to approve of it. Labour representatives and social democrats were less clear-cut. Dispersal weakened urban solidarity, threatened to push down wage rates, and represented an interference in working-class life. The working men on the early LCC might be thought to have spoken out against it, but their leaders were heavily implicated in moral reformism. In particular John Burns, though he fathered the first Town Planning Act, seems never to have expressed a plain attitude on the subject. Thus was established a pattern whereby the pace was set by middle-class reformers, while the working-class communities directly affected by the policy looked in vain to their leaders for any sort of concerted attitude.

The LCC Labour Group, like the Progressives, consisted of an alliance between union representatives and middle-class radicals, but policy was set more centrally, through the London Labour Party. By 1920 the LLP had plumped wholeheartedly for dispersal. Here, as with so much to do with the Labour LCC, the personal attitude of Herbert Morrison was crucial. Morrison had lodged in Letchworth as a conscientious objector during 1917-18 and worked in a fellow socialist's market garden. Here he met his wife, a worker at the Spirella Corset Factory and a star performer in the decorous country dancing which took place at the Skittles Temperance Inn. He also re-encountered F.J. Osborn, a former schoolboy acquaintance and the most tenacious British propagandist for dispersal over the following fifty years.[23]

Morrison's Letchworth experience loomed large in his consciousness; arguably it was to prove critical to London's history. In 1920 he contributed an essay to *Garden Cities and Town Planning* advocating satellite towns rather than unchecked growth as the answer to London's expansion.[24] The same commitment to the garden city is pledged in Morrison's *Toryism: The Ratepayer's Enemy* of 1923. As Labour replaced the Progressives in the 1920s as the main opposition party on the LCC, its members made it plain that they objected not to suburban estates as such, but to the building of such estates outside a framework of regional planning, without their own industry and allocation of open space. In this more sophisticated attitude Morrison was backed by a growing band of well-briefed middle-class allies, notably Ewart Culpin, a professional planner, former official of the Garden Cities and Town Planning Association, and Labour LCC Member from 1925.

By the time that Labour captured the LCC in 1934, the garden city movement had fallen into the doldrums. Additionally, the emphasis of the

[23] Bernard Donoughue and G.W. Jones, *Herbert Morrison, Portrait of a Politician*, 1973, pp.41-3; Michael R. Hughes (ed.), *The Letters of Lewis Mumford and Frederick J. Osborn*, 1971, p.109.

[24] Herbert Morrison, 'A New London: Labour's View of the Satellite Towns', in *Garden Cities and Town-Planning*, May 1920. See also *ibid.*, June 1924, p.117.

national council-house programme was switched in 1935 from suburban development to flats on central sites through a change in government subsidies. These circumstances have obscured the degree of Labour's pre-war commitment to dispersal. Ever the pragmatist, Morrison was content for the time being to play the city boss and to bind his working-class allies and electorate with a show of efficiency in slum-clearance and rebuilding. It was in this capacity that the South London lawyer Lewis Silkin, later to preside over the creation of the post-war New Towns policy, gained his spurs as Chairman of the LCC Housing Committee. Once in power, Morrison opposed programmatic statements committing the Council to future policies without immediate prospect of implementation. So the LCC, for instance, proffered only statistical evidence in 1938 to the Barlow Commission on the Distribution of the Industrial Population, the first occasion at which the idea of government-backed satellite towns for London was seriously aired.[25] Pressure-groups like the Garden Cities and Town Planning Association (gradually being invigorated through the efforts of Frederick Osborn) and the Hundred New Towns Association made the running, with calls for planned dispersal on a scale never contemplated before. (The Hundred New Towns body airily threw about a target for reducing London by no less than two million people.) Throughout all this the LCC politicians kept cautiously in the background, content to shelter behind those like W.A. Robson who were arguing with growing articulacy for a democratic Greater London or regional government.

When therefore Patrick Abercrombie, by way of preparation for his County of London Plan, asked the LCC what it had in the way of documents for future planning strategy, he could discover no preparatory work to help him. 'We looked into the bottom drawer to see what was there, and we found absolutely nothing', he recollected.[26]. Yet the LCC leadership's commitment to dispersal was never in doubt. Proof of this lies in the one practical influence it was able to exert in Outer London in the 1930s: the inauguration of the Green Belt.

The idea of a 'belt' or 'girdle' of open space around London was as old as the LCC itself. Lord Meath, first Chairman of the LCC Parks Committee and an inveterate dispersalist, fresh-air enthusiast and eugenicist, had brought it to the attention of his committee as early as

[25] The evidence given to the Barlow Commission was never published, but can be found in the series PRO, HLG 27. LCC statistical evidence, HLG 27/35; Garden Cities and Town Planning Association, HLG 27/54; Hundred New Towns Association, HLG 27/59; W.A. Robson, HLG 27/68.

[26] Sir Patrick Abercrombie, 'Twenty Years After', *RIBA Journal*, 59, March 1952, p.157.

1890 after visiting the parkway systems of Boston and Chicago.[27] From time to time the idea had resurfaced, less and less in Meath's guise of a narrow strip for healthy recreation, more often as a device to limit the size of London. The Green Belt took clearer shape in the deliberations of the Greater London Regional Planning Committee, set up in 1927 by the Minister of Health, Neville Chamberlain, in a first attempt to make sense of the increasingly confusing issues of planning in and around the capital (since the LCC at that stage was taking scant interest in doing so). Raymond Unwin, who had planned Letchworth and been the driving force behind the Addison Housing Act of 1919, was the committee's technical adviser; a former Fabian, Unwin was strongly in favour of dispersal, indeed of 'rebuilding something like half London'.[28] To this end, he advised establishing a wide belt of green land all around London with a string of satellite towns beyond it. This recommendation was embodied in the committee's report of 1929. But the hopes of getting government money to buy land for the Green Belt came unstuck with the financial crisis of 1931, when the committee lost status and impetus. To get things going and avoid further loss of open land on the outskirts of London to speculators, the Labour LCC took unilateral action when it came to power. In 1935 it set up its own scheme, whereby the LCC gave grants to help neighbouring county councils buy up open space and farmland with an undertaking to maintain previous uses. Morrison was prominent in this initiative, abetted by his successive lieutenants in charge of the Parks Committee, Richard Coppock and Ruth Dalton. By the time of the war, nearly forty square miles had been 'safeguarded' by this means and an act of parliament secured to guarantee the Green Belt. Later acquisitions brought the total up to fifty-six square miles by 1970.[29]

The establishment of London's Green Belt has always been judged one of Herbert Morrison's cardinal achievements at the LCC. In the nick of time, it delimited the size of the capital and inhibited the worst excesses of megalopolitan sprawl. But it could never be an isolated policy. Given economic growth on the scale seen all through the south-east in the 1930s and a continuation of the existing trend whereby some 325,000 people moved out of Central London per decade, future outward movement was going to have to leap the barrier of the Green Belt and find new homes beyond it. The Green Belt meant that people and jobs would now have to

[27] Earl of Meath, 'Report to the Parks and Open Spaces Committee of the London County Council on the Public Parks of America', 1890 (copy in LSE Library); Earl and Countess of Meath, *Thoughts on Imperial and Social Subjects*, 1906, pp.105-24; Earl of Meath, *Memories of the Nineteenth Century*, 1923, pp.259-60; David Thomas, *London's Green Belt*, 1970, pp.73-7.

[28] Raymond Unwin on garden cities in *The London Rotarian*, 15 Oct. 1932, p.10.

[29] Green Belt: *RIBA Journal*, 44, May 1937, pp.677-85; Thomas, *op.cit.*, pp.51-2, 77-83; Elizabeth Sharp in *Planning History Bulletin*, vol.2, no.2, 1980, pp.12-16, 18.

go further. And the LCC, as the only authority with practical experience of dispersal, would have to help them do so.

### *Abercrombie and After*

The Second World War supplied a great psychological boost to those who favoured the dispersal of Londoners. Well before its outbreak, anxieties about aerial bombardment had coloured views about London and accelerated strategies for decentralizing not only people but industry. Evacuation, in the planning for which the LCC played a key role, was from one perspective a trial run for post-war dispersal; from another, it marked the final triumph in the long tradition stretching back to Octavia Hill of middle-class reformers' endeavours to take slum-bred children away from their corrupting families and circumstances and into the improving country air.[30] The LCC's day-to-day operations were geared to education, health and housing and it numbered reforming teachers, doctors and officials amongst its most active members and officers. So the Council prided itself on the efficiency with which it planned and implemented its massive evacuation programme well before the bombs began to fall. Yet many evacuees – parents and children – returned, dissatisfied with makeshift circumstances and rural or small-town life, and proved reluctant to be uprooted again once the bombardment started in earnest. This, or indeed any real measure of attitudes to dispersal, was never taken into account once planning for post-war dispersal began in earnest, with the commissioning of the two Abercrombie reports for London, the County of London Plan of 1943 and the Greater London Plan of 1944.

How Patrick Abercrombie came to devise a plan for the County of London is not quite clear. The foreword to the plan explains specifically that it was commissioned by Lord Reith, during the year in which the latter was framing the bare bones of the Government's administrative organization for post-war reconstruction.[31] How far he imposed the appointment upon the LCC may never be known. Whatever the truth, Abercombie, an experienced practical planner in the mould of Unwin and author of a minority report for the Barlow Commission, was an unabashed advocate of dispersal. By accepting him as a consultant with wide powers, a broad brief, and no requirement to talk to union leaders or

[30] On evacuation see Susan Isaacs, *The Cambridge Evacuation Survey*, 1941, and Richard M. Titmuss, *Problems of Social Policy*, 1950, pp.23-44, 357-69.

[31] J.H. Forshaw and Patrick Abercrombie, *County of London Plan*, 1944, p.v. But Patricia Garside, 'Town Planning in London 1930-1961', Ph.D., University of London, 1980, pp.251-4, believes that the view that the County of London Plan was due to government sponsorship 'misrepresents the character of the LCC's relations with the planning Ministries between 1940 and 1943'.

industrialists, the LCC's leaders were acquiescing in a plan which was bound to recommend a large measure of planned dispersal. How much and on what grounds were the questions. As to grounds, the autocratic Abercrombie and his small team of assistants inside and outside the LCC felt no obligation to marshal statistics or proof on the point; they were almost wholly architect-planners to whom, with the wartime mess of London around them, the need for dispersal and the broad-brush replanning of the capital was self-evident. The whole document was an 'improvisation', as Abercrombie himself admitted.[32] As to numbers, Abercrombie was at first to prove more lukewarm on the subject than the extreme advocates of dispersal such as Osborn had expected. Osborn indeed was displeased enough with the caution of the County of London Plan ('a profound disappointment. It talks the language of "decentralization" and plans to slow up the process as much as possible')[33] to badger Abercrombie into a more radical stance on dispersal in the succeeding Greater London Plan. Ever the persuader, Osborn also took care to cultivate Lewis Silkin, who had moved at the outbreak of war from chairing the LCC's Housing Committee to take on its Town Planning Committee. The setting for this courtship seems to have been the Labour Party's wartime Reconstruction Sub-Committee. Silkin had not hitherto been deemed an enthusiast for decentralization, and his conversion marked an important turning-point. Elevated after the war to Parliament, he was to be given immediate charge of the young Ministry of Town and Country Planning and to embark upon the New Towns Policy with remarkable fervour.[34]

Abercrombie set out his concrete proposals for dispersal and for satellite towns beyond London's Green Belt in his Greater London Plan, which involved the LCC only as one of several partners with the Ministry of Town and Country Planning. Theoretically, everything worked out quickly and neatly. The New Towns Act, expeditiously squeezed through Parliament in 1946 by Silkin during a gap in Labour's legislative programme, was to be applied first and foremost to fulfilling Abercrombie's plan for relieving London, where enormous housing pressures were building up, especially in the blitzed LCC area. The LCC, working for the first time in close partnership with a Labour Government, was supposed to decide at what 'densities' it would rebuild the various parts of the County of London. From this quite abstract planning principle was to flow how many citizens and industrial jobs the LCC could relinquish from the different parts of the capital to the eight New Towns

[32] *RIBA Journal*, vol.59, March 1952, p.157.

[33] Hughes, *op.cit.* (n.23), p.39; see also *ibid.*, pp.40, 45-7, 64-5, 91.

[34] F.J. Osborn and Arnold Whittick, *New Towns, Their Origins, Achievements and Progress*, 1977 edn., pp.53-4.

around London, soon expected to come on stream.[35]

Alas for the LCC and for Londoners, this was not how things worked out. Committed to Abercrombie's figure of a drop in the County of London's population from four to three and a third million, with Silkin mired down in opposition over plans for the first New Town at Stevenage, with housing lists mounting and the threat of people dispersed by the war trickling back into inner London, the LCC felt it had no alternative but to fall back on the old expedient of out-county estates. It was a policy undertaken *faute de mieux*, with no illusions: it meant Becontree all over again, or worse. The LCC still had no powers to establish factories or promote proper communities, and with the New Towns and Development Areas in cut-throat competition with each other to attract industry, it had no hopes of securing any. Instead, the Council was once more building working-class dormitory suburbs, further than ever from the centres of employment and entertainment, and to a large extent within the very Green Belt which the LCC had itself pledged to hold sacred ten years before. Nor were these estates freshly laid out or designed. To get them going, their construction was entrusted not to the LCC Architect but to the forcible Director of Housing, Cyril Walker. The post-war out-county estates represented the fag-end of the LCC's cottage-housing tradition – row upon monotonous row of two-storey houses with a bare minimum of layout, few shops and no amusements. The largest of these estates was at Harold Hill, Essex, where 7,380 units had been built or were under construction in 1949, followed by Aveley (5,200), Oxhey (4,200), Borehamwood (4,180), Debden (4,013), St. Paul's Cray (3,905) and Hainault (2,779). Compared to these figures, the amount of inner London housing built in these years by the LCC was trivial.[36]

Early efforts to prevent these estates from becoming single-class ghettoes were unavailing. Together with the county councils, the LCC did manage to attract a few firms to the edges of the out-county estates, but the vast majority of workers who lived there were commuters whose young families found themselves isolated. After 1950, when workmen's fares began to be phased out, it was expensive too to travel to work on the increasingly crowded commuter trains. A study of the Oxhey estate undertaken in 1952-4 found no mass misery of the kind that some critics claimed, but confirmed and deepened Ruth Glass's pre-war picture of a bleak social reality during the early years of LCC suburban estates.[37]

[35] Density: Garside, *op.cit.*, Ch.17; LCC Minutes of Proceedings, 17 July 1945, p.955, and 28 June 1949, pp.401-7.

[36] Out-county estates: LCC Minutes of Proceedings, 28 May 1946, pp.329-30, 30 July 1946, pp.515-7 and 21 Oct. 1947, pp.602-4. Numbers are from Walter Segal, *Housing, A Survey of the Post-War Housing Work of the London County Council, 1945-1949*, 1949, p.12, and *London Statistics*, new series vol.7, 1965, p.102.

[37] Margot Jefferys, 'Londoners in Hertfordshire, the South Oxhey Estate', in Ruth Glass (ed.), *London, Aspects of Change*, 1964, pp.207-55.

According to another report, Oxhey had 'no churches, no church halls, no public houses. After three years there is one small café. To enjoy these amenities the Oxhey citizens have to leave the Estate and visit neighbouring towns and this not only adds to their expenses of living, but prevents the growth of a sense of community.'[38] The contrast beween the life of these places and the seeming warmth of the old inner-city communities was to be a powerful stimulus to urban sociology in the 1950s.[39]

The LCC never looked complacently upon these developments. 'We have really re-created in these post-war estates exactly the conditions which everybody is united in condemning', lamented Geoffrey Hutchinson, LCC Member and MP for the area where the Hainault estate was being built.[40] But what could the Council do? Committed to a policy of dispersal, it continued to be unable to house its citizens in the special towns with industry attached which had been promised for them by Abercrombie and Silkin. At the end of 1950 a sum total of 451 dwellings had been completed in the New Towns, and many of these were occupied by building workers.[41] Harlow and Crawley were coming along, but Stevenage (Silkin's private Waterloo) had hardly got beyond infrastructure and other of the New Towns for London had only just been designated. So long as Silkin presided over the Ministry of Town and Country Planning, the course which many people were beginning to see as the sensible alternative, that of enlarging existing towns in the south-east, received short shrift. So as a stopgap measure the LCC did what it knew how to do – it built suburban housing.

1950 was the year in which dispersal began to take on some semblance of order and humanity. Completions in the New Towns began to creep up, Hugh Dalton replaced Silkin, and his ministry at last came forward with a scheme for deciding how people who wanted to leave London could be encouraged to go about it and where they might go.[42] Outer London was divided into sectors and linked with particular New Towns, according to geographical proximity. The Ministry did not at first want the County of London zoned in this way, maintaining airily that 'movement from the central areas may take place as easily in one direction or another'.[43] (It was at this time that the Abercrombie-derived language of 'export', 'reception', 'movement of population' and so on began to assume an unquestioned status in the literature.) The LCC demurred at this and in

[38] Quoted by Lloyd Rodwin, *The British New Towns Policy*, 1956, p.134.

[39] See notably Michael Young and Peter Willmott, *Family and Kinship in East London*, 1957, contrasting Bethnal Green with the LCC estate at Debden (alias Greenleigh).

[40] Parliamentary Debates, 5th series, vol.502, 1951-2, cols.126-9.

[41] Rodwin, *op.cit.*, pp.72-93.

[42] LCC Minutes of Proceedings, 1 Aug. 1950, pp.524-6 and 28 July 1953, pp.397-8.

[43] *Ibid.*, 1 Aug. 1950, p.525.

due course a similar scheme of zones was adopted, in addition to the Government's 'industrial selection scheme', which in effect ensured that those with the greatest incentive to leave were London's most skilled industrial workers. In addition, London was obliged to pay for this loss by means of a substantial contribution for ten years to the rates of the New Town in respect of each nominated family successfully housed. Since five out of six houses in the eight London New Towns were let to Londoners in 1956, the sums involved were not insubstantial. To make this system work, encourage dispersal and ease communications, many LCC and borough councillors from the relevant zones found their way on to the boards of the corresponding New Town Development corporations. Stevenage, for instance, was 'twinned' with St. Pancras and other parts of north-west London. Monica Felton, a borough councillor and former LCC member, chaired its development corporation from 1949 to 1951 (when she was dismissed by Dalton for left-wing deviationism); and Evelyn Denington, prominent in the affairs of the LCC and of St. Pancras and long active on the housing front, sat on the Stevenage Development Corporation for many years and chaired it for the last fourteen of its existence.[44]

*New Towns and Expanded Towns*

Yet throughout the 1950s the LCC longed to do something substantial outside London on its own account. Its machinery for housing design and production had been reformed after 1950 with an influx of young architects and planners and seemed, on the strength of schemes like the great Alton Estates at Roehampton, to promise better and braver housing. As the Ministry's cherished New Towns at last became recognizable as places, many – not least the younger LCC architects – were sorely disappointed at what they saw. The growing animus against them was articulated by J.M. Richards and Ruth Glass in the *Architectural Review* for 1953, which condemned their loose 'prairie planning', found them not so different from the despised out-county estates, and called 'the bluff of those who conjure with density figures'.[45] The County of London Development Plan, the revised and elaborated version of Abercrombie's sketch to which the Council was working from 1951, reduced his figure for 'overspill' down to 385,000, mainly because less people had come back to live in inner London after the war than expected.[46] Even after allowing for the completion of the out-county estates and postponing much of this

[44] Jack Balchin, *First New Town: An Autobiography of Stevenage Development Corporation 1946-1980*, 1980, pp.21-2.

[45] *Architectural Review*, vol.114, July 1953, pp.29-31 (Richards) and Dec. 1953, pp.358-60 (Glass).

[46] LCC Minutes of Proceedings, 18 Dec. 1951, pp.764-70.

reduced figure, the LCC was committed to taking over 75,000 people out of its area in the immediate future. Armed with New Town powers and an up-to-date approach to planning and architecture, the Council felt that it could build complete new communities faster and better on its own. Reginald Stamp and William Fiske, the Labour members in charge of LCC housing and planning in the early 1950s, advanced these arguments on the basis of the Council's expertise, and because the pressure of numbers was then so crushing and housing so critical in the politics of London that they were prepared to back anything which would get roofs over heads. Behind the scenes, they were being egged on by a swelling band of officers who were eager to show their mettle. Give them a neighbourhood in a New Town, argued the architect-planners, or better still a whole New Town, and at last there would be something worth seeing.

The Ministry of Town and Country Planning (after 1950 the Ministry of Housing and Local Government) stood out resolutely against the LCC all through this period. Eight of the fourteen original New Towns had been assigned to London, much to the dissatisfaction of those who had believed that any shift of jobs and people should favour the more depressed areas of Britain, in line with the anxieties of the 1930s and the preoccupations of the Barlow Commission. When the Conservatives came back to power in 1951, the designation of any further New Towns at all, let alone ones to 'relieve' London, became remote. With existing New Towns slow to grow, it seemed madness to encourage fresh ones, especially a municipal one which the Ministry might not be able to control. In 1951 Evelyn Sharp, the civil servant who was to dominate housing policy for a decade and more, dismissed the LCC's ambitions for building outside London in robust fashion:

> He [the Minister of Health] has put up with it in the LCC out-county estates in order to carry them on till the New Town Corporations were ready to take over, but they are now, or will shortly be, ready, and there is no longer any need to let the LCC continue building out-county. They can now safely concentrate on their proper job – the redevelopment of London.[47]

The LCC had one last bite at this cherry. Amid worsening relations between the Council and the Ministry, and with the prospects of the Herbert Commission bringing the LCC to an end, its architects and planners went ahead in the late 1950s and prepared plans for a high-density New Town at Hook in Hampshire. For those in the political know, it was always likely to prove a drawing-board exercise. In the event Hook was slain, seemingly to the civil servants' satisfaction, by the expedient of

[47] PRO, HLG 90/289, memorandum from Evelyn Sharp, 16 Jan. 1951.

influential local landowners finding the ministerial ear.[48]

There remained one way for the LCC to promote dispersal in the 1950s, and this was the device of the 'expanded town'. In retrospect it seems the sanest solution. To induce working-class Londoners in the name of some abstract standard of urban open space and density to go and live in suburban fields without local facilities or employment, or to spirit them off to an as yet incoherent new community, was authoritarian to a now unacceptable degree. But Londoners were already moving of their own volition to smaller, long-settled towns. To encourage them to do so appeared a wiser course of action. Thus was born the Town Development Act of 1952, an all-party measure instigated by Hugh Dalton during his brief period at the Ministry and taken through the legislature by his successor, Harold Macmillan. It was meant almost entirely for London, and stemmed from work Silkin had commissioned for co-ordinating dispersal policy. To avoid the wrangles over local jurisdiction and compulsory purchase which had so much delayed the New Towns, it provided machinery for 'town development' by voluntary agreement between the 'receiving' and 'exporting' authority, and for the easier building of factories and other employment-generating buildings.[49]

After brief suspicion of this Ministry-inspired bill, the LCC politicians took it up. In Evelyn Sharp's words, the LCC

> set out to use the Act; and by patient negotiation, generous financial contribution and a vast amount of work managed to conclude several agreements . . . It has gained enormously in reputation among the smaller local authorities of the south east as a result of its work under the Act. Before the war the London County Council had been feared – and indeed hated – as it dumped its housing estates wherever it could in the Home Counties, with small regard for the views of the local authorities concerned. In seeking to conclude town development agreements the post-war Council has won the confidence of many small authorities whose representatives before the war would as soon have entered a lion's den as County Hall.[50]

Proof of this is the promptness with which the Council approached authority after authority in the south-east in search of these agreements. In May 1952, for instance, with the new Act scarcely passed, top LCC members and officers were asking Berkshire County Council about possible expansions at Didcot, Wokingham or Newbury. Ashford in Kent was another town over which there was prolonged early negotiation.[51]

Some of these initiatives came to nothing. But at Andover, Ashford,

[48] London County Council, *The Planning of a New Town*, 1961, pp.9-10; information from Lady Denington and the late Hugh Morris.

[49] Debate on expanded towns: Rodwin, *op.cit.*, pp.134-5, 148-57.

[50] Evelyn Sharp, *The Ministry of Housing and Local Government*, 1969, p.173.

[51] Interesting papers on early town-development negotiations are in GLRO, AR/CB/1/173-86.

Aylesbury, Banbury, Basingstoke, Bletchley, Bury St. Edmunds, Haverhill, Huntingdon, Kings Lynn, Letchworth, Luton, Swindon, Thetford and Wellingborough, all beyond the radius of the London New Towns, the LCC won permission to build small or large housing developments for Londoners which for the most part proved better-looking than the out-county estates and socially less fraught than the early New Town communities.[52] In some places like the Suffolk village of Haverhill, the scale of development and the influx of population changed the character of the community completely. In effect, the larger expanded town schemes amounted to very much the same thing as the New Town which the LCC had always wanted to build, but without the political control from London, implicit or explicit, which the Government always feared. Landowners and other locals might still raise the spectre of 'slum-dwellers' and their bad behaviour, as they always did wherever the arrival of Londoners impended, but the fact that the agreements had been freely negotiated by local councils and contained a degree of economic incentive dampened opposition. Small-town populations too were by no means all averse to developments which might prevent the last local cinema from closing. The stimulus of the agreements with the LCC led some towns on to a prolonged path of growth. At Bletchley, the dull suburb which the LCC added on to the town led on step by step to the designation of the new city of Milton Keynes. At Swindon (much the biggest of the expanded town schemes, with over 6,000 houses completed by the time of the LCC's abolition in 1965) the influx of people and industry and the foresight of one official turned the town by degrees from a declining old railway community to a thriving centre of new technology. In all these developments, much depended on the relation between 'receiving' and 'exporting' authority. At Andover, where technical faults in housing built by the LCC and GLC ended in large-scale litigation, the issue went back to bad blood between the LCC and the local council in the early stages of development. By the time that it was settled in the 1980s, the reasons why a London authority should have been building in the midst of a Hampshire town seemed lost in the mists of the political past.

[52] *London Statistics*, new series vol.7, 1965, pp.104-5; information from Lady Denington, Lady Pepler and David Wisdom.

## *Chapter 13*

# *Conservatives and the LCC after 1934*

Helen Jones

The 1930s are usually portrayed as a decade when there were distinct differences between political parties in Britain, while the 1940s and the 1950s in contrast are seen as years of consensus. Recent evidence suggests that there was far more disagreement between the parties during the war years than was previously assumed,[1] although the idea of post-war consensus has remained largely unscathed. How accurate a portrayal is this of the local London political scene? Bernard Donoughue and George Jones in their biography of Herbert Morrison, leader of the London County Council from 1934 to 1940, present the Labour Party, personified by Morrison, as dynamic with very different policies from the Conservatives,[2] while the London Municipal Society (LMS) has been painted as increasingly moribund from the 1930s.[3] In this chapter an alternative interpretation can only be pointed to. Conservative and Labour Party policies were far closer in the 1930s than either would have had Londoners believe: differences were of tone not substance. In the early years of the Second World War the parties co-operated closely; as party politicking re-emerged towards the end of the war this heralded a period of more genuine policy differences.

It was not however what Labour was doing in office which encouraged some Conservatives to dismantle the LCC, and create the Greater London Council but rather, the fact that Labour was in office at all, and some feared, would continue in it. In the 1930s when the Labour Party heavily defeated the Conservatives, many Conservatives believed that vigorous opposition and improved organization would restore Tory fortunes. In the post-war years, although coming closer to victory, many

Bibliographical note. The records of the LMS are kept at the Guildhall Library, London; records of the Conservative Party are in the Bodleian Library, Oxford.

1 Kevin Jefferys, 'British Politics and Social Policy During the Second World War', *Historical Journal*, 30, I, 1987, pp.123-44.

2 Bernard Donoughue and G.W. Jones, *Herbert Morrison*, 1973, pp.189-210.

3 Ken Young, *Local Politics and the Rise of Party: The London Municipal Society and the Conservative Intervention in Local Elections, 1894-1963*, 1975, Chapter 7, entitled 'The fifth wheel'.

Conservatives lost faith in their ability to win back the LCC. For this reason some Conservatives, with a wider vision than those in the metropolitan boroughs, revived the idea of a Greater London Council which would embrace more 'natural' Conservative voters, and so restore London government to them. A similar scheme had been briefly toyed with by the LMS in the immediate years after the First World War, but abandoned when it became clear that it had no political mileage.

Until 1963 the Conservative Party continued to be fronted in London by the LMS. Most other Conservative front organizations, many of which, unlike the LMS, had operated in conflict with the Conservative Party during the 1930s, had been swallowed up in Lord Woolton's post-war Conservative Party reorganization. The LMS from the 1930s had not shown signs of independence and LMS history is very much that of the party. London Tory politics are best understood, therefore, if placed in the wider context of Conservative Party experience.

### *The 1930s: Decade of Municipal Consensus?*

A whole range of welfare issues, education, housing, public health and public assistance have been discussed in terms of expansion, improved services and increased spending after 1934. Labour is portrayed as the party of action in contrast to the slow inaction of the LCC under the Municipal Reformers. Morrison has been quoted, uncritically, as saying that the period of Municipal Reform rule was one of uncertainty, confusion, indecision and negation while Labour was full of vigour, decision, efficiency, creativity and progressiveness. 'Obstacles which had impeded the Municipal Reformers seemed to melt away'.[4] Conservatives had warned of the terrible fate that would befall Londoners if the Labour Party was elected: 'Labour Socialists would devote more attention to the establishment of Socialism and the destruction of private trade than to the discharge of essential municipal services'.[5]

In practice, although the tone of London under Labour was different from the years of the Municipal Reformers, there was no sea-change in the substance of policies for health, public assistance or any other area of welfare. Conservatives roundly criticized Labour for providing free treatment to all tuberculosis patients and for lowering rents, and Donoughue and Jones have emphasized the more humane and expanding services for the blind and for hospital patients; this is typical of wider trends throughout much of the country in response to national legislation. It is doubtful whether the impact of local government on Londoners would have been very different if the Municipal Reformers had continued

[4] Donoughue and Jones, *op.cit.*, p.199.
[5] *The Ratepayer*, No.97, March 1934, p.81.

to rule. Certainly there were sections of the London Labour Party which were critical of the LCC under Labour for failing to introduce any radical changes.[6] The framework of social legislation laid down by central government precluded any great differences in social policy, although there was scope for pursuing those policies with varying degrees of propaganda, and greater or lesser vigour and effort, thereby giving the impression that Party differences were more substantial.

Labour's distinctive achievement in education has received particular praise.[7] However, although rustlings of change were heard in the London Labour movement throughout the 1930s, no significant changes were implemented. The National Association of Labour Teachers, which was strong in London, had published a document in 1930 in favour of a common secondary school for all children over the age of eleven. The Elementary Education and Higher Education Sub-Committee, of which Barbara Drake was chairman, proposed in 1935 introducing non-selective 'multiple-bias' schools and the following year Drake contributed to a New Fabian Research Bureau pamphlet in which she argued for multi-lateral schools alongside existing ones.[8] Nothing came of these proposals.

Both parties gave the impression, in public, of a sea-change in London education after 1934; in practice there was a good deal of continuity and agreement between Labour and the Conservatives. In the years following the Municipal Reformers' defeat in 1934 the LMS repeatedly criticized Labour over its education policies, although in private it was admitted that Labour had not introduced anything new to London's education.[9] The Conservatives' loudest criticism was that socialist ideology was being imposed in London schools. This was however a difference of tone rather than substance: the Conservatives criticized the LCC for changing 'Empire' to 'Commonwealth Day' celebrations in schools and for discouraging 'any worthy feelings of racial superiority or antagonism to the rest of the world'. The LMS also disapproved of a London Labour Party resolution to set up a committee to examine school text books so that those which were inaccurate and unreliable could be replaced by more impartial ones.[10] One of the most frequent Conservative criticisms of the Labour LCC was its placing a memorial tablet to Karl Marx on one of his residences and publishing a short biography of him which portrayed him

[6] London Municipal Society, *Two Years of Socialist Rule*, 1939, p.17, London Municipal Society, *One Year of Socialist Rule*, 1935, p.7; Donoughue and Jones, *op.cit.*, p.200; see chapter in this volume by Mark Clapson.

[7] Donoughue and Jones, *op.cit.*, p.201.

[8] Rodney Barker, *Education and Politics, 1900-1951: a Study of the Labour Party*, 1972, pp.66-71.

[9] K. Jefferys, 'The Educational Policies of the Conservative Party, 1918-44', Ph.D., University of London, 1984, p.264.

[10] London Municipal Society, *One Year of Socialist Rule*, 1935, pp.6-7.

as an industrious scholar who was fond of children.[11]

Despite some appearances of dispute over raising the school-leaving age and the shape of secondary education in the wake of the Hadow Report, the differences between the parties were over timing, not principle. Both parties believed that it was desirable to raise the school-leaving age, although Labour would have liked to do it immediately. Instead, Labour was constrained by the Conservative-dominated National Government. To some extent there were differences over the type of secondary schools children should attend. Labour wanted to introduce some multi-lateral schools, but also expand secondary schools. The LMS criticized this for laying too great an emphasis on academic education and not enough on practical and technical schools. Labour retorted that the Conservatives wanted to restrict a good academic education to those who could afford to pay.

How can these similarities best be explained? It has been argued that both parties worked under similar constraints while in office. For instance, elementary reorganization was hindered by the difficulty of incorporating voluntary schools into the system, even after the 1936 Education Act. Moreover, although Labour did have more money to spend on education as the economy improved, it was not so much more that it could transform London education. Strict financial control was exercised over all areas of expenditure by Charles Latham, Labour's chairman of finance, nicknamed the 'Iron Chancellor'.[12] All this was compounded by Herbert Morrison's lack of interest in education because he did not believe it to be a vote-catcher, and winning the 1937 election was of paramount importance to him.[13] One further factor helps to explain the continuity in the structure of London's education. Labour's strategy was one of changing the hidden curriculum, such as abolishing the cadet corps and scrutinizing textbooks. This was attractive because it gave the appearance of a policy which was different from the Conservatives and at very little expense.

As with education, there was a great deal of continuity in Labour's housing policy, which the Conservatives were in this case willing to admit publicly: Sir Cecil Levita, previously Chairman of the Housing Committee under the Municipal Reformers, affirmed in a lecture on LCC housing in 1936 that there was no great divergence between the LMS and Labour.[14] Ken Young and Patricia Garside in *Metropolitan London: Politics*

[11] London Municipal Society, *Two Years of Socialist Rule*, 1936, p.19. The same criticism was made for many years.

[12] Jefferys, 'Educational Policies . . .' (n.9), pp.266-7; Donoughue and Jones, *op.cit.*, p.192.

[13] British Library, Add. Mss. 59,697, Chuter Ede Diary, 4 February 1943, p.19; Lord Morrison of Lambeth, *Herbert Morrison: An Autobiography*, 1960, p.144.

[14] London Municipal Society, *LCC Housing: Lecture by Sir Cecil Levita, 29th June 1936*, 1936, p.3.

*and Urban Change 1837-1981* (1982), conclude that the only room for manoeuvre in housing policy was marginal change in the weight given to inner-city tenements and out-county cottages. 'Despite the claim in 1934 that Labour had decisively switched the emphasis in housing policy back to tenements and slum clearance, the retreat from cottage estates occurred six years before their election'.[15] As with education, LMS and Labour Party housing policies were subject to similar constraints. The problems with which Labour had to contend had already been faced by Municipal Reformers: efforts to find new sites for building were hampered by local opposition, large landowners, speculative buying, and the absence on desirable sites of particular features specified by the LCC. While the development of outer London was helped by economic recovery from the slump of 1929-31, the competition for scarce sites correspondingly intensified. Whereas economic recovery slightly helped Labour's education policy, it had the opposite effect on its housing plans.

While the LMS had favoured the building of 'cottage estates' in outer London to rehouse those moved by slum clearance, Labour favoured tenement blocks within LCC boundaries; this fitted in well with the subsidy system introduced by the National Government to encourage slum clearance. At the same time Labour continued the Municipal Reformers' search for suitable sites in outer London, which fitted in with a traditional Labour party concern with houses set in their own gardens with open spaces. Morrison gave lip-service to the idea but warned that it was not

> a political or municipal programme for London . . . it is not practical politics for today: it is a vision of the London of my dreams; the London I should like to see [which] cannot constitute a practical programme for either of the political parties at the next London County Council election, for then we shall not be able to ignore financial and other practical considerations, nor the legal limits on our area and Local Government powers.[16]

Young and Garside emphasize that both the LMS and Labour Party in office operated a policy of 'low cost opportunism'. 'Labour built more homes but the underlying assumptions of the LCC housing programme were remarkably unresponsive to political change.' Indeed the ethos of Labour's housing programme complemented Conservative sentiments, for Morrison emphasized compromise and agreement in building a London in which its inhabitants could feel 'civic pride'.[17]

In the early years of the Second World War party rhetoric subsided. In

[15] Ken Young and Patricia Garside, *Metropolitan London: Politics and Urban Change, 1837-1981*, 1982.

[16] Herbert Morrison, 'What I would like to do for London', *Evening Standard*, 9 January 1936.

[17] Young and Garside, *op.cit.*, pp.173-218.

1939 an Emergency Committee of six Labour and four Conservative members ruled London and all other committees were temporarily suspended.[18] The two parties co-operated closely, especially over air-raid precautions in the initial stages, but gradually Conservative criticisms of Labour's alleged incompetence in dealing with housing and the education of children in LCC homes re-emerged.[19] These criticisms were to herald a period of more profound disagreement than had existed in the party bickering of the previous decade.

### *An End to Consensus: The Early Post-War Years*

In the post-war years Conservative and Labour policies became more distinctive. The permissive factors for Labour were the economic situation and initially a Labour Government in Whitehall. The Conservatives never forgot Labour's alleged dirty campaign in 1934 while keeping up the attack on current Labour policies. 'We suffer from one disadvantage compared with the Socialists – we remember the people who have to pay for these services as well as those who benefit from them'.[20] Nevertheless both sides had carefully thought out a more distinctive policy than previously.

By the early 1950s the Conservatives claimed there were 'fundamental cleavages' between themselves and Labour over housing policy.[21] The key to this cleavage was the collapse of the pre-war private housing boom and Labour's policy of council-house building in concentrated areas.[22] Differences between the parties now went far beyond mere rhetoric; the two parties were pretty evenly balanced in elections but Labour's policy was seen as electorally disastrous for the Conservatives in the longer term as well as ideologically unsound. In vain the Conservatives called for a boost to private housing and the leasing of sites to organizations such as housing associations, so that 'a genuine mixed community' could be created.[23] There was also concern after the war that concentrated council-house building could affect the electoral chances of Conservative MPs. Housing policy was also vital to the Labour Party's fortunes nationally at this time too, because it was on this issue more than any other that the country judged the government's success. The Labour Party was conscious of the importance the electors placed on housing and the main thrust of the LCC Labour Group's Report in 1946 was Labour's housing

[18] *The Ratepayer*, September-December 1939, no.161, p.317.
[19] *The Ratepayer*, November 1944, no.176.
[20] London Municipal Society, *London's Local Government: The Work of the LCC*, 1949.
[21] London Municipal Society, *LCC Elections: 1952 Campaign Guide*, 3 April [1952].
[22] Young and Garside, *op. cit.*, pp.287-8.
[23] London Municipal Society, *The LCC Housing: LCC Elections, 1946*, 1946. pp.9-10; *The Londoner*, December 1948.

achievement.[24]

It was over education that the most substantial differences between Conservatives and Labour were to emerge. In 1954 it was claimed that Labour's plans to go comprehensive produced the first deep ideological division since the LCC had taken over responsibility for education from the London School Board.[25] The 1944 Education Act required local authorities to submit their plans for education, but did not dictate the form it should take. On 1 August 1944 (before the 1944 Act was passed) the principle of comprehensive education was put to London's Education Committee and later the London School Plan was published, setting out a system of comprehensive schools for the capital.[26] The plan was adopted by the LCC in March 1947 and the first moves towards comprehensive education were under way. It was not until 1954 that the first purpose-built comprehensive opened and even then grammar schools were prevented from being incorporated. The Conservatives, while urging the implementation of the 1944 Act in full, argued for the development of new schools, specializing in technical and 'modern' curricula, parallel with grammar schools and all on a par in prestige and amenities. Along with Labour, the Conservatives were keen to see a school programme which included both the building of new schools and the renovation of old ones. The Conservatives' main demands were for new buildings, smaller classes, more teachers, an extension of technical education, science and trade schools, and for all those with the ability to be helped to a university education. At the other end of the age range they underlined the importance of nursery education.[27] In the late 1940s they were critical of the way Labour administered the existing system, especially text-book shortages, inadequate meal-time accommodation, poor lavatories and the lack of new buildings.[28]

The Conservatives in the early 1950s were only willing to experiment with two or three comprehensives, and they had little faith in them. They doubted whether pupils would receive individual attention in the large schools proposed. American schools on a similar model, they claimed, showed lower academic standards than British grammar schools and failed to create social equality. It was also suggested that a comprehensive, by drawing pupils from one area, would actually reduce the social mix of London schools. Evidence from comprehensives in other

[24] *Wandsworth Borough News*, July 1946; *South Western Star*, 1946; *Clapham Observer*, March 1946.

[25] 'London Schools', *The Londoner*, July 1954, p.226.

[26] A Griffiths, *Secondary School Reorganisation in England and Wales*, 1971, p.32.

[27] London Municipal Society, *London LCC Elections, 1946*, 1946, p.9.

[28] Guildhall Library, London Municipal Society, MS 19,527 (Report of Executive Committee to the Council, January 1948, LMS and Ratepayers' Union, 47th Report issued by the Council).

parts of the country was hardly relevant to London; they ranged in size from 210 to 2,150 pupils, and at least half the comprehensives were in Anglesey and the Isle of Man. Conservatives questioned whether a comprehensive school in a rural area or a small island community was relevant to the vast, mixed urban life of London. They queried whether anyone indeed really knew the meaning of a 'comprehensive' school. Added to this was a condemnation of Labour's 'wanton destruction of the traditions and standards' by proposing the expansion of existing grammar schools into comprehensive ones.[29] The Conservatives believed that if comprehensives were introduced they had to be set in the context of selective schools: parental choice had to be maintained. So in 1953 the Minister of Education refused to sanction the merger of an LCC grammar school with an existing comprehensive on the grounds that it would change the nature and status of the grammar school.[30]

### *The End of the LCC*

Two themes constantly recurred in Conservative analyses of why they lost London in 1934 and failed to regain it three years later. Conservatives focused on what they believed to have been Labour's dirty campaign of labelling them 'Baby Starvers' and referring to Tories' 'brutal inhuman treatment' of applicants for public assistance (Labour thought the Tories' portrayal of the Labour LCC 'direct lies').[31] More significant in the longer term were complaints about the apathy of Conservative voters and their lack of interest in London's government.[32] Lord Jessel, President of the LMS, frequently referred to the 'lamentable' indifference of voters in local elections.[33] Complaints about the lack of interest in local government did not abate, although during the war years the Tories consoled themselves with the thought that Labour suffered from the same problem;[34] Conservative organization throughout the country was run down during the war, not just in London.[35] By the 1950s the lack of interest in London

[29] London Municipal Society. *LCC Elections 1946: The LCC Education Plan*, 1946, pp.9, 12-13; *The Londoner*, July 1951, 'Education in London', p.46.

[30] Michael Parkinson, *The Labour Party and the Organisation of Secondary Education, 1918-1965*, 1970, p.75.

[31] *The Ratepayer*, No.98, April 1934, pp.113-4, and no.99, May 1934 (Sir Samuel Gluckstein at Annual Council Meeting, 18 April 1934); The London Labour Party, EC 33(34/5), Executive Committee agenda for 4 July 1935, item no.5, 'Latest London Municipal Society Propaganda'.

[32] *The Ratepayer*, No.115, October 1935, p.261; Guildhall Library, MS 19, 527, Council Meeting, 8 May 1935.

[33] London Municipal Society, *Socialism in Local Government*, 1936, 1937 and 1938 edns.

[34] *The Ratepayer*, No. 168, March 1942, p.500.

[35] Ken Young on the other hand, believes the war to have been a period of activity and transformation for the Party: Ken Young, *Local Politics and the Rise of Party*, 1975.

government was being put forward as an argument in favour of the LCC's abolition.[36] Because of this lack of interest among Conservatives, the LMS found it difficult to recruit candidates of suitable calibre.[37] It was from the 1930s that Conservative activists' concerns over lack of interest in London Government, the absence of suitable candidates and the weaknesses of internal organization became firmly established.

In the late 1930s the Tories secretly began to examine their own organization. Initially, it was felt that publicity should be overhauled, but by the end of 1937 a full-scale review of London organizations, both for local and national elections was decided upon. A committee was set up under Sir Kingsley Wood, and although the report was never made public, Neville Chamberlain wrote to the LMS with a number of organizational suggestions, including more effective mutual aid, strengthening the Junior Imperial League and Young Britons, improving propaganda and fighting every seat at General and LCC Elections. Meanwhile the LMS newspaper was improved and its name changed from *The Ratepayer* to *The Londoner*, and endless discussions continued over changing the name of the LMS.[38]

To focus on these internal questions is misleading. Ken Young has emphasized the internal weaknesses of the LMS and its increasing redundancy in London politics. Yet, whichever organization had been in charge of London Conservatives, it would have faced similar problems. The LMS was, in all but name, interchangeable with the Conservative Party by this time. It had not acted independently from the Conservative Party as had some other Tory front organizations, and from the mid-1930s organizational matters such as financial support for LCC elections, the selection of candidates, the running of campaigns and the arrangement of meetings were dealt with by the Conservative Party.[39] In post-war elections candidates even stood under the name 'Conservative'.[40] To understand the significance of changes in London Conservative politics, it is necessary therefore to move away from the increasingly redundant LMS – because the Conservative Party had already taken over the effective running of local organization – and look to broader changes in London politics.

In the 1930s the Conservatives still believed that they could recapture London, despite a poor showing at the polls; in the post-war years their

[36] Robert Vigars, 'Local Government Reform in London', *The Londoner*, April 1959, p.72.

[37] *The Ratepayer*, No. 168, March 1942, p.500; *The Londoner*, April 1959 p.71.

[38] Guildhall Library, MS 19,527, Council Meetings 31 May 1937, 25 November 1937, 5 December 1937, 16 November 1938, 5 June 1939; MS 19,528, Executive Meetings.

[39] I should like to thank Dr. John Ramsden, Queen Mary College, London for offering me the use of his notes on which this information is based.

[40] Ken Young, *op. cit.*, p.196.

belief in the possibility for doing so receded, despite a much improved showing in LCC elections. Failure to recapture the LCC in 1947 was compounded by the 1947 Fulham by-election loss. In the 1930s Conservative analyses had focused on apathy, which was put down to demographic shifts, such as the number of new and temporary residents.[41] Gradually the focus shifted from the apathy to the demography of London.

It was after the Conservatives not only failed to regain London in 1952 but also lost another twenty-seven seats that serious analysis began. Central Office's concern was less over the organizational failures of the LMS than the demographic changes taking place in London. H.V. Armstrong, previously a Central Office Agent, presented an analysis of the subject in 1952. He realized that London was changing. From the 1930s businessmen and professionals were moving outside LCC boundaries into the suburbs of Middlesex, Surrey and Kent and their property was being turned into flats for working-class households. Demographic shifts were aggravated by organizational problems; lack of leadership, poor quality agents, and the absence of a community spirit among 'natural' Tory voters. The war intensified the trend; many who could afford to move out of London did so, and few later returned.[42] Inevitably there was a lack of local feeling in a conurbation like London; such individuality as constituencies had had in the past was now blurred and redistribution was further destroying it. The Conservative Party machine was localized and a lack of local feeling told against it. In contrast Transport House, the Labour Party's headquarters, was thought to be well placed to respond quickly and decisively. The Labour Party's organizational strength was seen to lie in its local trade union links. So, for instance, there were dock workers in riverside constituencies and railway workers in the St Pancras area. Moreover, after years of personal supervision by Morrison, the Labour Party machine was much stronger. The Conservatives had had no such continuity or inspiration and no leader of equal national stature. Local associations also complained about the apathy of Conservative voters and workers, although blame was also apportioned to the Labour Party for focusing on national rather than local issues and to ill-timed and unpopular government announcements.[43]

This was probably an accurate assessment; evidence from Bermondsey, a riverside community, shows the working class to have been well organized and strong supporters of trade unions. The co-operative movement also had firm roots. In Fulham trade unions were not

[41] *The Ratepayer*, No. 115, October 1935, p.261.

[42] Bodleian Library CCO/2/2/3, Appreciation of London Organisation, p.3; H.V. Armstrong to T.F. Watson, 24 April 1952.

[43] Guildhall Library, MS 19,528, LMS Meeting of the Executive Committee, 6 May 1952.

so active in the Labour Party but still strong, and the Fulham Co-operative Party and Women's Co-operative Guild were both affiliated to the Labour Party.[44] Conservative perceptions of a flight to the suburbs were also accurate.

Discussions over the future of London government had been under way from before the Second World War. The Ullswater Royal Commission had looked into the possibility of changing London's government but its report did not lead to major reforms. Just before the outbreak of the Second World War William Robson published a damning attack, *The Government and Misgovernment of London* (1939), in which he proposed a complete overhaul and a new and enlarged authority to run London.[45] The Conservatives returned to office in 1951 committed to a reform of local government, although they made no specific mention of London.[46] In July 1957 Henry Brooke, Minister of Housing and Local Government, announced to the House of Commons that a Royal Commission would consider the future of London government in a Greater London context. The Royal Commission under Sir Edwin Herbert argued that this was necessary in order that London government would reflect social and economic changes; on the whole London had grown as a 'single great city', outward from the centre, and the task of the Royal Commission was to mirror these changes in its recommendations.[47] Not surprisingly the 1960 Report recommended a Greater London Council as a strategic planning body for roads, industry, housing and education. The day-to-day running of services was to be in the hands of the boroughs, whose powers would now be greater than under the LCC. As the GLC's boundaries were more extensive than the LCC's, many boroughs previously beyond the sway of London government, were now to be included. The metropolitan areas of Essex, Kent, Surrey and Hertfordshire as well as the county boroughs of Croydon, East and West Ham were to be part of a Greater London government.

Despite growing divergencies over policies, at no time did the Conservatives link the Labour-controlled LCC's actions to their own future or the future of London government. Growing disquiet in sections of the party with the LCC related to the Tories' failure to recapture London, not what Labour was doing in London, even though there was enormous Conservative hostility to Labour policies.

Conservatives were interested in the future of London government in order to increase their powers. No single party line ever existed on the issue; the Herbert Commission actually commented on the divergence of

[44] John E. Turner, *Labour's Doorstep Politics*, 1978, pp.89, 93, 97, 144.

[45] William A. Robson, *The Government and Misgovernment of London*, 1939.

[46] F.W.S. Craig, *British General Election Manifestos, 1950-1974*, 1975, p.173.

[47] Royal Commission on Local Government in Greater London, 1957-60, Report and Maps, 1959-60 (Cmd. 1164), Vol.XVIII, p.19.

views between the Bow Group and the LMS.[48] No detailed planning on London government took place within the Party until after the GLC was set up.[49] Central Office wanted the Conservatives to control London and this involved the expansion of the LCC's boundaries to embrace more Conservative voters: 'Our concern is the *political control* of any future new type of local authority'.[50] Most Conservative metropolitan boroughs, supported by the LMS, hoped to increase their own powers.[51] There was not one, but various 'interests' within the Party, although Central Office was keen to cover this up in public and reconcile the differences in private.[52] It felt that 'some of the opposition [to the Herbert Commission's recommendations] expressed by the Councils did not make any attempt to equate local feeling with the problem of Greater London or the problem of the development of local government'.[53]

Central Office was concerned that some local borough Conservatives only thought in terms of their own immediate government, not London government as a whole;[54] no grass-roots Conservative desire for a London-based regional government existed. The Parliamentary Housing and Local Government Committee had indeed been anxious about the absence of a policy on the future of local governmental structure in London, fearing that as Labour spoke with one voice in favour of maintaining the existing structure, the Royal Commission would accept its case through the lack of any unanimous alternative.[55] Although the Royal Commission came out in favour of an enlarged Greater London Council this was not without its problems for Central Office, which in an effort to co-ordinate the Party, gathered the views of a range of London Conservatives.[56] It was hindered in drawing up a policy statement because of the divided loyalties of those best placed to help them, the agents. One illustration will suffice. It was feared that if the Ilford agent was approached, he would inform his council group that Central Office was looking to the overall interests of London; this information would be useful to Ilford Conservatives who intended to fight for county borough status, 'regardless of the consequences to other Conservatives'.[57]

[48] Royal Commission on Local Government in Greater London, 1957-60. Report and Maps, 1959-60 (Cmd. 1164), Vol. XVIII, p.58.

[49] John Ramsden, *The Making of Conservative Party Policy: The Conservative Research Department since 1929*, 1980, p.216.

[50] CCO/4/8/351, Horton 27 February 1958.

[51] CCO/4/8/351, Royal Commission on Local Government in Greater London.

[52] CCO/4/8/351, Toby Low.

[53] CCO/4/8/351, Royal Commission on Local Government in Greater London, p.2.

[54] CCO/4/8/351, 12 December 1958, from a confidential report issued to members of LCC.

[55] CCO/4/8/351, 26 June 1959, Graham Page MP to W.H.L. Urton.

[56] CCO/4/8/351.

[57] CCO/4/8/351, Horton, 27 February, 1958.

A committee at Central Office gathered the views of all the areas that might be affected by the Royal Commission's recommendations. An analysis of the reports from the South-Eastern Area, London Areas, and a combined report from the Home Counties North and Eastern Areas showed that there was a fair amount of disagreement between Conservatives. For example, there were differences between constituency associations and party members actively engaged in local government work. Differences also existed over the method of election to the GLC. In the main, county councils and a majority of Conservative members of Surrey and Kent County Councils opposed the Commission's proposals. Particular worries existed over the suggested allocation of resources to the GLC, especially for education. Most agreed that for certain functions such as planning, sewage, intelligence, drainage and roads, some form of overall authority was necessary. Areas like Bromley, Esher, Croydon North-West, Carshalton and Mitcham feared that really 'local' government would be replaced by an impersonal bureaucracy. The GLC's control of education was regarded as unworkable. Instead it was suggested that the Greater London boroughs should control primary and secondary education. The largest percentage of rate expenditure would thereby be under local control and the management of education closer to those affected. There was also strong feeling against GLC control of housing. It was argued that the boroughs should be responsible for owning and building houses and the overspill should be the responsibility of the Minister of Housing and Local Government.

Responses in the Middlesex and Essex areas were mixed. While thirty constituencies were broadly in favour of the Herbert Report (Chigwell Council group were in favour only if they were excluded), six constituencies opposed the report outright on grounds of the size of the proposed government and the slowness with which it would operate, two constituencies had doubts about how 'human' the GLC could be as a policy-making body, four wanted positive safeguards for 'freedom in local action' and three thought the proposed GLC should be split in two.[58]

Experience of a Labour-controlled LCC did not lead to a concerted attempt by London Conservatives to take over the running of London government. For most grass-roots Conservatives control over their own borough was of paramount importance. It was the professionals at Central Office who led the way in rethinking Conservative Party strategy and in reconciling conflicting Conservative interests. Central Office responded not so much to the experience of a Labour-controlled LCC, but rather to the experience of long-term opposition. Housing was the only area of Labour policy which affected Conservative thinking about London government and this was not because of Labour's alleged record of

[58] CCO/4/8/351, reports from various areas.

'failure', but the 'success' it was feared it might have in further changing the demographic structure of London to Labour's advantage. First and foremost it was the party managers' belief that class, rather than policies or organization, was the key to local authority control which prompted change. Ironically this was also the time when ideas about the 'death of class' and the 'embourgeoisement of the working class' were current, and the Conservative Party had expended much energy in the late 1940s on rethinking its policies and rebuilding its organization nationally.

The Conservative Government had to reconcile the different Conservative interests. In a White Paper published in November 1961 it accepted the broad recommendations of the Royal Commission, with certain changes. Legislation increased the powers of the boroughs at the expense of the new overall strategic authority. The outer boroughs kept control of education and a new Inner London Education Authority was created which was under the joint control of the new Greater London Council and the inner London borough councillors.

Boroughs became planning authorities which increased their powers, against the Herbert Commission's recommendations. Also, contrary to the Royal Commission's proposals, a number of Conservative areas such as Epsom and Esher managed to negotiate their exclusion from the new Greater London Council. Between the publication of the White Paper and the abolition of the LCC, strong opposition to government policy was mustered, culminating in the establishment of a Committee for London Government. There was bitter fighting in both Houses of Parliament, and over 1,000 amendments were put down during the committee stage of the Bill.[59] Bitter conflict at the local level spilled over on to the national stage, providing further evidence that the early post-war years were not ones of consensus and weakening class loyalties. The irony is that when the first GLC elections were held the Conservatives failed to gain a majority. The *raison d'être* of a Greater London Council for the Conservative Party died in the course of its creation. The abolition of the GLC twenty years later by a Conservative Government is perhaps less surprising, therefore, than its creation.

[59] Frank Smallwood, *Greater London: The Politics of Metropolitan Reform*, 1965, p.31.

## *Chapter 14*

# *Partnership Denied: The London Labour Party on the LCC and the Decline of London Government, 1940-1965*

John Mason

This chapter compares attempts by the London Labour Party to reform metropolitan government in the early 1940s with the lack of its effective response to reorganisation in the 1960s. These two episodes are linked by a discussion of the nature of the leadership of the London County Council in the intervening years.

There is, first of all, the special problem of London. The character of London government is corporate and oligarchic rather than local and democratic. Whatever the achievements of the Metropolitan Board of Works, the Metropolitan Asylums Board, the Metropolitan Water Board, Port of London Authority, London Passenger Transport Board and London Residuary Body, there has been no push towards popular representation. Indeed several of these organizations were established precisely to prevent such an occurrence. This gives a fragility to the history of London's own instruments of government which we do not find in Manchester, Leeds or Sheffield. The LCC and its successor, the Greater London Council, are to a certain extent implicated in maintaining this cosy and narrow state of existence, though the LCC less so in its early Progressive phase.

The birth of the LCC was itself a centralizing (or regionalizing) act designed to replace the chaos of nineteenth-century boards and the unevenness of individual vestries. The growth of London, split between scores of different agencies, had to be regionalized. From the beginning therefore, there existed a strong tension between the need to represent local communities and the necessity to amalgamate and rationalize, as suburban growth pushed London outwards.

There seems to be no problem in outlining the history of the LCC from Labour's remarkable victory of 1934. Firstly, came three years of concerted but gradual consolidation crowned by Labour's electoral triumph of 1937. This was followed by the period up to and including the war when the LCC, despite a diminution of its powers and a weakening of

*I wish to thank Mary Carter, Ellis Hillman, Susan Laurence, Ellen Leopold, Patrick MacDonnell and Susan Pennybacker for their assistance and comments.

members' control stemming from wartime exigencies, succeeded in maintaining a new found popularity. Then occurred the assumption and tenacious hold of power by the despotic (Sir) Isaac Hayward (1947-65). The final phase stretched from Labour's largest victory ever in 1958 to the report of the Herbert Commission and the subsequent abolition of the LCC.

The difficulty is to describe Labour's contribution to London's post-war reconstruction and the welfare of its citizens; to decide why – despite the size of its house and school-building programmes – this achievement seems so pale; and, to relate these findings to the underlying issues of London government.

During the quarter of a century spanning the period of 1940-65 the LCC exercised the widest influence on the lives of Londoners of any metropolitan 'civic' institution on the assumptions of a 'bureaucratic-rational' kind. Even those who, like the members of the 1960 Royal Commission, came to advocate its abolition, did so largely on planning grounds derived from the model of rational administration.[1]

According to this logic the rationality of the bureaucratic politics of Morrison and his successors was wholly consistent with the tasks of reconstruction facing London in 1945. Was the flaw that Morrison and his successors were not 'rational' enough? Or did the strength of the boroughs pull them back from the achievement of their true goals?

At every stage in the history of the LCC a number of interrelated themes recur. Examples are its relationship to Parliament and to national bodies, the problem of public utilities, only one of which – the trams – ever came under its control, and the issue of borough politics. The view of the LCC itself and the various attempts to review its structure, two of which are described here, was from the 'top down'. This does not necessarily push aside the borough problem. The strength of the Herbert Commission, for example, lay in its admirable commitment to *local* democratic institutions:

> Local government . . . is with us an instance of democracy at work, and no amount of potential administrative efficiency could make up for the loss of active participation . . . by . . . people elected by, responsible to, and in touch with those who elect them.[2]

The commission touched the raw nerve of Labour's problem – the failure to meet the need for a more representative politics. W.J.M. Mackenzie, perhaps its most influential member, commenting on the continued

[1] Royal Commission on Local Government in Greater London, 1957-60, Cmnd. 1164, 1960. The commission's analysis is more subtle than this suggests. Nevertheless, when it came to framing their proposals, planning considerations were uppermost. See, for example, their careful yet radical criticisms of the Greater London Plan, pp.83-93.

[2] *Ibid.*, p.59.

survival of the metropolitan boroughs, noted seven years previously that

> it now seems, fifty years after their birth that the Boroughs have made a secure place for themselves. Twenty-eight Mayors and a Lord Mayor . . . may be rather too much compensation for the very prosaic appearance of the LCC, but . . . their councils spread the responsibility of government . . .[3]

Labour simply never got the problem right. In 1922 the London Labour Party gave contradictory evidence to the Ullswater Commission. In the next thirty years it moved from advocacy of a new regional body for the capital to a conservative defence of the status quo. This identification with the LCC and, more recently, with particular boroughs has been extremely costly.

The party also failed to exploit the available opportunities. In a number of ways the LCC was 'closer' to the citizen than the body which superseded it. In particular its control over welfare and education, neither of which belonged to the Greater London Council, gave it a potential and powerful means of identification with Londoners. This was heightened by the impact of war which was greater than in most of the other large centres and bestowed upon the LCC an awesome authority.

The problem for LCC members was that their role was often closer to Members of Parliament than borough councillors. How could they convey the scope and activities of the Council and its massive organization in any sustained or serious manner? This difficulty was intensified by restrictions on press publicity and on attendance by the public at committees and sub-committees. Only proceedings of the Council itself and those of the full Education Committee enjoyed unrestricted access and coverage.[4] Although this reflected the conventions of the period it was intensified by the political leadership exercised by Morrison's successors at County Hall, Charles (later Lord) Latham (1940-47) and (Sir) Isaac Hayward (1947-65). Though the least important of the three on the national political stage, even Hayward was aware that 'the borderline between parliamentary and county council duties is neither clear-cut nor readily appreciated'.[5] No attempt was made to explore the tension implied by the word 'borderline'. Nor did Hayward try to define London-wide politics from a borough perspective. Morrison's brutal tactics, his increasing indifference to the boroughs, and the sporadic and impulsive nature ascribed to strong local feelings, meant that the needs of the boroughs and those of London as a whole were never defined or reconciled. These ambiguities were heightened by the 'disalignment' of metropolitan politics in that, for long periods, opposite parties at County

[3] W.J.M. Mackenzie, *Explorations in Government*, 1975, p.63. The quotation is from a paper given in 1952.

[4] Lifted by legislation in 1960.

[5] *Forward*, 11 March 1960.

Hall and Westminster faced each other across the Thames. 'I would quarrel with anyone [continues Hayward] who fought to make of County Hall a second Parliament to the detriment of the great services . . . which we are here to administer.'[6] Even this bland, managerial interpretation of its role cannot conceal the anomalous, exposed and interesting position of the LCC.

On a nostalgic visit to County Hall in 1961 Morrison demonstrated how this ambivalence intersected with the social and electoral geography of London. Speaking of the local elections of that year he told the LCC Labour Group:

> The result in Middlesex was regrettable but it was a marginal county. The LCC was famous for concentrating on its own London work and problems, its good administration and upright standing. At the next LCC election we must show that after thirty years we were still fresh and full of new ideas.[7]

The identification with a particular area irrespective of all social and geographical changes – though not intended by Morrison – marked the end of a single, separate authority for inner London. Labour failed to make an effective argument for sustaining the LCC's boundaries. In ignoring a growing area whose population was equal to 70% of that of the LCC, and in concentrating on their 'own London work', Morrison and the Labour Group had abandoned the problem of matching political organization and social change. The effectiveness of local opinion depended on the strength and nature of the ties linking local parties to metropolitan and, beyond, to national leaders and organizations. There were few effective links between the two levels of London government, and the Labour Party never changed its structure in any fundamental way to accommodate or build up these links. This criticism can also be applied to the internal politics of the boroughs. As a result the bureaucratic nature of the LCC loomed large in the lives of Londoners, without benefiting them in any way they could understand or truly claim as their own. Working-class London, the ostensible constituency of Labour, was excluded. The downfall of the LCC and, later, the Greater London Council reflected the critical division between political power and popular representation. The reforms of 1963 were an unrepresentative measure in that they ignored Labour's return to power over and over again at the polls and the popular mandate this enshrined for its politics. But, in the last analysis, the LLP did not wield that mandate for the benefit of those it was elected to represent and their views were never given imaginative political expression. Labour, under Latham and Hayward, demonstrated that it was working on behalf of London, but it failed to take up the opportunities

[6] *Ibid.* The remark is a thrust at those who opposed him during the 'Crown Prince Affair' described later on.

[7] LCC Labour Group Minutes, 19 April 1961.

opened up by that success.

Throughout its history, as Morrison's early career demonstrates, two achievements were necessary to expand the LCC's authority and power: an effective scheme for the reform of London government and a clear relationship of social policy to municipal structure and enterprise. The supremacy of Hayward, leader from 1947 to 1965, was achieved, at least in part, on the basis of the defeat of the first of these. The failure of the second is bound up with the decline of municipal enterprise as a consumer-based trading activity and the rise of nationalization, set in train by Morrison with the London Passenger Transport Board in 1931[8] and completed by the loss of the council's hospitals to the National Health Service in 1948.[9] The fate of Morrison's immediate successor, Charles Latham gives a historical dimension to both themes.

### *The Reconstruction Debate and the Future of the LCC*

Though Beatrice Webb, in the aftermath of the 1934 victory, described Morrison as 'a Fabian of Fabians'[10], she could with equal fairness have bestowed the title on Latham. His role as chairman of the LCC's finance committee under Morrison, his involvement in the legislative growth of the new planning system and his vigorous participation in the national party's attempts to examine local government echo similar themes in Morrison's early career – albeit within a narrower if more privileged framework with six years of Labour rule at County Hall behind him. At the end of 1940 Latham instigated and conducted the most thorough inquiry into the structure of London government ever carried out by Labour. This took the form of a joint committee composed of London Labour Party executive nominees and LCC notables, with some later, limited participation from the metropolitan boroughs. Its terms of reference drew together post-war replanning and the reorganization of local government in Greater London.

The review was not solely confined to the question of structure. Appropriate to the stage of development Labour had reached in London, it made a brave stab at future policy for housing, education and the hospitals.[11] It also sought to consider the impact of these changes on the distribution of functions between the two major, constituent parts of the

[8] At the time an enormous blow to the prestige and self-esteem of members.

[9] See James Gillespie's chapter in this volume.

[10] Norman and Jeanne MacKenzie, *The Diary of Beatrice Webb*, vol.4, 1985, p.330 (14 March 1934).

[11] But *in advance* of the wider debate about reconstruction. As a result those participating did not have an outline of the Greater London Plan, the Uthwatt Committee's report on the assessment of land values, or Beveridge's recommendations – affecting the future of public assistance and hospitals – to guide them.

structure, the metropolitan authority with jurisdiction for London as a whole, and the individual borough or local councils carrying out the principal services within a specific geographical part of this area. Latham sought to establish what may be described as a comprehensive form of socio-economic planning, which would find expression in a Greater London Authority, a metropolitan sub-region, to a large extent self-sufficient in all major functions. These embraced planning, roads, housing, main drainage, education, hospitals and public assistance, an important role in co-ordinating gas, electricity and water, and they even cast envious glances at the Port of London, River Thames and transportation as a whole.

Latham's problems began when the joint committee appointed three small sub-committees to work on the details for education, housing and hospitals (including public assistance). The analysis and conclusions of all three sub-committees served to undermine Latham's ambitions. They laid bare two sets of problems. The first was the inconsistency of asking for wider boundaries, more population and an extended bureaucracy when control over existing services was insufficient; the second was to reveal that the conception of how London should be governed cut an enormous swathe through the powers of the boroughs.

For example, Latham's blueprint envisaged a doubling of the population within the boundaries of a single metropolitan authority. The education group, though eager to support the new sub-region, was anxious that members knew too little about the LCC's current problems:

> If they had to deal with a population twice as large . . . Members would have to rely almost entirely on officers' reports with the result that practically all real power would be vested in a vast bureaucratic machine.[12]

In other words, they were prepared to double the scale of the LCC on the basis of their own admission that they were unable to cope with their existing responsibilities. The housing group wondered aloud whether councillors 'had or could have a picture in their minds of what was going on'.[13] They noted that members of the housing committee were at a disadvantage to their colleagues on, for example, the hospitals and mental hospital committees, who received advice from individual management committees. They asked whether decentralization and more local control would temper the threat of bureaucracy. Their answer to this question summarizes a crucial difficulty:

> it might, and . . . it might also contribute more variety to housing development. On the other hand housing operations would clearly need to be

[12] Joint Committee on the Replanning and Reorganization of Greater London, Minutes Book, 30 Oct. 1941, pp.49-50.

[13] *Ibid.*, 7 November 1941.

carried on with great regard to the needs of the Region as a whole.[14]

The use of the phrase 'On the other hand' effectively cancels out all previous talk of local control. Either the attraction of Latham's region was blinding them to the recognition of the need for decentralized control; or, they were simply restating traditional LCC views reinforced by the enormous programme of rebuilding necessitated by the blitz.

It fell to Lewis Silkin to flesh out the role of the new local committees. He envisaged that they would monitor local housing needs, advise on priorities and oversee the management of estates. 'In a way,' he concluded, 'I suppose their functions would correspond very largely with those of the Hospital or Institution Committees.'[15] It is necessary to add that a hospital management committee was however closer to a board of visitors than a democratic arm of government. Was the region to impose its policies on those boroughs who had chosen to elect a different party? The issue was acute as the new Greater London was not to be covered by parish councils, but by seventeen separate areas with populations varying between 265,000 and 874,000,[16] reducing within the smaller area of the LCC the existing twenty-eight metropolitan boroughs to six.

Another blow to the LCC supremacists came with the debate over the future of the hospitals, which ante-dated Labour's discussions of 1945-7. The direction of social policy was to remove hospitals together with public assistance from local government. Demands for minimum uniform standards made it difficult, outside a national framework, to bring together the voluntary hospitals with those of the LCC. This was compounded by hostility to municipal ownership and control from doctors. Significantly, these obstacles were never openly acknowledged.[17] Instead the joint committee's hospital group proposed placing general hospitals under area control leaving the LCC's special hospitals to the region.[18] Many of these institutions were located in the healthy environment of Surrey. Latham wished however to entrust both types of institution to the region using an awkward patchwork of area hospital committees. Essentially this was an attempt to build up Silkin's model of hospital management committees, handing over planning matters and disciplinary powers over staff to local representatives.

Public assistance in the new framework was to belong to the regions. The only real discussion of its future came from Bernard Sullivan, LCC

[14] *Loc.cit.*

[15] *Ibid.*, 5 January 1942, p.67.

[16] Latham's original nine units, co-terminous with the existing nine civil defence subdivisions, were increased to sixteen after special deliberation by the LLP organizer, Hinley Atkinson.

[17] F. Honigsbaum, *The Division in British Medicine*, 1979; J.E. Pater, *The Making of the National Health Service*, 1981.

member and secretary of the Tailors' and Garment Workers' Union. He insisted that the future of the service could not be separated from the fate of the old poor law institutions. By handing over sickness payments to the National Assistance Board and extending pensions to everyone over 65, the 'institutions' or former workhouses would be left to care for smaller numbers of the infirm and those with no dependents. Their numbers would in turn be reduced by rehousing in small dwellings on housing estates or in small hostels or bed-sitting rooms with communal facilities attached. Poverty would be effectively abolished by redefining it in a number of specialized categories, a recurrent theme in LCC thinking about social policy.

The hospital recommendations and Sullivan's paper on public assistance represented a direct attack on Latham. They had shown that the logic of his blueprint led not to a new form of metropolitan sub-region but to nationalization. *In toto* the new region can be seen as the power base for a perpetual, Labour-run miniature state. The size, scale and funding requirements of the new local state – to borrow a phrase from the 1970s – drive it further away from local government. The boroughs, though now equal in size to the other large towns, are stripped of everything but a mild, consultative role. This was the Prometheus of LCC centralism unleashed, and Latham as its protagonist was overwhelmed and rendered impotent as the details unfolded.

Members of the joint committee, with Morrison in attendance, failed to reach agreement on the final draft of the report in July 1942. In October the central recommendation for a regional authority was eventually endorsed with two dissident votes – Isaac Hayward and Freda Corbet. Four other members, including two former leaders of the Labour Group at County Hall, Cecil Manning and Lewis Silkin, could not agree with the distribution of functions – and therefore power – between the region and the new boroughs. All that could be forwarded to the LLP executive was the plea for a Greater London authority, and the need to encourage co-ordination. To this was added the necessity to combine replanning with administrative reform.

The differences over the draft proposals were intensified when the executive asked Latham to return to his colleagues for further discussion. The joint committee, still unable to reconcile their differences, 'had nothing further to add to the report and . . . considered their reference now to be discharged'.[19] On this note of stalemate ended Labour's most sustained attempt to resolve the twin issues of local government and social policy in London.

[18] For example, TB sanatoria, children's and isolation hospitals.

[19] LLP, Executive Committee Minutes, 24 Dec. 1942. The aftermath is described in the party's annual conference reports for 1943 and 1944.

### *Party Leadership under Hayward*

Assessing the blow dealt to Latham's prestige is a difficult task given the lack of information about him. The remaining five years of his leadership saw a closer integration of LCC administration with wartime needs. Key services such as the fire brigade were removed from the council's control, and new services such as the civic restaurants introduced to see Londoners through the war years. Meetings were often cancelled and the influence of constituency members diminished. The LCC Labour Group was a party whose only members remained solely within the confines of County Hall, where the difficulties of controlling huge staffs and masterminding the contribution to the war effort, and later on reconstruction, gave emphasis to the role of the policy committee. This lynchpin of party management created an oligarchy which fused the power of LCC leaders with the authority of chief officers, to the detriment of individual members or a strong constituency role. But there always had been strong oligarchic tendencies within the Labour Group, centring around the appointment of chairmen – an exclusive prerogative of the leader – and the power of the policy committee to discipline, curb and suppress dissent.

It is significant that the two figures most opposed to Latham's concept of a new metropolitan sub-region, Isaac Hayward and Freda Corbet, should have been elected leader and chief whip respectively, on his resignation as LCC leader for 'personal reasons' in July 1947. Complaints from individual councillors about party discipline and lack of communication now intensified, which Hayward attempted to dismiss as partly a consequence of war. This view implicitly lay much of the blame at Latham's door.[20] The new leader's subsequent history did little to alter this state of affairs. In 1947 he overruled a proposal for more frequent changes in the chairmanships of individual committees as damaging to the preparations for the 1948 elections, a pretext he had been invoking since 1934. In 1949 'the present difficult circumstances' made it appropriate to hold over changes until 1950. 'The situation', he told his colleagues, 'called for the utmost loyalty'.[21] This statement illustrates the sheer continuity of Hayward's tactics, emanating from a simmering autocratic disposition legitimated by appeals to loyalty and the (always) unique circumstances of the hour. To these can be added a tendency to personalize criticisms of policy for 'when objections were made it was

[20] Cf. W.G. Boys' remark that 'the former leader worked the system [of appointing chairmen and chairwomen] very badly'. LCC Labour Group Minutes, 7 Oct. 1949.

[21] *Ibid.*, 3 May 1949.

regarded as a motion of "No Confidence" in the present leader'.[22]

Miniature revolts surfaced in 1949 and 1953, with a more serious crisis in 1959, after which they subsided under pressure from the Herbert Commission. The two earlier rebellions were essentially expressions of back-bench resentment, seeking to put the appointment of committee chairmen to a vote of the group as a whole. Frustration was also directed at the requirement that members obtain the Chief Whip's permission to ask questions at full council meetings or committees open to the public. They were also obliged to table motions prior to group meetings routeing all criticisms through the policy committee. Within such a framework the scope for criticism was reduced and individual dissidents easily picked off. W.G. Boys, LCC Brixton member, failed to submit a motion to continue the financing of civic restaurants in 1953, refusing 'to alter his action in deference to the wishes of the Party'.[23] In a set piece drama Freda Corbet read out the rules governing party discipline and Boys was then 'warned' by Hayward. But the real job of reining in the recalcitrant Boys was undertaken by the policy committee. After an interview with them Boys promised 'not [to] speak or vote against the Party in future'.[24]

The 1959 revolt, in sharp contrast, came close to forcing Hayward's retirement. The background to it was Labour's overwhelming victory in the 1958 LCC election. The difficulties affecting the national party in the early 1950s had left the LCC unscathed. Morrison's careful sifting of recruits and the stress on exemplary Fabian qualities had created an organization balanced between a combination of right-wing trade-union officials and upper-middle-class intellectuals, with representatives of the co-operative movement caught uneasily in between. A study by the LSE of the 1961 election noted that 'the LCC, given the size of its Labour majority, is probably unusual in having such a high proportion of middle class members'.[25] None of the eighty-four Labour members elected in 1961 was semi-skilled (social class IV) and only one was unskilled (social class V). The largest occupational group consisted of barristers of whom there were eight. Within this system left-wing dissent was easily curbed. The spread of Labour's power to the outer reaches of the LCC's area paradoxically introduced a small, hitherto unknown number of left-wingers more in tune with the state of the national party.

The most prominent was Hugh Jenkins, member of the Campaign for Nuclear Disarmament, treasurer of the pressure group 'Victory for Socialism', supporter of the magazine *Tribune* and an inveterate letter writer to *The Times*. Jenkins attacked discipline at County Hall as

[22] *Ibid.*, 6 Dec. 1949. The remark belongs to Councillor R.W.G. Humphreys (Lambeth, Norwood).

[23] *Ibid.*, 28 July 1953.

[24] *Ibid.*, 6 Oct. 1953.

[25] L.J. Sharpe, *A Metropolis Votes*, 1962, p.42.

excessive and went on to urge a more realistic and progressive attitude to the reform of London government, to the extent of making an independent appearance before the Herbert Commission.[26] The fragile structure of power at County Hall was further unsettled when Tom Braddock, a new member for Holborn and St Pancras South, following an initial brush with the policy committee, advised LCC tenants to withhold rent increases. He held that as Labour had opposed any rent rises in the 1958 election it was outrageous to rush them through immediately after it.[27] This was part of a widespread battle in his own constituency against Conservative-imposed rises which Braddock could not have ignored, even had he wished to. The policy committee reacted by sealing up all previous avenues for critics, who were now threatened with expulsion if they made statements in the press or in the Council Chamber itself. In *Tribune*, Donald Soper, another CND supporter as well as Methodist preacher and popular broadcaster who had been made an LCC alderman in 1958, Francis Williams, former editor of *The Daily Herald* and others attacked 'the intolerant behaviour on the part of some Labour Councils'. Soper wrote that 'the LCC has become in some ways the worst of all offenders'.[28] It was rumoured that Attlee had described the LCC as 'the nearest approach to a totalitarian state in Western Europe'.[29]

In response Hayward announced in March 1959 that he would step down before the end of the year to enable a new leader to take the party into the 1961 election.[30] After the Council had recessed for the summer this pledge was however withdrawn. Opposition now fell to Alderman William Fiske, later chief whip and then leader of the first GLC administration. In the absence of any party meeting until October Fiske, with Hayward's informal approval, arranged to consult with a cross-section of thirty colleagues. As a result the issue was eventually raised in the Labour Group, and he was able to ask whether Hayward 'might be willing to devolve some of his responsibilities so that someone might be trained'.[31] Fiske was rewarded with the new post of Deputy Leader and all further attempts to get rid of Hayward were buried. The 'Crown Prince' affair was the closest to a palace revolution in thirty years of Labour rule. Significantly, the leader of this bureaucratic coup was incorporated dramatically and swiftly within the top power elite of the South Bank.

Hayward had by now consolidated his position, in a similar way to

[26] Royal Commission on Local Government in Greater London, Evidence, vol.5, 14 Oct. 1959, pp.2032-44.

[27] *Tribune*, 14 Nov. 1958. Letters from John Wobey (LCC Member for Hackney) and Braddock. See also Braddock's letter to the *Manchester Guardian*, 2 Feb. 1959.

[28] *Tribune*, *ibid.*

[29] *New Society*, 4 Jan. 1968, article on Morrison's legacy by R.L. Leonard. The source of this (unproven) remark appears to be Francis Williams: *Forward*, 22 Jan. 1960.

[30] LCC Labour Group Minutes, 3 March 1959.

[31] *Ibid.*, 15 Dec. 1959.

Morrison, by cultivating colleagues who would preserve the close connection between the LLP executive and the policy committee at County Hall. His longevity – a 'mere 75-years-old' – was no bar to his continued hold on power.[32] Nor was 'the immovable posture which [his] party has frozen into during 25 years of power' an obstacle.[33] Paradoxically the reason why Hayward was able to stay on for another five years was the Herbert Commission's recommendation to abolish the LCC.

### *The LCC and the Herbert Commission*

The commission was set up by the Conservative Government in 1956 to address the problem of readjusting county boundaries surrounding London and the effect upon these of future changes in the shape of Middlesex and the LCC. The insistence of the Middlesex Labour Party in remaining outside the parameters of London politics, and thereby evading LLP control, a merger first suggested in 1951, goes to the heart of Labour's failure to adapt and to win over by example.[34]

The position taken by the LCC before the commission was that the two-tier system and current boundaries should remain, with minor adjustments in functions to be settled by negotiation with the boroughs. A sub-committee of the LLP executive, chaired by Lord Latham, who seems to have remembered nothing of his previous efforts, considered resuscitating tenification, that is breaking London up into separate county boroughs. This was rejected by Latham and his colleagues 'as it would mean the end of London as an entity'.[35]

The commission attacked this evidence, and, to the horror of those who had come to see the LCC as indestructible, it proposed sweeping away the entire structure of 1889 in favour of a Council for Greater London. The coincidence of the Fiske episode with the publication of the report indicated Labour's increasing difficulties in London. To succeed Hayward had, firstly, to come up with a better scheme and, secondly, to prevent Labour boroughs and district councils threatened by absorption into the new Greater London from taking up different or contrary views. This meant an alliance with Surrey, Kent, Hertfordshire and Essex – all,

[32] *Evening Standard*, 25 Nov. 1959, 'A warning rumble for "Sir Ike" of County Hall', by J.W.M. Thompson, the paper's political correspondent – the fullest account of the episode.

[33] *Ibid.*

[34] LLP, Executive Committee Minutes, 21 Sep. 1950.

[35] Peter Robshaw, LLP secretary at LCC Labour Group special meeting, 17 Jan. 1958. 'A regional authority was also considered, but it was felt that was not *really* local government.' For Latham's contribution, see Royal Commission on Local Government in Greater London, Evidence, vol.5, 22 Oct. 1959, pp.2125-49.

but the last, strong Conservative authorities.

The key to the Labour Group's strategy, in which Fiske once again came to the fore, was a trade-off: the LCC would hand over traffic, strategic planning decisions, intelligence (a key function identified by the Royal Commission) and refuse disposal to a new advisory body overseeing an area of some 2,000 square miles. In exchange the Labour Group hoped to save the three fundamental existing LCC services – education, children's and housing. To buy borough support the LCC would devolve planning applications, personal health services and other welfare functions. Together the LCC and boroughs would oppose the new GLC, the break-up of education and changes in boundaries except by consent.[36]

The boroughs, however, were not so compliant. For the first time they had the upper hand and they were naturally in favour of having more powers devolved to them from the LCC. In amalgamating them into larger units, two and three times their previous size, the Commission was also shifting the balance of power away from County Hall. The linking of previously Labour and Conservative boroughs entailed the reshaping of parliamentary constituencies with, given population movement out of inner London, a loss of seats to Labour. The LLP was forced to take London's new boundaries seriously, because not to do so would jeopardize the party's electoral chances. The decision to participate in elections to the new GLC marked the end of active resistance. Arthur Skeffington, on behalf of the Parliamentary Labour Party, explained the LLP's true position apologetically to the Labour Group at County Hall, i.e. that the party had adopted no policy on local government reform. Labour's National Executive Committee had left the reconstruction of London government to the LLP whilst 'Mr [R.A.] Butler had always ensured that the Conservative Party views were put forward'.[37]

It is unfair to place all the blame for this failure on the leaders of the LLP. After all, Labour's national lack of success was in sharp contrast to its continued triumphs in London. But the culture of opposition within the national party had the advantages of keeping alive a habit of rethinking strategy and policies, which the complacent leaders of the LCC, with thirty years of power behind them to build upon, had lost. There had long been a tradition of jealousy between London and the national party's organizers.[38] The capital was also handicapped by its reputation as an affluent city. The result was to weaken support for retaining the LCC in the highest circles of the party. As the process of reform took a decisive turn after 1960 the LLP was wrong-footed. When the new electoral machine scooped up sixty-four out of 100 seats at the initial GLC elections

36 LCC Labour Group Minutes, 17 Jan. 1958.

37 *Ibid.*, 3 July 1962.

38 R. McKibbin, *The Evolution of the Labour Party, 1910-1924*, 1974, pp.170-4.

in April 1964, Hayward was ironically deprived by this victory of his last chance to sustain effective opposition.

On the penultimate day of the council's life (30 March 1965) two ceremonies took place at County Hall. Inside, Hayward was presented with a box of cigars; outside, the ashes of Morrison (who had died on 6 March) were scattered over the Thames. 'I have an immense admiration for the Morrison tradition of local government', wrote Richard Crossman who, with Harold Wilson, had been guest of honour at the farewell dinner of the LCC Labour Group, '. . . Nevertheless, what an inhuman show the London Labour Party is!'[39] One durable legacy of the LCC was to enthrone the professional leader in London politics. Morrison had sought to introduce a popular element into London politics and to confront what has been described as this 'city of people concealing their robustly antisocial desires behind a mask of formality'.[40] He did not, however, manage to develop a sufficiently flexible party to accommodate changes in the external development of London. The LCC and the GLC both failed to acknowledge that the key to successful political organization within London's unstable firmament, remains the balance between populist leadership, bureaucratic control and popular representation.

[39] Richard Crossman, *Diaries of a Cabinet Minister*, vol.1, 1975, pp.177-8.
[40] Kenneth Tynan, *Tynan Right and Left*, 1967, p.318.

# *Appendix*

Excerpt from Evidence of the Centre for Environmental Studies given to the Royal Commission on Local Government in Greater London, 1959. This section was written by Asa Briggs.

In the course of its history, the London County Council has established itself both as an instrument of effective local government and as a focal point of service and loyalty. The second achievement has been as important as the first. Indeed, it has been the precondition of the first. In any rearrangement, therefore, care should be taken not to disturb (for the sake of hypothetical advantages) the strong sense of 'self-governing community' in London.

The debate leading up to the foundation of the LCC was concerned with the fundamental question of 'whether London shall really become a self-governing community, and take the management of its own collective life into its own hands' (Sidney Webb, *The Reform of London*, 1892, p.3). Despite the many difficulties placed in the path of the LCC at the start, it succeeded in providing a positive answer to this question. For the pre-existing 'anarchy of London' there was substituted the sense of a genuine 'self-governing community'. The consequential political and social gains have been remarkable, and it is possible to underestimate them if emphasis is placed on administration alone.

The London County Council has achieved this sense of a 'self-governing community' without external trappings of a civic kind. The deliberate unconcern for civic ritual gave the Council its initial ethos, and throughout its later history there has always been more emphasis on service than on display.

The Council has always been able to draw upon the services of a large number of people who might not have been as anxious or willing to serve in smaller authorities. The large amount of time and energy involved in being a member of the Council has been commensurate with the administrative responsibilities. Partly for this reason women have been among the most active members of the LCC. From the start the question of the admission of women was made a matter of principle, and throughout the inter-war years and since 1945, women have continued to play an important part. The sense of participating in a large enterprise and of having exceptional opportunities to initiate policy has drawn in a number of people of considerable ability.

The quality of service (both voluntary and official) has always been outstanding, so much so that the point hardly needs to be made; it can be taken for granted. As Gibbon and Bell put it in their *History of the LCC*: 'the high level of service has won notable recognition in this country and abroad'. From the start the service has been associated with a strongly developed political sense. Indeed, the three most important themes in the history of the LCC have been (i) the growth of party government; (ii) the recognition of the importance of civic policy; and (iii) a sense of rivalry with Parliament in Westminster. Each of these three themes has given point and piquancy to London politics.

Whereas before the formation of the LCC the political horizons of Londoners were often far narrower than those of people living in the provinces, since the 1890s the position has changed. Whereas in the days of the Metropolitan Board of Works, political issues centred on small matters primarily concerned with jobs and vested interests, since the formation of the LCC, London politics have centred on big issues, including major issues of policy. The emphasis on policy (as distinct from technical matters of administration) can be traced back to the first big speech that Lord Rosebery, as Chairman, made to the Council when he talked of the necessity of a city as great as London having a 'policy', that is, a deliberate sense of direction in which to move. Questions of policy have stirred Londoners ever since in a way that would have been impossible had local government powers been concentrated in small units or in *ad hoc* bodies operating largely in secret.

The strength of party government in London has been a precondition of the particular kind of civic responsibility which has been involved. It should be regarded, therefore, as a strength and not as a weakness in relation to the organized life of a great city. Methods that would be appropriate in small places are quite inappropriate for an area and population of London's size. Both at County Hall and in the metropolitan boroughs there is a high degree of party organization. The 'Progressive Party' was highly organized from the start, and party feeling ran high even in the first debates of the Council. Since the early days the existence of well-organized parties has clarified the issues of local government and stimulated public interest. The organization of the Council (for example, the early formal recognition of the role of 'Leader of the Opposition') has registered the distinctive approach to party, which can be noted also at election times when there is a relatively high degree of participation and considerable public interest in the result even outside London.

As far as policy is concerned, the LCC has acted as a pioneer in many branches of policy making. Housing policy provides a good example. In the early years of the century many schemes were started which were far in advance of schemes in most parts of the country. Although in the 1920s London tended to lag behind, there was another great burst of building after 1934; while since the Second World War housing policy has been favourably commented on by experts from all parts of the world. Two features of the Council's recent housing policy have been particularly prominent – first, the refusal to regard large-scale public housing as merely an inferior service for the poor; and second, the concern for architectural as well as economic considerations. The very recent record of the LCC during the past two or three years should be taken into account in assessing its housing performance, for it is in the latest phase that some of the most significant achievements have taken shape.

Associated with housing policy and other branches of social policy, there has been a very marked improvement in health standards in London. The administrative County of London has a lower mortality than the other conurbations and urban areas. Indeed, the County's mortality is only slightly greater than that of the more openly developed outer ring of Greater London. For this distinction, which clearly rests on environmental factors, the LCC can legitimately take a considerable share of the credit. The position contrasts sharply with that in the days of the Metropolitan Board of Works. Discussions on policy are eventually expressed in services performed, and without the initial incentive, which has been effectively provided by the LCC, substantial results could not have been achieved.

Many arguments which on occasion have been used against the LCC – that it is too remote, for example – do not stand up to careful examination. The Council has been able to tackle some environmental and social problems more effectively than would otherwise have been the case because it has escaped the persistent pressure of small vested interests, and has been able to concern itself with policy based on principle. This is clear from the Council's record, on the basis of both historical and contemporary data.

In the evolution of policy, momentum has certainly increased as a result of rivalry with the Parliament at Westminster. Situated in the same city as Parliament, the LCC is one of the few local authorities in the country which is strong enough to hold its own against Westminster. It is significant that on more than one critical occasion in its history, the political complexion of the LCC has been different from that of Parliament. Thus while Unionist governments were in control at Westminster for most of the first seventeen years of the LCC's existence, it was the Progressives who controlled the Council. After the Liberal victory at the General Election of 1906, however, the Progressives lost their majority on the LCC at the election of 1907, and the Municipal Reformers took over. During the 1930s the Labour Party captured the LCC at a time when the National Government had a very large majority at Westminster. Labour Party control was reaffirmed in 1937 – two years after the General

Election had returned the National Government again.

The strength and purposefulness of the London County Council have served as an example for local government in the country as a whole. Battles waged in London, for example, over poor law in the 1920s and housing in the 1930s, have echoed in other local authorities, and decisions reached in London have influenced the tactics and policies of other local bodies.

The difference in political complexion between London and Westminster has been a source of energy in London politics themselves. It has inspired public interest and vitalized discussions on policy. Three major elections in the history of the LCC stand out. The election of 1907 was probably the most stirring election which has ever taken place in the history of British local government. It inspired the writing of Graham Wallas's *Human Nature in Politics*, which for the first time described realistically the problems of electioneering. The election of 1934 in a different kind of social setting stimulated equal excitement. The same was true of the election of 1937 when far more resources were devoted to the election than had ever been devoted to a previous one, and the Labour Party was again successful. Herbert Morrison's comment on the result is significant in that it goes far beyond straight party questions. 'The government let it be known', he said, 'that they wanted to decide what kind of a county council our citizens should choose. It was another of a long line of attempts to turn the capital into a Crown colony.'

The success of the LCC, not only in providing what is recognized to be efficient local government, but also in stimulating and maintaining public interest should be taken into account in considering any proposals for change. It is most unlikely that a new authority concerned with a wider area, would be able to continue with equal strength the traditions which have been developed by the LCC. The historical record of the Council, including its recent one, suggests that no new authority would be able, within the framework of local government powers and finance, to inspire such a strong sense of commitment, service and genuine public interest.

# *Index*